MUHAMMAD ALI

with Richard Durham

THE
GREATEST
MY OWN STORY

EDITED BY TONI MORRISON

GRAYMALKIN
MEDIA

BOXING WAS JUST A MEANS TO INTRODUCE ME TO THE WORLD.

—MUHAMMAD ALI

To Cassius Marcellus Clay, Sr.
and
Odessa Clay

Cash and Bird
With love

Published by Graymalkin Media

www.graymalkin.com

"I, Too" from *The Collected Poems of Langston Hughes* by Langston Hughes, edited by Arnold Rampersad with David Roessel, Associate Editor, copyright © 1994 by the Estate of Langston Hughes. Used by permission of Alfred A. Knopf, an imprint of the Knopf Doubleday Publishing Group, a division of Penguin Random House LLC. All rights reserved.

"Stand by Me" Words and Music by Jerry Leiber, Mike Stoller and Ben E. King. Copyright © 1961 Sony/ATV Music Publishing LLC. Copyright renewed. All rights administered by Sony/ATV Music Publishing LLC, 424 Church Street, Suite 1200, Nashville, TN 37219. International copyright secured. All rights reserved. Reprinted by permission of Hal Leonard Corporation.

"The Glory of Love" Words and Music by Billy Hill. Copyright © 1936 Shapiro, Bernstein & Co., Inc., New York. Copyright renewed. International copyright secured. All rights reserved. Used by permission. Reprinted by permission of Hal Leonard Corporation.

Letter from Bertrand Russell, printed in the May 5, 1967, issue of *Muhammad Speaks*, reprinted by permission of *Muhammad Speaks*.

This edition published in 2015 by Graymalkin Media

Originally published by Random House, Inc.

ISBN: 978-1-63168-049-6

Printed in the United States of America

1 3 5 7 9 10 8 6 4 2

ACKNOWLEDGMENT

In order for a prizefighter to be successful and come out with what belongs to him, he has to be two separate people in two different places at the same time—in the gym and in the lawyer's office, in the ring and in the accountant's office. And since no one can be two people, a prizefighter must have a partner, a brother, a friend, a counsel, a twin in thinking and aspiration who will be the other self he needs.

Herbert Muhammad is all of these things. There's been no single decision I've ever made, unrevealed or in the pages that follow, where he hasn't played the prominent and decisive part.

It was Herbert who, during the time I was completely barred from boxing, suggested that I should start work on my autobiography. I had been outlawed in the United States for three years from the only profession I'd every really worked at, and my passport had been lifted so I couldn't practice in any other country. When I first came to Random House to talk about doing a book, there was a strong chance that the only boxing I'd ever be a part of would be the fights in the past, and that I might even have to finish my story in jail.

I had just begun to look back over my life and put it together, thinking the Supreme Court decision would be the climax of it all, when Herbert's constant probing broke the boycott against me. He found an opening in Georgia, and like a Second Coming, the final, most important part of my life as a fighter opened up.

I first met Herbert, who has become my closest friend and counselor, and who eventually exerted more influence in the ranks of boxing than any manager in history, when I went to Chicago to have photos taken shortly after I won the World Heavyweight Title from Sonny Liston in 1964. The photographer had been recommended to me as one of the best in the city, and during our first picture-taking session in his South Side Studio, we talked frankly of fighters and what they are really, deep down, fighting for—their lives and the lives of their families and those they love and who love them. He was warm, friendly, but serious, and I was deeply impressed with his sharp business sense.

"I wanted to be a prizefighter myself," Herbert Muhammad told me, "and although my father asked me to give it up, I've never gotten it out of my blood. I came up in the days when the names Joe Louis, Sugar Ray Robinson, Ezzard Charles, Rocky Marciano were the great names in boxing. I got over the desire to get inside the ring, but I never got over the desire to help these great fighters outside the ring. I guess this was so because I could see what happened at the end of the careers of those great fighters, and what they had left after all those years. It shocked me, and I said if I ever got a chance to help a fighter who was worthy of the name, help him realize something out of what he fought for, I would try to do it."

While technically I already had my "eleven managers" in the Louisville Sponsoring Group, I knew none of them really had the time or background to understand my real ambition, to help me go as far as I wanted to go. And while I believed that I would continue to do better, I knew that if I was ever to maintain my position in the field of boxing, every thought, every move would have to be concentrated on training and developing my craft. I would have to discover, if I was lucky, someone who had the business gift and skills to work for me in those areas where sound judgment is needed—an agent capable of selecting lawyers, analyzing financial propositions, securing finances and maintaining the image of the fighter in a progressive way.

I approached the Honorable Elijah Muhammad who, although not in support of professional sports, understood the need for me, one of his followers, to be protected until I was able to retire from that profession, and asked if he would allow Herbert to act as my consultant in and out of the ring, to help make it possible for me to pursue my career and still be able to live the kind of life that can make contributions to freedom, justice and equality for the black man in America.

The Louisville Sponsoring Group, who were worried about the gap in communications between us, welcomed Herbert as a consultant, especially when they discovered his keen business instincts and devotion to my development. In a short while, he had mastered the fundamentals of business in the fight game.

When my Louisville sponsors' contract expired in 1966, Herbert took over as manager. Working as a unit, we decided on a division of labor. "It's your job to be champion of what goes on in the ring," Herbert said. "You concentrate on training and developing the skills and your own specialty for promoting. I'll concentrate on bringing you the finances that are due you.

"Promoters have a way of taking from a fighter," he explained, "closing off tributaries that should flow into a fighter's purse. I'm learning them all—hidden rebates, endorsements, hidden commercials, all monies that are created by the fighter and some portions of what should flow into the fighter.

"Interest in the Heavyweight Championship will never be as high as it is now—because of the way you have built it up and promoted it. After you go, it's bound to die down, because never in history has any fighter been exposed to so much of the world as you've been, in so many ways. When you came into Islam, you made an enormous number of people—who had never thought of boxing before, or very little of any sport, for that matter—conscious of the World Heavyweight Champion. Never before had the world focused so much attention on one athlete. This is your time. You have to benefit from it."

It was Herbert's aggressive outlook and imagination that brought about for the first time in sports history fights supported by governments, as in Zaire, Malaysia and the Philippines; attracted bids from such countries as Egypt, Saudi Arabia, Iran, Santo Domingo and Haiti; and set up promotions for matches in Ireland, Switzerland, Japan, Indonesia and Canada.

Herbert had a poem which went with the new strategy:

Invite Muhammad Ali to fight,
And your country will share the world spotlight.

I've been fortunate to have a manager with skill, integrity and devotion, and a friend who, although he helped mastermind my career, has been retiring and modest. He has made it possible for me to help change the history of manager/boxer relationships and is forever encouraging me, not only to give the best performance to the people, but to be a part of the struggles of the people, to be concerned with the progress of the people and to stand for the principles of peace, justice and equality—to show that in a profession which is mainly known for brutality and blood, a man can have nobility and dignity. It is not only I who owes Herbert Muhammad a debt of gratitude, it is the entire boxing and athletic world.

For these many benefits I thank Allah and the Honorable Elijah Muhammad, the servant of Allah—may the peace and blessings of Allah be upon him. And because of Herbert, a brilliant and dedicated man—whom I first met as a photographer, but who changed the picture of my future to make it brighter than it ever could have been —it is possible for me to share with you some of the highlights of my life.

Muhammad Ali

CONTENTS

CHRONOLOGY

1942   Birth date (January 17, Louisville)

1959   Golden Gloves Championship (Chicago)

1960   Golden Gloves Championship (Chicago); Olympic Championship (Rome); Reynolds offered two contracts (September); signed with Louisville Sponsoring Group (October)

1964   Announced membership in Nation of Islam six months after joining (February 28); marriage to Sonji (June 4)

1965   WBA rescinded boxing license (June 19)

1966   Divorce from Sonji (January 7); held press conference announcing Viet Nam sentiments (February 17, Miami); left Louisville Sponsoring Group and signed with Herbert Muhammad (October 26)

1967   Reported to Induction Center (April 28, Houston); boxing license rescinded by New York State Boxing Commission (April 28); received five-year jail sentence for refusal to join Army (June 25); marriage to Belinda (August 17)

1968   Birth of daughter, Maryum (June 18)

1970   Reversal of five-year jail sentence (June 20); birth of twins, Jamillah and Rasheda (August 21); received first state boxing license after exile (September 28)

1972   Birth of son, Muhammad, Jr. (May 14)

PROFESSIONAL FIGHT RECORD

1. WITH LOUISVILLE SPONSORING GROUP

DATE	MY OPPONENT	LOCATION	RESULT	MY PURSE
1960				
October 29	Tunney Hunsaker	Louisville	W 6[1]	$2,000
December 27	Herb Siler	Miami Beach	KO 4	200
1961				
January 17	Tony Esperti	Miami Beach	KO 3	545
February 7	Jim Robinson	Miami Beach	KO 1	645
February 21	Donnie Fleeman	Miami Beach	KO 7	913
April 19	Lamar Clark	Louisville	KO 2	2,548
June 26	Duke Sabedong	Las Vegas	W 10	1,500
July 22	Alonzo Johnson	Louisville	W 10	6,636
October 7	Alex Miteff	Louisville	KO 6	5,644
November 29	Willi Besmanoff	Louisville	KO 7	2,048
1962				
February 10	Sonny Banks	New York	KO 4	5,014
February 28	Don Warner	Miami Beach	KO 4	1,675
April 23	George Logan	Los Angeles	KO 4	9,206
May 19	Billy Daniels	New York	KO 7	6,000
July 20	Alejandro Lavorante	Los Angeles	KO 5	15,149
November 15	Archie Moore	Los Angeles	KO 4	45,300
1963				
January 24	Charlie Powell	Pittsburgh	KO 3	14,331
March 13	Doug Jones	New York	W 10	57,668
June 18	Henry Cooper (I)	London	KO 5	56,098
1964				
February 25	Sonny Liston (I)	Miami Beach	KO 7[2]	464,595
1965				
May 25	Sonny Liston (II)	Lewiston, Me.	KO 1[3]	361,819
November 22	Floyd Patterson	Las Vegas	KO 12[3]	300,078

DATE	MY OPPONENT	LOCATION	RESULT	MY PURSE
1966				
March 29	George Chuvalo	Toronto	W 15^3	$66,332
May 21	Henry Cooper (II)	London	KO 6^3	448,186
August 6	Brian London	London	KO 3^3	290,411
September 10	Karl Mildenberger	Frankfort	KO 12^3	211,576

Gross earnings with Louisville Sponsoring Group: $2,376,115

With Herbert Muhammad

DATE	MY OPPONENT	LOCATION	RESULT	MY PURSE
November 14	Cleveland Williams	Houston	KO 3^3	$405,000
1967				
February 6	Ernie Terrell	Houston	W 15^3	585,000
March 22	Zora Folley	New York	KO 7^3	275,000

(In Exile: April 1967 to September 1970)

DATE	MY OPPONENT	LOCATION	RESULT	MY PURSE
1970				
October 26	Jerry Quarry (I)	Atlanta	KO 3	580,000
December 7	Oscar Bonavena	New York	KO 15	925,000
1971				
March 8	Joe Frazier (I)	New York	L 15^4	2,500,000
July 26	Jimmy Ellis	Houston	KO 12	450,000
November 17	Buster Mathis	Houston	W 10	300,000
December 26	Jurgen Blin	Zurich	KO 7	250,000
1972				
April 1	Mac Foster	Tokyo	W 15	200,000
May 1	George Chuvalo	Vancouver	W 12	200,000
June 27	Jerry Quarry (II)	Las Vegas	KO 7	500,000
July 19	Al "Blue" Lewis	Dublin	KO 11	200,000
September 20	Floyd Patterson	New York	KO 7	250,000
November 21	Bob Foster	Lake Tahoe	KO 8	260,000
1973				
February 14	Joe Bugner (I)	Las Vegas	W 12	285,000
March 31	Ken Norton (I)	San Diego	L 12	210,000
September 10	Ken Norton (II)	Los Angeles	W 12	535,000
October 20	Rudi Lubbers	Djakarta	W 12	200,000
1974				
January 28	Joe Frazier (II)	New York	W 12	1,715,000
October 30	George Foreman	Kinshasa	KO 8^5	5,450,000

DATE	MY OPPONENT	LOCATION	RESULT	MY PURSE
1975				
March 24	Chuck Wepner	Cleveland	KO 15	1,500,000
May 16	Ron Lyle	Las Vegas	KO 11	1,000,000
June 30	Joe Bugner (II)	Kuala Lumpur	W 15	2,100,000
September 30	Joe Frazier (III)	Manila	TKO 14[3]	6,000,000

Gross earnings with Herbert Muhammad: $27,375,000

Gross earnings since returning to ring: 26,110,000

Total ring earnings: 29,751,115

Total estimated earnings for exhibitions: 1,500,000

Total lifetime earnings: $31,251,115

[1] I signed for this fight on my own before my contract with the Louisville Sponsoring Group.

[2] I won the World Heavyweight Title.

[3] I retained the World Heavyweight Title.

[4] This was for the Undisputed World Heavyweight Title.

[5] I regained the World Heavyweight Title.

SHORTY IS WATCHING

Louisville 100 miles. I barely see the sign in the rain.

"Won't make it by morning," Harold Hazzard, my driver, says. He has been at the wheel too long and is driving with just the edge of his mind.

"We will if I drive." I know every bend and curve in the road from here. When I take the wheel, Harold joins the rest of my camp crew in the back of the bus. Belinda and my daughter Maryum are back there too, fast asleep.

"Worse place in the world is an old hometown when you're down," Chris Dundee once warned me. "Let them remember you as a winner; never come home beaten."

Until now, I had always come home like the victorious hunter bringing back big game from the jungle: two Golden Gloves Championships, some AAU titles, an Olympic Gold Medal, the World

Heavyweight Title. Even exiled and barred from boxing, I came back as The Undefeated.

Now it's the spring of 1973 and I'm coming home after a defeat every man, woman and child in my hometown saw or heard about, just like everybody else all over the world. The press will crowd the sports pages with headlines that remind me: MUHAMMAD IS FINISHED! END OF AN ERA! ALI BEATEN BY A NOBODY! BIG MOUTH SHUT FOR ALL TIME! MOST THRILLING FIGHT IN HISTORY!

I want to come home. To rest. To see Bird and my father and old friends. To see where I am. To remember who I am, where I came from and where I want to go. I was born, bred and spent the first twenty-one years of my life there. I have to know if it's really "home"—the place you can go to when you're whipped.

The rain pours down heavier and I slow up to see the road better. Squinting out into the darkness, mile after mile, I keep going over the same scene, like in a movie: San Diego Sports Arena. The last round is over. I'm standing in my corner. The referee is collecting the judges' votes. He looks at them, calls off the scoring, glances my way for a second, then turns to Norton. "The winner by a split decision—Ken Norton!"

The stadium explodes. Wild shouts and screams come down from the bleachers. Some boo the decision, but the screams and cries of "NORTON!" "NORTON!" drown them out.

"We beat you, you bastard!" I look down at a heavyset white man who has jumped up on his chair yelling up at me, waving a newspaper. "We got you! We got you!"

Policemen leap into the ring, but people break past them, pouring in under the ropes. Joe Frazier is hugging Norton, who is his stablemate and sparring partner. A radio commentator is yelling for me to come over, "say something to explain it." But Angelo and Bundini are already moving me down the steps. I taste blood draining into my throat and the pain in my face and shoulders is growing. I remember pausing and looking over to where I know Belinda is sitting. I want to wave at her, give her some sign that I'm all right, but the police and the crowd are shoving against each other and I'm pushed toward the dressing room.

"Who's the prettiest *now?*" . . . "Who's the prettiest *now?*" A cluster of white women are shouting at the top of their voices and stomping their feet. The police move them aside.

My head feels as though it will drop off. The pain in the left side of my jaw is almost more than I can stand.

A man in a fireman's uniform breaks through the police line: "You finished, loud-mouth! You finished!"

The police form a wedge in front of me, forcing the crowd back until we get out of the arena and down the hall. The hecklers follow, screaming, chanting, booing while the ushers try to open the dressing-room door. Finally it opens from the inside and one by one we squeeze through—Herbert Muhammad, my manager; Bundini, my assistant trainer; Dr. Pacheco, my ringside doctor; Captain Joseph Yuseff of Temple No. 7, who I've known since the first day I joined the Nation of Islam; Angelo Dundee, my trainer; Lloyd Wells, an old friend; Eugene Kilroy and Hassan Salami, my aides; Howard Bingham, my photographer; Dick Durham, my writer; Reggie Barrett, another friend; Pat Patterson, security guard; Walter Youngblood, assistant trainer . . . Even after we're in, they keep pushing the door open to make sure I can hear them: "Who's the greatest *now?*"

At last the door is closed and Angelo is leaning against it, exhausted. He can't believe the hatred and fury in those voices. "Savages!" is all he can say.

Kilroy is picking up the robe that dropped from my shoulders, THE PEOPLE'S CHAMPION across the back of it—a gift from Elvis Presley, who had it made when I fought Joe Bugner. He comes over and wraps a towel under my chin and over my head to ease the strain on my jaw.

"This is Norton's town. Norton's people," someone is saying. "Like Louisville is your town, Ali. Just a hometown reaction to a local boy."

But I know those faces, those voices out there are not just a "hometown reaction." It's the reaction of most of White America. I'm used to having half the audience come to see me get beat, regardless of who my opponent is. I've denied them this day for a long time, and now that it's here, they're making the most of it. They haven't had much to cheer about since Frazier dropped me with a left hook in Madison Square Garden. And this defeat is much sweeter to them because I'm beaten not by Frazier or Foreman, internationally qualified monsters, but by a "local boy."

"They're not local boys when they fight you," I hear Herbert saying in our private conference just before the fight. "You are thirty-two years old. That's old for a fighter, but now you're facing fighters rougher and tougher than those you fought when you were young. This is their chance for instant fame and fortune if they beat the braggart everybody in the world heard boast, 'I'm the greatest fighter that ever lived.' All fighters you face come out inspired. Your boasts inspire them. They fight harder against you than anyone they meet. You make them ashamed not to."

Always, before a fight, Herbert and I find a secluded spot, give blessings to Allah and take a final look at what I'm about to face.

"You broke every rule for good conditioning in the book," he said of this fight. I thought about postponement. "I'm ready for Norton," I told him. "You'll see." I didn't want postponement.

I'm sitting on the dressing table, looking around at the faces near me, the people slipping in and out of the room, and feeling as though I'm in a strange place. Then I understand why it's strange—it's not the winner's room; it's the loser's room. I've been in one only once before. No one knows what to say in the loser's room.

Why did I lose? I think back to the second round when Norton got in through my guard and crashed a left up against my jaw. I know exactly when the blow came. I felt a snap and a sudden gush of blood in my throat. When I come back to my corner, I ask Bundini and Angelo, "How can you tell when your jaw is broke?"

"When you open it like this"—Bundini demonstrates—"and it clacks, it's broke."

I open it and hear the clack. A sharp pain goes around my face. I spit the blood trickling down my throat into the bucket and wash out my mouth, but more comes gushing in.

"If it's broke," Bundini is saying, "we've got to stop the fight."

But he knows I won't stop. There are thirteen more rounds to go, and I can win. I glance down ringside, I see Joe Frazier and Archie Moore looking up, puzzled. They're here to coach Norton. I'd like to see them leave disappointed.

Before the bell rings, Bundini whispers in my ear, "Shorty is in the living room, watching. Shorty is sitting down, crossing His legs and watching you. Just remember that."

"Shorty" is Bundini's name for God. And during the whole time I'm struggling to take Norton out before another blow crushes into my jaw, Bundini is screaming, "Shorty's watching! In the living room! On TV in the living room! He's watching you!"

I go through round after round, see openings, but I know I can't rumble with Norton in the corners any more. I can't afford to exchange blows. Even when I throw a punch and it lands, the pain goes through my hand as though I've got arthritis.

Afterwards, people want to know why I didn't stop—didn't I know I could have got my face torn off? Even now I can't explain it. Maybe because I didn't think it was really broken that bad; maybe because I didn't believe Norton could beat me, even with a broken jaw; maybe because I've never backed off from a fight. Then, in the ring, under the heat and excitement, my jaw didn't feel as bad as it does sitting here cold in the dressing room. Every throb is like a toothache.

Someone is banging on the door and shouting, "Let the doctor in!" It's the California Boxing Commission doctor. He walks over to me and gently touches my head and neck, feels the side of my face and throat and underneath my chin. There's a deep frown on his face.

"Is the jaw broke?" I ask.

He says nothing at all. The room is quiet.

I try again. "How bad?"

"The only way to be sure is to take x-rays," he says, and turns to Dr. Pacheco. While they talk to each other in low tones, I'm listening for another knock at the door. Someone else should be trying to get in.

"Where's Belinda?" I ask.

Nobody answers. I know something is wrong. Nothing would keep her away from me when I'm hurt.

Finally, Captain Joseph speaks up. "She's in the next room."

"Go bring her in here," I say.

"Well, she's in a room down the hall," he says. And then, "She's in shock."

I hear the California doctor saying, "Muhammad, we've got the car waiting. The plastic surgeon is standing by. You've got to go right away."

But I'm pushing away from him, through the door to the hall, down toward the room Belinda is in. Both doctors follow me. The clusters of hecklers cheering my defeat have grown thicker, and when they see me a roar goes up.

"That loud-mouth finished! Norton beat that nigger! Norton beat that nigger!" Only this morning Norton was a "nigger" like me. But tonight he's The Great White Hope.

The catcalls and screams follow me to my wife's room. After we get in and close the door, I just stand there looking at her. Whoever wanted revenge for all my bragging and boasting has it. Norton's blow is nothing to what shakes me now. Belinda, strapped down on a dressing table, is clawing, straining, screaming, rolling her head from side to side. Youngblood and four other men are holding her down.

While I stand there, she struggles and twists so hard the straps fly open. The men scramble to keep her down and get the straps fastened again.

I move slowly over to a bench and sit down beside her.

"I've given her a heavy sedative," Dr. Pacheco explains. "But she resists it. I'm afraid to give her any more."

Belinda's companion is Suzie Gomez, a young Mexican student. She sits down next to me.

"What happened?" I ask.

"I don't know," Suzie says, "She just went wild when they announced that Norton won. At first, she just sat there. Very quiet. Very still. But I could tell something was wrong with her." She stops and looks a long time at Belinda. "Before the fight she said she had a premonition, but she wouldn't tell me what it was. Then when they announced the decision she started to raise her hands, as if she was going to put them over her eyes, but they never got that far. She just held them in the air. I thought she was going to stand up, and some man sitting next to her did, too. He tried to help her but she hit him."

Belinda has taken karate lessons for two years, and I have seen her lashing out with the skill and power of the Black Belt that she is.

"People in back of us jumping up and down on seats and shouting," Suzie goes on. "Everybody pushing and shoving. We saw you come down from the ring, and we tried to get through to reach you. Then Belinda started fighting her way through. She hit a policeman and she was screaming all the time, screaming, 'Muhammad Ali is dead! They killed him!' "

"She thinks I'm dead?" I reach over and put my arms around Belinda, trying to hold her still. We had married in 1967, when she was only seventeen years old and I was in exile. For the first three years of our marriage there were no trips across the world to fight, no build-ups for fights, no training for fights. It was the worst time for my career but the best time for my family.

I feel her forehead; it's blazing hot. I make them loosen the straps that are cutting into her arms. Then I lean down and whisper to her, "Everything's all right. Pretty girl, Muhammad Ali's all right."

"Muhammad Ali is dead. He's dead." She's crying.

I lean closer and put my mouth to her ear. "No, he ain't, pretty girl. I'm right here. I'm all right." I look into her eyes; they're wide open, but she's looking right through me to something far away.

The California doctor comes over to me. "You've got to leave for the hospital now," he says. "The quicker we get x-rays, the better."

"I want her with me."

He shakes his head. "There's another hospital that's much better for her. Seeing you lose must have traumatized her. She identifies so closely with you. It's like she's fighting the people who were glad you lost, or else she's fighting Norton for you. I don't know, but something shocked her."

I get up from the bench and lie down on the table with her, whispering, "Pretty girl, I'm not dead. They can't kill me."

Both doctors are trying to pull me away, but I stay until she's quiet. Then I ask Suzie to go to the hospital with her and to come back and tell me how she is.

They take me to Claremont General, a long one-story hospital that has no private room. All they can do is keep the bed next to me empty. When the x-rays are taken and the diagnosis made, they wheel me into the operating room and an anesthetist comes to put me to sleep.

"When you wake up," the doctor says, "it will all be over."

I remember thinking to myself, "I'll stay awake and watch what's going on. When they stick the needle in, I'll resist, like Belinda did. I won't let them put me out."

The next thing I remember is waking up with my mouth feeling like it's full of barbed wire. The pain is gone. A doctor is looking at my x-ray and pointing to the fracture. "You were hit a direct blow that landed right here at the site of a recent tooth extraction, on the weakest side of the bone."

I lift my hands to my mouth and feel the wires that hold bone fragments together and keep the teeth lined up.

"It will take three, maybe four months before it heals," he says. "But then it should be as good as new."

I try to say something.

"Oh, yes," the doctor says, smiling, "you won't be able to talk for a while, only through your teeth."

I muster up enough strength to open my mouth and say, "That's the worst punishment of all. Now I really got to pay Norton back."

They laugh, but I know the worst punishment is not mine. I reach up and feel my numb jaw. I think of Maryum, my six-year-old, who is bright and sharp and loves to throw her arms around my head and hug it as tight as she can. And the twins, Jamillah and Rasheda, and my son, Muhammad Ali, Jr. How long before they can take running leaps into the bed with me and crawl around my head?

Bundini comes in every day with the latest news. This morning he says, "Howard Cosell is predicting you're finished. He's saying that three and a half years' exile took too much out of you. The sucker is taking you cheap. Only yesterday, he was saying how great you were."

"Don't blame Cosell," I strain and say through my teeth, "blame me. Only a fool stays with a sinking ship."

I had always been the one who picked up all the stragglers and stray followers. Now I can see them swimming over to Norton, shifting to Norton. It's a cold feeling, and I'm surprised that I'm prepared for it. Herbert, who spends most of his time shuttling back and forth between my hospital bed and Belinda's, says this is the least of my worries, and all I need to do is rest and heal.

On the afternoon of the second day Kilroy tells me there's a call from Eddie Futch, Norton's manager. "He says Norton wants to come and pay his respects. Is it all right?"

Captain Joseph jumps up, furious. "What does Norton want here?" And Bundini shakes his head and growls, but I say let him come. It will be the first time in all my eighteen years of fighting that a victor comes to visit me.

I have already heard that the night after the fight Norton dressed his flashiest—black skintight pants, a blazing red, low-cut Italian shirt, wide open to show his chest—and paraded around the lobby, boasting about breaking my jaw. I understand it. The victor has to have his day.

When the nurse brings Futch and Norton in, we speak of the fight as though we had watched it happen between two other people, not us.

We talk lightly. I tell Norton that Futch is a good manager. "But I've beaten all his fighters before. You're the first he's coached to take a decision from me. What's his secret?"

"I guess he likes me." Norton smiles.

"I never take on a fighter I don't like," Futch says. "If I find myself with a fighter I dislike, I get rid of him, no matter how much profit in it. I've seen managers who subconsciously hate one of their fighters, and actually enjoy seeing him beat. If, after a few months, I haven't fallen in love with my fighter, I drop him, let him go. You've got to love your fighter like your own son. Otherwise, it's dangerous. You'll send him out and get him mangled or killed just for money. Now I'm sixty years old. I waited a long time for a spot like this. I got Norton set to fight for the Heavyweight Title."

"You're about to fight George?"

"They're putting up a million for it now." Futch beams. "Sadler is going to take it."

I feel suddenly hot inside. I see something being snatched from me. "You're a good fighter," I tell Norton. "You throw some heavy bombs. If you win the title, give everybody a shot. Don't duck. Don't hide from nobody."

Norton had been up to my camp and admired my strong, special-built heavyweight punching bag. "I like the feel of that bag," he says when we talk about it now.

"It's yours as a gift," I say. I turn and tell Youngblood to see that he gets it right away. Blood's eyes are blazing. Everyone in my camp will oppose my giving it to Norton, but I insist.

Right before they leave, Futch says he wants to take a picture of me and Norton together. "Just for my family album," he says. "Just for my children."

"We ain't taking no pictures," Bundini mutters, but I have no objection, and Norton poses by the head of the bed.

Then I discover that the pictures were never meant for the Futch "family album." By "chance" Futch has brought a professional photographer with him. Norton and his manager have set it up so the photographs will appear in publications all over the world. The conquerer and the defeated. The man who broke the jaw of Muhammad Ali standing next to his victim.

I resolve—no matter what, even if I have to fight free—I'm going to pay Norton back, and in the morning I see my chance: Dick Sadler and his lawyer, Harry Barnett, come by. I first met Sadler when I was seventeen. The Louisville Sponsoring Group had sent me up to Archie Moore's camp right near here in San Diego. Sadler was to help train me. Now he's the manager of the World Heavyweight Champion, George Foreman. He takes off a little jockey cap and rubs his bald head, sighing like all the world's problems are his.

"What's the matter?" I ask. Like everybody else, I knew Sadler had trouble directing George.

"They offered him five million dollars to fight you. We had an offer of five million for an Ali-Foreman fight, but he backed out of it. You're the biggest draw there is in sports, Ali. Can't no athlete make five million unless he fights you. Now, I come to tell you don't let this little setback bother you. You going to get a title fight. When your jaw gets well again, don't take on anybody else. Just wait for George. The world will still pay five million to see you fight him. Then we can all go out and dance and celebrate and spend the money." He does a neat soft-shoe on the tile floor. "I'm dancing on five million dollars, Ali. Don't let no broken jaw worry you. You fight George next." He keeps on dancing.

"I'm going to fight Norton next."

Sadler stops dancing. "Hell, no! You don't need to prove nothing. Don't fool with five million. They was ready to put it up. They still ready. You want more?"

I shake my head. "I want a rematch with Norton."

"Look," Sadler says, "I'm your friend."

He comes close to the bed, and though it hurts me to talk, there is something I have to say. "Please, if you my friend, let me fight Norton before you put George on him. I know he's due to fight Norton next. Just give me a chance at him. I want this more than anything else." My throat is hot, my head is aching.

"We fight this game for money, not revenge," Sadler says. "Why take a chance with a fool like Norton a second time? I tell you, you still the only fighter that can draw five million."

"It ain't the money," I say. "You know it ain't the money. Just let me fight Norton before Foreman takes him on."

Sadler brings his flat nose directly up to mine. I can read his mind. He's thinking that Norton might beat me a second time and all the money possibilities will go down the drain.

"It ain't a matter of money," I say through closed teeth. "It's me." I know that Sadler can go to Madison Square Garden anytime and get a million for a Foreman-Norton fight. Especially after what Norton has done to me.

Slowly Sadler makes up his mind. "All right. If that's what you want, all right. You got Norton next. I know you're better than Norton, but it's a matter of styles. He's got a style that'll bother you, but it won't bother George. George would smash him like a roach. But I believe you can beat him, too."

"How long you think before I'll be ready?" I ask Sadler. He's been a fighter, a manager, a trainer. He knows the ways of fighters better than the doctors do. He's seen hundreds of boxers beaten, broken, skulls cracked, ears busted, noses smashed, teeth knocked out, eyes cut, and he knows, in the way that a fighter knows, how long it takes to heal them.

Sadler looks up at the ceiling for the answer, putting his little jockey cap back on top of his head. "If you stay quiet, don't agitate your mouth too much, it should be maybe three months, maybe four. You should be ready. When you get out of here, go home and get some rest. That's the best medicine. A good long rest away from the newspapers, from the gyms, away from all the ring business. Go somewhere you can think. Go back home to Louisville."

With that, he whips off his jockey cap, bows low to the nurses, to the aides, to me, and does a soft-shoe dance out of the room, Barnett behind him.

Now I can look past Norton. Sadler will keep his word. He'll match George with other contenders until I fight Norton. When I do, it'll be close but I will even the score. I can regain my title, if I ever get George in the ring. George is on a long string of easy victories. I know how fatal that can be.

Several times a day I get reports on how Belinda is doing. As soon as I feel steady on my feet, I get out of the bed and look for my clothes. The doctor comes in as I'm getting dressed and reminds me and my aides that I'm supposed to stay quiet. They take my clothes away from me, but when I start walking out naked, they change their minds and let me get dressed.

Kilroy drives me to the hospital and I take the elevator to Belinda's room. A nurse opens the door, saying, "She is not allowed visitors. Who are you?"

I bare my teeth to show the wires and say, "Dracula." Then she recognizes me and I step into the room. Belinda is writing notes on a piece of paper and passing them to her mother, Sister Inez, who has flown up to be with her.

"She might not want to talk yet," Sister Inez says, but she gives me an encouraging look. She has been my strongest supporter since I entered her family.

I remember what Suzie said when she first reported back to me at the hospital: "I told them to give her a simple room, to take out anything that might set her off, but when we went in, there was this large crucifix on the wall. She screamed until they took it away."

Herbert is the one who helps her most. Belinda has known him since she was three years old, and it was Herbert who introduced us. He sits with her for two nights in a row, holding her until she is quiet. Twice she stops breathing. The first time they bring her around by hitting her on the chest, but the second time they have to call for the respirator unit. They work for an hour before they get her breathing on her own again, and whenever she gets to a semiconscious state, she opens her eyes and asks, "Who won the fight?" At first the doctors and nurses try to humor her by saying, "Muhammad won. Your husband won." But that makes it worse, and she starts screaming again, "No! Ali is dead! Muhammad Ali is dead!"

Through it all, Herbert studies Belinda carefully. He is afraid that unless something snaps her out of it soon, her malady might be too deep to overcome. Finally he calls his father, the Honorable Elijah Muhammad, tells him the circumstances, and his father phones Belinda, speaks to her as only he can, consoles and reassures her. "His voice made me remember what I was living for," she will tell me when she looks back on this. "My children and my husband came into focus . . . and then I saw you come into the room."

I am standing there looking at her, realizing that when a fighter is beaten, everybody who believes in him is beaten too—his family, his friends, his children, the people who cheer him on, who give him their love, their hope, their pride. As for me, I know no fighter can survive if he feels sorry for himself when he's defeated. When I accept a fight, I accept the consequences. I do everything to make the fight come out my way, but if I'm defeated I have to get up and come back again, no matter how humiliating the loss.

Though she's still paying hardly any attention to me, I bend down and say, "Pretty girl, I'm not dead. They can't kill me, don't you know that? They can't kill Muhammad Ali, baby. Haven't I told you that? Never mind what you hear. Never mind what they say. I won't die. I'll be back up there." I see her eyes on me and I put my arms around her. "We're going home in a few days. You ready?" She looks up and I smile. She's staring at my mouth and then I remember that no one has told her my jaw's been broken. I hold my breath for a moment, wondering how she'll react. Then I bare my teeth and say, "This is the way Dracula kisses in the movies." I lean over and kiss her neck.

In the weeks ahead, when she talks about San Diego, Belinda will say, "Maybe I'll never go to another one of his fights because I identify too much with him. It's like when the blow hits him, I feel it in my stomach. I can feel all the blows myself. I can feel his exertion and the pull of his arm when he's tired. I feel tired when the blows that come to him, come out to the seat and hit me. I think about the pain in his hand when he strikes a blow and I wish he could use my hands, which are painless. When I see him jabbing a certain slow way, I know he's doing it because his hands are hurting. I wish I could get in the ring and jab for him. The feeling almost overpowers me. Maybe I will never go to his fights again."

But she will go and I will help her avoid the blows. When I fight Norton again, she will be as calm and confident as though the outcome was certain, and in the fights to follow she will be by my side cheering me on, safe and solid.

"I ain't been beaten," I whisper to her, "I've been chastised. Allah gave me a little chastising for not obeying the rules. I didn't train right. I didn't rest; I played all night. Fighting is a serious, dangerous business, and I took it lightly. Allah wanted to wake me up and remind me of what my mission is. Remind me that I had strayed away from my mission to our people. This is the best thing that could happen to me.

"I'd started believing I couldn't be whipped, that I didn't have to work hard, train hard, discipline myself, dedicate myself in order to win. Now I know that too many easy victories can ruin a fighter just as much as a long line of defeats. Since Frazier, I started back. I beat Jimmy Ellis, easy, Buster Mathis, easy, Jurgen Blin in Switzerland, Mac Foster in Tokyo, George Chuvalo in Canada, Blue Lewis in Ireland, Bob Foster—all easy. When you win so long, so much, you forget, you think your name will win. You forget the sacrifices, the work that goes into winning. Now I'm down, way down. They say I'm finished. They're celebrating. But I'll come back. I can win my title back. Don't worry, pretty girl. Muhammad Ali is not dead, and nobody will ever kill me.

"We're going back to Louisville. I want to go back home for a while. I need to find my old compass, find out who I am, where I came from, where I'm going, how I got where I am. We'll go back to Louisville and start off where I left my Gold Medal. I'll come back and whip 'em all over again."

She has been looking down at the paper on the table, but she slowly raises her head. There is recognition in her eyes. Just recently she had her twenty-second birthday. Now she looks even younger. She hugs me tight.

Finally the doctors examine me for the last time: Dr. Michael G. Kilty, from London, and Dr. Lancaster, the plastic surgeon who had wired up my jaw. They look at the x-rays.

"How do you feel?" an intern asks.

"My jaw," I say. "Will it always be this numb?"

Dr. Lancaster takes the x-ray, points to the fracture. "There is a nerve here that goes through the bone. It's been severed. Until that nerve connects, until it has healed, that part will always be numb."

"How long will I have to drink my dinner through a straw?"

"Maybe three weeks. It's hard to tell. When you get to Philadelphia, you'll see Dr. Lester Cramer at Chesterhill Hospital. He'll follow you through.

"The main thing is put no strain on the jaw. Cramer will adjust the wires every now and then to keep them tight, take x-rays to see if it's healing right. If it heals right, it should be as strong . . . stronger than it ever was. When you get those two missing teeth replaced, you'll need a special mouthpiece that fits. Had those teeth been replaced earlier, your jaw probably would not have been broken."

"How do you feel?" Dr. Kilty wants to know.

"Like somebody with lockjaw," I say.

"With people who have lockjaw, it's different," the doctor says. "Nearly half of them die. You'll be better than ever." Then he asks me to autograph my x-ray. "There are some kids back in London who won't believe that Ali got his jawbone broken. I have to have proof that you're human."

When I'm ready to leave the hospital the nurses hand me a stack of mail. One message stands out. It's addressed to me and written on the back of a brown bag:

THE BUTTERFLY HAS LOST ITS WINGS
THE BEE HAS LOST ITS STING

You are through, you loud-mouthed braggart. Your
mouth has been shut up for all times. It's a great day for America.
You are finished.

I read it aloud to the embarrassed nurses. There is something about the poem I like. I read it again and again:

THE BUTTERFLY HAS LOST ITS WINGS
THE BEE HAS LOST ITS STING

Later I tape it up on the wall of the gym so that every day I train, I remember that the butterfly has got to get back its wings and the bee has to get back its sting. Of all the messages that came in to me while I was at Claremont Hospital, this is the one I like best. It's funny, but those who hate me most sometimes inspire me the most. As long as I know they're out there.

Before I get out of the hospital, Bundini comes to see me. He rushes in with a big shopping bag and pours its contents at my feet.

"What's this?" I ask him.

"These are buttons," he says, grinning. "Your buttons."

I pick one up. THE PEOPLE'S CHAMP, it says in big black letters.

"I got them from Big Mo, the photographer with George Foreman," he tells me. "He been around there selling them and he asked me if I wanted to buy some cheap. I took all of them. I even snatched off the one he had on. He gave them to me for half price. I asked him why he was selling them so cheap and he said, 'Nobody wants these any more. You all are through.' He thinks we're through, Champ! He really thinks we're through."

Bundini rocks with laughter. He knows I'll train harder than ever now. I've got to show Big Mo and everybody else who doubts me that they can't count me out.

I have gone through the most important fight of my life, and I can sense that somehow it will help me regain the World Heavyweight Title. It was also the most dangerous, and one that could have destroyed me altogether. It was the fight that left me looking inside myself, where before I had been looking on the outside, talking outside, thinking outside. I had not regarded the loss to Frazier as a defeat. I left believing that I had outpointed him, that I should have gotten the decision. But no matter how close the fight with Norton was, a broken jaw has a way of convincing a fighter that he lost. It showed me that a long line of victories can destroy a fighter's sense of what is real. I will draw on this when I fight George Foreman.

George is out there like an overfed lion, fat with victories, overconfident. My old hungry feeling is back. Now only the World Heavyweight Title will whet my appetite. I look forward to Foreman.

LOUISVILLE TEN MILES. I've driven the bus at almost full speed. All night I go over the fight, mile after mile, following the road by instinct until I look up and it's early morning. I'm on the Ohio side of the river and coming up to the bridge that crosses into Louisville. All my crew is asleep, my daughter and Belinda, Harold and Kilroy. And I stop the bus in the middle of the bridge, get out and go over to the side.

It was thirteen years ago when I last stood here with my Olympic Gold Medal. It was a turning point in my life and the starting point.

A panel truck is coming from the Louisville side, and the driver stops and calls out to me: "Is that you, Cassius?" An elderly white man in a security guard's uniform is getting out of the truck. A younger man, who looks like his son, is following. "Is that Cassius Clay?" Something about the voice sounds familiar and suddenly I recognize old John Mayberry, a white policeman who patrolled the black district when I was a boy. He chased my gang down the streets many times. But I am even glad to see him. He turns to the young man beside him and says, "Didn't I tell you that was Cassius Clay?"

I resent him insisting on my "slave name."

"It's Muhammad Ali," the boy says meekly.

"Cassius Clay!" the old man shouts without concealing his joy. "So you finally got your jaw broke. I saw it on the TV. Didn't I tell you you was going to meet your match?"

"How'd it happen?" his son asks softly.

I give him the old joke Sonny Liston used when Marty Marshall broke his jaw: "I was in the ring with this clown, and I started laughing and I had my mouth open."

The boy smiles.

Old man Mayberry sees nothing funny. "You had it coming a long time. You're through boxing now."

"I'm just getting started," I answer. "I just come back to see my people."

"How long you expect to stay?" he asks.

"Just long enough to get my bearings, then I'm going to get the title," I answer.

We're blocking traffic, the car horns are blowing, and I get back in the bus. His son screams out as I pass, "Welcome to Louisville!" But old man Mayberry steps on the gas and moves on, giving me a look as chilly as the rain.

I almost pass my old church before I see it. Mount Zion Baptist Church, where I was baptized in the days when I was a Christian. I thought it had been torn down, and my surprise at seeing it turns to pleasure. I want to go in, but Belinda refuses. She is firm about not visiting Christian churches.

I park the bus anyway and go up to the door alone. It's open, and I see children inside, singing. Young children, standing at attention, holding music books and singing a song I sang when I was their age.

I love children. I can never pass them by without saying something to them. They make you want to start life all over again. Everything I know, I want to teach them—the boys and the girls. Before my son was born, the doctor kept telling us that we were going to have a girl. The first boy Belinda had was premature and died. And the doctor knew we had three girls and wanted a boy. When it was time for delivery, he said, "Let's go watch the girls." They put a mask and apron on me, and I stood there looking and listening to the doctor saying, "Here's the girl; here comes the little girl." But when the lower part of the baby's body came out, and I saw it was a boy, I got so excited I didn't know what to do.

"I would have given anything to have been able to get a picture of you," Belinda later told me. "Your eyes got as red as fresh blood and tears started coming out."

I tried to leave the delivery room but I couldn't find my way out. "Don't go anywhere, just come here and look at the baby," the doctor said gently, grabbing my arm. I stayed for a while, and when I finally left I had to go to Belinda's room and lie down before I was calm enough to go home.

Now I step into this little church and look around for the pew I used to sit on, for the pictures that my father had painted on the walls, a job for which he was paid twenty-five dollars and a chicken dinner. The pictures are gone, but the bench is still here with my initials, C.C., that I had carved into the wood.

The children stop singing and look shyly at me.

"This is Cassius Clay," Miss Davidson, their choir leader, says. One boy speaks up sharply. "His name is Muhammad Ali."

"Yes," she agrees. "Muhammad Ali, our great fighter. This is the church he used to attend when he lived in Louisville." Then she turns to me. "We call ourselves The Buds of Praise. Can we sing anything for you?"

"Just sing what you were singing when I walked in. I used to sing it myself."

Bashfully, the children look into their music books, giggly at first, then stronger, filling the church, they sing, "God Gave Different Things to Different People."

> . . . *What is God to you?*
> *We are not perfect, living in the way we do.*
> *But God knows just what we have been going through* . . .

I'm eight years old again. I'm one of them, singing in the choir, listening to the long sermons, the sisters shouting, waiting for it all to end so I can get outside with my gang and roam the streets.

Suddenly everybody knows I'm here. They begin coming out of the shops, out of their homes. The cars stop. They follow my bus, and whenever I park it on the street, they come out and call me. They surround it.

"It's Muhammad Ali!" some children run down the street yelling. "The World Heavyweight Champion!" they shout, as though they hadn't seen me beat on TV.

A thin, gray-haired woman timidly tries to get through the crowd. It's Miss Murphy, who taught me English at Central High School, and I hear her asking, "Is it all right to call him Cassius? Will he get mad if I call him Cassius?"

"You call me anything you want, Miss Murphy," I tell her. "Whatever you call me, it's all right." And she comes over and I put my arms around her. Home is the only place in the world where most people still call me Cassius and I know they love me.

"You always said you were going to be the Heavyweight Champion of the World," she says. I flinch. Did she see me fight Norton?

People come up for autographs when I get out of the bus and walk around. Some come up grinning as though we share some secret together, some still timid and shy, but most act as though I left home yesterday.

I steer the bus to the home of my parents, Bird and Cash. "He calls me 'Bird,' " my mother tells everyone, " 'cause he says I look like one—pert and pretty. Now everybody calls me that. I started calling him 'GG' 'cause those were the first words I ever heard him say. When he got older, he told me he was trying to say 'Golden Gloves.' He was born right here in Louisville at General Hospital."

The first horror story I ever heard was one my father used to tell about how I was born. How I almost killed my mother in the process.

"She was so long overdue," he said, "the doctors couldn't figure the thing out. It was because of his big head, his head was too big to come out. They tried everything. Pulling it out, pushing it out, but his mother stayed in labor. We didn't know at that time that her pelvis was too small.

"Finally enough of the head was showing so that the doctor could use forceps to pull him out. It left those scars on his cheek. They're still there."

My mother would add, "That wasn't bad enough, but then, after he was born, I almost lost him. They put the wrong baby in my bed. I was satisfied that it was my baby for a while, but then I noticed that the tag said 'Brown,' not 'Clay,' and I called the nurses.

"Where is my baby?" I asked them. "This is somebody else's. They went back and got Cassius. I knew there was something wrong, because the other baby was a quiet, nice baby. Once I got Cassius, he cried so much he could touch off all the other babies in the ward. They would all be sleeping nice and quiet, then Cassius would start screaming and hollering. And the next thing every baby in the ward would be screaming."

Black Louisville is divided into three sections: the worst is East End, we call it "Snake Town"; the California Area is the better section; and the most populated is West End, where I grew up. From my parents' house, we have to drive through town to get to West End. Bird looks out the window, pointing out things about Louisville she thinks I've forgotten.

"Don't talk, G. Doctor says let your jaw heal up. Anything you want to know about in Louisville, ask me. Just drive and listen. Things've changed in Louisville, even since you been here last. It ain't the same Louisville."

"It looks about the same to me, Bird."

"No, G, when you were growing up, Louisville was segregated, you remember? Colored couldn't stay in the hotels until 1960. Only one movie theater for colored. Most big stores downtown wouldn't serve you food or drink. Not even that five-and-ten out there."

I stop for a red light across from a five-and-ten-cent store.

"That one," Bird says. "When you were a little boy, you stood outside that five-and-ten crying for a drink of water. I took you in and asked the clerk for some water, but she was too scared. 'If we serve Negroes in here, we lose our jobs,' she told me. And the store guard came up to get us out. You kept crying. You cried all the way back to West End.

"That wasn't the worse time, though. I used to hate to bring you downtown, especially when you got to be around seven or eight years old. You'd look around, see only white faces in the stores and offices and start crying, asking me over and over, 'Bird, where do the colored people work? Bird, what did they do with the colored people?' And you would cry your little eyes out until we got home. I hated to see you cry like that.

"Me and your father both worried about you. When you'd hear about some injustice against blacks, you'd lay up in your bed, cry all night. Remember? Rudy would cry 'cause you cried. Then your father'd come home and dramatize what happened, make it worse. Like the thing about Emmett Till. You remember when they lynched Emmett Till in Mississippi, how upset you were? Your father talked about it night and day. I told him not to upset you. You remember you were always asking ain't there something we can do to help Emmett Till? We worried from the time you in grammar school till you out of high school. If boxing hadn't come along, Lord knows what you would've got into . . . Why you stopping here, G?"

I've pulled the bus up beside an old railroad station and I get out.

"Train don't stop here any more." Bird is puzzled. "G, this station's been dead a long time."

I know it has. I walk over the tracks and look down the curve the way I did when a train was coming down twenty years ago.

Emmett Till and I were about the same age. A week after he was murdered in Sunflower County, Mississippi, I stood on the corner with a gang of boys, looking at pictures of him in the black newspapers and magazines. In one, he was laughing and happy. In the other, his head was swollen and bashed in; his eyes bulging out of their sockets and his mouth twisted and broken. His mother had done a bold thing. She refused to let him be buried until hundreds of thousands marched past his open casket in Chicago and looked down at his mutilated body. I felt a deep kinship to him when I learned he was born the same year and day I was. My father talked about it at night and dramatized the crime.

I couldn't get Emmett out of my mind, until one evening I thought of a way to get back at white people for his death. That night I sneaked out of the house and walked down to Ronnie King's and told him my plan. It was late at night when we reached the old railroad station on Louisville's West Side. I remember a poster of a thin white man in striped pants and a top hat who pointed at us above the words UNCLE SAM WANTS YOU. We stopped and hurled stones at it, and then broke into the shoeshine boy's shed and stole two iron shoe rests and took them to the railroad track. We planted them deep on the tracks and waited. When a big blue diesel engine came around the bend, it hit the shoe rests and pushed them nearly thirty feet before one of the wheels locked and sprang from the track. I remember the loud sound of ties ripping up. I broke out running, Ronnie behind me, and then I looked back. I'll never forget the eyes of the man in the poster, staring at us: UNCLE SAM WANTS YOU.

It took two days to get up enough nerve to go back there. A work crew was still cleaning up the debris. And the man in the poster was still pointing. I always knew that sooner or later he would confront me, and I would confront him.

I PULL THE BUS up in front of Aunt Eva's Barber Shop and look through the dusty storefront window. Aunt Eva, my father's oldest sister, strapping her razor to shave a grizzly old man on one of four chairs, shouts when I walk in: "I don't believe my eyes . . . Cassius!" Her customer jerks his head and the shoeshine boy climbs all over me. She hugs me so tight the wires holding my jaw hurt. "Ain't it about time you through fighting?" she says when she sees me flinch. "Ain't you had enough? Cassius, you know how long you been fighting?"

"Twenty years!" the shoeshine boy cries out. "You been boxing twenty years. Your aunt told me."

"How much longer, G?" she asks.

"Until I win the title back," I say.

"They'll never let you get it back," she says. "You scared them when you had it, turned the Army down, joined the 'Black Muslims.' They ain't gonna let you get no more title."

Aunt Eva was taught to cut hair because there were eight boys and four girls in my father's family. In those days only girls wore long hair, but the boys' hair grew just as fast and my grandfather said barber charges were too high to pay for eight heads. Aunt Eva was trained to cut the family hair and she went on to become a licensed barber.

When I tell her I'm going to Aunt Coretta's for a family reunion, she says she'll close up shop early and come on over.

It's been years since I've driven down the narrow street where Aunt Coretta's little two-story red brick house sits back from the lawn with a sign planted: CORETTA'S HOUSE OF GOODIES. Long ago she converted the place into a notion store, a restaurant, an apartment, a bakery and a candy kitchen. Aunt Coretta lives in the front and there's an entrance on the side for customers to get to the restaurant and the bakery.

All the old memories come back. This is where I first learned to walk, run and talk. I spent so much time here because it was the best place for my mother to leave me on her way to work. Here, where all my father's relatives assemble, get acquainted with each other's children, gossip, and since Coretta was known as the best cook in the Clay family, enjoy the food. My mother's family was small, only her father, who was bedridden, and a brother, who had moved to Chicago.

In singles, in pairs, my cousins, aunts and uncles come into the small living room, greet my broken jaw with hugs and kisses. They want me to eat a piece of everything: baked and fried chicken, beef and lamb, kale and spinach, mustard greens, macaroni and cheese, carrots and peas, fresh oven-baked breads and cakes, a variety of Aunt Coretta's famous taffy. It is here that I decide to take Aunt Coretta back to camp with me. She'll be my cook, along with Sister Lana Shabazz, as long as I'm fighting.

"There was a time," Aunt Coretta says as I pick over the food, "you'd eat everything in sight, including hay and oats with the horses." She points to an old photograph of me, taken when we lived only half a block from Churchill Downs, watching race horses train. I'd fallen in love with horses. "You remember that?" she asks. "You remember when you started fighting, you'd go out to the track in the morning and race the horses?"

I'd run ahead of the trainers, until one day a horse went beserk. His rider swerved to get out of my way and was thrown to the ground. "Boy, I told you to stay off this track," the supervisor shouted at me. But that didn't keep me from coming into the stables. I wanted to live and sleep near the horses. I loved the smell of horses and hay and the sight of their beautiful bodies. Somehow it inspired me to train harder so my body could be in condition like that.

"It's a shame," I hear my uncle saying. "You getting whipped like you did, your jaw broke. I saw it on TV."

"I never saw you fight so poorly," Aunt Coretta says. "Getting beat by somebody I never heard of." As though that was the worse disgrace. "At first I thought somebody put a mickey in your coffee. I was lying on the bed, looking at the TV. You just weren't yourself. I called everybody in the house—'Will you look at this! Come up here! Cassius getting beat!' "

"Who you fighting next?" my uncle wants to know.

"The same fella," I say with a mouthful of mashed potatoes.

"Oh, my Lord! Let us pray!" one of my cousins screams, and breaks out laughing.

"Cassius is stubborn that way," Coretta explains. "Takes after his grandfather, Herman." She nods at a picture on the wall. My grandfather was a husky, well-built man. There he is, in black pants and white shirt, shoulders proud and muscular. "That's why he never spanked any of his children," she goes on. "He was so strong, he was afraid he'd hurt us. My mother did all the spanking, but if he was in the house, he wouldn't allow it. He'd just talk to us. He liked to talk. You took that after him, I'd say."

I look at Grandfather Herman and remember the way he talked —clear, direct, colorful. He was a good baseball player, but in those days blacks were not allowed in the major leagues. I remember his death and how shocked and disappointed I was. He died the year I started boxing and I wanted to show him, above all, how good a fighter I was.

"We came up during hard times," Coretta says. "In those days, they paid black laborers near slave wages in Louisville. He worked downtown cleaning cuspidors for twenty-five cents a week for years. Then he made a business of his own, selling ice and wood. He never forgot how the whites treated him, would never let a white man come in the house."

Next to him is a picture of my grandmother, painted by her nephew, Sedgwick. "She was a very handsome woman," Coretta says.

After I defeated Liston, I had flown home to stand with her at the Broadway Temple Methodist Church, where she was being honored as the oldest member. She was proud of my father's artwork and used to encourage him: "If you become a great artist, you can get out of the South. Go to New York, Chicago, somewhere. The South ain't no place for a colored artist."

Relatives keep coming in and everybody knows and remembers something about me that I've long forgotten.

"This is where you first started boasting and saying, 'I'm pretty,' Coretta says. She points to the edge of an old dining room table. "You bumped into this table and tore the skin over your eye. It started bleeding, and when your father saw you, he said, 'My God! I hope he didn't mess up that pretty face!' Your father was always saying you were 'pretty as a picture' and 'Don't mess up that beauty.' And the next thing I know you're looking in the mirror and saying, 'I hope I don't mess up this pretty face.' "

I listen all evening and I feel better for having come back. We've been a close family. The only thing that shook them up was when I quit Christianity and became a follower of the Honorable Elijah Muhammad. But somehow they've all gotten over it and are even inspired by it.

Except when I leave, I go through Aunt Coretta's bedroom and there above the bed in massive print is a sign:

ONLY ONE LIFE,
IT WILL SOON BE PAST.
ONLY WHAT IS DONE FOR CHRIST
WILL LAST.

So few people seem to know about life for blacks in Louisville that when I became Champion I was surprised to hear people speak of my "middle-class upbringing." One writer even wrote: ". . . For he was no child of the slums. His mother was a gracious pale-skinned lady, his father, a bitter wit, pride-oriented on the family name of Clay—they were descendants of Henry Clay, the orator, on the white side of the family, nothing less. . . ."

The truth is that most of my life in Louisville was one of poverty —semi-poverty. How much a child of the slums I was can be judged by the facts that stared me in my face most of my life.

While there was a black "middle class" in Louisville, even some affluent blacks, and the neighborhoods were not as ghetto-looking as in some big cities, my part of the Clay family was not among them until my ring earnings made it possible.

I remember the summer of 1956. School was out, and my brother Rudy and I were roaming the streets all day and we'd come home hungry. My father was somewhere across town painting signs and we looked down the streets every few minutes hoping we'd see Bird come with a bag of groceries, maybe hamburger and hot dogs. Maybe, if she spent all her day's pay, chicken and potatoes. Usually she kept only enough for bus fare to go to work the next day for some white lady in the Highlands I never met. She'd get up early in the morning, walk four blocks to catch a bus, ride up where the white folks lived, clean house, clean toilets, cook food, take care of babies—all for four dollars a day. Sometimes she came home too tired to cook.

There was seldom enough money for Rudy and me to have bus fare for school, not both of us at the same time. This is the real reason why I began to race the bus to school. But since my ambition was to be the World Heavyweight Champion, I could say I wasn't racing the bus because I didn't have any money, I was running to get in fight condition.

We never owned a car that was less than ten years old, or even new tires for it. The neighbors could at least buy new tires. Daddy's tires kept blowing out. If we had gotten any money, it wouldn't have gone for cars or tires. It would have been used to fix the house. The rain was coming in through the roof and walls; for four years, the toilet needed a new flush unit; for eight years the front porch had been falling apart. The construction man told Dad it would cost two hundred dollars to have it propped up temporarily. That was too much, so we lived with a front porch ready to fall any day.

Most of the clothes we got came from Good Will, including the secondhand shoes that cost maybe one or two dollars. My father had become an expert at cutting out cardboard and putting it in the bottoms. Now and then there would be a new shirt, and once I remember Daddy buying a cheap little suit for me to wear to church and Sunday School.

IT ALL COMES BACK NOW, driving the bus down Walnut Street, 22nd Street, 34th Street, Shelby Street, Jefferson and Market, 12th and Kentucky. All over Louisville, I see the signs Dad has painted—signs on billboards, on cleaners' trucks, on bakery trucks, on taverns, above factories.

Once Dad painted a picture of Moses on Mount Sinai. It was so striking that other churches started calling for his services. I'd stay up all night in churches watching him paint murals on the wall about John the Baptist, the Lord's Supper, the Holy Angels, the Virgin Mary. His Crucifixion made you cry.

I drive past an old four-story building, the sign on top painted by my father. I helped him one winter as bucket boy, running up and down the ladder, bringing him the paint. He taught me something about the art of sign painting, but it was cold and we could only work twenty minutes at a time, going down to a truck to get warm, then back up again.

Watching him work, the great care and pride he took in painting, whether it was a sign or a whiskey bottle or a mural on a tavern wall, made me admire him, though I knew I wouldn't follow in his footsteps. And he didn't want me to. "You be a lawyer or a teacher," he'd say. But after he saw me in the ring, that changed. He was the first to shout: "This is gonna be the next World Heavyweight Champion!" I'd only had one fight. It startled me. When my father believes something, he dramatizes what he believes. "Let's get ready for it," he said. "Get down to business. I've got another Joe Louis!"

For some strange reason, at least two biographers have written that my father never came to see me fight until I turned professional, which is totally untrue. My father's loud and dramatic encouragement spurred me on. He attended almost every fight I had in Louisville, only missing the ones that were out of town because we couldn't afford the travel expense. One writer of a picture book on my life even said my father beat me throughout my childhood, a claim that had all the Clays in Louisville laughing. My father raised his children like my Grandfather had raised him. We were not to be struck by anyone inside the house or outside.

In the evening after work, Dad usually came home and practiced singing. He was a natural actor. He would imitate the movie stars, especially the lovers. He had a voice that sounded like a cross between Nat King Cole, Bing Crosby and Russ Columbo, and when company was around, he'd sound like all three. Around the neighborhood, he was known as the fanciest dancer in Louisville, and the other dancers would stop, get off the floor and watch him glide. But it was while watching him that I came to the conclusion early in life that there was little future in Louisville for talented black artists. Dad was one of the most gifted men I've ever known. I always thought if he could have grown up where blacks had freedom and opportunity, how different life would have been for him. It was one of the reasons I was determined to leave my Louisville sponsors, even though they were good, fair-minded liberals. Nowadays the South is different and changing, but when I was coming up, I wanted to leave it.

Insofar as being a proud descendant of Henry Clay, "on the white side of the family, nothing less," the fact is that in my part of the family there was very little knowledge, if any, of "white blood" from any source. During the days of slavery, slaves became automatically known by the name of their slave holders: Jones, Williams, Robinson, Smith, Davis, etc., and if slave holder Clay's blood came into our veins along with the name, it came by rape and defilement.

In the old days, when whites had to acknowledge some achievement by blacks, rather than recognize black ability, genius or talent, they'd search for some evidence of "white blood." If the black, no matter how mixed the blood was, happened to be a burglar, a drunkard, a dope addict, a drifter, or just on welfare, they would ignore the "white blood" and he was classified as pure black.

If white blood had anything to do with superior ability, those sixty whites I fought should have beat me to a pulp. The Russians and the Poles in the Olympics should have slaughtered me. Jerry Quarry and Karl Mildenberger should be the World Heavyweight Champions.

Whatever pride I may have felt in the name faded when I found out a little more of what abolitionist Clay thought about black people. One of my teachers at Central High, proud that I had the name, would constantly say to me: "Cassius Marcellus Clay, if you could just follow in the footsteps of that great friend of Abraham Lincoln, that fighting abolitionist whose name you carry . . ." And when I finally showed some curiosity, he directed me to a book, *The Writings of Cassius M. Clay*, by Horace Greeley.

The next week, I brought it back to him and read out loud what the great Clay had said about race: " 'I am of the opinion that the Caucasian or white is the superior race; they have a larger and better formed brain; much more developed form and exquisite structure. Modern discovery proved that the builders of pyramids and Egyptian founders of signs and letters were white. And this long disputed problem is now settled. Historians now unite in making the Caucasian race the first in civilization through all past time.' "

The teacher was embarrassed, took the book, read it himself. That was the last time I was ever called on in school to follow white Clay's footsteps. He had gotten rid of his slaves, but held on to White Supremacy.

Actually, though, I liked the way the name sounded, and I hadn't thought of changing it until I went deeper into black history and heard the teachings of Mr. Muhammad. Then I asked why should I keep a name handed down to me by a slave master, liberal or not? Why should I keep my white slave master's name visible and my black ancestors invisible, unknown, unhonored?

But a barrage of letters from good white friends kept coming at me, urging me to reconsider. The Philadelphia *Sunday Bulletin Magazine*, June 7, 1970, carried an "Open Letter to Cassius Clay": "Now, Champ . . . why not salute your big-hearted, two fisted Kentucky namesake for his great battling for civil rights, by reclaiming the Clay name, thus conceding that what the world needs is more—not fewer —Cassius Marcellus Clays?"

THE NEXT DAY I head the bus toward Grand Street and the house where I grew up. Along the way Bird points out places in the old neighborhood where I used to play.

"There's the fence, the one he used to climb up on. He first walked in his grandmother's house. She used to keep him when I went to work. You know, I worked for Vertner Smith once, way long time ago. I was just a girl of fifteen."

Vertner Smith, my mother's old boss, became one of the Louisville millionaires who sponsored me.

A group of children are standing on a street corner waving, and

I pick them up and drive them with me to East End to find the house where I spent most of my life. When we reach Grand Street, I get out of the bus and stand outside the old house. It's for sale. "I want to buy it," I say. "I want to keep it as a memorial."

I climb the steps and knock on the door. A woman opens it slightly and peers out.

"Wait and come back when I'm dressed and I'll talk to you about it." Mrs. Arvin, a big woman with hair dyed red, is dressed in a purple robe. She tells us she has been feeling poorly, and it's not the weekend. "Only on the weekend do I have a chance to clean it up. It's too messy for you to look at now."

Later, she lets us into the tiny living room heated by a stove. The house looks better than it did when we lived in it. I go into the room I shared with my brother, and it looks smaller than I remembered it. In the kitchen I see that the sink is the same one my father made, and the back porch is still unfinished and the rafters still exposed.

"How would I go about buying this house?" I ask Mrs. Arvin.

"Well, it's for sale. Anytime you want to buy it, it's for sale."

Driving around the old streets reminds me of a time when I was afraid to walk them. I was sixteen. In the gym, in boxing tournaments, in Central High, I was recognized as The King. I took on any fighter. I walked proud and confident, except when I heard Corky Baker was out on the streets. Whenever I walked through Snake Town or West End, with or without my gang, Corky was undisputed Lord of the Streets and wouldn't tolerate any rival.

I had the Golden Gloves ahead of me, the AAU, the Olympics, all of which I was confident I'd win. But the crown that would make me feel most confident as a fighter was held by Corky. He terrorized everyone, including me, and beat up everyone, including me. Already I'd made it known that my ambition was to become the World Heavyweight Champion, but this made Corky laugh. He couldn't see a boxer being anything but a sissy. "Cassius," he told everybody, "ain't got nothing but a big mouth." I would never feel really confident as a fighter until I stopped dodging Corky.

Corky was older than I was, shorter, stocky and bowlegged, but built from the waist up like Mr. Atlas in those "How To Get Strong" advertisements. In his spare time, he lifted weights or tore up four-inch-thick books with his hands. The first time I saw him, he was holding a member of Central's football team upside down, shaking him until the money fell out of his pocket. When you walked near Corky's street, you had to detour unless you wanted to pay a toll for the privilege of walking past him. His steady job was bouncer for the Dreamland Tavern, where he lifted rowdies and drunkards by the scruff of the neck and tossed them out. He made side money betting how high he could lift the front end of Cadillacs from a flat stance, or occasionally a truck if the bet was good enough.

I'd had several run-ins with him, and each time I came out on the bottom. It was beginning to shake me up. I had the feeling that unless I could whip Corky, with all my training, roadwork, and boxing science, it really wasn't much use going into boxing as a profession. On the other hand, I felt if I could whip Corky, I could beat anyone in the world.

I had enough confidence to brag about how I might whip him if we ever got into the ring, but someone overheard me and went back and told Corky. He was outraged, indignant, insulted; in fact, he got mad. For weeks, rumors circulated around Louisville's black community about the coming bloody showdown between Cassius Clay and Corky Baker. It created as much stir in the little town as a big fight did years later between Joe Frazier and me, and in its way it was just as important to me.

It might not have come about, but my "friends" kept egging me on until I walked past the tavern where Corky was standing, his chest bursting through his T-shirt, his arms like hams. It took half the patrons in the tavern to keep him from tearing me apart until they could lay down a heavy bet that in spite of all my boxing medals Corky could whip me in one round, anywhere. "You stand for that, Cash? You hear that?" The roar went up and I took the bet.

I knew it was suicide to fight him on the streets with no rules or referee or regulations, so I took him on for a fight on *Tomorrow's Champions* in the Columbia Gym. "That's not real fighting," Corky said, but the hecklers laughed at him and he quickly accepted. They put us in the ring for a three-round bout, the winner of which would be recognized in Louisville as the real champion fighter. "Corky'll break his spine, fracture his skull and tear his ribs out," the tavern patrons said joyfully. "Corky'll shut his big mouth."

When the bell rang, Corky rushed out, swinging rights and lefts that nearly took off the referee's head, but missed mine. By then I had perfected the art of leaning back, circling, jabbing, and in a few minutes I was pouring lefts into his face from every angle, while nothing he threw hit me. When the round ended, he had thrown so many punches so fast and furious that he was breathing like he had gone ten rounds. My right crosses had blackened his eye and bloodied his nose, and his mouth was bleeding. Before the second round was over, he suddenly stopped in the middle of the round, screamed out, "Hell, no! This ain't fair!" and staggered out of the ring into the dressing room, got his clothes on and left the gym.

My classmates from Central High shouted and jumped for joy,

lifted me up on their shoulders. "The King is Dead! We all free now!"

I was the new King of both the gym and the streets.

It was a victory of no financial importance, but when I was sixteen the battle with Corky Baker was big. It told me something I needed to know.

Later, I asked Lawrence Montgomery, an old friend who grew up next-door to me, where Corky was now. Through the years Corky had kept up with my career and we'd gotten to be friends of a sort. I wanted to hear what he thought of my fight with Norton.

"Corky's dead," Montgomery said. "Got killed a week ago."

"What?"

"In a tavern on Warner Street. He shot it out with the police. He went out the way he came in, fighting in the streets."

BEFORE WE HEAD for home, we drive over to a Catholic school that was called Nazareth College when I worked there, dusting the stairs, cleaning the floors and taking care of the library. A sister in charge of admittance says the nun I've asked for, Sister Allen, is no longer there. I ask for Sister Christina, but before she goes off to find her, she tells me she has read about me and that the college has a picture of a chair with a sign underneath it: THIS IS WHERE CASSIUS CLAY SLEPT.

"I remember you would never pass a mirror without shadowboxing," Sister Christina says.

We drive through Chickasaw Park, where day after day, every morning, I ran. Now I take the same path that I used to run around five times.

When we get back to my parents' house, friends and relatives begin calling and coming by. These are my streets. These are my people and I know I am part of them, and they of me. My defeat? "It's like a mis-cue," a friend says, "on a pool table. In any game there's got to be a mis-cue."

I meet more people that I haven't seen in years.

"How is the family? What's been going on? What kind of work are you into now?" I ask them. It's a funny feeling. They don't have to ask me about what I'm doing. They all know it. People that I grew up with and they all know so much about me and I know so little about them.

Across the street from Nazareth College is Columbia Gym, where I first started boxing but not where I learned the science of it.

The story that my boxing career began because my bike was stolen is a true one, as far as it goes. But that was only a part of it. I was twelve years old, and me and Johnny Willis, my closest buddy, had been out riding around on our bikes until the rain got too heavy. We were looking for something else to do when Johnny suddenly remembered seeing an ad for a black business exhibition at Columbia Auditorium on 4th and York. The auditorium is a big recreational center, with a boxing gym and a bowling alley. Every year the black people in the city hold a big bazaar, the Louisville Home Show, at the Columbia Gym.

At first I didn't want to go to the Home Show very much, but when we read the leaflet we saw that there would be free popcorn, free hot dogs and free candy. Besides, my father had bought me a new bike for Christmas, a Schwinn with red lights and chrome trim, a spotlight in the front, whitewall tires and chrome spokes and rims, and I wanted to show it off.

At the show we focused in on the food, and we hung around eating until seven o'clock, when everybody was leaving.

The rain was still coming down heavy as we left, so it took a while for us to notice that my bicycle was gone. Angry and frightened of what my father would do, we ran up and down the streets, asking about the bike. Someone told us to go downstairs to the Columbia Gym. "There's a policeman, Joe Elsby Martin, down there in the recreation center. Go and see him."

I ran downstairs, crying, but the sights and sounds and the smell of the boxing gym excited me so much that I almost forgot about the bike.

There were about ten boxers in the gym, some hitting the speed bag, some in the ring, sparring, some jumping rope. I stood there, smelling the sweat and rubbing alcohol, and a feeling of awe came over me. One slim boy shadowboxing in the ring was throwing punches almost too fast for my eyes to follow.

"You'll have to give me a report," Martin said calmly, and wrote down what I told him. Then, as I was about to go, he tapped me on the shoulder. "By the way, we got boxing every night, Monday through Friday, from six to eight. Here's an application in case you want to join the gym."

I was about 112 pounds, skinny, and I'd never had on a pair of boxing gloves. I folded up the paper and stuck it in my pocket, thinking it was a poor thing to take home instead of a bike. That night my father bawled me out for being so careless. And for once I was in total agreement with him. I told him I was sorry, and I meant it.

That Saturday I was home looking at a TV show called *Tomorrow's Champions*, an amateur boxing show, and there was the face of Joe Martin, working in the corner with one of his boys.

I nudged my mother. "Bird, that's the man I told about the bicycle. He wants me to come and box. Where's that application?"

She had taken the paper out of my pocket when she washed my clothes, but now she went and got it. "You want to be a boxer?" She was serious.

"I want to be a boxer," I said.

"How you going to get down there? It's a long way off. Your bike is gone. There's no carfare for that."

"Oh, I'll borrow somebody's bike," I said. "And I don't have nothin' else to do."

I remember my father looked uncertain. Then someone outside opened the door and yelled, "Johnny Willis's out here waiting for Cassius."

That decided it. "Well, boxing is better than running around with Willis and that gang," my father said. "Anything will beat that. Let him go."

When I got to the gym, I was so eager I jumped into the ring with some older boxer and began throwing wild punches. In a minute my nose started bleeding. My mouth was hurt. My head was dizzy. Finally someone pulled me out of the ring.

At that moment I was thinking I would be better off in the streets, but a slim welterweight came up and put his arms around my shoulders, saying, "You'll be all right. Just don't box these older fellows first. Box the fellows who are new like you. Get someone to teach you how to do it."

But there was hardly anybody to teach me anything. Martin knew a little. He could show me how to place my feet and how to throw a right cross, but he knew very little else. I was fighting like a girl, throwing wild, loopy punches. But something was driving me and I kept fighting and I kept training. And although I still roamed the streets with the gang, I kept coming back to the gym.

"I like what you're doing," Martin said to me one day. "I like the way you stick to it. I'm going to put you on television. You'll be on the next television fight."

Thrilled at the idea of being seen on TV all over Kentucky, I trained the whole week. They matched me with a white fighter, Ronny O'Keefe, and I won my first fight by a split decision.

All of a sudden I had a new life. Inside the gang, I was getting recognition as a fighter. My father walked up and down Boston Street after my first victory, predicting, "My son is going to be another Joe Louis. The World Heavyweight Champion, Cassius Clay." Bird began to see how I resembled Louis. "Hasn't he got a big round head like Joe Louis?" she asked my cousins.

And from then on she would recall how I used to jump up in the bed and say, "GG." "Those were the only things he could understand.

The two letters, GG." And I would make the joke about how I was trying to tell her I was going to be a Golden Gloves Champion.

Even the gap in her two front teeth, she would now attribute to me. "When he was a baby he had the fighting instinct in him. I was spanking him and he got mad and swung at me and knocked both of my two front teeth out of place. He was only a year old then. It shows how hard he could hit from the start."

And each week Joe Martin would book me on *Tomorrow's Champions* because in the ring I flailed away, even after I was exhausted, and I was winning. Not because I was so skilled but because I never stopped. The other fighters would go down or quit or get discouraged.

But it was while fighting in my first Kentucky State Golden Gloves tournament that I learned more from a defeat than from all the victories I had been accumulating under Martin. In that tournament, a black fighter beat me decisively. I was hurt, but I knew I had been beaten by a better boxer and I knew where he came from. Grace Community Center, a boxing gym over in the all-black part of town, under the guidance of a trainer named Fred Stoner.

I had already noticed that the boys from Stoner's gym were better boxers than those at Martin's. They were counterpunchers, with better rhythm. Their timing was better, their punches sharper.

Martin's strict rule was that there be no association with Stoner. I was getting four dollars every time I boxed on *Tomorrow's Champions*, and Martin would not allow Stoner's boys to box on the show. Most of Martin's boys were white, and most of those he tried to seriously recruit were white.

One evening, watching Stoner's fighters outclass and outstyle boxers that had come in from another state for an exhibition, I was so impressed that I decided to take the chance. With Rudy, I walked all the way up to Grace Community Center and went down into the basement gym and met Stoner.

A slightly built, quiet black man, he was very intent in his work, watching every move his boxers made. I looked around. He didn't have the facilities that Joe Martin had. In the winter the basement of his church would be cold, while it was warm in Martin's gym. And his handbags and equipment were inferior to Martin's.

"If you want to come in, come on," he said.

"Have you seen me on TV?" I asked.

He nodded, unimpressed. "You got courage," he said. "You got the will, but you don't have the skill. We train here at night from eight to twelve o'clock. If you can get here, I'll show you how to fight."

The next morning, when I walked into the Columbia Gym, Joe

Martin called me aside. "I heard you were over there training with Fred Stoner."

For some reason, I was frightened. He talked to me as though I had done something criminal.

"You know the rules in this gymnasium," he said. "No one can be with Stoner and be with me. It's up to you. Either drop Stoner or I'll drop you."

I felt my heart sinking. I needed the four dollars I was getting for boxing under Martin, but I also needed the science and skill Stoner was teaching. All of the black professionals—Jerome Dawson, Billy Williams, Bill Hestor, Green Gresham and Rudolph Stitch—had been molded by Stoner.

I remember standing in front of Martin, sweating and feeling degraded. I agreed to stay away from Stoner's gym.

But that year Fred Stoner's boys went to Chicago and brought back most of the amateur titles. They were beautiful fighters. Boxers. They had sharp hooks and they danced. They could jab, hit, move. They had pretty footwork. They could duck and weave. Some were even younger than I was, but their bodies looked mature. How did they get their bodies that way? I had to find out.

I remember one hot Saturday morning, making the long walk from 32nd Street to the gym on 6th Street where the boxers for *Tomorrow's Champions* assemble. I'm thirteen years old. I stop on 18th Street to watch boys and girls splashing around in a big swimming pool. As I stand there, a skinny boy in ragged tennis shoes, holding an old pair of dirty underwear-looking trunks, comes up next to me. I hold on to my own black and white striped trunks and we look each other over carefully.

"Where you going?" he asks, eyes on my trunks.

"I box today," I tell him.

"Who you fighting?"

"I don't know. I'm supposed to fight on a show, *Tomorrow's Champions.*"

"That's funny. Me too."

"Who you fighting?"

"I don't know," he says.

And then a friend of his comes up on a bike, and he gets on and rides off to the gym, ahead of me.

By the time I get there, he's coming out the door, and he pushes me and says gruffly, "Well, you won't fight today." I rush over to find Joe Martin, and he points to the same boy and says, "That's the fellow you're supposed to fight, Jimmy Ellis, but he don't weigh enough."

I walk over to him. "You Jimmy Ellis?"

"You Cassius Clay?"

"Why don't you gain some weight," I say, as if being skinny is his fault. Tears are in his eyes. "We both lost four dollars because you're too skinny."

"We lost four dollars because you're too heavy!" he shoots back. "You're too young to weigh that much."

I can see he feels as bad as I do. I am two years younger than Jimmy, but I am also heavier. Later, we will fight even in an amateur tournament. He'll win one and I'll win one and we joke of someday fighting to break the tie. When I become Louisville's first World Heavyweight Champion, I will use Ellis as my main sparring partner. When I am stripped of the title, he will win the WBA's Heavyweight Elimination Tournament and be recognized by them as the World Heavyweight Champion. For a while little Louisville will have produced two Heavyweight Champions in a decade. And only when I am climbing back into contention, do we fight our final "rubber match," to break the tie.

It will come in Houston. He is the first fighter I face after my loss to Joe Frazier. And it's crucial that I beat him to prove I can come back. It's crucial for him to prove that he's more than just my sparring partner, but a real champion. A defeat by Ellis would mean extinction for me. Fortunately, I was always a little heavier and better than Jimmy.

By the end of that year, I knew I wanted to be a fighter. I decided to go down to Grace Community Center and learn the science of it, even if it meant cutting off a good source of income.

After school I would go to work four hours for the Catholic sisters, then train at Martin's gym from six to eight in the evening. From there I would go to get the real training at Stoner's gym from eight to twelve at night.

The discipline in Fred's gym was tough. Roadwork was like religion, and Fred was relentless in making me develop certain muscles which he believed were necessary for survival in the ring. He made us shoot left jabs, two hundred straight, sharp left jabs at a time without stopping. If we got tired, he made us start all over and count to a hundred, one, two, three . . . shooting jabs until we could do the two hundred without feeling it. Then he made us shoot and jab and a right cross. Then come back with a hook, jab, left hook and duck; a jab and back up, a jab and move forward. He taught us to block, to shoot right crosses, and we went over it again and again. We did a hundred push-ups and a hundred knee bends.

In Martin's gym, all that was required was to punch the bag, jump ropes and jump in the ring and flail away at each other. All the publicity about my boxing origin and the early development of my boxing skill describes Joe Martin as the incubator. But my style, my stamina, my system were molded down in the basement of a church in East End.

I am fourteen years old, riding my little two-horsepower motor scooter. I am coming home in the rain from the basement gym at Grace Community Center in the East End of Louisville. I have been there all afternoon with Fred Stoner.

It begins to rain harder and I am driving, head down, zipping past parked cars until I pass one with its radio up loud and hear a roaring crowd. I put on the brakes, skid around and come back to hear more. A heavyweight boxing match is taking place. The car is too crowded for me to get in, but they let me put my head inside so I can hear. I have gotten there just in time to hear the announcer crying out above the noise, "And still the Heavyweight Champion of the World, Rocky Marciano!"

A cold chill shoots through my bones. I have never heard anything that affected me like those words: "Heavyweight Champion of the World." *All* the world? And from that day on I want to hear that said about me.

I pull my head out of the car and stand there in the rain. "Still Heavyweight Champion of the World, Cassius Clay!" I get back on my scooter and ride on, hearing that announcer's voice coming through the wind: "And still Heavyweight Champion of the World, Gene Tunney, Joe Louis, Ezzard Charles, Rocky Marciano, Floyd Patterson . . . Cassius Clay!"

I start dreaming: I can see myself telling my next-door neighbor, "I'm getting ready to fight for the Heavyweight Title of the World!" And coming back the next night to say, "I'm now the Heavyweight Champion of the World!" The rain is cold and pouring down harder, and I ask myself, "Can I?" At this time I can't even beat everybody in my own gym. I ask Jim Martin. He shakes his head doubtfully. "You hardly weigh a hundred and fifteen pounds soaking wet. You know how big a heavyweight is? Maybe you could be a lightweight."

But I want "heavyweight." Somehow, although no one on either side of my family is that big, I feel I will be. I turn from him, and the next day I start training in earnest. I start watching fights on TV with more interest. What catches my eye is the way fighters trade punches with each other. I see Ralph "Tiger" Jones, Hurricane Jackson, Carmen Basilio, Gene Fullmer, and watch how they stand, and get hit with the same punch. Or jab each other over and over. And I know I can beat them. Even when I see Patterson. Even when I see Archie Moore. I know that one day I will be able to whip these men very easily, because they are not moving, not circling. Not moving backwards at the right time. I know I can learn to hit without getting hit. And every day in the gym I practice pulling back from the punches. I jab and then lean back. I learn that you can't dodge most punches by weaving, bobbing and ducking—not from short range.

Professionals around the gym tell me, "Someday you're going to get your head knocked off." But the wiser ones remember that Jack Johnson also leaned back.

Soon I develop a built-in radar. I know how far I can go back, when it's time to duck or time to tie my man up. I learn there is a science to making your opponent wear down. I learn to put my head within hitting range, force my opponent to throw blows, then lean back and away, keeping eyes wide open so I can see everything, then side-step, move to the right, or to the left, jab him again, then again, put my head back in hitting range. It takes a lot out of a fighter to throw punches that land in the thin air. When his best combinations hit nothing but space, it saps him.

Throughout my amateur days, old boxers think I'm easy to hit, but I'm not. I concentrate on defense. I concentrate on timing and motions and pulling back. When I throw a jab, I know my opponent will throw a punch, and I pull back.

"I'm going to train harder," I told Stoner one night. "I want to know everything you can teach me."

Stoner was looking me hard in the eye, as if to see how serious I was. Then he said, "You're quick and you got the talent. Some of the best pros in the country are in town now. You get down to business, and when they hold the tournament in the fall, you will come out a champion."

A minute earlier my hands had been burning, my arms and legs aching, but what Stoner said was healing them faster than all the alcohol and iodine he had poured over them.

"You think I can win the Golden Gloves?"

"Not only the Golden Gloves, you'll take the Olympic Gold Medal in Rome." Stoner said it as though it was inevitable.

I had been winning most of my matches without much coaching, but after Stoner's lessons I was certain I would defeat my opponents. In 161 amateur fights out of 167, I did.

Both Martin and Stoner kept the gold of the Olympic Medal shining in my eyes: "It's worth a million dollars to a fighter. When you win that, you're a national hero. You're celebrated like Lindbergh. And the governor, the mayor, the police, even the President honors you. It's something you'll remember for the rest of your life."

They were right. I remember winning the Golden Gloves tournaments and the AAU titles. But what I remember most is the summer of 1960, when I came home from Rome to a hero's welcome.

THE GOLD MEDAL

When I came home from Rome, Joe Louis would have been my first choice as manager, but Louis didn't like to talk much, didn't like loud-mouthed, bragging fighters, and predicted that I would lose every fight I had.

Then I wanted Sugar Ray Robinson, and went to New York to search for him and offer myself as a prospect. Ray was near the end of his career, and I thought he might like to handle mine. When I finally cornered him and forced him to notice me, he brushed me off. "Look, kid, come back, maybe in a couple of years, okay?"

All day I followed him around Harlem, dancing, jabbing, shadow-boxing, showing him how fast, how quick I was. Ray was too busy.

Years later, when we became friends, he would shake his head sadly over "what might have been" if he had taken me on. Now, looking back, I'm glad he didn't. I respect Sugar Ray in the ring as one of the greatest of all times. But he stayed out of what I call the real fighting ring, the one where freedom for black people in America takes place, and maybe if he had become my manager he might have influenced me to go his way. I'm glad he had no time.

Those who did have time for me were mostly rich white Southerners. The expectation in Louisville, and all through the South, was that I would be managed by the millionaire William Reynolds. In fact, when I came home from Rome, I found Reynolds being praised across America for what he was about to do for me. His personal Man Friday and my trainer Joe Martin had met my plane in New York. They had arranged for me to stay up at Reynolds' private suite at the Waldorf-Astoria. Reynolds' man took me on my first shopping tour in Manhattan, let me buy four hundred dollars' worth of watches as gifts for my mother and father. Then he took me to a restaurant and said, "All the steaks you can eat." I ate six.

"Why would any normal Kentucky boy who wanted to get ahead in boxing turn down a millionaire benefactor with the generosity, affluence and connections of William Reynolds?" a Louisville newspaper would editorialize a few years later, after I had been outlawed from the ring. They were looking back to see where I had gone wrong. "When he turned down Reynolds we should have realized how twisted and misguided was Black Cassius, this same young man we Kentuckians once loved and respected so much. This was the turning point."

In a way, my relationship with Billy Reynolds was the hidden turning point. It was Martin who first wanted to be my manager and came with a contract. In all the years he trained me it was the only time he visited my house. "Well, here it is," he said, and dropped the contract into my father's hands. Dad wanted to have a lawyer look at it, but Martin said it had to be signed immediately. It guaranteed me seventy-five dollars a week for ten years. I wanted to take it because I was making so little money at the time. My father screamed, "Nobody buys my son for seventy-five dollars a week for ten years! The slave trade is over!" And he told Martin what to do with the contract.

Martin blamed the rejection on Dad's "hatred for white policemen," and that version of the story circulated around the world. The truth is different. Until now, I've kept quiet about why I never signed that contract or the more important ones that were offered later by Reynolds. I still see myself that spring of 1960, a tallish eighteen-year-old boy in sweat shirt and khaki pants, standing outside the big iron gate of the William Reynolds estate in Bridgeton, Kentucky, one of the richest suburbs of Louisville. I had been sent there by Joe Martin, who said Reynolds was interested in me and might give me a job. I got up at 5 A.M., did four miles of roadwork around Chickasaw Park, then caught the bus to Bridgeton.

When Martin first announced that I might get a job with Reynolds, a sort of excitement had gone through the gym; it signified that the millionaire was interested in becoming my manager, and "looking after me." A millionaire backer for a boxer. That was the dream in the gyms.

"You need somebody who ain't hungry," Martin had said. "Reynolds got money like Fort Knox. His family owns all that aluminum. Reynolds pots, Reynolds pans, Reynolds steel, Reynolds railroad cars. He knows you're the best heavyweight prospect that's been in Louisville for a long time."

Martin had met him through Reynolds' brother Jerry, a sportsman who once managed the flyweight Spider Thomas. "As a policeman, you get to escort a lot of important people around town," Martin always said with a wink. "They want a good investment. Cassius is the best fighter in the gym."

I may have been the best fighter, but I was also the poorest. I owned one T-shirt, two pairs of pants, several pairs of shoes with holes in them. My jackets were torn and patched, and hardly a day went by when my pants didn't split somewhere. And although I had won nearly all my fights, and was on the verge of turning professional, I had never been able to afford a first-class mouthpiece to protect my teeth. I had to wait until other fighters finished so I could borrow their headgear, or their trunks or bandages. I wanted my own training gloves, my own gear.

"Reynolds will see that you get suitable work this summer, and after the Olympics, go professional," Martin had said with great pride.

I couldn't help grinning and feeling good.

"No prizefighter's got a manager like Reynolds," Martin had explained. "I hope he's big enough for your dad," he said sarcastically, referring to Dad's first rejection. "He'll greet you like his own son."

Reynolds' house was in the center of the estate, a three-story gray building, with stairs sweeping up to a high porch with huge white pillars. The beauty and size of the place were breath-taking. Like in *Gone with the Wind*. I halfway expected to see slaves picking cotton and rows of cabins at the foot of the hills.

I kept pulling the bell cord, and when no one answered I pushed back the iron gate. It swung easily and I walked down the lane toward the big gray house.

A heavy voice cut in behind me. "Say you! Nigger! You know you on Mr. Reynolds' private property?"

I turned, and coming down on me was a hefty red-haired white man with a shovel. And coming up behind him was a stoop-shouldered, elderly black man who I later learned was the gardener.

"Nigger, do you know where you are?" The hefty man was now standing over me, his shovel in a tight grip.

"Yes, sir," I said.

"Look, that road goes that-away." The man pointed back to where I had come from.

But I stood still, my eyes fastened tight to his. He was moving toward me, raising the shovel, when the black man came up and said gently, "I think that's Cassius Clay, sir."

The big man turned toward the gardener. "John, you know this nigger?"

"Yes, sir." The gardener nodded his head. "Mr. Reynolds told him to come. He gonna hire him." He spoke almost apologetically, as though he didn't want to offend the white man, even with the truth. "Yes, sir, this is the boxing boy." The black man's eyes had a glint of pride. He had a kind, soft voice, and he motioned for me to follow him. When we were alone for a minute, he said cautiously, "Did he scare you with that shovel?"

I said no.

"You really a good fighter?"

"Yes, sir," I said. He seemed to like me.

"You got good manners, son. You'll make it good here. Mr. Reynolds' folks is nice people. You keep them good manners. Most young ones coming out of Louisville, they talk louder than the bosses."

"Is Mr. Reynolds here today?" I asked as we passed the front porch.

The gardener nodded. "He ain't down yet, but he's here. See those cars?" He pointed to the garage. "All around here, them's his cars. What kind of job Mr. Reynolds gonna give you?"

I couldn't tell him what I expected. I was good in mechanical drawing and had learned something about drafting and art from my father. I walked along thinking that in all of Reynolds' far-flung businesses surely there would be something in one of them for me to do. Maybe I could learn drafting, have a second trade besides the one I'd trained for.

"How long before I can meet Mr. Reynolds?" I asked.

The gardener shook his head. "You don't worry about that. Mr. Reynolds told me to introduce you to the manager of the house, his aunt. She runs the place. She's got something in mind for you already."

We'd come to steps leading to the kitchen. A tall, scrawny, white-haired old woman in a dull gray dress came out and looked me up and down. Finally she said, "I'll show you what you gotta do."

And every morning she showed me what dust to remove, what garbage to dump, what floors to scrub, what toilets to wash, what porches to sweep. And I'd ask the gardener if I could see Mr. Reynolds, but he would shake his head cautiously and say, "He's a very busy man. You'll see him, but he don't spend much time here, not Mr. Reynolds."

Then one day, while I was sweeping the back porch, I heard someone say: "The next Olympic Champ of the World! The next Olympic Champ, Cassius Clay!"

It was Mr. Reynolds. Shorter and fatter than I had expected, but vigorous. He looked exactly like STP Granatelli.

"Mr. Reynolds—" I began.

"Call me the future manager of the World Heavyweight Champion."

Already I felt better, and that week I mopped the floors harder, trimmed all the hedges, washed all the windows, and looked forward to the rare times that I could see and maybe talk to my "manager." He'd come in and out, take a bite to eat, dash back to his office, give me a wave now and then. "Martin tells me you're improving." Or, "Be sure you win that Olympic Championship. It's worth a million."

"Thank you, Mr. Reynolds," I'd say, "but may I talk to you for a minute?"

"Not now, my boy, but later on."

One day, when he had a little time in between two cups of coffee, he called me into the kitchen. "Cassius, I'm going to see that you get a chance few fighters ever get. Is there anything special you need?"

I thanked him and asked, "What kind of work do you think I should be doing now, while I'm training?"

He was already hurrying out of the house, and he pointed to his aunt. "She'll tell you what-all there is to do, Cassius. She's got it mapped out. How's he makin' out, honey? How you like him?"

She looked at me without any special approval. "He walks around like a cat," she said. "Like some jungle animal. He don't even walk like a houseboy. He'd be all right if he'd stop daydreamin' so much. He daydreams too much."

Mr. Reynolds laughed. "Feed him good. He needs it. Build up his body. He's a fighter." And he left.

Of course I was well fed. Each day his aunt brought my lunch out on a tray and put it on the porch, the same as she did for the dogs and cats. Only mine had been deliciously cooked in expensive pots in the beautiful marble-walled kitchen. As I ate she would call out, "Soon as you get through, Cassius, I want you to scrub those toilet stools down in the basement. You missed those yesterday."

When I needed water, they brought out a pail and sat it on the porch. "It's not that they don't want you in the kitchen," the old gardener explained, "only your clothes are so sweaty and dirty. It's better to eat out here in the fresh air."

It seems strange to me now, but I really didn't mind then and I made friends with some excellent breeds of dogs. But I knew I was being treated like any good animal, or good race horse, worth feeding and investing in.

I was in better condition than most athletes, but I could only go on with the grind of getting up at five every morning, the roadwork around Chickasaw Park, the one-hour bus ride to the suburbs, the rush to the gym to train for two hours, then back to finish the houseboy duties, by holding my dream of becoming the World Heavyweight Champion in front of me.

"When you win the Olympics, Reynolds will make you an offer, the biggest offer any fighter ever started out with," Martin would remind me.

This kind of talk drove me on, but somehow I still wanted to talk to Reynolds, and I asked his aunt if there was any way I could do it.

"Can't you see he's busy?" she snapped. "If you want to impress him, do your work. You don't do half the things I ask you. Go on. And don't let me catch you daydreaming again."

One day Mrs. Reynolds' black Fleetwood was blocking the driveway, and I got in to back it into the garage. I'd never been in a car so big, lush and pretty. It was blazing hot outside, so I rolled up the windows, cut on the air conditioner and leaned back to soak it all in. I rubbed my hand over the soft seat covers, felt the black leather interior. I began backing it toward the garage, amazed at how easy it steered.

Then someone was screaming. "Help! Help! Stop him! Somebody stop him! Help!"

I smashed on the brakes. A thief was coming on the grounds! I threw open the door to dash out to save the family jewels.

"Nigger, how dare you! Git out of that car!" Mr. Reynolds' aunt shouted at me. "That's Mrs. Reynolds' private car! Nobody is allowed to touch that car!"

Her screams had brought the old gardener running up. He understood her in a way that surprised me, and he patted her on the shoulder as though soothing a spoiled child.

"Cassius didn't mean no harm, miss. Remember what the doctor said about your blood pressure. The car ain't worth gittin' yourself upset about."

"That car," she said, "is worth more than that nigger will ever be worth in his lifetime. And I don't want to see him in it. I told you he was a daydreamer."

I apologized, but she was bitter. "Why don't you do your work like you supposed to do, instead of sitting around in a white man's car daydreaming?"

I went away to clean the ring around the bathtubs. I felt no resentment against the old woman, but I felt uneasy about the prospective manager of the World Heavyweight Champion, a feeling that never left me.

Reynolds was excited over my Olympic victory, but afterwards, when the plane landed in New York and his Man Friday and Martin took me to stay in his private suite at the Waldorf—next-door to the suite of the Prince of Wales, above the suite of General Douglas MacArthur and adjacent to that of former President Herbert Hoover —a suite more lavish than his Fleetwood, he didn't seem to be the real Mr. Reynolds. He seemed more real when I sat on the porch eating with the dogs.

His Man Friday handed me a contract and said, "Take it home to your father to look at. It's a good one. You're the Olympic Champion now. You deserve it."

I took it home, and even though Dad was not sympathetic to Reynolds, he wanted to accept it. "It's the best contract that's been offered," he said. "It's almost as big as the one the millionaire group is offering, and it could be better."

But I refused it.

It takes pride and a tiger's drive to build up the confidence, the ego, the power to defeat an opponent in the ring. It struck me as peculiar that the man who wanted to manage the tiger wanted him home on a leash as his houseboy.

So what I remember most about the summer of 1960 is not the hero welcome, the celebrations, the Police Chief, the Mayor, the Governor, or even the ten Louisville millionaires, but that night when I stood on the Jefferson County Bridge and threw my Olympic Gold Medal down to the bottom of the Ohio River.

A few minutes earlier I had fought a man almost to the death because he wanted to take it from me, just as I had been willing to fight to the death in the ring to win it.

It had taken six years of blood, blows, pain, sweat, struggle, a thousand rounds in rings and gyms to win that medal, a prize I had dreamed of holding since I was a child. Now I had thrown it in the river. And I felt no pain and no regret. Only relief, and a new strength.

I had turned pro. In my pocket was my agreement with the ten Louisville millionaires, our "marriage contract" for six years. I felt as sure as day and night that I would one day be the World Heavyweight Champion. But my Olympic honeymoon as a White Hope had ended. It was not a change I wanted to tell the world about yet. I would be champion. My own kind of champion.

The honeymoon had started when my plane touched down at Standiford Field. They opened the door and my mother rushed up to hug me. Then my brother Rudy and Dad. I had been gone for twenty-one days, the most time I'd been away since the day I was born.

Then came the celebrations: the long police escort all the way downtown; black and white crowds on the streets and sidewalks; WELCOME HOME CASSIUS CLAY signs from my classmates at Central High; the Mayor telling me the Olympic Gold Medal was my key to the city; plans under way for me to have my picture taken with President Eisenhower.

Time magazine saying: "Cassius never lets his Gold Medal out of his sight. He even sleeps with it." They were right. I ate with it, and wouldn't stop sleeping with it even though the sharp edges cut my back when I rolled over. Nothing would ever make me part with it. Not even when the "gold" began to wear off, leaving a dull-looking lead base. I wondered why the richest, most powerful nation in the world could not afford to give their Olympic champions real gold.

One Kentucky newspaper described my medal as "the biggest prize any black boy ever brought back to Louisville." But if a white boy had brought back anything better to this city, where only race horses and whiskey were important, I hadn't heard about it.

In later years, when I fought and did exhibitions around the world, in Zurich, Cairo, Tokyo, Stockholm, London, Lima, Dublin, Rio de Janeiro, I was given welcomes and celebrations that were much greater, more colorful. But when you've been planted like a tree in one town, and suddenly become recognized and acclaimed by the other trees, it is unlike any other experience you are likely to have. In fact, I'd written a poem about it on the plane, "How Cassius Took Rome," which I sent to the black newspapers and later recited to my classmates, a poem expressing my love for Louisville.

And although I was still hit with some of the same race hostility I'd known all my life, my spirits were so high I felt whoever was against me would change. Even those whose resentment made them go through the acknowledgments half-heartedly or with no heart at all. Those who came only out of curiosity, and looked disgusted when they learned they had to honor a black boy.

I was deeply proud of having represented America on a world stage. To me the Gold Medal was more than a symbol of what I had achieved for myself and my country; there was something I expected the medal to achieve for me. And during those first days of homecoming it seemed to be doing exactly that.

I remember the crowds that followed us down the street where we lived. The porch of our house was decked with American flags, and my father had painted the steps red, white and blue. Photographers yelled, "Hold it! Hold it!" And I posed for a minute, arm-in-arm with my father as he sang "The Star-Spangled Banner" in his best Russ

Columbo style. We stood proud. Everybody cheered.

Through most of that summer the crowds kept coming around the house. Louisville lit up. Congratulations every day from city officials. Even handshakes from the Chief of Police. A slap on the back from the Governor of Kentucky, who reminded me, "Boy, I know you proud of that name 'Cassius Clay.' I know you proud to carry that name."

In the evenings we sifted through offers from professionals to "manage" me. One telegram from Archie Moore: IF YOU DESIRE TO HAVE AN EXCELLENT MANAGER CALL ME COLLECT. From Rocky Marciano: YOU HAVE THE PROMISE. I CAN GIVE YOU THE GUIDANCE. From Cus D'Amato, Floyd Patterson's manager. From Pete Rademacher, former Olympic Champion. We examined every offer until a lawyer came representing ten (later eleven) Louisville millionaires, who put together the contract my father and family approved. It was to run from 1960 to 1966, and it did. The main feature was a $10,000 advance. The Louisville group, to start off, was to get 50 percent of all my earnings, in and out of the ring. At the time, $10,000 seemed to me a huge amount. The only frame of reference I had to "big" sums of money was the worn-down little house we lived in. Sold to us on installment for $4,500, it was taking my father his lifetime to pay for it. Most of the $10,000 went to repair and pay off the house.

In those first days after my return from Rome, I was proud to boast of my millionaire sponsors. It looked like solid evidence that the pain and struggle I had undergone to win national Golden Gloves titles, state and AAU championships had brought me to a point where I could make money from boxing, not only for myself but for my backers. I felt fortunate having so many people in town who wanted to give me what they called the "right kind of moral and ethical environment" for launching a career. As far back as I could remember, boxing was associated with stories of "gangster control," "fixed fights" and "backdoor deals," some of it brought out by Kefauver Committee investigations while I was fighting in the Golden Gloves.

The Sunday after I signed, the Reverend Isaiah Brayden, of the Ship of Zion Baptist Church, preached a sermon about it, and said, "May Cassius Clay be eternally grateful for what those kind Christian millionaires are doing for his black soul." Every newspaper account I read described the event in the holiest light, with ten white angels tending charity in the jungle. Not as the good, hard, common-sense business deal it was.

And if I could not always manage to act humble and thankful, maybe it was because, even though arithmetic was not my best subject at Central High, I could figure that $10,000 from ten millionaires who had shared equally in the funds (Bill Faversham got in free) meant that each had chipped in $1,000. (A little more, but not much, was later added to cover training fees before my second fight; after that, the money rolled in.) If $1,000 each had come from poor people like my father, I would have felt humble. But I had been around Louisville hotels and the Kentucky race tracks, and I had seen rich guys, without shedding a tear, blow that much in a weekend on a girl friend or lose twice that on a long-shot horse. And I was different from the Kentucky horses. I would win. More and longer.

When I filled theaters throughout America, Europe and Canada, the Louisville Sponsoring Group won acclaim around the world and was featured repeatedly in every major sports magazine and newspaper. But it disturbed me then, even as a teenager, that they claimed the venture was "strictly altruistic," "not for money." I had never heard of anyone that did not want more money, whether it was Rockefeller or the U.S. Government. They made it seem as though they were doing me a one-sided favor, and whenever I refused to carry out their commands—as later I did, especially when they ordered me to drop my religion, or have my championship fight with Sonny Liston canceled —I was pictured as insolent, ungrateful, an unmanageable racist who hated all whites.

As it turned out, their $1,000 investment netted each a sizable amount in the six years of our association.

Somehow the gap between me and my Louisville sponsors widened until there was hardly any direct communication. It remained that way until Herbert Muhammad accepted the post as consultant in charge of handling all affairs surrounding me. After that the real responsibility of managership was transferred into Herbert's hands— unofficially at first, and officially when I ended my contract with the Louisville group in 1966.

Following that first contract session, I caught glimpses of them mainly at my fights as I sat on my stool waiting for the bell to send me out for the next round. One or another would wave at me from his ringside seat, wave a cigar or nudge a girl friend or an associate, as though saying, "There's our horse." And I'd gallop out into the ring to bloody up the other white manager's horse, a horse who probably had no more real, personal or social relationship with his rider-manager than I had.

This common black-white work relationship did not stop one biographer, John Cottrell, from telling the world: "Clay the unproven professional was entirely happy to put himself in the hands of these eleven fairy godfathers, and it was an atmosphere of complete trust."

Actually, my most intimate look into the group occurred during that first meeting, with my father and mother and brother there, beaming happily. Details would later be worked out by Attorney Alberta Jones, a brilliant woman lawyer from Howard University. A thoughtful secretary whispered to me a quick who's who when I was introduced, and typed a letter with all their phone numbers and business connections so I could refer to them.

"Call us. Anytime you need anything," Bill Faversham, the son of an English actor and the real coordinator of the group, would say. And the others would amen, "Call on us anytime. We're here to help you."

"I'm proud to sponsor anyone with a name like Cassius Marcellus Clay," another said. "Lean and hungry . . ."

I kept their names in my pocket, ready to pull them out as proof of my status as a top-sponsored fighter, and I meant to display them as much as my Gold Medal.

I had the list for display one afternoon when I rode my new motorbike down to the Mayor's office to let him show my Olympic Medal to some visiting dignitaries. Along with me was Ronald King, a close friend, a good student, one who I copied off of in class.

The Mayor introduced me. "Cassius is a typical Louisville product," he said. "Our next World Champion."

The visitors applauded.

"Y'all hear what Cassius told that old Russian in Rome?" The Mayor was warming up. "Read 'bout that? This old Russian had the nerve to ask our boy how things were for Negroes in America. G'head, Cassius. Tell 'em. Don't be shy."

I saw what was coming. A remark I'd made in Rome, one I regretted. But the Mayor went on.

"He brushed off that Russian reporter like dirt. Tell 'em, Cash. Why, Cassius stood up tall, 'Look here, Commie. America is the best country in the world, including yours. I'd rather live here in Louisville than in Africa 'cause at least I ain't fightin' off no snakes and alligators and livin' in mud huts.' He sho' told 'em!" He put his arms around me. "He's our own boy, Cassius, our next World Champion. Anything you want in town's yourn. You hear that?"

I heard him, and I heard something else inside me that turned over in shame. Of all the things I had said at the Olympic Village, this remark was most quoted in newspapers and magazines, on TV and radio, and repeated month after month, and the instant I made it I felt I had gotten caught up in some big white net. I had given the answer the white reporters, who were listening, wanted to hear a black athlete say. I knew nothing of Russia and little of Africa, except what I'd seen in Tarzan movies. Yet the effect of my answer had been brought home to me my first day in Louisville. A young Nigerian approached me as I was talking with some friends, and asked if I'd been quoted correctly. When I acknowledged that I had, he said, "I thought we were brothers. You don't understand."

I never met him before or since, but his sadness shook me. And I knew I had been slanted in the wrong direction. Later, when I did travel many times to Africa, I was even more ashamed that I had grown up so brainwashed about the history and life of the people I descended from.

Most of the Africans I met and mingled with were far better educated than me, many spoke five and six languages and all spoke English better than I did. I saw modern cities, met talented, artistic people and got to know something of the culture and contributions Africa had made in the ancient and modern worlds. I learned how Europe and America had robbed, raped and enslaved its people for centuries, and were still plundering and draining its wealth.

That Nigerian's criticism made me cautious about not allowing myself to be groomed, deliberately or not, to become a "White Hope." Of course I understood they would prefer that the White Hope be white. But, Hopes having come upon hard times in boxing, I could see they would settle for a Black White Hope, as long as he believed what they believed, talked the way they talked and hated the people they hated. Until a real White White Hope came around.

Eight years later, barred from boxing in America and forbidden to travel outside the country, I watched the 1968 Olympic boxing matches in Mexico City. I saw George Foreman parade around the ring waving an American flag after his Olympic victory. Not that George usually went around waving American flags. I've never heard of him waving a flag before or since. But he had been put up to it to offset black athletes like Tommy Smith and Carlos Jones, who dramatized before the world their objections to American injustice with their Black Power salute. There was hardly a black or fair-minded white who did not admire Smith and Jones, or who did admire Foreman. And despite his considerable ability as a fighter, his image as an Uncle Tom stuck with him.

Yet I can understand where George was coming from. I had been there before him. It took me a while to learn that while the slave masters cheer for slavery, they get a freakish thrill making the slave cheer for slavery.

That afternoon I left the Mayor's office resolved that if I could not change my remark before the public, I would change it for myself. Little did I know that the first act in this "correction" would begin before I had finished my bike ride.

It was getting cloudy, and Ronnie and I raced our motorbikes across downtown Louisville. There had been a forecast of high wind and heavy rain, and the first sprinkle came when we passed a newly remodeled restaurant. I slowed down.

"Not there, not there!" Ronnie warned and kept his motor going.

But I stopped and parked near a line of big Harley-Davidson hogs. Their owners, a leather-jacketed gang, were sitting at tables near the window with their girl friends. Nazi insignias on their backs, Confederate flags painted on the front, a style popular with some whites in the East End. One they called "Kentucky Slim" I'd seen at my fights. Slim gave me a nod. Their leader, a big redhead with doubled-up leg chains hanging from his shoulder, sat with his arms around a heavy blonde. "Frog," as we knew him, never looked up, although I knew he saw me.

I found two empty seats at the counter, and as Ronnie caught up I sat down and picked up a menu. A young waitress quickly came up and placed napkins, silverware and a glass of water in front of us.

"Two hamburgers. Two milk shakes, vanilla," Ronnie said, but as the waitress moved back to the kitchen a big, beefy man with a hungover stomach motioned for her to come where he sat near the cash register.

Whatever his words, they were brief. The waitress disappeared inside the kitchen, and after what seemed a long time, appeared again, talking to one of the kitchen help, an old, thin-faced black woman who just stood at the door, looking down my way and trying to say something.

In those days most of the restaurants, hotels and movies in Louisville, as in all of the South, were either closed to blacks or had segregated sections.

The white girl finally came back and whispered as though she had something confidential to tell me. "We can't serve you here."

Ronnie muttered under his breath, and I nudged him to be quiet. It felt good to be so calm and prepared for what I thought was coming. My Gold Medal would be the solution to the whole thing.

This was not the first time Ronnie and I had entered a "white only" place, just the first time as "home-grown" Negroes. Once, for Halloween, we had a seamstress make us a couple of African turbans and flowing gowns. We used them for months to masquerade downtown. We would speak "foreign" English and talk to each other in a fast homemade language to get ourselves admitted to "white only" places as foreigners. One time at a movie house a suspicious doorman stopped us, but the white manager called back to him, "It's all right. They ain't Negroes."

Now I felt I had grown. Now there was no need to masquerade as a foreigner. I had whipped all the foreigners to bring the Gold Medal to America. I would use my native language.

"Miss," I began politely, believing she was acting out of ignorance. "I'm Cassius Clay. The Olympic Champion."

Ronnie proudly pulled the medal from under my T-shirt and adjusted the red, white and blue ribbon. He flashed it to show the

Italian word PUGILATO. Oh, how he admired and loved it. Maybe even more than I did.

The waitress was impressed. Without hesitation she dashed down the counter to The Owner, and spoke in urgent, hushed whispers. He never turned around.

"I don't give a damn *who* he is!"

The voice boomed with such force that everyone's head jerked up from their plates.

"I done told you, we don't serve no niggers!"

She put her hands over her face as though she had been hit, backed up, hurried to me and began repeating the message, as though I hadn't heard it. It got real quiet.

I remember looking directly into the eyes of a white high school boy with a Manual High sweater, no older than myself, who'd been admiring my medal a minute before. Manual High was a rival school to my own Central High, and he played on the opposing teams. He looked down at the floor.

My heart was pounding. A minute before, this had been a noisy, chatty place with thirty or more customers. I pushed away from the counter. Ronnie went through every motion with me as though we'd rehearsed the act. I stood up. Knives, forks and chitchat stopped, and all eyes were on me. My mouth felt hot and dry. Never in a hundred fights did I feel blood rushing to my head as I did then.

I tried to meet the eyes of the whites along the counter, but the only eyes looking into mine were those of the old black woman from the kitchen. She came through the door, a large cross hanging from her neck, trying to get my attention by waving a small book that looked like a prayer book.

Then The Owner, arms folded, his huge stomach bulging over his apron tie, started out from around the counter as if to give me a personal message. I backed off to the center. For an instant I had an urge to dig a right cross in the pit of his stomach, then a left hook to his mouth, then uppercut . . . and to this day I wonder if I shouldn't have obeyed that urge.

But my outlook on "fighting" had undergone a total change since the days when I scrapped in the streets and schoolyards at the slightest excuse. I had already signed for my first professional bout. It's part of the pride of a truly professional fighter not to indulge himself, not to be caught dead or alive in a free-for-all.

Most important, I had in mind another approach, one I was sure would work. I would make them feel ashamed of what they were doing. If necessary, I would stay here until they took me to jail.

I got myself together to tell them everything I'd been thinking. "This is supposed to be the land of the brave and the home of the free, and you're disgracing it with your actions. You all know me. I was born in General Hospital, only a block away. I was raised here. I went to Central High. And now I've brought back an Olympic Gold Medal for *all* the people of Louisville. I fought for the glory of my country and you should be ashamed of what you're doing. You serve any foreigner here, but not an American Negro citizen. You'll have to take me to jail, because I'll stay until I get my rights. You should be ashamed . . ."

But I never said a word.

The words wouldn't come out. Something there wouldn't let the words come out. Instead of making them feel ashamed, I felt shamed. Shamed and shocked and lonesome.

The kitchen woman was wiping her face with her apron as though about to cry. The motorcycle gang had taken a sudden interest in the action, and some walked down to where The Owner was, and leaned against the counter. I saw Ronnie move his hand to his right side pocket where he kept his pearl-handled switchblade, a long, wicked weapon he'd taken off a dying pimp, "Jailhouse Sidney Green—meanest pimp I ever seen." Just as many hours as I had put in punching bags, sparring with partners and learning the art of boxing, Ronnie had spent training himself to handle his blade with frightening skill.

"You take The Owner, I take Frog," he whispered.

I shook him off. In a one-on-one, two-on-one, maybe three-on-one, I could whip most of them. But the insult was so deep and painful no simple fight with fist or knives would be enough. I needed more—much more.

I had been standing there for less than a minute, but it seemed like a year. Ronnie was saying, almost in disbelief, "They don't really know who you are. They just don't know you The Champion! I ain't scared to tell 'em." Then, almost like an announcer in the ring, "Folks, this is The Champion! Louisville's Olympic Champion! Just back from Italy."

I heard my stomach growl. "Ronnie! Shut up! Don't beg. Don't beg!"

"You got sponsors," Ronnie said. "*Call* them sponsors." He reached inside my pocket for the list of the millionaires. "Go 'head. Call 'em up, tell 'em what's happening. They can buy and sell this little funky place with their pocket change. Watch their faces when Mr. Viceroy tells 'em."

He gave me a dime and pushed me toward the phone on the wall. I fumbled for the paper. An uneasy frown came on The Owner's face.

"Don't stop, go 'head," Ronnie urged.

I was investigating the list, trying to figure which one was likely to respond. The first name was James Ross Todd. No trouble remembering him. Youngest of the millionaires. Only twenty-two.

Ronnie was dubious. "Chicken. Still chicken. Would he know what to say?"

Next phone number, William Faversham, the coordinator. But he never made a move without the others. So I went on down the list.

William Lee Lyons Brown. Introduced to me as "the whiskey billionaire"—the man who produces Jack Daniels, Old Forrester and Early Times.

"Powerful," Ronnie approved. "Jack Daniels is powerful."

But then I remembered Mr. Brown: "Boy, this makes two generations of your family working for my family. Your mother was a cook for my cousin." I thought of the four dollars a day they paid Bird, and I knew I could never call him for anything under the sun.

George Washington Norton IV, millionaire oil man and horse breeder. "A direct descendant of Martha Washington," the secretary had whispered. "His nickname is 'Possum Norton.'" I shook my head; somehow I just couldn't call on Possum.

I moved to the next name. Patrick Calhoun, Jr., chairman of American Commercial Barge Line. "Largest inland boat company in the world," the secretary had said. Ronald pleaded with me to call, so I slowly dialed his number.

No answer. I felt relieved. But Ronnie wouldn't stop: "Go on! Go on!"

Archibald McGhee Foster. The only Northerner in the group. Would he carry any weight down here?

"Cash, call somebody! Anybody!" Ronnie was desperate.

William Sol Cutchings. The name Ronnie wanted.

"That's him," he whispered. "He owns Viceroy and Raleigh cigarettes! That's Brown & Williamson Tobacco Corporation. Call him."

I strained to remember what the secretary had said. It came back to me. "Mr. Cutchings is a direct descendant of a Confederate general," she had stated proudly. And I knew Confederate generals had fought a civil war to keep black people in slavery. And I knew what the Confederate flags on the jackets of the motorcycle gangs meant. I didn't feel I could call the Confederacy.

Vertner DeGarmo Smith and Robert Worth Bingham, "millionaire newspaper publishers and TV station owners," I'd been told. But I had overheard one telling the other a darky joke and doubling up in laughter.

J. D. S. Coleman, cattle and oil tycoon. He had been the coldest of all, had thought they were paying me too much.

The last name was Elbert Gary Sutcliffe. "His people run U.S. Steel," the secretary had said. Only because of Ronnie, I dialed U.S. Steel's number. Finally a soft, polite voice answered. "Sutcliffe residence. Yes?"

"Mr. Elbert Gary Sutcliffe?" I read the name off the paper.

"Who shall I say is calling, sir?"

"Cassius Clay."

Ronnie relaxed, smiling. Maybe we were getting somewhere.

After a bit, the voice of Mr. Sutcliffe came over, quick, business-like, steely. "Yes, Cassius?"

"Mr. Sutcliffe," I began. Then I stopped. What in the world did I want Mr. Sutcliffe to do?

"Cassius? What you want?"

"Mr. Sutcliffe," I started again, my throat hot and dry. There was a long pause in which I said nothing, nothing at all.

"If you want some expense money, boy, why don't you call Bill? He's the one who takes care of those things."

"Yessir, Mr. Sutcliffe," and I hung up.

Ronnie looked at me in disgust. "Nigger, you didn't tell him a thing! What's wrong with you?"

What was wrong? How could I explain I could never ask Mr. Sutcliffe to help me get a hamburger? I folded the letter and put it back in my pocket.

"What's wrong with you?" Ronnie kept asking.

How could I explain: my millionaires were the real rulers of Louisville. But I did not want to be considered "their" boy even in the eyes of those who hated me. I had earned my Gold Medal without their permission. It should mean something without their permission. I wanted that medallion to mean that I owned myself. And to call, seemed to me, to be exchanging one Owner for the Other. And suppose they did come to my rescue? Then I could come and go in the "white only" places, but other blacks couldn't. Then what would I be?

I moved closer to the door, keeping my eyes on The Owner. I felt a peculiar, miserable pain in my head and stomach. The pain that comes from punches you take without hitting back.

Whatever illusions I'd built up in Rome as the All-American Boy were gone. My Olympic honeymoon was over. I was back in my Old Kentucky Home.

I saw The Owner relax, move behind the counter and offer Frog a cigarette. They lit up and laughed, enjoying some great joke. Before I got to the door, someone was holding my arm. The black woman from the kitchen. Close up, her face looked even thinner, her eyes larger than any eyes I'd ever seen, soft and wet and looking directly into mine.

"Son, keep the faith," she said prayerfully.

"Don't say that, lady." Ronnie looked away from her.

"Such a nice poem you wrote for our paper." She put the thin little book in my hands. The poem I wrote on the plane had appeared that week in some of the black newspapers. She had it between the pages of her little book, and I glanced at it.

HOW CASSIUS TOOK ROME
By Cassius Clay, Jr.

To make America the greatest is my goal,
So I beat the Russian, and I beat the Pole,
And for the USA won the Medal of Gold.
Italians said, "You're greater than the Cassius of Old."
We like your name, we like your game,
So make Rome your home if you will.
I said I appreciate kind hospitality,
But the USA is my country still,
'Cause they waiting to welcome me in Louisville.

It only deepened my shame, and my eyes brushed by it. Her little book was not a prayer book, but a volume of Langston Hughes poems. I put it in my pocket.

"Mary!" The Owner's voice came as though he'd caught her in treason. "Mary! In the kitchen!"

She meekly followed orders and someone began laughing and the noise and chatter returned to the restaurant. Ronnie kept up a steady stream of curses. As I pulled him outside and over to the parking lot, we heard footsteps running in the rain behind us.

"Wait! Wait!"

It was the waitress and the white boy who sat next to me at the counter. They were waving menus.

"Mr. Clay, may I have your autograph?" They stood there dripping wet and panting, the rain coming down in sheets. "Please."

The boy in the Manual High sweater handed me a piece of red crayon. I scribbled "Cassius Clay—1960" on both. They grabbed them and ran, each one in a different direction.

"Hey, Olympic nigger!"

"You still tryin' to get a milk shake?"

The voices came from the gang of motorcycle riders coming over to the lot, climbing on their hogs. Frog, one arm around his big girl friend, looked over to where we were and said, "I got your milk shake, Olympic!" They cracked up, screamed, howled, imitated Frog's gesture. Frog helped his girl onto the back of the wheel and leaned over to Kentucky Slim, apparently giving some instructions. Then, with an exaggerated gunning of the motors, they took off, r-r-r-r-r-r-r-r-r-r-O-O-O-O-O-O-R-R-R-R-rrrrrrr, thundering past us single file, cursing, threatening, whooping.

We started our motors but sat still, our eyes on the gang. Suddenly, Kentucky broke from the pack, circled around, drove back toward us. One hand was held up like a signal and he didn't drop it until five feet from me. Ronnie moved his bike around and in between me and Kentucky.

"Clay." I can hear Slim's melancholy, nasal voice as he looked over Ronnie's shoulder. "I tried to save y'all. You done made Frog mad."

I said nothing, just waited for the real message, the settlement terms.

"Frog wanted to lynch y'all there in the restaurant," Slim confided, almost congenial. "But I said no suh. No suh! Let y'all go back where you belong, see? Just give Frog some li'l ole souvineer-like somethin'."

I understood exactly what he wanted, and I remember feeling tight and warm as though the bell had rung for the round.

"We fresh out of souvineers." Ronnie was cleaning his molars with a toothpick as if the restaurant had actually served him the hamburgers.

Slim pointed to my neck. "Frog wants that there ribbon and the medal for his girl. Li'l souvineer-like. And you kin go on 'bout your business." He waited. "What y'all say?"

"Slim," Ronnie said evenly, relieved the matter could be settled so simply. "Go tell Frog we give it to his mother—in trade."

Slim's mouth fell open, a bewildered, unbelieving look in his eyes. He brushed Ronnie aside to give me a reprieve. "Clay, it's yo' medal, not hisn. What you say?"

"See you later, Slim." I gunned my bike.

Flushed and furious, Slim gunned his hog, shook a prophetic finger at me and raged, "Frog gone kill you niggers for that!" He took off, screaming back over his shoulder, "You wait! You black bastards! You wait!"

Then I knew we had already waited too long. A good many young blacks had already been caught in white neighborhoods by this same gang, beaten, chain-whipped, some almost fatally.

If a drowning man's life parades before him when he goes down for the last time, as I had read somewhere, I was about to go under. All the years of sweat and struggle I had poured into becoming a champion flashed before me and I realized everything I wanted might go down the drain or be indefinitely delayed unless I submitted to Frog's "souvineer" hunt. A knock-down, drag-out battle with Frog's gang might leave me, if lucky enough to survive, too scarred and injured to continue as a fighter. My Gold Medal had lost its gleam in the Mayor's office and in the restaurant, but every ounce of my blood and marrow rebelled against paying it out as ransom.

I remember the rain was cold and had soaked through my sweater, down to my bones. But what made me shiver most was the awareness that in a few days my first professional fight was scheduled right here in Louisville's Freedom Hall. Against Tunney Hunsaker, a seasoned puncher who was also a police chief in Virginia. If I entered the ring with fresh cuts and scars, Hunsaker would open them.

Even though this match was made before the Louisville group entered the picture, they wanted me to drop Hunsaker and start off with an easier opponent. An old ring rule has it that a "promising amateur" must win his first professional fight if he is not to be scorned as a flash in the pan. Some commentators were not yet convinced I was for real and hopefully predicted I would be a flop against any "real professional" fighter. But I was sick of fighting "amateurs," and above all I wanted to test myself against a tough pro.

Ronnie, listening to Frog's big wheel as it circled the block, sensed what was going through my mind. "You got too much goin' for you to get messed up now."

My heart went out to him.

"I'll go on, make 'em fool with me. You get on down the other way. Go on now . . ." And he would have shoved off in Frog's direction, but I gripped his handlebars.

I had a plan. My guess was they expected me to head straight for the black neighborhood. But I planned to get to Jefferson County Bridge, a lonely area near rail junctions and highways, a dividing line between Kentucky and Indiana. I could cross to the Indiana side, run parallel with the river for a few miles and come back into Louisville over another bridge.

With Ronnie tight behind me, I cut across a vacant lot, shot up a side street and down an alley and for a while weaved through every intricate passageway I could find until the sound of the big motors died out.

We drove with our heads down. Straining our bikes against the wind and rain, hardly saying a word. There was no need to talk.

Ronnie King was one of my best friends from the time I started in junior high school to my second fight with Liston. He had an uncle he called "Tootie" who operated a dry cleaner's in Louisville, and he was always talking about him. "Tootie gonna take me fishing" . . . "Tootie goin' hunting" . . . "Tootie got a motorcycle." So I just named him "Tootie."

When I first met him, I was walking to enroll in classes in DuVall Junior High School, way down in the West End of Louisville on 34th Street, about fourteen blocks from my home. He was walking with his grandmother, a heavyset lady with gray hair. She introduced us and said, "Well, will you walk with my little grandson?"

So Tootie and I walked on together. "This is my lunch," he said, noticing me looking at a paper bag he was holding. "You want it?"

"What is it?"

"Aw, an ole hamburger," he answered, frowning. "My mother always makes me take hamburger sandwiches on this homemade wheat bread with mustard and onions and a pickle. And I want me a peanut-butter bun and some cookies and milk. I don't want this."

This boy must be crazy, I thought to myself. A big ole fat juicy beefburger, onions, pickle, and he's talking about he want some cookies and a peanut-butter bun.

"How much you want for it?" I asked.

"Gimme a nickel."

I gave him a nickel and took the sandwich. At lunchtime he came out with a peanut-butter bun, cookies and milk, and he was happy. I still had a nickel change from my lunch money, so I bought a couple of cartons of milk to go with my beefburger.

Every morning for almost two years after that, I'd be on the corner just in time, waiting to get that beefburger. If I missed him in the morning, I'd catch him in the lunchroom. We got to be pretty tight.

Since we both lived in the same district, we were assigned to the same classroom and we got seats right by each other. He was always a little smarter than me. He could read fast, spell good, add and subtract. I had my mind so wrapped up in boxing, I didn't work too hard in school. All I could think about was getting home, getting on my bike and going to the gym. I'd be shadowboxing from the minute I woke up in the morning. And I'd stop in a little drugstore, get a carton of milk and break two raw eggs in it because someone had told me this would help build up my wind and my lungs.

So Tootie did most of my schoolwork for me. A lot of times I'd look over and ask, "What's the answer to number four?" Or, "What's the answer to test number six?" And he'd always give me the answers. This is how I got by.

After school Tootie would come with me and my brother to the gym. We would ride all the way on my bicycle, one of us trotting while the other two rode, then switching around, taking turns.

This went on for about four years and we became fast friends. Ran with the gang together; fought in the streets together; sought girls together. We'd even gone into boxing together, but Tootie quit early. He got tired of getting his long nose bloody, his big eyes puffed: he said it jeopardized his chances of ever becoming a hustler, a career which brought him to an early death, fighting over a woman on a New York street.

I was thankful that he was by my side now. I had gym buddies like Jimmy Ellis, Donnie Hall, Tommy Jones, Maceo Bell and my own brother who, by ring rules, were far better fighters. But Ronnie was a natural demon by street rules, with the knack of making all his brawls seem like life-and-death choices. And so far, faced with such alternatives, most of his opponents had chosen "life" without a fight.

I could have phoned my policeman trainer, Joe Martin, but the thought of calling on a white Louisville policeman to help me with some white boys never entered my mind. I had known law officers in Louisville, but nothing I ever saw, heard or experienced left me with the impression that Martin, or any white policeman, would do anything but wink if I was in trouble with his white brothers and they had the upper hand. Biographers who have described Martin as being "like a father to Cassius" don't know anything about the South, white police and a black boy.

I remember how relieved I felt when I got within sight of the bridge. The rain had slackened, and I decided it was safe to swing from the passageways and hit the bridge from Main Street.

It turned out to be a mistake. No sooner had I struck the street than I heard wild, faraway screams. "There they is! There them niggers!" A woman's high-pitched cry. "You black bastard! We got yo' ass!" Frog's bellow.

At first I could only see Frog's machine. He had apparently sent his scouts to check the route to the black neighborhood, but he was cunning enough to suspect that I might try to get over the bridge into Indiana, and had come to seal it off. Comparing our relatively slow speed with his, and judging the distance to the bridge, it was obvious Frog would be on our backs by the time we made the top.

Ronnie leaned over, his face, like mine, wet far more from sweat than from rain. "They want you the most. Not me. You go up ahead. I'll be behind. You dig?"

I dug it. We hit the bridge and I began weaving from side to side, Ronnie dropping behind me, slightly to my right. I glanced over my shoulder, could see still another hog now, directly behind Frog. Kentucky Slim.

But Ronnie was right. Frog was almost parallel with him yet ignoring him, still concentrating on me, whirling his chain like a cowboy ready to lasso a loose steer. "Hey, Olympic nigger! So you a fighter—"

He may have said more, but with perfect timing and in a coordinated move Ronnie leaped off his machine, hurling it with all his strength underneath Frog's front wheel. Frog saw it too late, made a frantic jerk, cut to the left, skidded up against the cement mortar, smashing himself and his woman on the bridge column. The woman let out a painful scream. Badly hurt and bleeding, her blouse ripped, she scrambled over to help Frog, who hung dazed against the rail.

Kentucky was coming up behind them, whirling the same kind of chain, aiming at my head. Then and there occurred one of the two split-second moves in my life without which my career would have been forever altered. The second happened during my first championship fight with Sonny Liston, when in the fifth round, with my eyes blinded and burning from something on Liston's glove, Angelo Dundee pushed me back in the ring only a split second before the referee was about to award the fight to Liston. That incident was highly publicized. The first was here on Jefferson County Bridge.

Slim whipped his doubled-up chain at my head. Instead of slashing my face, the chain wrapped around my shoulders. Instinctively, I shot my hand out and gripped the chain and jerked with all my might. The force snatched Slim off his hog and hurled us together in a violent impact. His head struck mine and stunned me, but not enough to stop me from smashing my fist into his face. His body hit the ground, blood spurted from his nose, his empty hog careened over to the rail.

The woman was screaming, "They gonna kill Frog! They gonna kill Frog!"

Ronnie had a half nelson around Frog's neck, choking him, his blotched face even more distorted by the veins popping from his temples. The switchblade was pressed against his throat. "Get back! I'll cut his goddamn neck off! Get back!" He started ripping Frog's leather jacket as though it was tissue paper.

The girl dropped down on her knees, sobbing and pleading. Two other riders were coming up, one I remember with a flaming red, polka-dot neckpiece and a World War II German helmet.

I shouted to the girl, "Tell 'em stay off the bridge. Get 'em off the bridge!"

She sprang up, flew down to the end of the bridge, waving her arms. "Y'all go back! Go back!"

They slowed down, but kept creeping up cautiously.

"Let Frog tell 'em. Loosen up so Frog can tell 'em," I told Ronnie.

He eased his grip. Frog sucked in all the breath he could, and with more force than I expected he cried out, "Y'all g'on home! G'on! G'ON!"

For a second his riders just paused at the bottom of the bridge, confused. "What you want us to do, Frog?"

The girl shouted back, "Do what Frog tells y'all! You hear? Do what he tells you!"

The rider in the German helmet pulled out what looked like a .45, and I kept my eyes on his face for the slightest flicker of what he might do. They could have overwhelmed us for certain. But just as certain they knew Ronnie would rip Frog's jugular vein.

"Lighten up," I whispered to Ronnie. Frog was our only hope. "Let Frog talk."

Frog screamed, a throaty, desperate gurgle. "I done told y'all, g'on back! G'on back home. You too, Slim! G'on!"

Slim pulled himself together like a drunkard and limped with his machine back to his battalion. They consulted briefly, looked up at us, then slowly retreated down the street.

I didn't move. Just watched until I heard the girl crying, "They gone now. What you gone do with us?"

Ronnie released Frog and let him crawl over to his wheel. Like a hunter who chased what he thought would be a bunny rabbit, only to corner it and discover it to be a tiger, Frog's single thought now was escape. His girl struggled to help him mount the hog, but he kept slipping off. I stood there looking at them, feeling no anger, pity or hatred, just tension. Neither of them could ever make the hog go without our help. I moved over to the girl, and she cringed as though she expected me to hit her.

"Help us get off." She spoke very low, very desperate. "We ain't comin' back. Honest! We'll keep goin'."

I straightened the bent fenders so they wouldn't rub against the wheels, and fixed Frog's fingers on the handlebars. He was weak, unsteady, coughing as though his throat was still in Ronnie's grip. His blood, oozing through the shredded slits Ronnie's blade had made in his jacket, soaked all the way through my T-shirt as I helped him.

Ronnie and I held the hog on each side steady enough to run it down the incline and give it a mighty push. The electric starter was shot, but the hog sputtered, caught and slowly moved off, swaying a little. We watched to see if Frog would regroup the gang. But what the girl had said was true. Frog rode by them and they all fell in behind. We stood there until they disappeared, until all we could hear was rain and the shuffle and rattle of trains on the Kentucky side.

"Better get the hell away from here." Ronnie was wiping his knife on his sleeve like a violin bow. "My bike's wrecked." He surveyed what was left of it, a mass of twisted metal. Then something about my face must have stopped him. "You hurt? Goddamn—they got you?"

I shook my head. Physically, I had come off better than I expected, but the miserable pain in my head and stomach that I felt in the restaurant had returned. Give-and-take punches, like the blows exchanged with Frog's battalion, are bearable. But I was feeling the aftereffects of the blows I'd taken from The Owner, the Mayor, the millionaires.

"Let's wash off all this mess. You'll feel better," Ronnie concluded. We tested my bike to see if it would carry us both. "We get the blood off, we feel better."

I followed him down to the river, and hung the Olympic medal on a pier piling, the red, white and blue ribbon thick with Frog's blood. Some of it had stained the gold.

Ronnie picked it up tenderly. Even before washing himself, he washed the medal. Rubbed the luster back into the gold, rinsed the blood off the ribbon and hung it lovingly around his own neck.

I stopped and watched. This was the first time the Gold Medal had been away from my chest since the Olympic judge hung it there that day I stood on the podium, a Russian on my left, a Pole on my right. And for the first time I saw it as it was. Ordinary, just an object. It had lost its magic. Suddenly I knew what I wanted to do with this cheap piece of metal and raggedy ribbon. And as soon as I knew, the pain in my stomach eased.

We quickly rinsed, and Ronnie put the medal back around my neck, followed me to the bridge to get the bike.

I remember thinking that the middle of the Ohio was probably the deepest part, and I walked over to the center of the bridge. And Ronnie, with that extra sense people have who have known and loved each other for a long time, anticipated my actions. Dropping the bike, he ran toward me, yelling. But I had snapped the ribbon from around my neck. I held the medallion just far enough out so that it wouldn't tangle in the bridge structure, and threw it into the black water of the Ohio. I watched it drag the red, white and blue ribbon down to the bottom behind it.

When I turned, Ronnie had a look of horror in his eyes. "Jesus. Oh, my God!" Then tears came down his cheeks. "Oh, my God. You know what you did?"

"It wasn't real gold. It was phony." I tried to put my arms around him. He was wet and cold and stiff. "It was phony."

He wasn't listening. "Why you throw it in the river? Why?"

How could I put the answer together? I wasn't sure of all the reasons. The Olympic medal had been the most precious thing that had ever come to me. I worshiped it. It was proof of performance, status, a symbol of belonging, of being a part of a team, a country, a world. It was my way of redeeming myself with my teachers and schoolmates at Central High, of letting them know that although I had not won scholastic victories, there was something inside me capable of victory.

How could I explain to Ronnie I wanted something that meant more than that? Something that was as proud of me as I would be of it. Something that would let me be what I knew I had to be, my own kind of champion.

"We don't need it," I said. "We don't need it."

"You crazy fool!" He turned against me with a hostility he had never shown before. He held the neck of my sweater in a fierce grip.

"They gonna let a nut like you be Champ? What you gonna tell the sponsors? They supposed to take your picture with the medal. What the papers gonna say?"

I loosened his hands from my sweater and held his arms firmly. "You won't say nothing, I won't say nothing. Nothing at all."

The medal was gone, but the sickness had gone too. I felt calm, relaxed, confident. My holiday as a White Hope was over. I felt a new, secret strength.

I tried to console Ronnie. "Wait until we win the real World Heavyweight Championship Belt." I gave him the same description an old boxing trainer had once given me of the championship belt. "That's real gold. Gold with diamonds and rubies in it. Weighs twenty pounds. The same belt handed down by Heavyweight Champions John L. Sullivan, Jack Johnson, Jess Willard, Jack Dempsey, Jack Sharkey, Max Baer, Joe Louis—a belt made for the great champions. Not phony gold."

Ronnie would never see the "gold and diamonds" of the real World Heavyweight Championship Belt I won in Miami. And he would never hear the story of its disappearance. My cornerman, Drew Bundini Brown, took care of that. One night, while I was in exile, I called him in New York to ask about it and I got the answer:

Hello, Champ. You want to know what I did with your belt? Well, Champ, I kept it safe and sound since the night Malcolm X was murdered. You remember the night your apartment burned in Chicago? Four hours after Malcolm X was murdered? And me going up in the burning building and bringing out your World Heavyweight Championship Belt? And taking it back to New York for safekeeping? Well, to make a long story short, Champ, I pawned it . . . What? . . . Please . . . I thought you'd understand, Champ. I got broke . . . Please . . . My car note was due. My rent had backed up four months. My woman had left me. I'd already pawned every piece of jewelry I owned. So I looked at your big old gold belt. The most valuable thing I had in the house. And so I went to the best pawnbroker in New York. By experience I expect them to give me less than what I ask, so I ask for more than I expect. I told the pawnbroker: "Give me fifteen hundred dollars on this."

I told him the belt belonged to you, Champ, Cassius Clay, Muhammad Ali, the real true World Heavyweight Champion. They'd taken your title, but here's the belt. I told him thirty other world champions owned it before you became the greatest. All the clerks and customers in the shop gathered around and looked. Everybody in the pawnshop was raving over it. Only one of its kind.

But the pawnbroker hadn't put the little thing in his eye, he hadn't peeped down on it. And when he got the glass and peeped at it, he threw it back at me. "I can't give you a dime," he said. I said, "What you mean! Can't give me a dime! On the World Heavyweight Champion Belt, you can't give me no money?" He said, "This thing ain't worth a nickel." I said, "You got to be wrong." He said, "Just keep on talking if you want to. This ain't nothing but gold-colored metal with some printing of the names of some old fighters and the words 'World Heavyweight Championship Belt.' All it's got is sentimental value."

Champ, it wasn't worth more than the headlines on the newspaper they give you next morning with your picture in it. In fact, the man didn't give me a dime. So the newspaper's worth more than the belt.

Champ, I was not only disappointed that I didn't have subway fare back home, I was disappointed for the name of boxing. Boxing ain't for glory, it's for money. All the millions and millions big-time promoters from Tex Rickard and Mike Jacobs to Jim Norris—places from Madison Square Garden to Chicago Stadium—made off heavyweights from Dempsey to Joe Louis, Walcott to Marciano, they didn't think enough of the symbol them heavyweights were knockin' their brains out for to make it worth a dime.

I thought about how you dropped the Olympic Medal in the Ohio. I should have dropped the belt in the Hudson. But I pawned it . . . How much? Like the pawnbroker said, it had sentimental value. Champ, I found somebody sentimental . . . Champ, please . . . Champ, don't hang up on me . . .

I made that telephone call to Bundini eight years after I stood on the Jefferson County Bridge. But that night in 1960 the World Heavyweight Championship Belt was still a golden hope.

It rained all the way back, and after I dropped Ronnie off and got home, all my family was in bed asleep. I went to my room to tell my brother Rudy what happened, but he was sleeping so sound that I stood by the bed and watched him for a while. Only thirteen months separated us. I loved him since the day he was born, and we're seldom apart. He has the name my father wanted to give me: Rudolph Valentino Clay. I didn't get it because of my mother's objections. She insisted he name his first son after himself, she liked the name.

"Whenever I tried to spank Rudy," my mother would tell everyone, "Cassius would break in and start hitting me and saying, 'Stop spanking my baby! Stop spanking him!'"

He had followed me into boxing, was the fighter I sparred with most in the gym, and was my companion most mornings when I did my roadwork. But even as I looked down on him sleeping, I knew I would try to prevent him from becoming a fighter.

He had the courage, he could punch, but he wasn't gifted at it. He was getting hit too much. Fighting is too dangerous a trade if you're not gifted for it.

I decided to talk to him in the morning, and I tiptoed out of the room. I felt too fresh and stimulated to sleep. I would stay up till daybreak, do my roadwork around Chickasaw Park, keep in shape for Hunsaker.

I remember sitting on the worn-down old sofa, pulling out the little book the woman in the restaurant had given me. I read a poem by Langston Hughes she had underscored:

> I, too, sing America.
> I am the darker brother.
> They send me to eat in the kitchen
> When company comes . . .
>
> But I laugh,
> And eat well,
> And grow strong.
>
> Tomorrow,
> I'll be at the table
> When company comes.
>
> Nobody'll dare
> Say to me,
> "Eat in the kitchen,"
>
> Then.
> Besides,
> They'll see how beautiful I am
> And be ashamed—
>
> I, too, am America.

A few years later, I would meet Langston Hughes in a Greenwich Village poetry session where I had been invited to read my poems. I thanked him for his poem and asked him if he had any more. He gave me three books. His were the kind of poems I liked, straight, simple, and at least half of them were in rhyme.

When I got back from roadwork that morning, I still felt stimulated. I was about to have my first professional fight and I knew that with all the publicity and all the shouting I'd done, the sports world would be watching every blow I threw.

But I was so confident—so confident, in fact, that I ate a full dinner only one hour before the fight. I paid for it in the third round when Hunsaker hit me with a heavy blow in the pit of the stomach. It was all I could do to keep from vomiting. Somehow I kept out of his reach until my stomach settled. Then, in the final rounds, I shook him up so much he was groggy at the end.

I had won the first one. When I got back to my dressing room to celebrate, there was no champagne, no alcohol, but my sponsors, my family, all my boyhood friends were there, and my Olympic teammate, Wilma Rudolph, the sprint champion, winner of three Gold Medals, whom promoter Bill King had flown in to help publicize the match.

I'd kept secret the fact that I was deeply in love with Wilma, and in Rome I had tried every way I could to attract her. My problem: I was too shy and timid. As bold as I'd shout "I'm the greatest," and roam up and down the Olympic Village, challenging and predicting, I could hardly utter a word in front of Wilma—or any other pretty girl, for that matter.

While my talking and boasting had caught the attention of the newspapers, and they publicized my defeat of Belgium's Yvon Becus, Russia's Gennadiy Shatkov, Argentina's Tony Madigan, one of the few amateurs who'd ever defeated me, and my final victory over Poland's Zbigniew Pietrzykowski, as well as my tours with Bing Crosby and Floyd Patterson, the one whose attention I wanted was the chocolate-brown girl with the long, graceful stride and bright brown eyes. I'd hang around the American Embassy, where the women on the team lived, just to catch a glimpse of her when she walked out. I'd search for her whenever the team got together, but when she stood near me I was tongue-tied.

To make it worse, she had a boyfriend, Ray Norton, the sprinter, who was always ahead of me. I'd see Wilma occasionally drop something, a towel or shoe, and I'd rush to pick it up, but Norton was there a second ahead of me. I'd see her in the cafeteria and I'd dash to get her food tray, only to find that Norton had beaten me to it. I wanted to get Ray Norton in the ring. I'd take care of him.

I wondered if I'd ever get up enough nerve to speak to her and tell her what was on my mind.

Now here she was in Louisville, celebrating my first victory, and I wanted to say something about what I felt in the past and what I'd like to see in the future, but I was too bashful to do that and in a few hours the opportunity was gone.

Years later, I met her in Los Angeles, where she was teaching school, and I told her about my secret crush. She was surprised. By then she had married and was a mother. When I came back from exile to fight Quarry, she flew down the day of the fight with her two-month-old baby to wish me luck.

• • •

The day after the Hunsaker fight, I met with my Louisville sponsors to discuss who would be my trainer. Angelo Dundee and Archie Moore were being proposed.

I first met Angelo when I was out gunning for his fighter, Willie Pastrano. I was seventeen. I had defeated every amateur in my weight, in tournaments across the country. I wanted a test against a professional.

Every week I watched them on TV, and I was convinced I could beat most of them, but I'd never been in the ring with a pro. One I admired was Pastrano. He was fast, clever and a good boxer, and although slim, he had power. I had seen Angelo on TV in the corner of a number of top fighters, Carmen Basilio, Luis Rodriguez, Yama Bahama, Isaac Logart.

And on the day Angelo brought Pastrano into Louisville to fight George Holeman, I went up to his hotel and called his room. When he came to the phone, I introduced myself, "I'm going to be the World Heavyweight Champion, and I got to talk to you."

"Why?" I heard Angelo say.

"I admire Willie, and I want to meet him."

A long silence. Then Angelo said, "Well, come on up."

When I got there, I inhaled the strong scent of oil of wintergreen and alcohol. Angelo had been giving Willie a rubdown. Willie was flopped across the bed in his undershirt, a pillow under his head, digging into a bowl of ice cream. I was impressed with Willie's slimness, the size of his shoulders, his big muscular legs. He looked so mature, confident, strong.

He was the third-ranked light-heavy in the world, and would soon become The Champion.

'Why you lay around like this?' I asked him.

He rolled over on his stomach, looked up at me. "I can't be running around in the streets all day like you, kid. I just lie here and soak up strength. Nice meeting you," he said, dismissing me.

I turned to Angelo. "If I came down to the gym, could I box with Willie?"

Angelo said something about not wanting to get me hurt, that I looked like a nice kid. But I persisted. He and Pastrano exchanged glances slyly and Willie smiled.

"All right," Angelo agreed.

The next day, I was in the gym before they got there. I wanted to impress them. I was whipping the heavy bag hard. You could hear the bag pop all over the gym. Pastrano came in and glanced curiously at me and kept watching me while he shadowboxed. When it was my turn to get in the ring with him, Angelo decided I would work out two rounds.

The bell rang, I eased out and circled him. Pastrano was fast, shifty, smooth, but I was faster. My jab was better. My reach was longer, and I tagged him. Suddenly it dawned on me that I was tagging a pro, and a feeling of excitement came over me. I was tagging him with lefts and rights, cutting at his head, bouncing him around, and I saw the confused look on his face as he was unable to evade either my left or my right.

"That's enough! That's enough!" Angelo cried out.

I had cut into Pastrano as though he was another amateur. I had always believed I was as good as the pros I saw on TV. Now I was sure.

"Enough of that!" Angelo cried. "Willie's got a fight coming up!" He took me aside and said, "Look, kid, that's enough for today. Willie's got other sparring to do."

"With who?" I asked.

"Anybody but you," Angelo said. "When you turn pro, kid, look me up."

A year later, when I did turn pro and my Louisville sponsors asked me to choose a trainer, I had forgotten Angelo. I suggested Archie Moore, the "old man," because I liked his style in the ring and especially out of it.

I remembered the way Archie gained a title shot from Marciano by using colorful gimmicks that forced Rocky to respond. He had run ads in newspapers with a picture of Marciano in convict clothes and a headline that read: ONE HUNDRED THOUSAND DOLLAR REWARD FOR ANYBODY WHO CAN GET MARCIANO INTO A RING WITH SHERIFF ARCHIE MOORE.

My Louisville sponsors contacted Moore and arranged for him to take me over, give me the benefit of his wisdom and instruct me in the ways of the best boxers.

Moore wanted me to fly out, but in those days I avoided planes as much as I could and I rode the train all the way to San Diego, where Patrick Calhoun, one of my sponsors, met me and drove me to Archie's place.

Archie had a big modern house overlooking the San Diego Expressway, and when I got there he came out and hugged me. "Pick up your luggage and follow me," he said. And I went up to the second floor, where he put me in a little room. "This'll do until you get to be Champ," he said. Although he was one of the oldest active ring warriors, I liked the fact that his face was not badly marked and he still had all of his gleaming white teeth.

I remember walking around the house and looking over at the

Expressway, seeing cars pass by, blowing their horns, people waving and looking down on Archie.

"They'll be doing the same for you when you get to be Champion," Archie said. "Everybody'll know you, respect you. All you got to do is work hard, follow my instructions.

"In the morning, we go to the gym. You get some rest now. My daughters and wife, they do the cooking for us, but when we get up to the gym we do our own."

The next morning, we took his little half-ton truck and drove up into the hills on a long dirt road for nearly twenty or thirty miles until we came to the camp. It was designed strictly for fighters. I hadn't seen anything like it; big boulders surrounded the place and on them he had written the names of the immortals, Jack Johnson, Rocky Marciano, Sugar Ray, Joe Louis. Years later, when I built my own camp, I would use the same idea.

"There's still some walking to do before we get to the gym," Archie said, tightening his suspenders. He liked to wear blue jean outfits, with the pants and shirts all made together, and he bought one for me, too.

Just walking up the hill with him excited me, just to be walking next to one of history's greatest fighters. I couldn't wait to get in the ring with him and try to whip him. It was the only way I thought I could impress him. Archie was treating me rather casually, and I wanted him to know I was no ordinary amateur.

"Let's run to the top of the mountain," he said. I said okay and I dashed up. For a half-mile, I ran straight and fast and he followed me, taking his time in slow rhythm. But suddenly I was so tired I almost collapsed, and when I looked back he seemed cool and calm, running in stride, in rhythm. When he got up to me, he said, "Lesson one. Learn to pace yourself. You'll go longer."

The gym consisted of a little garage-like barn. The most prominent thing about it was a huge bucket nailed on the front, painted with blood trickling over it and the words "Bucket of Blood" in crimson red.

I stripped down and was eager to jump into the ring and spar with some of the fighters I saw around, and especially with Archie Moore. But he warned me against it. "Take your time. It's got to be discipline. I told the Louisville people I would train you right. One step at a time. You want to leap before you've learned to walk. There's other things to do besides box. Now, we eat out here once a day. After we eat, we wash the dishes. You sweep the floor and then you keep the place clean. This is the way I build up discipline right away. In about four years you'll be ready."

Archie and I began to oppose each other. It was here that I first met Dick Sadler, one of the most skillful trainers in boxing. Sadler kept the gym alive, dancing, playing boogie-woogie piano, cracking off-color jokes and driving the fighters on beyond their endurance. Each day I had my chores and I urged Sadler to get me in the ring with Archie. "He don't want that yet," Sadler said. "You better wait. He don't want that."

But one day Sadler found a way, and Archie put on the gloves with me. I took out on him my resentment of all the mopping, all the sweeping, all the scrubbing I had been forced to do during the weeks I had been there. I was jabbing him and moving, circling, whipping in uppercuts, stunning him with right crosses.

When I look back at it now, that was nothing to brag about, because Archie was twice my age. But I had gotten tired of the existence. Archie thought it would take me many years to get "ready"— but I knew better. I was turning against training. Out there in the woods and the mountains, there was nothing to do but listen to birds, watch rabbits cross the highway and jet planes going by every once in a while.

I decided that if I was going to be a fighter, I would have to train around people. I'd have to be around women and children, near barbershops, see people getting their shoes shined, watch the traffic, watch people go in and out of stores, hear them talk and talk back to them. And above all, I wanted to be associated with the instructor who would use his instructions on someone else. Not me. I had gone far past the training period. I wanted to fight, only to fight.

The next week, I left the "Bucket of Blood," mainly because I wanted to go where the blood flowed freer. I wanted to get back to Louisville the quickest way. I had already formulated my way of fighting and my own plans for bringing myself into a title fight.

"You're going to have to fly, son, if you want to be a fighter, fly to places all over the world." Sadler knew I had a fear of flying. "It's a strange fear," he said. "But to you it's real. You've got to either overcome it or give up boxing."

Many times I've searched my mind to find where the fear originated. Maybe because my father would dramatize the same fear and I'd inherited it from him. Maybe because on my first flight, a trip from Louisville to Chicago, the little twin-engine plane went through so much turbulence when it ran through a storm that some of the seats were torn from their bolts on the floor. The fear was so great that after winning the Olympic trials in San Francisco, I was scheduled to fly back to Louisville but I refused. I asked Joe Martin to loan me money to catch a train. "Either fly or walk!" he said. "You've got to get over this." And he flew back home without me. One of my prizes was a gold watch, and I pawned it for train fare and rode back to Louisville, disturbed that I had this fear, wondering how I could overcome it.

When I look back now, the same fear almost kept me out of the Olympics—and, of course, everything that resulted from it. When the team was ready to go to Rome, I told Martin I wouldn't fly. I'd be willing to take a boat, but the thought of flying over the ocean sent chills up and down my spine. Martin explained that a boat would be too slow, and he sat down with me and talked long and earnest about the benefit of being an Olympic Champion, especially if I was to become a professional fighter. "Think it over," he said. "You don't have much time."

What I was afraid of most was the plane crashing, and nothing would satisfy me until I called the Air Force and asked them to give me a record of plane flights between Rome and America. They said they couldn't even remember the last time one had crashed. That calmed me down enough to take the flight to Rome.

In a few years flying would become automatic. I would enjoy sitting in the cockpits with the pilots. I would plan to buy my own plane, and a helicopter.

"Fly and be well-fed or stay home and be hungry," Sadler said.

I flew home to Louisville.

SEVEN AND TWO

I used to hear handlers, trainers and managers, during my amateur days, commenting on the poor showing of certain fighters with sad shakes of the head. "Serves him right. I told him to stay 'way from that stuff." Listening to them, I prayerfully resolved to avoid sex at all costs. And up until the 1958 Golden Gloves, I was glowingly successful, without even a struggle. What I wanted in life was to be a spectacular, winning performer. And if turning my back on sex was what it took, I would be like a nun.

Many doctors and researchers have come to entirely different conclusions on the matter of sex and the athlete. But when I first entered competitions, we younger fighters listened with rapt attention to the old pros who testified on the evils of sex. One or another would account for his defeat or near-knockout by telling some hot, juicy tale of his fatal encounter with an unexpected piece, while the managers and trainers would nod amen.

If they saw us younger fighters, their "protégés," trying to make it with a girl, they'd take us aside and say, "Kid, you got to make her think you're dead. Stay away or it'll ruin you." Then they'd glide over to the girl, take over, and leave us wondering why sex could be so bad for us and so good for them.

"You don't know how to handle it yet," Donnie Hall, my best friend among the older boxers, would patiently explain. I had grown up in Louisville with Donnie, a tall, well-built black, heavy with beautiful teeth and flashing eyes, who defeated opponents with the same ease with which he acquired the prettiest girls.

"How do *you* handle it?" I asked him one day when we were preparing for the Golden Gloves trials. He had won Louisville's heavyweight division and I had won in the light-heavy.

Donnie glanced around to see if anyone was listening. "When we get to Chicago, I'll show you." He winked. "Right now, play it cool. Don't fool around with women. Keep your strength." With that, Donnie, who was four years older than me, strolled off to join his latest girl friend.

I hardly needed the warning; I had just turned sixteen, and I was miserably shy and bashful. It took all the courage I could muster to even approach a girl. If that's to be my only problem, I thought, I've got the championship in the bag.

It was a cold February in '58 when our team got to Chicago and huddled together in the St. Clair Hotel, a few blocks from icy Lake Michigan. There were six of us who wanted to go on to become pros: Ed Whitaker, Davie Hilton, Elmer Dennison, Bill Wikstrom and Donnie Hall and me. To us, winning the Golden Gloves meant getting the "master's degree" we needed for professional work.

I had already lost one shot the previous year when I was taken out in Louisville because the doctor found something irregular about my heartbeat. It cleared up, whatever it was, but too late for me to enter the tournament. And this year, most of all, I wanted to return home a champion.

The huge Chicago Stadium, with three boxing matches going on simultaneously under those hot white lights, with screaming, cheering, booing crowds, was the most awesome spectacle I'd ever participated in. Half the states sent fighters to Chicago, the other half to New York. And the eight winners would fight each other for the national title.

Certain cities became known to us for the caliber of their fighters. We'd say, "Ooooooowwweee, he comes from Cleveland. He must be tough." Or Detroit, Omaha, Toledo, Dayton, Chicago, Wichita. Little two-by-four towns were put on the map by the courage of their unknown fighters. And I wanted to put Louisville on the map for something other than whiskey and horses.

So I studied fighters in those rings like an honor student would his textbooks. Some wild, unorthodox; some poised, polished like the best professionals. I examined styles, stances, moves, feints, jabs, crosses, hooks, bobs, weaves. And I adopted all I could from those who made the trade, bloody, vicious and savage as it might be, an art. As Sugar Ray, Kid Gavilan, Johnny Bratton had done. They were the Picassos among fighters, and they made it all seem a thing of pride, poise, courage, strength, class.

In the Golden Gloves they arrange for the lighter fighters to eliminate each other first. Then they bring out the heavies. After my preliminaries I went up to Donnie's room and found him standing flatfooted, touching his toes before the mirror. He showed me an article forecasting my next night's battle: "A fight coming up that should be of main bout caliber sends Kent Green against Cassius Clay of Louisville. Clay was a standout performer last night."

Donnie laughed and slapped me on the back. "You can take this guy with one hand tied behind you. I got mine made, too. Let's go out." When I asked where we were going, he said, "I wanna see if you can handle it. How you been doin' with it, anyway?"

"Fine," I said, not daring to admit I hadn't been doing anything with "it." I don't know why I was so eager to follow him, instead of resisting and sticking to my rigid resolve not to break training. Maybe because the heaviest load a fighter carries between fights is the boredom, the weariness, that comes from waiting, waiting.

We caught a cab on Michigan Avenue, and when the driver asked where we wanted to go, Donnie said, "Where the women are."

The driver did a double take and said, "How much you expect to pay?"

"Well . . ." Donnie sounded smooth, hip. "Just take us to the best place you know."

"This'll cost you extra," the driver said before he pulled his flag down. He drove us to the South Side and let us out near 47th and Calumet. Donnie paid the fare, slipping in something extra, and the driver said, "Just start walking."

We were in front of a corner pawnshop under the el. An old woman in a knit cap, galoshes and a man's overcoat was standing on an orange crate, preaching the Gospel to people rushing by to catch the train. We started walking.

A few blocks down Calumet Avenue, two prostitutes came up behind us, one black, the other white. The white one looked at me with a fixed smile: "You looking for some fun?"

I said, "Yes . . . Well, no, ma'am, we just walkin'—"

But Donnie cut me off. "Sure, ba-bay, we lookin' for some fun. What's it gonna cost?"

I envied the smooth, self-assured way he took over and wished I could handle myself that way.

"Well," she was saying, "what do you want to pay?"

Donnie hedged. "How much you want?"

"Seven and two," she said.

Donnie turned to me as though I was Mr. Authority. "Cash, is seven and two all right with you?"

"Sure," I said, without the slightest idea what it meant. A few minutes later, when I learned it meant seven dollars for her and two dollars for the room, I couldn't believe the high price.

They took us back to a building we'd just passed, up three flights of rickety wooden stairs with grafitti-covered walls. We reached a hallway where an old white man, sitting in a little cashier's cage, closed his window tight when we came up.

The white woman calmed him down. "Dad, everything's all right," she said, and we stepped up and paid the seven and two.

Donnie started popping his fingers and asked in a loud voice, "Which one you want?"

I was too ashamed to speak so loud. It didn't seem right. Wouldn't one feel slighted if she wasn't chosen first? So I whispered in Donnie's ear, "I'll take the colored one." She was the best-looking of the two— younger, about thirty, a little neater. But when she started toward a door down the hall, I told Donnie I was going back to the hotel. "Got to get up early. Exercise!"

The woman saw me pull back and said, "Awww, don't worry, honey, everything'll be all right. Just don't worry." Her manner wasn't sexy at all, more like a nurse telling a new patient not to be afraid of a minor operation.

Donnie went down the hall and pointed for me to follow my woman, who had gone into a room near the top of the stairs. I got just outside the door and stood there, sweating, nervous, miserable.

I'm back in Louisville . . . seven or eight years old . . . running up and down alleys with the gang, looking into bedroom windows that had the shades or blinds up . . . disappointed in never really seeing anything, but peeping in anyway. We never see what we're looking for. Donnie's mother calls us "bad little rascals."

"Let's find us a new bedroom tonight," somebody says.

"I know us a good place. I saw a place down the street with no shades up or nothin' and last night I saw everything that went on."

And I say, "C'mon, man, let's go see that!"

So we run for about four or five blocks. In the dark we go up to the window and we peep and peep and don't see nobody. And it gets real late. Then the man and woman come in and start taking off their clothes, and just before they get them off, the man turns the light out. That makes me mad.

I TOOK A DEEP BREATH, went inside and closed the door. She was sitting on the bed, opening a pack of cigarettes.

"Hurry up. We haven't got all night."

"Hurry up what?" I said.

"Take your clothes off."

I crossed the room to the light switch and cut all the lights out.

"What you cut them lights out for?"

"I gotta take off my pants," I said.

"Well, goddamn, don't you think I know that? Why'd you cut them lights out?"

All I could say was the truth: "I don't want you to see me with my pants off."

She sat there stone-quiet for a while. I had managed to slip my shoes and socks off before she struck a match to light her cigarette.

"Wanna smoke?" She offered me the package.

"No, ma'am. I don't smoke. Prizefighters are not allowed to smoke, ma'am." The match had lit her face up and I could see her eyes on me in the dark, wide and wondering. "I'm in the Golden Gloves," I went on, trying to get myself on familiar ground so we could at least have something to talk about. "I'm going to be Light Heavyweight Champion, and then—"

"Nice," she said. "Ready?"

I follow Sandra Hanes and Charley Heard all the way home from a party . . . I watch them kiss and kiss and kiss for what seems hours. And when I see Charley in the hall next day at school, I say, "How did you ever get Sandra Hanes to go out with you? She won't go out with me."

He just looks at me with pity and says, "Look, man. You can fight, but you got to learn to talk. Talking is where it's at. Words, words, man. The way you hug the background, you never be hip. You got to step on out and get it. Talk, talk, talk, man. Talk to people. I can't fight a lick. Women like words. Talk."

THE MATCH had burned out and it was pitch-dark again and I was about to take off my long underwear. Then I thought I saw a tiny ray of light from the window. I went over and pulled the shade down tight, to shut out that little light still coming in.

"What the hell you pulling the shades down for? You some

kinda . . ." She was surprised, maybe even a little frightened.

I said, "Don't I have to take off my underwear?"

She was stone-quiet again. I just stood there against the wall, my eyes getting accustomed to the darkness. Then I saw she had stripped off her clothes and was lying on the bed. The blood went to my head. It was the first time I'd seen a woman naked. What was I supposed to do?

Gwendolyn . . . the first girl I ever kiss . . . lives in a little two-room frame house around the corner from me . . . I'm fifteen and devoted to boxing. Every week I'm on *Tomorrow's Champions.* I pass her house: "Oh, Cassius Clay. I watch you all the time on TV." She beckons me to the porch, where she has a record player going, and we listen to the Platters, Little Richard, the Dells, Ella Fitzgerald, and she has me come back week after week.

One night as I'm leaving, she says, "Cash?"

"Yes?"

"Don't you ever kiss anybody?"

I'm startled. I stand like a tree.

"Well, at least hug me," she says.

And I slowly press her body against mine, surprised how warm and good it feels.

"Kiss me, Cash."

I don't know what to do. I feel faint, but I finally put my lips against hers. Then I back up and say, "Well, I'll see you tomorrow." And I walk about a half-block before looking back. And there she is waving. My fight is scheduled the next day on *Tomorrow's Champions,* but I don't sleep all night . . .

"WHAT DO YOU intend to do?" the woman on the bed asked me. "Make up your mind what you want to do . . ."

I couldn't move. How could I tell her I didn't know what to do? What was I expected to do?

Aretha . . . the first girl I really love . . . I see her in the halls of Central High, too frightened to say anything to her. To attract her attention, I come to school with a size-too-small T-shirt on, to make my muscles look like they bulge. But she walks right by me. Then I try to get her attention by taking my friend Ronald King's head and pretending to ram it into the lockers: *B-o-o-o-m-m . . . B-o-o-o-m-m.* She should say, "Ooooeee, what's he doing to that boy?" and come over to see. But she keeps on going.

I don't know how to talk to girls, how to approach them. I ride my motor scooter real fast, turn the corners like I'm going to fall off, all to make Aretha look at me, make her think I'm brave and daring. She keeps on walking.

Then one hot summer night after a basketball game, after Central High beat Flagg J., I come out the big front entrance and see her walking home by herself. I hurry up to catch her on the corner, and force myself to say, "Is your name Aretha?"

"Yes."

"My name's Cassius Clay."

"I know. I've seen you around."

She's so pretty, beautiful black eyes, warm dark face, thick eyelashes. I just say, "I'm going your way. Can I walk with you?"

"If you want to."

And we walk. She has on perfume and the smell is wonderful. My heart is pounding real fast. I've never liked a girl before the way I like Aretha. She lives in Beachwood Apartments, one of the housing projects, on the second floor. When we get there, I get up my nerve. I don't care whether she slaps me or not. I have to kiss her. It must last for a minute and a half, and when I come up for air I'm so dizzy I reel, fall back and hit my head against the steps. I hear her scream. When I open my eyes, she's leaning down and patting me on the face to bring me around.

"What happened?" she asks. "Are you serious? You fainted. I thought you were just playing."

I say I don't know what happened. "I just passed out." Then I run all the way home, to the other side of town, thirteen miles away . . . people are looking at me like I'm crazy . . . and I just run all the way.

It takes about three days before I have enough nerve to face her again. Finally I lose track of her. I get so wrapped up in boxing, in the Golden Gloves, that I concentrate all my attention on that. I don't have time for girls or parties, because every morning I have to get up and do my roadwork. If I don't win a national Golden Gloves, then I'll never get to the Olympics. And I have to be The Champion . . .

"COME ON, let's do it," she said softly.

"Yes, ma'am."

She pulled me to the bed and said, "Do you want a trip around the world?"

"A trip around the world?" I asked. "What's a trip around the world?"

"Well, that's some of everything."

"Some of everything? What are you talking about?"

She never answered, just leaned over and bit me on the neck and put her tongue in my ear, and started biting my back. "Well, come on," she said. "Let's do it."

I got on top of her but I still didn't know what to do. I felt panicky. "Why don't you cooperate a little?" she asked.

I told her the truth: that I'd never been with a woman before.

She grabbed me with both her hands, pulling me to her. "Just push," she said. The panic left and all of a sudden I felt like a man. In a man's position. "Just go up and down," she said. So I went up and down, up and down, until finally she asked, "Aren't you through? Hurry up. Aren't you through?" But I just kept on going up and down. She said something like "Did you? Did you reach your climax?" I didn't know what she was talking about. "Didn't you get a ticklish feeling? A sensation?" I said, "No." There was nothing else to say.

She pushed me off, and I got up right away and started to put on my pants. She stood up and cut the lights on.

I hollered, "Hold it! Hold it!" And I cut the lights right back off.

"What's the matter with you?" she shouted.

"I don't have my clothes on yet," I explained. I couldn't look at her.

When I got dressed and went on back downstairs and stood in the hall waiting for Donnie, I began to feel miserable again. What had I done wrong? I must have left out some of the steps, because it was another half-hour before Donnie came down, walking like he was in pain.

"What's wrong?" I asked.

"She took too much out of me," he said with pleasure.

"What could she take out of you?" I said. "Can't you handle it?"

"She really laid it on me," he said as we got in the cab. He went to sleep on the way back. And all he said before he went to bed that night was "Boy, she really put something on me."

I'll never know for sure whether the experience had anything to do with my performance the next night with Kent Green, but he defeated me on a second-round TKO. Maybe it was only the feeling of guilt because I hadn't followed the rules of the trainers, but it was a painful defeat. And Donnie, also favored to win, lost badly too.

I really wanted to win the Golden Gloves. Already I'd begun to love having my name known. In Louisville, when my name first started getting into the newspapers, I'd run to the neighbors and say, "Hey! My name's in the paper. My picture too."

"Which one you?" an old woman once asked me when I showed her a group of Golden Gloves applicants. "About a hundred in the picture. Which one you?" she said, adjusting her glasses.

"Can't you see? That's me, right there in the middle," I said, surprised she didn't recognize me.

Even if I was just one of a hundred, I was there.

That year, even though I hadn't won the Golden Gloves, I felt a new pride walking the halls of Central High. All those girls I used to look at, wondering how they looked without clothes . . . I now had some idea. "Well," I thought, "now I know. I feel better. I been with a woman. I know." It was enough for a while. But gradually I found myself wanting to see another. Could I be so sure the non-prostitutes looked exactly like my prostitute? Because that prostitute was really too old. And these younger girls looked better. I'd always wondered before why men could become so easily upset over women. Ice cream, pop and hamburgers were far more attractive. But now I found myself going to parties, learning to talk, losing my inhibitions.

Then one day I got whipped by Jimmy Ellis, my only amateur loss in Louisville, and as I sat the next morning nursing my wounds I realized I had been with a woman the night before that fight, too.

"What relation does sex have on a fighter's performance?" I once sat with a group of reporters, fighters and handlers who were asking Harry Wiley that question. Wiley, a brilliant trainer, worked with Sugar Ray Robinson for twenty-four years, had been in the corners of Baby Joe Gans, Kid Chocolate, Henry Armstrong, Joe Louis, knew the habits of Jack Johnson, Sam Langford, Jack Dempsey, Harry Wills, had been an Olympic boxing coach and had come to camp for my 1970 fight with Ellis. I was amazed at his detailed knowledge of every aspect of a fighter's life.

"On sex activities for fighters," Wiley admitted, "I'm of the old school. You find most prizefighters have enormous sex drives. I've seen the time when you had to feed some of them saltpeter to keep them cooled off. They build up this tremendous store of vitality and drive, and just a few rounds in the ring is not enough release."

"How about Liston?" someone asked. "How was he?"

"One of the worse," Wiley said. "Liston used to take his sex drive out on opponents. I heard they told Liston that Lena Horne would see him if he whipped Patterson, that the only thing standing between him and Lena was Floyd. He slaughtered Patterson in the first round in both fights. Patterson was lucky he came out alive. They used to tease Liston, telling him a beautiful woman was out there waiting for him, but if he didn't knock his opponent out by the third she wouldn't see him. Then they'd set a woman at ringside, and at the end of the second round she'd get up and walk down the aisle and they'd whisper to Liston,

'Well, there you go. You lost your chance.' Liston would hurry to get the fight over."

"I heard you had trouble with Sugar Ray," one reporter said.

"Don't believe it. At his peak, Sugar Ray was the best-disciplined fighter in the trade. He valued his looks too much to take a chance on getting hurt in the ring. When it came time for him to stop, his will power was like iron. He could sleep next to Venus without touching her. But some of my others . . ." Wiley groaned. "Uncontrollable."

"Kid Chocolate?" someone asked.

"Kid Chocolate was bad, an awful hound. Joe Gans was, too. But the worse I ever had was Henry Armstrong. How he ever won and held three world titles with all the women he went through . . ." Wiley shook his head. "A glutton. Almost as bad as Sonny Liston. I blame a big part of Joe Louis' decline on his getting too much.

"The only fighter I ever saw just the opposite was Light Heavy Champion John Henry Lewis. I remember John Henry Lewis' manager, Gus Greenlee, calling me in, telling me how upset he was over Lewis' listlessness, his unresponsiveness. I took Lewis aside, asked him when was the last time he'd had a woman.

" 'Over a year,' he said.

"I screamed to Gus, 'Listen, this guy's got to get laid!'

"Then we got a woman. Like good medicine, he got better. Of course, Lewis was unusual like that." He turned to Pacheco, who had known me ever since I first came to Miami. "You heard of cases like that, Doc?"

Pacheco laughed. "The closest I could come to that was Muhammad Ali and those days when he was Cassius Clay. His Louisville sponsors had him staying at a hotel on Second Avenue, a hotel loaded with pimps, hustlers and prostitutes going after him every day. They'd come up to him, asking, 'What you want, kid? You want a broad or a sissy? Let me get you somebody. Whatever you need, we got.' And he'd turn 'em down stone cold, not even a bit of interest. Even when they tried to trick him to take a picture with his arms around a broad, he'd jump away as if they'd asked him to pose next to Hitler." He shook his head as if those days were long gone. "In fact, it got so bad around Second Avenue that for years hustlers thought he was funny.

" 'You know, I think this guy may be a little queer,' one hustler told me. 'Maybe he don't know it yet, but I think we could turn this guy.' He winked. " 'Man,' I told him, as I knew this hustler, he had come in my office many times to get a shot or prescription, 'man, leave the new kid alone, for Christ's sake.'

" 'But the guy won't do a thing with women,' the hustler tells me. 'This guy got to be funny.'

"Ali's not like John Henry Louis, but in those days he had only one thing in mind—winning The Championship. That's why the gamblers bet on young Cassius. I knew the best gambler in Tampa, and I wish I'd taken his advice. When he first sized up Cassius, he came and told me, 'There's a kid just come down here named Cassius Clay. If you bet on him every time he fights, you'll be a rich man, 'cause he won't lose a single fight. I believe his thing is sexual control. And he's got it.' In those days, Sonny Liston was considered the coming power, Floyd Patterson had the title, but the gambler told me this kid would go through Floyd and Liston and he'd go through every heavyweight up there or who was coming up. He'd never lose a fight. 'I tell you, I go by his sex control,' the gambler said. 'I believe in it. Any kid who can control his sex can win the title. I believe it. If you double on everything, you'll win on Cassius and you'll come home rich.'

"I wish I had listened to that guy. There was one guy, a headwaiter at a big hotel in Los Angeles, who did just that. He started out with a hundred-dollar bet on Cassius. Then he doubled the winnings every fight. Soon he had enough to buy himself a Cadillac convertible, and his wife a Mercedes-Benz, and all that before Cassius fought Liston. After the Liston fight, I saw him and I said, 'You must have really gotten well with Sonny Liston's fight.' He just smiled and said, 'Man, don't even talk about it. I don't think I'll work for the rest of my life.' He said that discipline and self-control was the thing that would make Cassius a champion. It's the discipline and self-control that makes it."

"I don't agree with that at all," Bundini cut in. He had been sitting silent all the time and listening to the trainers. "It's not that at all. It's freakishness that makes a champion."

They all turned and looked at him as he sat there with his bleary eyes and baby face, the only thing innocent about him; otherwise, he's the most thoroughly profane person I've ever met inside boxing circles and out.

"Every fighter I've ever known is a freak," he said as though he was the undisputed authority. Then he named the great fighters he had been associated with, names I won't mention only because they would be shocked to be defined like this. "Freakishness crawls out of their little finger. It's in all their bones and down to the tip of their toes. They can't help it. That's the thing that makes a champion. Now, you take Mel Turnbow over there." He pointed to Turnbow, one of the strongest fighters in the ring, but one who has always had trouble keeping himself from being knocked out.

Turnbow, six-foot-six giant from Ohio, heard Bundini and came over with his odd walk and his pants that always seem too tight and never quite long enough for his legs.

Bundini frowned. "You're built too strange to be wearing store-bought clothes. You ought to have your clothes tailor-made. Ain't no store-bought clothes in the world that'll fit your ass and size."

"I buy 'em off the rack just like you do," Turnbow retorted.

"That's why you look so peculiar," Bundini said. "It's a good thing you're a prizefighter and you're strong. The way those pants make your ass jog—God! Let's hope you never get put in jail—all that round eye goin' to waste, you turn even me into a sodomite."

Turnbow stood up defensively as though Bundini was really prepared to rape him.

"What I was going to say," Bundini went on, "is that even with all those muscles and power, long arms, the thing that's missing from Turnbow is he's not a freak. There's not a freakish bone in his body." He shook his head sadly, as though he was giving a profound opinion.

When Wiley wanted to read opinions on the subject from scientists, he was shown the response from Dr. Warren R. Guild of Harvard Medical School, who had done extensive research on the effect of physical intercourse on athletes. Dr. Guild wrote: "If I were Muhammad Ali's physician (which obviously I am not), I not only would not discourage him about sex, I would be on the positive side, definitely recommend and encourage him to have intercourse with his wife a night or two before the bout to insure better sleep and have increased vigor for the competition. The above response is a summary of our studies on this subject, the details of which I will not go into as they are too complicated. Physical intercourse," Dr. Guild concluded, "does not in any way sap one's strength or make one weak."

Then a reporter told Wiley that Masters and Johnson and Washington psychologist William Harper supported Dr. Guild's thesis.

The old trainer who had eaten, slept and worked in the corners of the greatest fighters for two generations sat thoughtfully for a while, said he was reanalyzing the case of Baby Joe Gans, of the Armstrongs, the Langfords, the Harry Willses, and finally concluded, "I don't believe the doctors understand what builds up inside a fighter. A little piece to an average athlete is all right, but prizefighters don't play around with small-size pieces. They never researched real prizefighters. I have."

Angelo Dundee nodded in agreement. "Without it a fighter gets mean, angry, willing, anxious to fight. With it he purrs like a pussycat. It's psychological, maybe, more than physical. You keep a fighter away from women, keep him in camp pounding bags, punching fighters day in and day out, and when he gets in the ring he's ready to take it all out on his opponent.

"Who wants to fight after good loving? All wars are brought about by leaders who never had good loving. Take Hitler, Mussolini, Napoleon. How about all those war hawks?

"A fighter who has sex regular, the way these doctors talk, would be a placid, easygoing pussycat with no drive, no resentment, no anger. The doctors don't know the fight game."

Now that I am near the end of my career, the controversy rages on just as it did when I stepped into the ring at age twelve. The only difference being, now when I climb the steps for the fight, I hope the scientists know what they're talking about.

THE FIRST COMING

I remember that morning, three days before my fight for the World Heavyweight Title, coming out of my house at 4610 Northwest Fifteenth Court to go over to the Fifth Street Gym. I have this eerie feeling that I'm at the crossroads of something I have to pass through or I'll never come this far again. In a few hours, I'll find out what it is; this fight will come closer to being canceled than any of my fights before or since.

Six months ago, I bought a bus in Chicago and drove it directly to Louisville, where the best sign painter I know, my father, painted it orange, green, red, yellow and blue, but mostly red, with WORLD'S MOST COLORFUL FIGHTER: CASSIUS CLAY on one side, and on the other side:

SONNY LISTON IS GREAT,
BUT HE'LL FALL IN EIGHT.

I named it "Big Red" and drove up and down and across the country, reciting poetry, predicting Liston's downfall. I've campaigned for this title fight harder than most candidates campaign for a Presidential election. "Feats of Clay" is my favorite campaign poem:

> *It all started twenty years past.*
> *The greatest of them all was born at last.*
> *The very first words from his Louisville lips,*
> *"I'm pretty as a picture, and there's no one I can't whip."*
> *Then he said in a voice that sounded rough,*
> *"I'm strong as an ox and twice as tough."*
> *The name of this Champion, I might as well say,*
> *No other one than the greatest, Cassius Clay.*
> *He predicts the round in which he's gonna win,*
> *And that's the way his career has been.*
> *He knocks them all out in the round he'll call,*
> *And that's why he's called the Greatest of them all.*

In the last six months, I've dogged Liston's every step, challenging, predicting his doom, calling him "The Big Ugly Bear," making it impossible for him or the newspapers to ignore me. In all my campaigning, I found a way to force the promoters to give me a title fight, but through it all I discovered something new and even more valuable to me than the World Heavyweight Championship.

The first inkling I get that this day will be different from any day of my life comes when Angelo bursts into the dressing room, a look of horror on his face. "Do you know who's out there?" He half-opens the door and points to Malcolm X standing near the ring, looking at old fight posters. "You know what will happen if the newspapers pick that up? They'll denounce you! They'll condemn you! They'll wreck the fight! Please! Please!" His eyes are wide with fear. "We've got to get him out of here! If the newspapers know you're associated with Muslims like Malcolm X, your career is over. Do you hear me?"

I've been as close to Angelo as I've ever been to a white man up to now. The only thing he doesn't know is that Malcolm is not the only "X" in the gym. I am Cassius X. I too am a follower of the Honorable Elijah Muhammad.

Angelo sees he is making no impression and abruptly turns away and leaves. I learn later that he called his brother Chris, and Chris relayed the information quickly to Bill McDonald, the promoter who had assembled the hundreds of thousands of dollars to stage what was being billed as "The Biggest Heavyweight Title Match in Boxing History."

Chris walks up to me: "Cassius, you got a minute? McDonald wants you in his office."

"What about, Gangster?" I ask. Although Chris and Angelo are friends as well as trainers, I always jokingly refer to Chris as "Gangster," mainly because his biggest days in boxing covered the period when gangsters had their tightest control.

"Won't take but a minute," Chris says very low, as though he wants only me to hear it.

I put my clothes on, and in a few minutes I'm walking across Washington Street with Chris and my brother to Convention Hall, where McDonald has his office. It's a bright, sunny day, people stopping me on the street for autographs, giving me advice about Liston or calling out, "Good luck, young man!" Chris keeps glancing at his watch, muttering, "McDonald's waiting."

When we get to the office, I hold back for my brother to step in first but Chris stops him. "McDonald wants to see you, not your brother," he says to me. I hesitate. What could it be my younger brother can't hear? But Rudy steps aside politely. Not at all concerned, he says, "I'll wait outside." And Chris and I go into the promoter's office.

McDonald, a huge man with brown hair and a big reddish face, tells Chris to close the door, then turns to me: "Cassius," he begins, lighting a fat cigar Chris has given him. "Is it true you flew into New York a week ago and visited the New York Mosque of the Nation of Islam, that you were seen publically surrounded by 'Black Muslims,' that you spent the entire day there and that you defended them to newsmen who asked you about them?"

"It's true," I say.

McDonald goes back behind the desk, his face grim, his voice firm. And from then on he talks like a prosecuting attorney piling up evidence to justify execution by any means at hand. "Is it true that Malcolm X out there in the gym is here by your invitation?"

"Yes, sir," I say. I look directly at him, and see a tinge of real fear in his eyes.

At the time, Malcolm was an outstanding minister of the Honorable Elijah Muhammad; his face, his voice were known throughout the country from the numerous TV debates where he denounced the "white devil" and discrimination against black people and upheld the programs of the Honorable Elijah Muhammad. Looking back on those days, it seems almost unreal, although it's only ten years ago. But a veritable witch hunt was out against the followers of the Honorable Elijah Muhammad. Some whites thought they saw in the Nation of Islam overdue "black avengers" of all the injustice inflicted upon the blacks against those who segregated them into ghettos and who upheld

White Supremacy. And they saw Malcolm as the most visible spokesman.

McDonald continues with the prosecution: "I also understand you have a Captain Samuels in your camp and a security guard on your sponsors' payroll, and 'Black Muslim' women cooks in your camp. Is this true?"

"Yes," I answer.

I explain to him that Captain Samuels is the Muslim minister in Miami who has been helping me. A big, strong man with a pleasant smile, Captain Samuels has been so cooperative that even Chris, who had begun to suspect that I was associating with "Black Muslims," thought he could confide in him: "Look," Chris said. "You're a nice guy. I know Cassius listens to you. Well, you've got to tell him to stop hanging around those 'Black Muslims.' It'll ruin his career. Talk to him. Tell him those 'Black Muslims' are too controversial. Please do that for me." He kept this up for maybe a month, until one day he saw a boy he knew was a Muslim walk up to Samuels and salute him in the Muslim manner. Chris almost went through the floor. Later he told me, "I sunk and walked away. You kept this thing hidden all this time."

"The sisters cook for me," I tell McDonald, "because I only eat kosher food and they're trained in preparing it. I won't let them go."

McDonald tries a new approach. "Maybe you don't know it, but the World Heavyweight Title is the greatest prize in sports. It makes a fighter famous just to get a chance to fight for it—much less win. Instantly, you're a part of world history. The doors open up for you. Everybody in the world understands a fighter and a champion, and I'm giving you this opportunity at the cost of millions of dollars to myself, and do you know why I'm doing that?

I knew exactly why.

"You came in as a fresh breeze in boxing. You were flamboyant, yes, colorful, cocky and confident. You know how Morton Sharnick, the *Sports Illustrated* editor, described you after you won the Olympics? He said you were the 'real All-American Boy.' You were the Johnny Appleseed of America. Everybody loved you. You were the Jack Armstrong, the natural attraction, everybody's hero. That's what I was basing this fight on. The good guy versus the bad guy. Everybody knows Liston's background. He's a thug, the menace, the monster. You would be like Little Red Riding Hood and he would be the wolf. That would be a good money fight. But you as a 'Black Muslim,' they'd pray for the wolf to win. And they'll stay away. That would wreck my promotion.

"Do you know that since it's leaked out that Malcolm X is in the camp, there're stories that the 'Black Muslims' are manipulating you? Already this fight is jeopardized. I've got to have a chance to make my profit back. And there's only one way and you've got to do it now, today. You've got to clean house. First get rid of those Muslim cooks, those 'Black Muslim' security people, Captain Samuels, all the others. Then you got to get on the radio, on television, tonight. You got to deny you're a member of the 'Black Muslims.' I'll give you a public relations man to work with. You got to say you were misquoted, it was all a mistake. You declare yourself clean. Then we can go on." He picks up the phone and starts dialing.

"And if I don't do that?" I say.

He turns around, looks at me, slowly puts down the phone. His face is grim and hard, no trace of bluff. "If you don't," he says softly, "the fight's off. I'm calling it off. You're through. You're finished. But I know you've got better sense than that. I know you've worked for this all your life. It's not too late to save it. I told you my public relations man would help you. You'll go on TV this evening. You'll tell the world you're not a 'Black Muslim.' You haven't joined anything. You've been misquoted. You're a true patriotic loyal American. You always were and always will be. Maybe you were tricked into signing something you know very little about, but if so, that's all over with. We'll arrange a press conference. We'll clear the air. Then the fight will go on. It's still a gamble, but only on those conditions can the fight go on."

I stand up and look at him and shake my head. "I can't do that. I appreciate the opportunity you've given me to fight Liston for the championship. I know I can beat Liston, and I don't want to call the fight off, but if you have to call it off because of my faith, then the fight's off."

"Why don't we all forget about it," Chris cuts in nervously. "Forget about the whole thing until after the fight."

"There's not gonna be a fight," McDonald says finally. His phone rings and he picks it up. "The fight's off. Tell the press. Tell everybody the fight's off."

He's still on the phone when I walk out the door. Chris is holding on to me, urging me to stay. But I've looked into the promoter's face and I know he isn't bluffing, and neither am I. My head is ringing so much that when I pick up my brother, I hardly say anything but go straight to the gym. I gather up my things and head back across the Causeway to the Miami side, and drive up to the house and park behind Big Red.

I'm shaken up because I know, deep down, that McDonald really wants to cancel the fight and means everything he says. But no sooner do I get in the house than the phone rings. It's a call from one of my Louisville sponsors, Worth Bingham. He already knows about the cancellation.

"Look, Cassius," he says, "I know your side of the story, but whatever you do, get this fight on. What does Mac want you to do?"

"He wants me to disavow my religion," I say, "make a public statement."

"Then make it! Do it! Go ahead. What've you got to lose? They'll never let you get a chance like this again. McDonald's been trying to get out of this fight for days. Don't let him off the hook! Don't give him an excuse!"

"I'm not going to denounce my religion, not even for the fight."

"Will you listen to me! The public climate has changed against you. You win the title and things will be different. If you want my advice, I'm giving it. Do what McDonald wants! I'm telling you, McDonald wants an excuse to back down. You're giving him the out he wants. Don't let him have it. Pull the rug out from under him. Your religion is not in your public image. Who'll know what's really in your heart but God . . . er, I mean Allah? Your conversion is only a few months old. Allah will understand." With that, he hangs up.

I feel alone. Years later, when I look back at this moment, I will try to think how I felt. I remember a sense of resignation. What they thought of as a conversion "only a few months old" was actually much deeper than that, for in the Nation of Islam I saw the liberation of black people from subjugation and slavery to freedom and equality and justice, and I could never explain that to my Louisville sponsors or to McDonald.

Most of my crew have overheard the phone call and know what I'm up against. Bundini is standing in the doorway. "What are we gonna do now, Champ?"

"We're leaving," I say. "There's no championship fight. We're packing to go home."

"What does going home mean?"

"It means you get no money," I tell him.

"It means you ain't no phony, and I stay with you money or no money. Pack the suitcases!" he screams. "Get the show on the road! Pack up! Big Red's gonna roll again!"

And the crew start packing the trunks, the suitcases, getting my gear and taking it to the bus.

I call my mother and tell her the fight's off and I'm coming home. I know by her voice she's heartbroken. It's the end of a long, long road for us all. I help Bundini lift a heavy footlocker full of boxing gear onto the bus and I sit at the wheel, thinking back on how it all started.

Even before Liston had become World Heavyweight Champion, I knew he was the fighter I would have to beat if I were ever to be recognized as what I declared I was: The Greatest.

I had always stalked the professional fighters, trying to get into their gyms to spar with them, and I used to watch Liston, but his managers would never allow me to train with him. I just stood there and watched him. He was everything they said he was, a mass of muscles, power, force. "He's the King Kong of boxing," John Cottrell, the English writer, once said. "A savage, glaring-eyed gorrilla with mighty muscles—the ultimate weapon in unarmed combat, a human destroyer with bone-crushing fists that measured a fantastic fourteen inches round the Knuckles and needed special-made gloves to cover them. They call him old stone face, a man without pity in his hard brown eyes."

On the scale of dinosaurs, as the old trainer, Reverend Williams, would say, Liston would be the biggest and baddest that ever shook the ground: the brontosaurus.

He had been recognized as the "Uncrowned Champion," even when Floyd Patterson held the title. After my first feeling of awe and fear wore off, I watched him in the gym with keener eyes. In those days the only thing the newspapers had against him was his association with outlawed racketeers, and the fact that Senator Estes Kefauver had once said, "If Liston won the title, we'd face the ugly prospect of having the World Champion revert to Mob control." But I was to find that they considered it a worse prospect to have it under "Black Muslim" control. Between the White Mafia and the "Black Muslims," they would prefer the Mafia.

But the more I watched Liston in the gym, the more I began to see something the others didn't see, something that let me know I could take him. Anytime I wanted to.

Now, sitting in Big Red, having it packed to leave Miami without a fight, I know it might take years before I get another title shot and this time I might have to come back the hard way, fighting the other contenders who are ahead of me: Eddie Machen, Harold Johnson, Cleveland Williams, Zora Folley, good fighters who sometimes can fight with brilliance. It would be just my luck to catch one of them when he was determined not to lose, no matter what.

McDonald had said I talked myself into the fight, I had brought it about. And in a way he was right. I'd been doing that since I was fourteen, as an amateur, flailing away at another boy in the center of the ring, the people screaming and calling to my opponent: "Shut his mouth! He talks too much! Stop him!"

I had fought before, but now the crowd was calling my name, calling out against me. What mattered was that they were alive to me. Before the fight, for the first time I'd talk openly about beating my opponent, telling not only him but everybody else, and the word got around that "Cassius is bragging." But when they came to the gym, they gave me all the attention I wanted. I kept calling out, "I'm The

Greatest! I can't be beat!" I'd seen good fighters carry on bloody brawls with hardly anybody caring which one won or lost. At least now they were interested in my fights, even if they wanted me to lose, something I had some control over. Best of all, it made fighting more attractive to me, more challenging, and by the time the Olympics came, I was better known than most professionals.

I picked up the art of talking to my opponent during the Olympic Trials, after I fought Allen Hudson, who talked to me during the whole bout, made fun of my mistakes, rattled me. And even though I beat him, in the end we were both talking to each other.

I can understand how it works. No one likes a blowhard, an immodest braggart. It gets on your nerves. I had started announcing myself: "I'm the World's Prettiest Fighter! I'm the World's Strongest Fighter! The World's Fastest Fighter! The only fighter who can predict what round they'll fall in!" And almost overnight everyone wanted to see me fight. When I flew into Las Vegas, I found I was on the right track. I was awed by the glitter and the girls and the gambling, but mostly I was struck by Gorgeous George. He was doing what I had been doing. I was fascinated.

Gorgeous came into the TV studio where Duke Sabedong, my opponent, and I were being introduced. He made his entrance combing his long blond hair like a movie idol, two pretty girls holding up the ends of a ten-foot-long robe so it wouldn't drag. "Look at my velvet skin," he purred. "Look at my pretty hair. If that bum messes up my hair tomorrow night, I'll annihilate him!" When he snatched the microphone, the announcer cautioned him, "Hold it, Gorgeous. This is not your show!" "It is my show!" George said, and he walked in front of the stage and spoke into the mike. "I want all of you out there to come to the Sports Palace early because I'm gonna mop the floor with this bum. If he beats me, I'll cut off all my golden hair and throw the hair out in the audience and go bald."

Instead of resting for my fight that next night, I was at the Sports Palace along with a standing-room-only crowd, wanting to see what would happen to George. I saw how his strategy had worked, just as mine had been working. When George came down, they were booing him, calling for his opponent to shut his mouth. They cursed him and threw paper cups at him, but in the end he won.

After Las Vegas my plans for going after the World Heavyweight Title match were set. I only had to do more of what I'd been doing. I was predicting the round my opponent would fall in each fight with an accuracy the papers found unbelievable. I created a poem for every opponent: "They'll all fall in the round I call!" I shouted.

And each time the boos for me were getting stronger and stronger. But I won and I kept the World Heavyweight Title in focus. The louder the boos, the surer I was that some promoter would see that there was more money to be made with me fighting a title match than any so-called contender above me.

Up until I fought Archie Moore, I hadn't had an opponent who would draw world-wide attention. And when they told me I would fight "The Old Man," I knew my drive for a title match would open up. Archie Moore was the first real great fighter of world fame, the first ex-Champion I'd been put up against, and I had to make a prediction that would stick. I wrote on the blackboard in my dressing room, "Moore in Four." And I went on TV with poems:

> When you come to the fight,
> Don't block the halls,
> And don't block the door,
> For y'all may go home,
> After round four.

I predicted knowing Sonny Liston would have a ringside seat. After Moore, I would beat Liston in eight.

Fighting in Los Angeles was almost like fighting in Archie's home-town. They screamed and called for Archie to wipe me out. "Shut him up, Archie!" . . . "Hit him in his big mouth!" But Archie was long past his prime. I take no great credit for blasting him down. He had had more than two hundred fights in his career. And he'd won most of them in twenty-seven years. He was at the end of the line. He fell in four as I predicted.

I was still campaigning: "Now who can say I'm not one of the greatest? Everything went just as I said it would. I could have taken 'The Old Man' out in the first round—but I believe in doing things on schedule. Moore did better than most. Not many men could go four rounds with me. He's a great old fighter. Archie should blame the crowd for stirring me up."

Someone shouted, "How does it feel to be booed, loud-mouth?"

"It's a good feeling to enter the ring with thousands of people booing you," I said. "Especially when you know you can deliver what you predict. I'm ready for Sonny Liston right now."

> King Liston will stay,
> Only until he meets Cassius Clay.
> Moore fell in four,
> Liston in eight.

I said this at the victory party with Liston looking on. He gave me his coldest stare and said, "You go eight seconds with me, little boy, and I'll give you the title." He walked away, but I knew the promoters were listening.

"You can't predict no rounds! You fixin' 'em! You a phony!"

It was the night before my fight with Doug Jones, and I was in my hotel room, talking to a tall, thin black man in a red T-shirt and blue jeans, with a processed hairdo, and a long cigar in his mouth. Sugar Ray Robinson's brother-in-law, Bobby Nelson, had sent him to me. They called him "Fastblack," or "Bundini," Nelson had said. Fastblack had been with Sugar Ray for five years, but he admired everything I did.

"You can't be predictin' all them rounds," he said. "Tell me the truth. Y'all git together and fix them fights, don't you?"

He had a strange way of saying unexpected things that made you do a double take and look hard at him. He would stand there with a grin on his odd half-moon face, a long scar across his cheek. And even though he told you, you still wondered where he came from and how he got here. He had papers showing that he had been a merchant seaman at the age of thirteen, that he had grown up in St. Petersburg, Florida. "I've been paying my own rent since I was nine years old," he said, and he'd been out on his own since he was eleven; been in sea camps, reform schools, prison; been around the world a dozen times; was a hustler who hustled the hustlers; worked the streets of Harlem; had been converted to the Jewish faith; had a son, Drew Brown, Jr., whom he adored; had a way of throwing his whole life and soul into every project he believed in.

"You gotta be fixin' 'em, or else you couldn't tell Archie Moore when he was fallin'. You couldn't have told Powell. You got to be a phony!" He took his cigar out of his mouth, knocked off the ashes and pinned his eyes on me as if he were giving me an x-ray. "You either a phony or either Shorty's in your corner," he finally said. "I been with Sugar Ray. I was with Johnny Bratton. I never heard of anybody predictin' weeks in advance the round they're gonna win in. Tell me the truth!" He sat down on a pillow with his legs crossed Indian fashion, looking up at me. "Tell me the truth!"

I sat down next to him. "You know what the truth is?" I said. "The truth is, every time I go into the ring I'm scared to death."

He looked at me as though he was shocked. Then tears began to flow down his cheeks. "I knew Shorty was with you. Shorty had to be with you." He grabbed me and kissed me on the jaw. "You mean you actually scared out there? Why?"

"I'm scared," I told him, "because after all that poppin' off, all that predicting, all those people wanting to see me get whipped, I know I'm in trouble. If I lose, they'll be ready to run me out of the country.

I'm out on a limb and I know I gotta win. I'm on the spot when I'm out there . . . and I'm scared to death. Now that's a fact that only you and me know."

"You and me and Shorty," Bundini whispered. "What you predictin' about your fight tomorrow? You gonna whip Doug Jones?"

"Round six, but I don't know whether I can do it or not."

"You gonna win that fight!" he shouted. "I don't know if you gonna knock him out, but you gonna win. Put me in your corner."

"Why?" I asked.

" 'Cause you got the power and I got the spirit. You a heavyweight Sugar Ray. You gonna be the next Champion. You'll beat Sonny Liston, all right. Am I in your corner?"

"All right," I told him. "You be in my corner if you want to be."

That was the first I'd seen of Drew "Bundini" Brown, who would become one of my crew and is with me even today.

But the next night my prediction on Doug Jones failed to work. The resentment against my bragging, my predicting, my declarations —"I'm The Greatest! I'm The Prettiest! I can't be whipped!"— brought nearly twenty thousand people into Madison Square Garden, and when I came out they drowned the announcement in boos, which must have inspired Jones. He turned out to be the toughest fight of my life. I'd taken him too lightly.

When I missed my prediction for a six-round knockout, the stadium went wild. "Get him, Doug!" . . . "Shut his fat mouth!" they screamed. He was pressuring me all the way.

"Snake-lick 'em! Snake-lick 'em, Champ!" I heard Bundini shouting as I began peppering Jones with quick jabs in the eighth round. "Whip him, Champ! Take it to him!"

When it was over, I had won, but it was close and the audience threw everything they had in their hands into the ring—cups, bottles, peanuts, even a switchblade. And they booed me all the way to the dressing room and clutched at my robe. I had just made more enemies, and every one of them would find a way to see me fight again.

"What's your next fight? We've got so many choices to fight now," Faversham said happily. "Madison Square Garden wants you to fight the Swedish Champion. You've got offers to fight Doug Jones again, Eddie Machen, Thad Spencer, Ernie Terrell . . ."

"All I want is Liston," I said. "All I want is Liston."

"Now I'll make a prediction. If you stop Henry Cooper, it'll be your last fight before Liston. You've never fought outside America. It's time you saw the rest of the world and the rest of the world saw you."

I flew to London; I fell in love with the people in England. I had never been treated so warm, so friendly, and I had always said England was my second home. Even though I'd come to destroy their Champion, they treated me with a kindness and courtesy I had never felt in Louisville or any city in America. They even criticized the Queen for meeting with Henry Cooper but not with me. And years later in Las Vegas when I fought Joe Bugner, the present English Champion, hundreds of Englishmen flew in to see the fight. "Cheer for Bugner because he's your country's Champion," I told them as they crowded into my training quarters. "But after I beat Bugner, come on back over to my side." When they shouted back, "We will . . . it's just for this fight!" I felt better about whipping Bugner as thoroughly as I did.

On the night before the Cooper fight, I had announced that I was the uncrowned King of the Heavyweights. And Jack Solomon, the old English promoter, took me to a theatrical outfitter, who made up a king's crown for my head and a royal robe. I wore it at the weigh-in and announced to the crowd, "I'm King of the World. Henry Cooper is only a warm-up—just a stepping stone for me to get my real crown! You know that I'm the next King, the King of all Boxers!"

Now that I look back, I'm surprised at the sense of humor they had. They seemed to understand what I was doing even more than the people back home. They knew I was campaigning: "This ain't no jive, Henry Cooper will fall in five." I had the figure "5" printed on a large card and flashed across the room. And I held up five fingers. "Cooper will fall in five!"

But the next night Cooper came out throwing punches with all his might. I outboxed him, and when I started whipping my right to his head, jabbing him with combinations, the blood began gurgling out of a cut above his eye.

It was the third round, and I moved back because my prediction called for the fifth and I wanted to be on time. I dropped my guard and glanced down at ringside at a screaming woman—Elizabeth Taylor, with her husband, Richard Burton—and suddenly something exploded against my jaw. I was down on the floor. I was dazed and numb. The stadium was roaring. The referee was counting. But before he said four, the bell rang.

Back in my corner, Angelo discovered that the seam of my boxing glove was busted. The cushion was coming out, and the rules and regulations in boxing are strict—the gloves must be in good condition. It took nearly a minute to make the replacement.

Many times I've been asked if I needed the extra minute it took to get the glove, but the truth is I wasn't shaken up that much. I believe a regular minute would have been enough to clear my head, but, of course, the extra minute gave me new vigor, and I came out shooting jabs and hard, straight, slashing rights across to the head. The cut over Cooper's eye opened again, and in the clinches I could see the blood pumping out, gushing out. It was a warm night and the odor of blood was everywhere. It splattered on my chest and trunks, across his face. I looked around for the referee to stop it.

Elizabeth Taylor and the women at ringside with her were screaming louder, "Stop it! Stop it!" But some of the audience still had hope for Cooper. "Come on, Henry! Come on! Get him!" But for me, the fight was over. I decided to go no further. The referee finally came up. No human being should have to take that kind of beating just to please a bloodthirsty crowd.

I was still washing the blood off my chest when Faversham came into the dressing room with Jack Nilon, Sonny Liston's manager. "He's bringing us a message from Liston," Faversham said.

"I've flown three thousand miles just to tell you that Liston wants you," Nilon said, "and he's got a message for you. He says to please drink your orange juice and your milk shakes. Stay well and healthy. You talked yourself into a World Heavyweight Title fight. Now your wife can be a rich widow."

I'M SITTING behind the wheel of Big Red as Bundini and my crew load the last of the trunks and suitcases inside. If the talk I did got me the fight with Liston for the World Title, the talk they want me to do now to have it come off will never be done. I look back and call to Bundini, "Is everybody on?"

"Let 'er roll, Champ!"

A horn is blowing outside, a car has pulled in front of the bus. It's Chris. He jumps out almost breathless, holds his hands up and says, "Wait! Don't leave! We're talking to McDonald. Don't leave!"

I open the driver's window to hear him.

"Look, don't leave. If you go, it'll all be over. That's all McDonald needs. He wants you to go. You stay here while we talk to him. We're trying to talk to him! We've got people calling him on the phone telling him the fight's got to go through. Don't leave!"

"How long will it take?"

"Give us an hour," Chris says. "Give us another hour and we can tell. I'm telling him you're not leaving. He wants to know if you can make any concession on that talk."

"Tell him there's no change," I say. "There's no change in that at all."

I had climbed into the ring in Chicago when Liston won the title in his first fight with Patterson. I had cried out a challenge to Liston. And while Liston was training for his second fight with Patterson, I asked my Louisville sponsors to fly me into Vegas where I could talk to him, watch him train, let the world know that the real clash had not taken place yet.

And I remember one evening Liston turned the tables on me. I had been talking that morning to Willie Reddish, one of Liston's trainers. He told me Liston was down at the Thunderbird, gambling. "Why don't you go over and spend a little money, too?" he said.

The promoters had given me money to use on the gambling tables, to help stimulate business. I had been looking for Sonny and I had a new poem that I wanted to read to him. "I'll be there in about an hour," I told Reddish. "But I'm not coming to spend money. I'm coming to run him outta the saloon."

When I got to the Thunderbird, Liston was deep in a dice game. I started shouting at him, "Come on, you big ugly bear! Let's get it on! Come on!" Liston kept rolling the dice, hardly looking up. "I'll whip you right now!" I said. "Floyd Patterson was a nobody. You'll knock out Floyd Patterson, but I'm the real Champ. I'm too fast for you, and you know it! Put up all your money, Sonny! If you think you can whip me!"

He was still playing it cool, rolling the dice. But all the gambling had stopped. People were leaving the slot machines, the blackjack tables, the keno areas, coming over to see what was going on.

I walked straight up to him. He was still trying to roll the dice. "I want you out of town by sunup tomorrow," I said, giving him some Western talk. "Las Vegas ain't big enough for both of us."

Suddenly he reached in his pocket and pulled out a long black pistol, pointed it straight at my head, pulled the trigger: BANG! BANG!

I ducked. A chill went through my spine. BANG! BANG! He was still aiming at me. I leaped over the blackjack table, then the dice table, scattering chips and cards all over the floor, ducking and dodging all the way out in the streets, and behind me the pistol: BANG! BANG!

When I got back to my hotel room, I threw myself on the bed, panting. My heart was beating fast, my hands were shaking. I was thinking maybe I should leave Liston alone. I knew I was only acting crazy, but he might be crazy for real. I was still shook up an hour later when a reporter came and told me that Willie Reddish was laughing. They said the joke was on me. Liston's gun was loaded with blanks. Willie had set it up. He told Liston I was coming and prepared him with a blank pistol.

I had to laugh myself, but it did my campaign no good to have Liston get the up on me. I instantly made up my mind to get back at him. By now the papers were picking up every conflict between us and billing the match as "The Greatest Grudge Fight in History."

When I got back to Chicago, I convinced Clay Tyson, a black

comedian and a friend of mine, to drive to Denver with me to visit Liston. "I've got to make it look like I want Liston so bad," I told Clay, "that the world would be anxious to see the fight come off. When the public wants it strong enough, the title fight will have to come off."

Clay agreed to help me, and along with Rudy, Ronnie King and my photographer, Howard Bingham, we got in Big Red, headed for Denver. About two A.M. we came to the outskirts of the city. I got on the phone and called the numbers of some newspaper people my Louisville sponsors had given me. I spoke in a nasal voice, as though I was white: "Cassius Clay just drove into Denver. He's at Sonny Liston's house and he's getting ready to break in."

A black filling station attendant knew the exact directions to Liston's house, which was in a fashionable white neighborhood, and we drove there. The timing was perfect. As we neared Liston's front yard, I could hear police sirens. I sent Howard up to knock on the door and yell for him to come out. Howard banged on the door as loud as he could while we blew the horn as loud as we could. The whole neighborhood woke up.

Liston stuck his head out the window, cursing, saw us and growled so deep it sounded like a lion's roar: "Hey! Get out of my yard, you black bastard!"

His white neighbors were sticking their heads out the windows and doors, and I was blowing the horn louder and louder, and Howard was banging on his door. Suddenly Liston came storming out in polka-dot pajamas, waving a poker from his fireplace. I locked the bus doors just before he smashed one of the windows and started beating on the others with his iron.

A squad car screamed up and a policeman and his dog jumped out. Two of the policemen came over and pulled Liston back into the house, but another one recognized me: "Boy, if you're not out of this town in the next hour, you're going to jail!"

I started the bus and got ready to pull off, but not before I screamed at Liston, standing in his doorway: "You big ugly bear! The policemen and those dogs saved you. You no Champ! You a chump! You gonna fall in eight 'cause I'm The Greatest!" And I went off calling to him as the newsmen came up, "I'm The Greatest!"

I drove through the cold foggy night, feeling warm inside thinking of the look on his face.

The next day the story was spread all over the papers that I'd raided Sonny Liston's house at two in the morning, woken up all the neighbors, and it took ten policeman and six police dogs to break us up and I was run out of town. But I felt good about it. I knew people would be anxious to see Liston shut my big mouth.

I remember when the fight was finally signed in November of

1963. I felt as though it was a dream come true.

When Sonny was asked what he felt about it, he said, "My only worry is how I'll get my fist outta his big mouth once I get him in the ring. It's gonna go so far down his throat, it'll take a week for me to pull it out again. That's my only worry—that loud-mouth. Otherwise, he means a lotta money to me—I just hope he keeps well and I sure hope he shows up."

NOW IT'S TIME for Chris to show up. I look at my watch. More than an hour has gone by. I ask Bundini to check the house and see if everything is out, but he comes back. "There's a phone call."

When I go in, it's Chris. "The fight's back on!" he says. "McDonald is gonna have it. Everybody talked to him. You don't have to disavow your religion."

"That's the only way I'll go," I say.

"The fight's on. We'll talk about the details later. Now it's up to you. It was always up to you. You know what the odds are."

The headlines in the Palm Beach *Post* declare: LISTON SEVEN-TO-FOUR FAVORITE TO PROVE CASSIUS IS A HOAX. The *Gazette:* THE NEWS-MEN BACK LISTON FORTY-THREE TO FOUR."

Of all the controversies surrounding my first war against Liston, the weigh-in ceremony will be the least understood. I'll be labeled as "frightened to death" or "hysterical" or "terrified." The truth of the matter is I've rehearsed and planned every move I make that day. Usually, weigh-in ceremonies are dull, routine little affairs in the Commissioners' office, but Liston has announced that he will annihilate me in the first round and I've decided I won't wait for the first round. I'll attack at the weigh-in. I'll act totally crazy and so will Bundini, who is an expert on craziness. "I'll jump him, and when I do, you hold me back," I tell my my brother and Ronnie, and we march into the weigh-in room to play our part. Sugar Ray has flown down to be by my side, but he knows nothing of the plan and is embarrassed by the whole act.

We burst in through three hundred photographers and reporters, scuffling and pushing and shoveling to get close to us. "We're ready to rumble! We're ready to rumble!" we scream. "Float like a butterfly, sting like a bee!" we shout together. "This is it, you big ugly bear!" I shake my fist at Liston when he comes up to the scale in his white terry cloth robe. "It's all over! You'll be mine tomorrow night. I'm through playing with you. It's all over now."

Liston turns a stone face to mine. I lunge at him, but my crew holds me back. I make a mighty effort to break through. "Let's get it on!" I scream. "Let's get it on right now!" I'm surprised to see a confused look cross his face. He speaks very low, for only me to hear: "Don't let everyone know what a fool you are." I'm delighted. He actually believes I'm a fool.

When I move up to the scale, I continue to shout. And then we face each other eye to eye. For ten seconds there's nothing but silence. Reporters and photographers back away as though they expect a fight. Finally, I break the silence. "Would you look at this big ugly bear?" Liston steps back. "You're not The Champ, you're The Chump. To-morrow night is your last night." Bundini's screaming along with me, Ronnie's laughing and shouting.

It's my turn on the scale. I weight two-ten, and when the doctor checks my blood pressure and pulse, his eyes widen in surprise. "Your pulse rate is one-twenty," he says, "more than twice your normal rate."

Jimmy Cannon, whose column appears in the Miami *Herald Reporter*, steps in with his pencil and pad. "Does that mean he's fright-ened, Doctor?"

The doctor nods. "He's in mortal fear or he's emotional. We'll have to call the fight off if his pressure doesn't come down before he goes into that ring."

My crew march out of the room shouting and screaming, and I go back to my house. It's hard to stop laughing. I have a tape of the words of the Honorable Elijah Muhammad, and finally I turn it on and play it and lay back relaxed and thinking. I'm resting quietly when Dr. Pacheco comes in. He takes my blood pressure and finds it normal. He looks amazed. "Liston has been boasting he's afraid of no man alive," I tell him. "But Liston means no sane man. Liston's got to be afraid of a crazy man." With that, I go to sleep.

They've got me in my dressing room nearly an hour before the fight. Over the loudspeaker the announcer is saying Rudolph Clay is about to fight, and I throw my robe around me and dash out. Angelo tries to stop me, but I snatch away. My brother's fighting, I've got to see it. I'm always worried about Rudy when he fights.

I rush up to the bleachers, stand next to a woman who says to me, "Young man shouldn't you be down in the dressing room getting ready? We came here to see you fight Liston." But I'm yelling encour-agement down to Rudy, hollering at the top of my voice. "Jab him! Jab him! Keep moving, Rudy! Keep moving!" The sweat is pouring off me. I feel Dr. Pacheco tugging at my arm. "Champ, you need all the rest you can get. For God sakes, you go on in thirty minutes."

Rudy wins the fight by a split decision, and I hear the boos. They're booing him because he's been announced as my brother and they want to take it out on him. I want to call to Rudy, "Come on out of that ring, little brother, you don't have to fight no more." I'll do the fighting." And when he gets in my dressing room I put my arms around him and I say, "You're through fighting. I'm going to be The Champ tonight. You're not going to have to fight any more." But it will be a long time before he listens to me.

Now they're calling for me to come out. There's a roar going up and through the stadium. They want to see if I can live up to all the boasting and predictions. They want to see someone kill the predictor. Of all the fights that I will have, of all the crossroads I have come through, this will be the most crucial, and even months after the fight, after the storm has raged and subsided, I find myself still trying to put the pieces together. I'm with Angelo and Bundini at the home of Dr. Pacheco, who's saying, "What always puzzled me is why you were so suspicious of your white friends that night. We were all together—you, me, Angelo, Rudy, Bundini. We were in that room and the doors were locked, waiting for the fight to start. No one could get in, no one could get out. That's how much suspiciousness was in the atmosphere. And all your water bottles were taped, as they should have been. You told Rudy not to take his eyes off the water. When you'd ask him, 'Have you been watching the water bottles?' and Rudy would admit that he had left them alone for a few minutes, you'd say, 'Take the tape off, throw the water out. Put fresh water in and tape it up again.' And I kept thinking to myself, how is anyone going to get in the room to put anything in the bottle? What was going on? What was happening?"

I look back on that night and I see Pacheco and all of us sitting in that room, and it isn't only Liston that I feel on guard against. "The truth is," I tell Pacheco, "I wasn't trusting Angelo at the time. I wasn't trusting you, Dr. Pacheco. I trusted only my brother and the Muslim Captain Sam. All week I had been getting phone calls at my house saying, 'Nigger, you'll not win that Sonny Liston fight.' That morning of the fight I'd gotten calls saying, 'You'll be lucky if you make it in the ring, you loud-mouth bastard.' Then the caller would hang up and another caller would say, 'If Liston don't get you, we're gonna get you! You'll never be the World Heavyweight Champion.' At first I didn't pay any attention, but Captain Samuels said, 'The White Power structure wants you whipped. You were up in New York with Malcolm X a couple of days before the fight, and it's out that you're a follower of the Honorable Elijah Muhammad. You're a 'Black Muslim.' It's all in the press now. We'll get Rudy to watch everything, especially your water.' I knew that only a few months earlier it had been published that Harold Johnson, the fighter, had been given a doped orange by someone and he was groggy in the ring. The Kefauver Committee had exposed how corrupt and treacherous the Syndicate operations had been inside boxing. It was my first big fight and I knew I was hated more than Johnson."

"But why wouldn't you trust a man like Angelo, who had been with you since the first days?"

"Why? Because history shows people change. People in my own family had turned against me when I became a Muslim. Other people's families had turned against me. Why is it necessary for me to trust a white man just because he worked in my corner? I was twenty-two years old then. The only ones I could trust would be those closest to me. All I wanted that night was to make sure I got in that ring without being doped. I wanted the security of being satisfied. My insurance was to have only my brother, my blood brother, watch the water. No one else. I never thought Angelo was a crook. The only thing that could hurt me, I thought, was something coming through the water. And in the fifth round, when I was blinded, at first I felt again it was something coming in through the water.

"The first round was exactly as I had planned it. I could see my strategy paying off. Liston's coming at me like a bull, throwing wild punches. He wants to do me in the way he did Floyd Patterson, and I lean back and dance away. He tries to catch me on the ropes, but I duck under his punches and spin around. I wait until I'm halfway through the round before I even open up on him. Then I sting him with left jabs, right crosses to the head. And when that round ended, I knew I had him.

"I remember the middle of the third round. In the clinches, I can feel the pace is telling on him. His face is swelling up from my jabs. I throw more right crosses and I open a cut under his left eye. I see he's shocked, confused, bewildered. He had never been cut in his entire career. Now his own blood is spilling into the ring for the first time. I see him come at me like a wounded animal, throwing hard shots to my body, but I catch most of them on my elbow, and when the bell rings I put my hand on his shoulder and push him away.

"And on into the fourth, I keep sticking him, moving and sticking him. Then the fifth round comes up. I felt at ease and relaxed, he was still doing everything I thought he would do. But in the fifth round, I would later find out he had been having some shoulder trouble and they had been rubbing him down with a liniment, and by brushing up against me and trading punches, some of the liniment got on my forehead, and when Angelo sponged my face between rounds, it dripped down into my eyes. 'I can't see!' I cried out when I came back. 'My eyes are burning! I can't see!' And I couldn't see. It's like if you put a drop of hot liniment in your eye, for a while it will burn and burn. Angelo was trying to rinse my eyes with the sponge, but that didn't help. That's when I said, 'Cut the gloves off. Show the world there's wrongdoing going on.' I was whipping Liston from the first round on. His eye was cut and bleeding. I knew what the press would say, that I got scared and quit. But why would I get scared and quit when I was winning the fight so easy? I started to quit because I couldn't see. Th-y'd want to say I quit because I was getting slaughtered. They'd say I was using that for an excuse. Then Angelo said, 'This is the big one. This is for the title shot. You gotta go back out there. You're winning.'

"When the bell rang, Angelo pushed me back out into the ring, only ten seconds before the referee was about to give the fight to Liston. I could hear Bundini yelling, 'Don't let him knock us out! Use the yardstick on him! Yardstick 'em, Champ!' I went out with my right eye closed. Liston was lunging at me, throwing wild hooks that just missed me. I could barely make out his image, but I ducked, pedaled and danced away.

"I wiped my eyes as Liston charged, trying to catch me with vicious punches that barely missed. He was going all out. Whenever he got within range, I reached out and put my hand on his head. My arms were longer than his and I knew he couldn't hit me as long as I kept him an arm's length away.

"Then I heard somebody scream from the ringside: 'Beat that nigger's ass, Sonny! Beat that nigger's ass!' Somehow that stimulated me, and it made me more determined to hold on. And by the end of the round my eyes started to clear, and I went back on attack, snapping his head back with sharp jabs.

"When I got back to the corner, I knew everything would be all right. In the sixth, I went out and Liston was a changed man. He'd thrown his best stuff and he hadn't been able to do his damage. I felt his breathing. He was tired and I was still strong, and he knew he had no protection against my lefts or rights.

"When the bell rang for the start of the seventh round, he stayed in his corner. He sat limp on the stool, staring blankly across at us. Angelo and Bundini were screaming at me: 'You The Champion! You The Champion!' I leaped into their arms. The long campaign was over. I had come into my own. I had fulfilled my prediction."

In weeks ahead, things would happen which I could never have foreseen: I would fall in love and marry the most beautiful woman I'd ever met, and while my new marriage was being torn by religious quarrels, I would prepare for my return match with Liston.

I would learn how narrowly Angelo came to being roughed up when the fight was over: "I thought your guys were going to kill me," he said, speaking of Ronnie and Archie. "They thought I had done something to the water. I saved myself by grabbing the bucket and drinking some of the water and rubbing it in my eyes to show them that my water was all right."

WHEN IT'S ALL OVER, there's one final talk I want to make—to the press. When they gather in front of me, it's hard to forget that nearly all of them had considered me a hoax. They start to shoot questions at me, but I cut them off: "Hold it! Hold it!" I say. "You've all had a chance to say what you thought before the fight. Now it's my turn. You all said Sonny Liston would kill me. You said he was better than Jack Johnson or Jack Dempsey, even Joe Louis, and you ranked them the best heavyweights of all time. You kept writing how Liston whipped Floyd Patterson twice, and when I told you I would get Liston in eight, you wouldn't believe it. Now I want all of you to tell the whole world while all the cameras are on us, tell the world that I'm The Greatest."

There's a silence. "Who's The Greatest?" I ask them. Nobody answers. They look down at their pads and microphones. "Who's The Greatest?" I say again. They look up with solemn faces, but the room is still silent.

"For the LAST TIME!" I shout. "All the eyes of the world on us. You just a bunch of hypocrites. I told you I was gonna get Liston and I got him. All the gamblers had me booked eight-to-one underdog. I proved all of you wrong. I shook up the world! Tell me who's The Greatest! WHO IS THE GREATEST?"

They hesitate for a minute, and finally in a dull tone they all answer, "You are."

I'm up in Chicopee, Massachusetts, training for my return match against Liston. Malcolm X has been assassinated in New York early in the year. There are rumors that some of Malcolm's associates are out to retaliate against me as one of Mr. Muhammad's loyal followers. "Everywhere in the city there's a rumor that some avengers are coming up to kill you to get even for what happened," a reporter tells me. "Since you're the most popular Muslim in the Nation of Islam, they've picked you as a target."

I ignore the rumors, continue training, because I want this return match to come off. It was postponed for five months when I had to recover from a hernia operation.

When I get into town, reporters come up to my room and ask for my prediction. Sharnik remembers my dream. "Is it still the same as the dream you had on the bus?"

I laugh. I'm not sure. Two months ago I told Sharnik that I

dreamed I was sitting in my corner waiting for the first round to start in my fight with Liston. The bell rang and I jumped up and ran out and hit him with a right hand. I leaned back and moved away as he pursued me for maybe a minute. Then all of a sudden I saw him coming in and I hit him with a right hand—BAM!—right on the chin and The Big Bad Bear fell on the floor. I stood over him, yelling, "Rise and shine . . . rise and shine."

"I remember the dream," I tell Sharnik, "but I make no predictions this time."

The rumors keep circulating that two carloads of men armed with rifles are on their way from New York to try to kill me, either while I'm training or while I'm in the ring. All week the papers report that my life's in danger. "Gunman Stalking Clay," one says, and "Contract Reported on Clay's life." "Black Muslim War Endangers Muhammad Ali."

The first week I'm in camp, five FBI men come to my hotel. They show me their credentials. "We believe there's some truth in the rumors," one says. "We're posting a twenty-four-hour guard outside your door. There'll be a police escort for you in the morning."

From then on, each morning two police cars follow me to the track, and before they let me run, five policemen cross the field to make sure no one is planning to ambush me. Every five or six hundred feet I see a policeman with a rifle hiding in the bushes.

When I go to the gym, plainclothesmen circulate through the crowd. Somehow I have a deep resentment against the guards, I don't believe anyone is out to get me. And I find it a dangerous distraction from my training.

Three days before the fight, I'm sparring with Ellis when he lands a sharp right cross to my ribs and the pain from it almost makes me double up. I know something is deeply bruised, if not broken, but I believe if I go to a doctor the fight may be postponed again and I'd lose a chance to convince my critics that my victory over Liston was no fluke. Instead I go home irritated, my temper short, and I clash with Sonji because she's smoking cigarettes and refusing to wear the dress required in our religious guidelines.

"I'm tired of this!" she shouts. "I told you I can't follow all these rules. I love you, but I don't love this religion and I don't want to be a Muslim." What she's saying hits me as hard as Ellis's blow in the gym.

"Well, honey," I finally say, "all you have to do is be honest and we can get a divorce." It was the beginning of the end. That night I sleep with a pain in my rib and in my heart, knowing that my life with the first woman I'd ever loved is almost over.

Somehow Liston has ceased to be the most important thing on my mind in the first offense of my title. When the gates open for the fight, women's pocketbooks are being searched for concealed weapons and some newspapermen have ordered bulletproof shields that stick from behind their seats.

When the bell rings for round one, I feel comfortable circling Liston. I feel as though I know every move he's likely to make. I open with a left jab to his head and dance away. I move in, land another short left to his head. He answers with a hard right to the body that I catch with my elbow. Then he lunges forward to follow with a jab, and I see an opening. He's coming in off balance and moving toward me. I shoot a hard right to the side of his head that lifts him up in the air before he crumbles on the canvas, lies flat on his back. I stand over him and I scream down at him: "Get up off that floor, Sonny! Come on, this thing ain't even started good yet! Get up and fight! You're supposed to be so bad!"

But Sonny never gets up until long after the count is over, and when he does I see his eyes are dazed. And there are cries of fix, fix, fix, and boos, but the fact of the matter is there was never a fight less fixed.

Why did he fold up? I believe all the pressure, the FBI, the rumors of assassination, and rifle-carrying policemen, all directed at me, somehow was transferred to Liston. He must have felt that somebody really planned to do some shooting. I believe while he was looking out around the ring at all those bulletproof shields, he thought if somebody was out to shoot me I'd be dancing and moving so fast they wouldn't be able to get a target. That they might miss me and hit him.

All I know for sure is that I hit him hard enough to knock out any man.

When it's over, Sharnik, who always thought there was something eerie about my predictions, comes over and asks: "Was the dream the father of the fight or was the fight the dream?"

"The dream was the father," I tell him.

THE PROPHECY OF SELL-OUT MOE

Of all the poems I wrote, all the words I spoke, all the slogans I shouted—"I'm the greatest!" . . . "I'm the prettiest!" . . . "I can't be beat!" . . . "He must fall in five!"—of all the controversies that aroused people against me or for me, none would have the effect on my life or change the climate around me like the "poem" I read on a TV hookup one warm February afternoon in Miami, 1966.

I was in training and looking forward to my third defense of the World Heavyweight Title. This time against six-foot-six Ernie "The Octopus" Terrell, so named because he wrapped his long arms like tentacles around his opponents, smothering their blows and hugging them half to death.

I had come out into the front yard of the little gray cement cottage that my White Southern Christian Millionaire Sponsors had rented in my name in the black section of Miami. A TV reporter had been set up to ask my reaction to the fact that the Louisville Draft Board had just promoted me from 1-Y, deferred status, to 1-A, making me eligible for immediate induction into the U.S. Army.

I gave it: "I ain't got no quarrel with the Viet Cong." Later, when they kept asking the same question, I rhymed it for them:

> *Keep asking me, no matter how long*
> *On the war in Viet Nam, I sing this song*
> *I ain't got no quarrel with the Viet Cong . . .*

I said more than that, of course, much more, and all evening, but those were the only words it seemed the world wanted to hear from me. They broke out in headlines across America and overseas—in London, Paris, Berlin, Zurich, Madrid, Hong Kong, Rome, Amsterdam—and for years afterwards their echo would rumble in the air around me. In fact, the rumbling began even before I got to sleep that night.

After the reporters left I took a ride over to a Miami Beach steakhouse, and when I came back my brother was in the doorway. He was beckoning me in a way I understood to mean he wanted no reporters to follow.

"The phones won't stop," he whispered as I brushed past him. "They gone crazy."

We had three phones and all three were ringing. I was reaching for the nearest one.

"Wait a minute." He tried to restrain me. "Let me answer. They all insane."

But I was already hearing a hard, mean voice on the other end of the line: "This you, Cassius?"

"No, sir," I said, feeling he should at least acknowledge my name. "This is Muhammad Ali."

"Muhammad, Cassius—whatever you call yourself, I heard you on TV!" he shouted. "You cowardly, turncoat black rat! If I had a bomb I would blow you to hell! I've got a message for you and your kind . . ." I hung up, since I had already gotten the message, and picked up the kitchen phone. A woman's voice was hysterical: "Cassius Clay? Is that you? You better'n my son? You black bastard, you! I pray to God they draft you tomorrow. Draft you and shoot you on the spot! Listen to me . . ."

I let her go to pick up the phone in the bedroom. This time it was a voice I knew. A deputy sheriff named Murphy who had escorted me around Miami Beach many times. He had a soft drawl, like a fatherly bigot: "Now, Cassius, you just done gone too far now. Somebody's telling you wrong. Them Jews and Dagos you got around you. Now, some of my boys want to come down and talk to you, for your own good."

I hung up and took the phone handed to me by my sparring partner, Cody Jones. There was only heavy breathing. Then: "You gonna die, nigger, before the night's out! You gonna die for that!" and more heavy breathing.

Those who had always wanted me to disappear from the scene reacted quickest. The first calls came mostly from the white side of Miami. But as the news spread across the time zones, other voices were saying, "That was mighty fine." . . . "I'm glad you said that." . . . "It's time someone spoke out."

And in the days that followed, calls came in from Kansas City, Omaha, St. Louis, Las Vegas, New York, Philadelphia. Housewives and professionals and plain everyday people—who I never heard from except when I pulverized somebody in the ring—thanked me for what I said. Students called from campuses, urging me to come and speak. It was a strange new feeling, and now, without planning or even wanting it, I was an important part of a movement I hardly knew existed.

For days I was talking to people from a whole new world. People who were not even interested in sports, especially prizefighting. One in particular I will never forget: a remarkable man, seventy years older than me but with a fresh outlook which seemed fairer than that of any white man I had ever met in America.

My brother Rahaman had handed me the phone, saying, "Operator says a Mr. Bertrand Russell is calling Mr. Muhammad Ali." I took it and heard the crisp accent of an Englishman: "Is this Muhammad Ali?" When I said it was, he asked if I had been quoted correctly.

I acknowledged that I had been, but wondered out loud, "Why does everyone want to know what I think about Viet Nam? I'm no politician, no leader. I'm just an athlete."

"Well," he said, "this is a war more barbaric than others, and because a mystique is built up around a champion fighter, I suppose the world has more than incidental curiosity about what the World Champion thinks. Usually he goes with the tide. You surprised them."

I liked the sound of his voice, and told him I might be coming to England soon to fight the European champ, Henry Cooper, again.

"If I fight Cooper, who'd you bet on?"

He laughed. "Henry's capable, you know, but I would pick you."

I gave him back a stock answer I used on such occasions: "You're not as dumb as you look." And I invited him to ringside when I got to London.

He couldn't come to the fight, but for years we exchanged cards and notes. I had no idea who he was (the name Bertrand Russell had never come up in Central High in Louisville) until two years later when I was thumbing through a *World Book Encyclopaedia* in the *Muhammad Speaks* newspaper office in Chicago and saw his name and picture. He was described as one of the greatest mathematicians and philosophers of the twentieth century. That very minute I sat down and typed out a letter of apology for my offhand remark, "You're not as dumb as you look," and he wrote back that he had enjoyed the joke.

A short time after I fought Cooper, when I had another fight prospect in London, I made plans for Belinda and me to visit him, but I had to explain to him that the outcome of my fight against being drafted to Viet Nam might hold me up. The letter he wrote back was sent to me in Houston:

> I have read your letter with the greatest admiration and personal respect.
>
> In the coming months there is no doubt that the men who rule Washington will try to damage you in every way open to them, but I am sure you know that you spoke for your people and for the oppressed everywhere in the courageous defiance of American power. They will try to break you because you are a symbol of a force they are unable to destroy, namely, the aroused consciousness of a whole people determined no longer to be butchered and debased with fear and oppression. You have my wholehearted support. Call me when you come to England.
>
> Yours sincerely,
> Bertrand Russell

By the time I got his letter I had been convicted and my passport lifted, just as his had been in World War I. Four years later, when my passport was returned, the friend I had made with my remark in my front yard had died. I thought of him whenever I visited England and for years I kept a picture of his warm face and wide eyes. "Not as dumb as he looks."

When I first got to Miami, my mind was on the coming showdown with "The Octopus." So I wasn't very interested when a TV reporter, Robert Halloran, came to me one night saying he had news that would shake the camp: "Something's going to hit that'll make you forget all about Terrell."

I had let Halloran sit on my bed for a few minutes before curfew, and I had started "snoring" to hasten his exit.

He leaned over and whispered, "I got a leak from the Louisville Draft Board. You're being reclassified 1-A. It'll be announced tomorrow morning."

"I heard 'em say that before." I was getting sleepy. Since announcing that I was a member of the Nation of Islam, not a month went by without a rumor that I was about to be drafted. "Why me and why now?"

"You're in good health, single, twenty-four years old. They want your class first. To get you before you get to be twenty-six. After twenty-six you're out of reach. They got to find a way to shut you up."

"Look." I turned over. "I flunked the draft exam twice. The passing point was seventeen and I made sixteen. I even had major surgery for a hernia since then, and haven't had another exam."

"I know." He nodded wisely. "But they dropped the passing point down to fifteen and that makes you in." He chuckled.

"Will that stop the fight?" I was a lot less sleepy now.

He shook his head. "It won't hurt this fight. This is February 17. Your fight's for March 29 in Chicago. They won't be ready that quick, but after that . . ."

"Why you come here telling me this?" I was a little suspicious.

"I'm the only one who got the tip," he said. "I want your okay to have a TV crew here in the morning when the announcement is made. Exclusive. All right?"

"I'll think about it," I told him.

Even though I had been expecting the news about my draft status, now that it was here I was surprised. So the blanks I had filled out six years ago were about to come due. I thought back to the day I was in Joe Martin's gym, whipping the speed bag, preparing for the Olympics in two weeks. Another boxer reminded me I was due at the Draft Board, and we rushed out, grumbling over losing valuable training time.

All I knew was what I had been taught in school: that every war fought by America was for "freedom" or to "make the world safe for democracy" or to "preserve the peace." Had I been drafted then, I probably would have gone without a murmur, only asking time for the Olympics. It was after I got back from Rome that I began to change.

As early as I can remember, I noticed the difference in the way black people and white people lived. Louisville was a segregated, racist town; the smell of the old Slave South hung as heavy as the smell of famous whiskeys and horses. And it hung over my White Christian Millionaire Sponsors. As "nice" as they tried to be to me, many of their actions reminded me that they were part of a system I wanted to escape from. Once Joe Louis, never known as a critic of White America, said of my sponsors, "They live in a different world from Clay. They don't know what they got ahold of. They don't know what makes him go. He's outgrown them already."

Although my outlook was changing, during the first two years after the Olympics I was still a horse with blinkers, fighting and training, fighting and training, concentrating only on what it took to get the championship. As for the draft, my millionaires assured me there was nothing to worry about. Why should there be? Deferment for top athletes was common if your sponsors had pull and power, and mine had. Professional baseball, football, basketball couldn't keep going without deferments. I hadn't heard from the Draft Board since the day I registered.

Then a week before my first fight with Liston, I was called to take an examination at the Induction Center in Coral Gables, Florida, and I drove down with Bundini, who sang all the way up to the door:

> The Old Master Painter from the faraway hills
> Who painted the violets and the daffodils
> Say don't draft The Champ from Louisville . . .

An Induction Center supervisor told him to shut up. I went through the test and signed it with a big "Cassius X," the first time I had used that signature.

"What does the X mean?" the supervisor asked after scoring the results.

I told him I was a member of the Nation of Islam and that we rejected the names handed to us by our former slave masters and X took the place of our real but unknown black names.

He puzzled over that awhile and called me into the back room. Showed me a long list of organizations under the title "Subversive" and asked which ones I belonged to. As Islam wasn't on the list, I said, "None."

He turned to my scores and said the results were "inconclusive." "You failed the mental aptitude part. You skipped over questions."

"I did the best I could," I told him.

"Nobody in their right mind'll believe it. You'll hear from us."

I did. Four weeks after I became World Heavyweight Champion and had announced that I was a follower of the Honorable Elijah Muhammad, I was tested in Louisville, with the same results, classified 1-Y, and the uproar began.

A "Draft That Nigger Clay" campaign was started by a Georgia lawyer. He had been the sponsor of the national "Fire Your Nigger Week" campaign, addressed to whites who had black employees, and he was among the first to turn his guns on me. But his guns were weak compared to the bombardment coming down on the Louisville Draft Board from all over the country. The late Congressman L. Mendel Rivers of South Carolina went on a speaking tour, preaching with a passion: "Clay's deferment is an insult to every mother's son serving in Viet Nam. Here he is, smart enough to finish high school, write his kind of poetry, promote himself all over the world, make a million a year, drive around in red Cadillacs—and they say he's too dumb to tote a gun? Who's dumb enough to believe that?"

It was around that time that Worth Bingham, youngest of my Louisville sponsors, summed things up: "They're calling for a Senate hearing with your case in mind. They say you flunked the exam on purpose."

"I only said I was the greatest, not the smartest," I said. He laughed, then got down to business.

"Look, Cassius, let's work this thing out. They don't want you in the Army as much as they want the title back in 'patriotic hands.' Let's get them off you. You pick any service you want: Army, Navy, Air Force, Marines—you name it. You go in for five, six weeks basic training. We'll swing a commission. You come out in the reserves, special services. You never go near a battlefield. It's done every day."

"Does that mean I'm part of the armed services?" I asked.

He nodded. "Technically speaking." Then, seeing that I was unimpressed, he tried to end the conversation on a hopeful note. "You don't have to answer now. We've got a little time. But think it over."

I HAD TWO YEARS to think it over, and when the question came to my doorstep I gave an answer that had been partly the result of the day's events. It happened the morning after my conversation with Halloran.

I woke up fresh and early, got my sparring partner out of bed, walked over the Miami Beach Causeway to the golf course and circled it five times before dawn came up over the ocean. I had always used early-morning roadwork to clear my mind as well as keep in shape. It seemed to help me sort things out. As I ran I was trying to think of how to react to the announcement they said was coming.

When I got back to my cottage around 7 A.M., camera crews had set up tripods in the yard, but no announcement.

My only message was a poem from Moe Fleischer, who assisted Angie's brother, Chris, over at the Fifth Street Gym. Moe and I shared a common interest in writing "predictions of things to come" in poetry and he had sent one over:

> The Army may call
> The heavens may fall
> But it's way too late
> To stop a million-dollar gate
> You've had your say

> *That way let it stay*
> *No matter what they hate*
> *Keep yourself in shape . . .*

I'd see Moe when I got to the gym, so I had a shower, drank juices, looked at TV awhile and took a nap until it was time to take the long walk across the Causeway.

If Halloran thought his "leak" was exclusive, he was mistaken. Before I had gone six blocks I was hailed by three policemen, two tamale vendors, four cabdrivers, one whore and a drunk—all asking, "Champ, they gonna make you 1-A today?" . . . "You going in the Army?" And by the time I got to the gym a parade of reporters was following, wanting to know, "What you gonna say when the Army calls?" . . . "Are you going in?"

"For God sakes, don't say nothing, nothing at all," Angelo whispered as the reporters followed me into the dressing room. He knew they had surrounded my cottage and were waiting. "Send them to me," he said. "Let me talk to them."

"I'll do my own talking, Angie," I reminded him quietly. The thing that kept Angie and me tied together in friendship as well as business was his understanding that I am my own spokesman—and more than that.

Since the first day I decided to become a fighter, I challenged the old system in which managers, promoters or owners looked upon fighters as brutes without brains. I'd known fighters to be the most human of humans and among the most talented people to be found anywhere. But when I first came into boxing, tied up as it was with gangster control and licensed robbers, fighters were not supposed to be human or intelligent. Just brutes that exist to entertain and to satisfy a crowd's thirst for blood. Two animals to tear each other's skin, break each other's nose, and bleed and bleed, then get out of sight while the managers and the lawyers and the promoters announced it all, judged it all and profited most from it all.

A fighter (and most athletes, for that matter) was seen but hardly heard any issue or idea of public importance. They could call me arrogant, cocky, conceited, immodest, a loud-mouth, a braggart, but I would change the image of the fighter in the eyes of the world—and certainly the image of the World Heavyweight Champion.

And I wouldn't do it accidentally; I would do it deliberately. Not only outside the ring, but inside as well. I hated the sight on TV of big, clumsy, lumbering heavyweights plodding, stalking each other like two Frankenstein monsters, clinching, slugging toe to toe. I knew I could do it better. I would be as fast as a lightweight, circle, dance, shuffle, hit and move, zip-zip-pop-pop, hit and move back and dance

again and make an art out of it. And unlike the Dempseys, Tunneys,
Louises and Marcianos, I would seek advice and cooperation from all
those around me—but not permission.

"Whatever you do, it'll come out all right," Angie was saying. He
pointed toward the ring. "Look what we got in for you today."

Three towering sparring partners were limbering up in the ring.
Mel Turnbow, out of Cincinnati, Dale Hayward from Atlanta, Tom
Jones from Philly. All over six feet four inches, hand-picked because
they could imitate Ernie Terrell.

I took three rounds with each. Long ago I had established a
reputation of being "easy" on sparring partners because in the gym I
work mainly on defense. I have never been able to see the sense or need
for top fighters—like the Joe Fraziers and Sonny Listons—to crush or
destroy their sparring partners. Why pulverize a hired hand? What
does that prove? But now I felt a deep resentment at something unseen
and I found myself unleashing all hell against Turnbow like he was a
tree and I was an ax, stomping Dale Hayward like he was a nail and
I was a hammer, and pounding them all till I heard the trainer shouting,
"Time! Time! Lighten up, Champ! Have mercy!"

After the workout I lay down on the rubbing bench, and Angelo's
educated fingers examined each muscle. Solemnly, he pronounced his
judgment. "You ready right now. If you fought Terrell tonight, you'd
demolish him. Wouldn't last four rounds. You in top shape now and
it's early. Here on in we take it easy. You're ready." A chorus went up
from the trainers and handlers looking on: "Amen! Say that again!
Amen! The Champ's ready! Woo-ee-ee! Let's get it on! Get it on now!
Watch out, 'Octopus,' here come the shark! Watch out!"

I got up and shadowboxed nude before the tall mirror, watching
my own reflexes, checking out balance, and I knew they were right. The
best feeling in the world is when all your body's fit, when the muscles
and blood and bones feel strong. You get a kind of glow and your spine
tingles. Then even your thoughts seem to create new energy. I knew
I was ready. I wanted "The Octopus." Bad!

Moe was bringing in the new posters for the fight. They were
huge. "Muhammad Ali versus Ernie Terrell in Chicago," he announced, and held one up. "It'll be bigger'n Dempsey-Tunney, bigger'n Louis-Schmeling, and I ought to know."

Moe Fleischer, nicknamed "Sell-Out Moe," the oldest match-
maker and boxing historian, had been Kid Chocolate's trainer; had set
up fights for such immortals as Panama Brown, Abe Attell, Tony
Canzoneri; had worked with the great Joe Gans, Harry Greb, Battling
Levinsky, Benny Leonard; but his genius was in his knowledge of
human nature—what people will buy and what they will sell. He had
staged forty straight fights in which all the tickets were sold out in

advance. That's how he got his nickname, though I had heard a fighter or two say he got the tag in another way.

Moe's unfaltering prediction was for a two-million-dollar gate. He chuckled as he always did when he thought of turnstiles. "I'll have to write you a poem about it."

I liked Moe. Not that he was always on my side; he was always on the side of the turnstiles but I was the fighter that kept them moving.

"I congratulate you on talking this fight into life, Muhammad," he was telling me. "I've known all the big promoters, Doc Kerns, Tex Rickard, Jim Norris, Mike Jacobs, and I give credit where credit is due. You're the best. You've made the world think Terrell's got a chance."

Moe was right. I had campaigned for a "showdown" with Terrell because I knew a big section of White America was in the mood to pay a high price to see me beaten in public. Where Floyd had failed, three months ago in Las Vegas, they thought Ernie could succeed. After all, "The Octopus" had heavier weapons, longer guns and as much courage.

They had banked heavily on Patterson performing the miracle, totally ignoring the fact that "The Rabbit" had been knocked out in one round *twice* by Sonny Liston, the same Sonny I had *twice* defeated, and *still* they went into a rage when I chastised Patterson. I had talked to Patterson throughout the fight because I wanted to make it clear to him that the blows weren't really meant for him, my black brother, but for White America. Somehow Floyd missed my point.

But Billy Rose, the Broadway showman, seemed to understand what I was doing. I had been invited to appear on Jack Parr's show to read my poems with Liberace playing a piano in the background, and I read:

> It all started twenty years past,
> The Greatest of them all was born at last.
> The very first words from his Louisville lips
> "I'm pretty as a picture and there's no one I can't whip."

> Then he said in a voice that sounded rough,
> "I'm as strong as an ox
> And twice as tough."

> The name of this Champ,
> I might as well say,
> No other than The Greatest,
> Cassius Clay.

> He predicts the round in which he's gonna win,
> And that's the way his career has been.

He knocks them out in the round he calls,
And that is why he's called The Greatest of Them All.

I had another one:

This is the story about a man
With iron fists and a beautiful tan.
He talks a lot indeed,
Of a powerful punch and blinding speed.

The boxing game was slowly dying,
And fight promoters were bitterly crying
For someone somewhere to come along
With a better and different tone.

Patterson was dull, quiet and sad,
And Sonny Liston was just as bad.
Along came a kid named Cassius Clay,
Who said, "I'll take Liston's title away."

His athletic genius cannot be denied.
In a very short time,
He spread far and wide.

There's an impression you get
Watching him fight.
He plays cat and mouse,
Then turns out the light.

This colorful fighter is something to see,
And the Greatest Heavyweight Champion
I know he will be.

Immediately I got a storm of letters. Half the people enjoyed the fun, but the other half expressed the great hope that I would be beaten and stomped by my next opponent. A Chicago alderman denounced me for what he termed my "immodesty and obnoxiousness."

"Keep it up," Rose said. "The more obnoxious you are, the more they'll pay you to fight some White Hope. They'll pay high to see you beat. Remember, the bigots got most of the money in this country."

Every time I stepped into the ring, at least half the audience was so anxious to see me slaughtered, they would cheer and scream and stomp for every punch an opponent hit me with. So much so that they became hysterical when I frustrated those dreams and hopes.

The morning after I whipped Patterson in Las Vegas, most of the sportswriters were enraged. I assume they had some hidden hope that Floyd would perform a miracle.

Red Smith called me a "practicing sadist." Art Walden asked

boxing authorities to "outlaw this cannibal Clay." And Jimmy Cannon described me as "streaked with savagery." I knew these were all qualities they secretly wanted my opponent to possess.

I had hardly wiped Floyd's blood off my arms that November night when some of the audience started chanting, "Terrell! Terrell! Fight Terrell!" They thought Terrell could succed where Floyd had failed.

Later, when they gave me the microphone, I spoke as modestly and quietly as I could under the circumstances: "Well, if you want me to, I'll fight Terrell next. If the public wants it."

Terrell and I had looked forward to this encounter for some time. In 1965, when he won the WBA's version of the World Heavyweight Title, the title that had been stripped from me, Terrell had come up to my hotel room in New York. He was depressed. "I didn't get a dime for that last fight," he groaned. "They said it didn't draw. The only way a heavyweight is going to make money is to fight you, Clay."

I told him to see what my manager thought of the idea, and he went to Chicago and found that Herbert was already making plans for a fight between us. He had both Terrell and me pose for publicity pictures to make it look like we were dying to attack each other, and in a few weeks the fight was sold to Madison Square Garden, billed as "The Clash of Champions."

Terrell flew back into New York with his manager, Bernie Glickman, an associate of the notorious Frank E. Carbo, exposed by the Kefauver Committee as a key man in the syndicate that once controlled boxing. The New York State Athletic Commission immediately called for an investigation of Terrell's management and wouldn't allow the fight in New York.

But it was a good fight, with high profit potential, and investors in Chicago came forward and picked it up.

Now A HUSH seemed to fall over the room and I realized that uppermost in the minds of everyone in camp was the outcome of today's Army announcement.

Someone brought Moe a telegram. He tore it open and read it, and his usually bloodhound-sad face creased with smiles. Then he handed it to me like it was a certified check. "Didn't I tell you the fight would go through?"

His telegram was the Chicago promoters' first response to my 1-A reclassification. It said: ALI-TERRELL FIGHT STILL ON. WE KNEW CLAY TO BE DRAFTED. WE DIDNT KNOW WHEN. NOW PLENTY TIME TO GET FIGHT IN. TICKETS SALE GOING GOOD. BRITISH RIGHTS SOLD $200,000.

I was ready to leave, but Angie couldn't resist the last word.

"Muhammad, I know you'll handle it, but don't get me wrong. They want something to blow up big. They haven't got over the way you whipped Liston and Patterson. One question will lead to another. They'll ask you all kinds. I'm not trying to put words in your mouth. But if the Army announcement comes, I would just say, 'No comment.' Leave it at that. 'No comment.'"

"Thanks, Angie," I said and started downstairs, but I looked back at my trainer's worried face. Maybe "No comment" would have been the best way out that day, but Angie knew that was not exactly my way of responding to questions.

I took the long walk from Miami Beach back to the black side of town, with children calling me, following me all the way. Then something happened that would shape my response to the big question.

It would be more than a year before a reporter asked me about it. In a restaurant high up in the Houston Astrodome, where the fight with Terrell was finally to come off, the New York *Post*'s Milton Gross was thinking back to that day and asked how it came about. "How is it you never said anything about the Viet Cong before? I kept up with your public statements. What brought that out? Was it those children you saw playing in the street that day?" He knew about the incident and was only probing. Gross, along with most of the white columnists at the time, had a habit of distorting every event surrounding me to prove that I was "bad" for boxing, although he later became my staunchest supporter. I withdrew from the conversation.

But he was right. Up to the time of my statement, outwardly at least, the extent of my involvement in the war had been as a TV spectator. But I had seen a series of pictures in a magazine showing mangled bodies of dead Viet Cong laid out along a highway like rows of logs and a white American officer walking down the aisle of the dead taking the "body count." The only enemy alive was a little naked girl, searching among the bodies, her eyes wide, frightened. I clipped out that picture; and the face has never quite left my mind.

Children are a special love in the life of a heavyweight champion. They have a way of making him know what love is. In the days when my exile seemed permanent, children would flock around me, calling out, "Champ! The Champ!" They tore up the isolation that was meant for me. Of all the glories of being World Heavyweight Champion, the greatest was the recognition and acceptance by children wherever I went. To be known by them, to be allowed to love them in return, was often worth all the blood and bruises, the years of being ostracized, the heavy years under threat of imprisonment or the abuse and denunciation hurled by those who hated me for what I was and for what I said. Children treat a champion fighter like a valuable member of the family. Like the little children who came every day outside my cell when I was jailed for seven days in Dade County, calling to me through the bars, "When you coming out, Champ? When they gonna let you out?"

Or like the morning in a Dublin hotel, where I was weighing in for my fight against Blue Louis. When I got off the scales, a handsome young boy broke through the crowd to get my autograph. I could see he was an American, and I asked him his name.

"Michael Reagan," he said.

And as I wrote "To Michael Reagan" I said, "The only Reagan I know is Governor Ronald Reagan of California."

"Yes. That's my father."

I looked up and he blushed, then held up his fist in a Black Power salute, and smiled. A little later I saw his father waiting for an elevator and overheard him complaining to his friends, "I don't know what happened to Michael this morning. Muhammad Ali was down here weighing in and I couldn't keep him in the room." If his father recognized me, he gave no sign, nor did I expect it. He had done everything he could in California to bar me from boxing as an "ungrateful," "unpatriotic" slacker. He had threatened to pass a law to prevent me from boxing in California. They kept me out of California for four years. But there was something he was unable to pass down to his son.

Or like the night in New York a few weeks after my jaw had been broken by Ken Norton. I was walking through Lincoln Center as the Metropolitan Opera audience was coming out. Some evening-gowned patrons had me autograph their programs, among them Mrs. Ethel Kennedy and some of her family. Her late husband, Senator Robert Kennedy, went out of his way to let me know he supported my right to fight and to have my own views. One little ladylike girl reached up and kissed me squarely on the jaw, put her arms around my neck and in a tough little voice, totally out of keeping with her ladylike manner, whispered, "You get that guy who broke your jaw! . . . You sock him for me! . . . Knock his head off! . . . Beat him to pieces! . . . Don't let him get away with it!" As soon as I winked and released her she resumed her aloof, sophisticated posture and went along.

So walking back home from the gym, I enjoyed the children calling to me, "Hey, Champ!" . . . "You gonna get Terrell?" . . . "Beat him up!" . . . "You The Champ!"

Usually when I crossed over the Causeway the children who had started out with me on the Miami Beach side fell away, to be replaced by others nearer to my neighborhood. This time I walked quite a while before I saw any of them. First I heard them screaming as though in a wild fight. Then, turning a corner, I found a gang of them hurling bottles and stones in the direction of three frightened, running children. Before I got up to them they had hemmed in the little group and were pelting them with sticks and stones. I took one child by the collar and asked him what was the matter.

"We just playing," he said sheepishly.

His buddy explained, "They Viet Cong. We Americans. We just playing."

Then they all recognized me and broke up the game. I went over to one of the little "Viet Cong"—the one who had been especially frightened—and lifted her up on my shoulder. One stubborn boy was still protesting, "She on the Viet Cong side. We against them, ain't we, Champ?"

"No," I said. "We ain't. We ain't got nothing against no Viet Cong. They just like you and me."

He looked at me to make sure I was serious, decided I was, then turned around, informing the other children, "We ain't got nothing against no Viet Cong."

I held the little girl, whose name was Patricia Ward, on my shoulder and carried her to her porch. She was the raggediest of a group of raggedy children. At first she only looked at me with big frightened eyes, and I saw a strong resemblance between her and the little Vietnamese girl in the magazine. I always sought out the shy girls who hid in the background and picked them up, as I did Patricia, and smothered them with kisses and hugs; when they sullenly wiped the kisses off I would attack, growling, "No girl wipes off The Champ's kisses and gets away with it, take that and that," and I would shower them with more until they began to laugh. The same way I made Patricia forget for a while the cruel game the others had played on her.

I knew that the Honorable Elijah Muhammad in his newspaper had described the war as the personal business of the Vietnamese and not the Americans.

Herbert and I had discussed it often and he had pointed out that it was a fight "inside the Vietnamese's own family," one in which our country had no right to use military force to impose its rule on either side. We were both shocked at the awful slaughter of innocent men, women and children.

Coming up to my cottage, still thinking of the children's war game and how easily they stopped when they saw that the World Champion did not go along with it, I heard someone call, "Hey, Cassius."

Deputy Sheriff Murphy was sitting with friends in his car. "You ready to go after them gooks?" he shouted gaily. "I told them reporters, wait till ole Cassius goes after them gooks!" and he whacked his thigh and roared.

I got to my door. Halloran was waiting inside by the phone. It was now late afternoon. Teams of photographers and reporters had come down from Chicago, New York, Philadelphia. Bob O'Hara, a little hawk-faced reporter I'd known from Louisville, called me aside, guardedly looking around. "The buzzards smell an animal about to breathe his last. Be careful what you say." Then he told me what he wanted. "Give a hometown boy a break. What're you gonna say when they draft you?"

I was about to answer when I heard a yell from the doorway. "The Army has just announced it!" Halloran was crying out. "What I told you! You've been reclassified from 1-Y to 1-A. They expect you in the Army in a month."

A Washington reporter shoved the microphone in front of me, but Halloran pushed it aside and we walked into the center of the yard before the cameras.

Children, who had caught the excitement, danced around the yard, and now there were more children than newsmen. I looked over and recognized some of the children I had just stopped from playing war.

A reporter was asking me if I would accept the draft. The children were looking at my face and I was looking at theirs. I shook my head and repeated the remark I had already made to them. Some of the reporters rushed off to file their reports. They had enough. Others kept asking, "How does it feel about to be drafted?"

"Well, for two years the Army labeled me a 'nut,' " I said. I felt relaxed and adjusted to whatever was to come. "And I was ashamed. They embarrassed my parents, even my ex-wife. Everybody was asking them if I was some kind of a nut that couldn't pass an Army exam. Now, without even testing me to see if I've gotten wiser or worser, they tell me I'm all right. It's as if in the two years they left me alone I became one of the thirty smartest men in Louisville."

They laughed, and as the evening wore on and the cameramen left I talked frankly about my position on the war, on integration and why I had become a Muslim.

"All I want is peace," I said. "Peace for myself and peace for the world. My religion is Islam. I am a follower of the Honorable Elijah Muhammad. I believe in Allah. I think this is the true way to save the world. There're five hundred million Muslims all over Asia, Africa and the Middle East. I'm one of them. And proud of it."

Most of the calls that poured in were so friendly I almost forgot the hatred of the first ones. Some nights I'd talk to the callers, and other nights we would take the phones off the hook in order to sleep sound. It was after such a night that I almost missed an important call. Just before dawn I was leaving the cottage for the run around the golf course. Rahaman had the phone and yelled to me, "It's from Chicago."

"Tell 'em I left for roadwork," I shouted back, and kept going.

But before I was out of the yard, he called in alarm, "Champ, he says forget roadwork! The fight's gonna be canceled!"

I rushed back and snatched the phone and heard Wendell Smith, a black *Sun-Times* reporter who also worked with Mayor Daley's political machine, saying, "I tried to get through last night. Your lines were tied up."

I was impatient. "What about the fight? I don't have time to be joking."

"Listen, Champ, Mayor Daley saw you on TV." Wendell was deadly serious. "He hit the ceiling. So did Governor Kerner. They've denounced you as a traitor. And that's not the worst."

"What's worse?"

"The Mayor told the Governor to have the Illinois Athletic Commission review the permission given you to hold the Heavyweight Title fight with Terrell in Chicago."

I had taken it all in and I knew the Athletic Commission would do whatever they thought the Mayor or Governor wanted them to do. But I didn't want to believe it. "You're sure?"

"I been waiting all night to get to you." Smith sounded exhausted. "You know that setup I had for you with President Johnson in the White House won't come off if the fight's out." Wendell, who had strong connections high up in Democratic party circles, had been working on a public relations gimmick where the winner of the Ali-Terrell fight would be invited to the White House as the undisputed World Heavyweight Champion. It was an invitation I had neither sought nor cared much about at the time, but Wendell insisted that it was an acknowledgment customarily extended to the reigning World Heavyweight Champion by American Presidents, as Louis had been invited by Truman, as Tunney by Hoover, Patterson by Kennedy, Marciano by Eisenhower, Braddock by FDR, Foreman by Nixon. Wendell said, "Frankly, Johnson is pulling for Terrell, but his wife and daughters think you'll win."

As it turned out, my first visit to a Western "White House" would be upon invitation by Ireland's Prime Minister, Jack Lynch. When his Parliament members crowded around me for greetings and autographs he asked if the same commotion had occurred when I visited my own country's White House. I answered that I was especially honored because Ireland had given me the first invitation from a Chief of State in the Western World, although I had received invitations from the heads of state of Ghana, Nigeria, Egypt, Saudi Arabia, Libya, Mali, Kuwait, Somali, Uganda, Pakistan, Indonesia, Sudan and Morocco. The Prime Minister was surprised. He said my visit to Dublin had set off as much commotion as when President John F. Kennedy had come over.

Only after I had knocked out Foreman in Africa, regaining the World Heavyweight Title, was I asked to visit the White House, a visit arranged by Eugene Dibble, a Chicago business consultant for the Nation of Islam. I met President Ford in the Oval Room. The President overlooked the fact that I had opposed the war he strongly supported. And I overlooked the fact that he had supported my being barred from boxing.

"My meeting presidents of countries is complete now," I told him. "You made a big mistake in letting me come here, because now that I see it, I'm going to have to run for your job," I joked.

The President smiled back. "Sometimes with the problems I have, I think you can have it."

For the first time I visited Congressmen and Senators, who congratulated me on regaining the title, including Senator Gene Tunney, whose father had bitterly denounced my refusal to enlist in the Army.

A banquet for me was hosted by Senator Walter Huddleston of my home state, Kentucky, who at the end raised his wineglass: "I propose we all stand up and I propose a toast to our guest," he said. "Let us drink to the best damn nigger in the world." The Senator was in a mellow mood, it was all supposed to be in good humor, but somehow I was glad I had left my Old Kentucky Home.

What I thought the Senator missed, nine-year-old Shelly Sykes, of P.S. 40, Class 5335, made up for in the poem she had ready for me when I visited her grammar school on Muhammad Ali Day in New York:

> There was once a man named Cassius Clay,
> He fought for the title and came a long way.
> He became a Muslim, changed his name,
> As Muhammad Ali, he grew proud of his fame.
>
> The trouble began when he refused to fight
> The Vietnamese, who happened to be non-white.
> The boxing commissioner tried to destroy his fame,
> By taking his title and filling it with shame.
>
> The Black people were mad because he was treated as bad,
> They thought he was the greatest fighter they ever had.
> So Muhammad went from place to place,
> Preaching that war was a racial disgrace.
>
> When the war was over they let him fight,
> And he tried to win with all his might.

First he lost, but he didn't stop,
Until he was back on top.
Now here's the latest,
Ali is the greatest!

Wendell had worked hard for his White House invitation and I felt sorry for him. "There's only one way we can head the whole thing off," he was saying now, hesitating.

I waited.

"If you could fly to Chicago and appear before the Commission. Maybe say you were misquoted. I could go to the Mayor. I could talk to him."

There was a long pause. "Thanks, Wendell," I said finally.

"Well, think about it," he said without much hope. "They don't meet until the weekend."

When I hung up I turned and saw my sparring partners, my cooks, my helpers, all looking at me, stunned. They had pieced together enough to be alarmed.

"Don't stand there with your mouths open," I snapped. "We got roadwork to do."

But nobody moved until I heard my brother say almost apologetically, "It's raining, Champ."

I glanced outside. A thin Miami rain was falling, but it just made me more determined. "What did we bring rain togs for? Let's get them out on the double! That fight's on. We're running."

When I got on the golf course the rain was coming down hard but the ground was not slippery. I took off, my sparring partners silently trailing behind, single file. It was dark as night. I remember making an effort to push every worry out of my mind so that I could run and think clearly. Now that I had won the title, I wanted to show that it was in the right hands. The World Heavyweight Champion is the real Mr. America, I'd heard old fighters say.

And not only "old fighters." One day, after my morning roadwork on Miami Beach, Ronnie and I are driving along the Fifth Street Crossway, the freeway that connects Miami and Miami Beach.

I'm looking at the sleek yachts and big tourist boats in the bay when Ronnie grabs my arm. "Dig that cat out there with the boxing gloves."

I put the car in reverse and back up to the curb to see what he's talking about. A long black Lincoln Continental is parked in a short cutoff drive that surrounds a wide grassy area. A white chauffeur is standing stiffly in front of it, holding a shiny gong in one hand and a mallet in the other. A young blond woman is sitting in the back seat and a middle-aged woman is standing nearby, holding a towel.

They are all watching an old white man, who appears to be in his early seventies, squaring off near a flower patch. He is wearing red trunks, red-and-white boxing shoes and white socks, and is throwing frail awkward punches at a huge heavyset black man. The black man is barely bothering to even block the old man's punches.

Suddenly the chauffeur strikes the gong and a loud *bong* echoes across the bay. The old man drops his guard, nods to the woman for his towel and walks off to the side where the chauffeur is waiting for him.

"Good Gawd, ain't that Jelly?" Ronnie thinks he recognizes the black punching bag, but the man is too far away to be certain.

It looks like they're practicing for some kind of show. I walk over to the black man and he stares past me as if I don't even exist. But then his eyes meet mine and there's a flicker of recognition. I've seen him at the Second Avenue Barber Shop, where it's rumored that he works for a wealthy white man on the beach, but nobody seems to know what he does.

"Jelly?" I speak low so the others can't hear. "What in the world you doin'? Is this a movie?"

"Why don't you mind your own business," he mumbles, again shifting his eyes away from mine.

"Why don't you hit him back?" Ronnie whispers. "That will make him stop."

He shoots us a glance, but then looks quickly past us at the old man, who is tugging at his shorts with his gloves.

"I'm training him," Jelly says as the man does a couple of creaky knee bends and looked expectantly toward the chauffeur.

"For what?" I ask, surprised. "Who is he?"

"He's the World Heavyweight Champion," Jelly says without cracking a smile.

"Burns," the old man says sternly, turning to his chauffeur.

"Yes, sir?"

"Your timing is off." The old man pulls a stop watch from under his stool. "You must keep better time."

"Yes sir," Burns answers, and strikes the gong again.

I step back as the old man moves into Jelly, flailing away with all his might. I can see that Jelly wants me to leave, but I wait and go over to finish our conversation when the round ends. This time the old man notices. "Young man, you're interrupting my training session!" he says peevishly. "Please remove yourself."

I'm about to answer him when I glance around and see alarm in the eyes of his attendants. They motion for me to leave.

"I know you were sent here by my challenger to spy on me," the old man snaps. "Well, you go back and tell him that I'm going to knock him out in the first round."

Something tells me to leave, but I have held the Heavyweight Title too briefly to go without saying anything, "Sir, do you know who I am? I am the Heavyweight Champion of the World."

The others stiffen at my statement, but the old man smiles tolerantly. "There's only one World Heavyweight Champion. There's never two, and the world knows it's me." He looks around at his servants and from them across the bay before turning back to me with a look of pity in his eyes. "The world will not be fooled."

The young woman gets out of the car, comes over and gently puts her arms around him. Then the chauffeur bangs the gong again and the old man goes back to his "training."

"My uncle is sick," the girl says quietly. "You understand. Please leave."

In the days that follow, I not only become acquainted with this rich old man, but I also get to know two of his sons, who will later become two of my most ardent fans. They will never speak of their father's strange behavior. But I understand.

THAT MORNING, when I had finished the run and gotten back to my cottage, Captain Samuel, a close aide and the head of Muhammad's Mosque in Miami, handed me a telegram that had already been opened.

YOU HAVE DISGRACED YOUR TITLE AND THE AMERICAN FLAG AND THE PRINCIPLES FOR WHICH IT STANDS.

It was from the former World Heavyweight Champion, Gene Tunney.

APOLOGIZE FOR YOUR UNPATRIOTIC REMARK OR YOU'LL BE BARRED FROM THE RING.

"Shall I send an answer back?" Sam was anxiously watching my face for my reaction.

Months later I invited Tunney to appear in a public debate. The Black and White of the World Heavyweight Champions, debating the issues of justice, equality, freedom and "patriotism." What was "patriotism" and what was treason. He never responded. I wasn't surprised. Tunney and Dempsey, when they were champions, had refused to face a single black contender. They had never dared to speak out against the lynching terror against blacks in the South which was raging while they held the title. They had always been "White Champions."

The phone was ringing and Captain Samuel was still waiting for me to answer. I shook my head and answered the call. It was Ben

Bentley, the Chicago promoter. He had asked Herbert for permission to contact me and he came directly to the point. "Champ, the Athletic Commission is holding a meeting Friday—a special meeting on you."

I told him I knew about it already.

"There's something I can't talk to you about on the phone. Can I see you in the morning?"

"Where?"

"At the airport. I'll fly into Miami tomorrow morning. Right after you finish roadwork. Is it all right? Don't tell anybody I'm coming. Okay? Just you."

"Okay."

I had known Bentley since my days as an amateur boxer. He was a dapper-dressing, cigar-smoking publicist and promoter who had always been around boxers and athletes, and most of them respected him. He would later become public relations chief for the Chicago Bears football team and Chicago Bulls basketball team.

The next day Bentley was already at the airport when I came up, still in my roadwork clothes. We took a table in the coffee shop, and he fumbled awhile in his brief case. Finally, he brought out some papers and clippings, and in spite of his nervousness he got right down to business. "Muhammad, I'm about to be ruined."

He spread the clippings out on the table.

"If the Athletic Commission meets Friday and you're not there, they cancel the fight. Everything I've got goes down the drain. Look at this: the American Legion has notified us that they're going to boycott all closed-circuit outlets unless you explain. You know that. But I've gotten the Mayor, the Governor and the Chicago *Tribune* to agree to back off and support us if you satisfy the Commissioner."

A waitress brought his coffee, and his hands shook as he lifted it to his lips. I looked over the clippings.

One from the New York *Post* held up the example of Joe Louis and asked readers to urge me to be like him. "Joe Louis said America will always win because this is God's war," they said.

One from Jim Kernaghan of the Toronto *Star*, with the headline CLAY IS HATED BY MILLIONS!

Jim Murray of the Los Angeles *Times*, describing me as a black "Benedict Arnold" and warning me "not to go near the statue of Lincoln. Those will be real tears running down his cheeks."

Jack Dempsey: "Muhammad Ali is finished as a fighter. Regardless of the outcome of his next fight, he is finished. He should be careful. It's not safe for him to be on the streets."

Although most of the clips had been shown to me by Angie or Chris, I felt an urge to declare even more strongly why I felt the war was unjust and why I would not let myself be used to help it in any way. Those who were denouncing me so bitterly had never said a single word against the injustices or oppression inflicted upon my people in America. I felt they were saying they would accept me as the World Heavyweight Champion only on their terms. Only if I played the role of the dumb, brute athlete who chimed in with whatever the Establishment thought at the moment even if it was against the best interest of my people or my country.

One clipping read: "A member of the Black Muslims, a race-hate sect, cannot be tolerated as world heavyweight champion." How could they say that my religion, Islam, was a "race-hate" religion after all the plunder and enslavement and domination of my people by White Christians in the name of white supremacy?

It was as though I had touched an electric switch that let loose the pent-up hatred and bitterness that a big section of White America had long wanted to unleash on me for all my cockiness and boasting, for declaring myself "The Greatest" without waiting for their kind approval. For branding their Christianity a farce and flaunting my own religion, for preaching, among my own people without apology, a "black-is-best" philosophy. For frustrating their desire to see me whipped "for the good of the country" and joyfully marching off to the bank with the fruits of it and setting them up to try again. In the days ahead, the same people who had found me a "fresh breeze to boxing," who had found my poetry "humorous" and my quips "funny," would agree with Bill Gleason of the *Sun-Times* that "he isn't funny, he's tragic" or, as one writer put it, "dangerous for the youth of America."

Those who had opposed me from the beginning had not been an organized group, had been divided among themselves as to just how to cut me up. Now, without knowing it, I had given them the one thing they could get together on: a holy, patriotic crusade.

Bentley was watching me, and when I looked up his eyes were wet. "If we let them get away with blocking you now, they won't stop until you're dead so far as boxing is concerned." And when I still seemed unmoved, he said, "Muhammad, everything I've got in the world is tied up in this. I'm finished."

It was an appeal I understood. "What do you want me to do?"

He wrote down a phone number. "Call the Commissioner in Chicago at one o'clock. Tell him you'll make the meeting Friday. Tell him you'll apologize." And when I said nothing, he said, "All they want is some assurance you're a patriotic citizen. Something for them to save face. If you do it, the fight will go through."

"Do they know you're talking to me?" I asked.

He nodded. "They're waiting to see what I come back with."

I walked him to the gate for his return flight. In spite of my resistance, his appeal had reached me.

In the gym that afternoon I worked three rounds with Jimmy Ellis. My mind was so far away that Ellis, one of the most skillful boxers in the ring and one who would one day be recognized by the WBA as "World Heavyweight Champion," got to me with telling blows. When I left the ring, Moe grabbed me. "I hear you might go to Chicago to talk to the Commissioners."

I said I didn't know yet.

"If you go," he said, "I got a poem I want to give you to read on the plane."

I nodded, but my mind was far away from poems and predictions. I was still thinking of Bentley's appeal.

I believe in a fighter's obligation to perform in the ring, in the same way an actor believes "the show must go on." I have known fighters, even some great champions, who would postpone or cancel on the slightest excuse. We had already established a policy unheard of in American boxing—to deliberately go after the toughest opponents anywhere in the world—and once I agreed to a match I went through with it. There was never a fight I backed away from once the money was up—with one exception: when Bill McDonald gave me a cold ultimatum to either publicly disavow my religion or cancel the first Liston fight. The choice was no choice at all, so the cancellation was in the promoter's hands, not mine.

I felt uneasy all that day. This time I was not so certain that the responsibility was not on my side.

"The choice is nobody's but yours, Muhammad." My New York lawyer, Edward Jocko, was now calling me every hour on the hour. "It's up to you."

The Chicago investors were pleading with me to "fix things up." My Louisville sponsors wanted me to "work things out." People around me, who depended on me, wanted the fight to take place.

"What do the Commissioners want me to say?"

"I'll tell you what to say." Jocko was ready. "Here's the song to sing." Jocko always carried his piano in his brief case. "Just pick up the phone, call Chairman Triner, say sure you spoke hastily. Sure you popped off. Sure you'll apologize. Go on. Make the call."

So at the appointed time I found myself phoning the Illinois Athletic Commission and asking for Commissioner Triner. He had been waiting for the call. I went through the notes Jocko had given me: I was sorry for whatever embarrassment I had caused. I had popped off out of turn. I was calling to apologize.

The Commissioner was pleased—in fact, a little triumphant. He thanked me but said he was not empowered to accept or reject my apology. Only the full three-man Commission could do that, and he was inviting me to come to the special meeting Friday. Could I present myself to the Commissioners to answer the questions which they were empowered to ask under Code 6, Chapter 9 of the Rules and Regulations of the Illinois Athletic Commission, which read that a prizefighter "must satisfy the Commissioner that he is a person of good, stable, moral character not likely to engage in acts detrimental to the public or the honesty of boxing?"

I couldn't answer for a second, thinking of what he wanted. As none of the other points applied to me, I gathered that my "no quarrel with the Viet Cong" statement was considered "detrimental to the public."

"Will you appear?" The Commissioner was a little uneasy.

There was no appearance I wanted less to make. But I had promised lawyers, friends, trainers, sponsors, associates, everyone connected with the Terrell fight, that I would follow through. "I'll be there," I said finally.

"Good. We meet at twelve noon, Mr. Clay." He was pleasant again.

I felt a peculiar kind of exhaustion when I hung up, as though I had gone fifteen rounds with some overrated fighter I should have wiped out in two.

My Louisville sponsors called, congratulating me for "clearing up the misunderstanding." Bentley called, joyous and thankful, saying he would meet me at the airport. Jocko called, like a coach rallying the team star: "Now you're on the road back! The fight's too big to kill over a little thing like an apology. Too big."

All around was an air of relief that led me to feel that perhaps I had spoken too fast.

With Angie, Sell-Out Moe and a carful of camp aides, we drove to the airport. Moe looked gloomy and downcast. Before I boarded the plane he handed me one of his little envelopes. "It's the poem and the prophecy," he said. "Read it on the plane." I stuffed it in my pocket and we took off for Chicago.

When we landed, Bentley shoved his way past the reporters and got to my side. He had a can of Band-Aids, and knowing how nervous he was over what I might say, I pasted some across my mouth. The reporters called it my new "closed mouth" policy and roared with laughter without pressing me with questions.

Bentley was on edge until he dropped me off at my hotel. He looked at his watch. "Only twenty-four hours to go before the meeting." He assured me it would take less than fifteen or twenty minutes once it got started. "Just say what you said over the phone and we'll get over this hurdle. Just don't say anything to reporters until it's over." He clasped my hand warmly.

That afternoon I conferred for hours with Herbert Muhammad

about my appearance before the Commissioners. We were on the eve of the most sacred day in the Nation of Islam: Savior's Day. I had decided to stay over the weekend to attend the convention. Herbert felt that whatever course I took, it would affect my life for years to come, and he suggested that I sit down with his father, Messenger Muhammad, for whatever counsel he would give me on the issue. The Messenger rarely, if ever, addressed himself to matters related to sport, but Herbert was able to set the meeting up for an hour before my appointment with the Commissioners.

In the evening, searching around for some quiet spot to escape prying reporters, I went into a little barbershop for a haircut, only to find all the talk was about tomorrow's meeting.

"What're you gonna tell them Commissioners, Ali?" my own barber wanted to know.

"What should I tell them?"

"Tell them to go to hell. You got a right to your own opinion about the war. That's no reason to stop a man from practicing his trade. Our white folks are getting out of hand!"

The barber at the next chair disagreed. "For God sakes, don't stop the fight. I'm betting a bundle and I know you'll come through."

The customers laughed. One came up to me with a newspaper and read aloud Red Smith's column, which predicted what I would say:

> To their credit Triner, the Commissioner, has not yet acquiesced to their boss Mayor Daley's demand for a reprisal against Clay. They did call a special meeting. Agreed to have him up in person for a hearing on Friday before making a decision. Cassius, who can be an extremely attractive young man if he chooses, will be winning and contrite. He has already conceded that he did pop off out of turn. He says he is not going to let newspapermen trick him into any more foolish statements.

"What does that mean?" my barber wanted to know.

The betting barber was delighted. "It means 'Put your money up, there's gonna be a rumble.' I'd give them the most humble apology I could find. Up, down, sideways. Then I'd go out there and tear Terrell to pieces."

My barber cut in. "The worse thing in the world you could do. Once they get you on your knees they'll never let you get up. The worse thing in the world!"

The argument raged back and forth just as it was churning in my own mind.

When I got to my hotel, I found Wendell waiting in the lobby, glowing with the news he had from Washington. "It's all worked out," he said as I got ready for bed. "Johnson has agreed the winner will be invited for a picture-taking session in the White House as soon as your apology is made."

Suddenly I resented him for assuming I had already made that decision. "I hope we'll still be friends after the meeting tomorrow," I said.

Wendell had been the black reporter credited with opening the doors of the major leagues for Jackie Robinson, and I knew he wanted to be the newsman responsible for opening the doors of the White House for me.

He looked helpless. "But you've already decided to apologize," he said, and handed me a newspaper with a headline: CLAY SET TO APOLO-GIZE. "Didn't the Muslims tell you? I thought you'd seen the Messenger and gotten it all straight."

I took the paper. It had an "exclusive story" by Jack Mabley, claiming to be based on "secret information from inside Muslim head-quarters":

> Clay's instructions, if pressed, are to give evasive answers. It is believed, however, that if it appears necessary, Clay may say at this stage that he would be willing to serve in the armed forces . . . if he finds it necessary to make this statement, it will be relatively simple for him to change his mind after the fight, but before he is inducted.

I read it through twice. I couldn't believe it. Where did these "instructions" come from?

In the morning I met Chauncey Eskridge, my lawyer and the tax counsel for the Nation of Islam, at the Messenger's mansion in Kenwood, and we sat down with him at a long dining table and had coffee and cakes. All of the conversation centered on a review of international and domestic affairs until we were about to leave and my lawyer finally explained the reason for my meeting with the Commissioners.

The Messenger was silent as we walked to the door. Then he turned to me and said simply, "Brother, if you felt what you said was wrong, then you should be a man and apologize for it. And likewise, if you felt what you said was right, then be a man and stand up for it." He said nothing more.

Riding along the Outer Drive to the Loop, I looked out at the rough water of Lake Michigan, half listening to Eskridge going over my alternatives. We pulled up across from City Hall at the Illinois State Building, and I remember my surprise at the enormous crowd gathered at the doorway. Almost blocking the entrance was a line of demonstrators in World War II Army uniforms, with signs reading: "Clay! Apologize to America!" . . . "Clay! Love America or Leave it!" Across the street a group of younger demonstrators had signs reading: "Give

The Champ a Chance!" . . . "We're with Muhammad Ali." . . . "We ain't got no quarrel with no Viet Cong." I noticed that those demonstrating for me were being treated much rougher by the police than those against me.

Inside the building, the corridors were jammed with photographers and reporters yelling as I passed, "Champ, what you gonna say?" Someone had my hand and was pulling me through the door. It was Jim Brown, ex-Cleveland Browns football star, who was now a part of Main Bout, an ancillary company that handled the closed-circuit operations of my fights. Jocko, who had flown in from New York, joined us and handed me a typewritten statement he had worked out.

We were pushed into an elevator and finally squeezed into the upstairs conference room. It looked more like a courtroom. Where I had expected to sit around a table and talk informally, I found the Commissioners sitting on a high podium like judges on a Supreme Court bench and myself in a chair looking up at them. Behind the podium were two huge photographs: on the left was Mayor Daley; on the right, Governor Otto Kerner.

"I understand you have a statement to read," Chairman Triner was saying.

I stood up and the room quieted down.

"Do you have something to say?" the Chairman asked sympathetically in the same voice he had used with me over the phone. Jocko was nudging me, slipping me a piece of paper. I pushed it away.

"I have no prepared statement," I said. "What I said in Miami, I should have said to the officials of the Draft Board, not to reporters. I apologize for not saying it to the proper people."

Chairman Triner looked puzzled. His eyes went from my face to my lawyer's face, and then Commissioner Joe Robichaux leaned over and cut through the preliminaries and got to the point. "To whom you made the remark is not important. It's the remark itself. Do you apologize for your unpatriotic remark, regardless to whom you said it?" His voice was loud and heavy.

I started to answer, but felt another nudge in my ribs and heard Jocko whispering desperately, "Tell them you apologize. Go on. Tell them!"

The Commissioner continued, "Cassius Clay . . ." He put special emphasis on my old slave name. "Do you apologize to the American people, to the Governor of this state, to the Mayor of this city? Do you apologize for your unpatriotic remark?"

He knew he had my career in his hands and he wanted me to know it, too. I found myself looking up at the photographs of the Mayor and the Governor. Jocko was almost pushing me aside, trying to answer for me.

Like an auctioneer on his last bid, the Commissioner sounded "Have I made myself clear?"

"No, I do not apologize for what I said. I do not apologize."

The Commissioners were startled. They looked down at my lawyer, then over at promoter Bentley. And one of them began again. "Cassius Clay . . ."

I cut in and corrected him. "The name is Muhammad Ali."

The glove was thrown and I had picked it up. I had no apologies inside me. The Commissioners were whispering among themselves, but I knew the hearing was over. I got up and pushed my way toward the door, Jocko frantically pulling on me, calling to me in desperate undertones, "Muhammad, come on! Come back!" But I had gone too far to turn around and so had they. Now either I would be free or they would put me in jail. And if I had to rot in jail, I felt I was ready for it.

I remember reporters shouting as I passed through the crowded halls, "Is the fight on?" . . . "What happened in there?" . . . "Is it all over?" I saw the blood-drained face of promoter Bentley. He had given up.

But my lawyer had not. When I got back to the hotel room the phone was ringing. It was Attorney Jocko. "Muhammad," he said, "we can still save this thing!"

"Let's leave it alone," I said.

"Look, for God sakes, listen to me! They haven't voted on you yet. We can turn this thing around. This town wants this fight. Even the Mayor wants it. All they need is something to save face."

"Jocko, I got something else to do, and I'm late!"

"Wait," he pleaded. "Please listen. You've got to go along with this or you're finished. Let me put it to you straight. What Gene Tunney and Jack Dempsey said was right. They'll hound you out of the country. They've been waiting to deal you a blow for a long time. Listen to me. Don't cut me off. Here's our next move. I'm calling a press conference in a few minutes. I'll say to the press that the Commissioners asked you loaded questions. Unfair questions. I'll say I just talked to you on the phone and you admit you didn't understand the meaning of some of the words the Commissioners used. For example, the word 'patriotic.' You remember Triner asking you if you were apologizing to the people of Illinois and to the Governor for your unpatriotic remark? I'll say it wouldn't have made any difference what you answered because you didn't know the meaning of the word 'unpatriotic'—had never heard it before. You get it?"

"Attorney, I tell you I got other things—"

"Let me finish!" he shouted. "Then I'll tell the Commissioners. I'll say you feel awfully bad about the whole thing. I'll tell them you're depressed and downhearted and dejected because of what happened and that you want another chance to come before the Commission, to meet the Commissioners, to meet the Governor, apologize in person. It's our only chance. You didn't understand those words they were saying."

"But, Attorney," I said quietly, since it was no use trying to outshout him, "I do know what the word 'unpatriotic' means, and if it's to be against the war, I am unpatriotic. I am that."

"You're not that!" Jocko shot back. "You're disappointing a lot of people who love you, who work for you, who depend on you. Let me come over where you are and we'll talk this thing out. Not over the phone like this. I'll tell you what the deal is. It's highly confidential. I'll be right over."

I was gone by the time he arrived. The deal he had described as being "confidential" turned out to be no secret at all. The phone he had been talking from had been bugged, and every word of what he said was printed the next morning in an opposition newspaper.

When there was no more reason for me to stay in Chicago, I began packing my things, throwing away clippings, discarding old notes, and I came upon the still sealed letter Moe had given me at the airport. I tore it open and saw one of his poems:

> Mayor Daley is king
> Of the Chicago ring
> Wants the Champ's name
> In the political game
> So the Governor can show
> That the Tiger is tame
>
> We stopped his holler
> With a million dollar collar
> Let him do his thing
> With his nose in a ring
> No Tiger no more
> Extraordinary whore
>
> But that won't be it
> The collar don't fit
> For in Miami that night
> The Champ was right
> He sings his song
> No quarrel with Viet Cong
>
> And is much too wise
> To apologize . . .
>
> Sell-Out Moe

I had to laugh; I could see Moe's long, bloodhound-sad face creased in a sly smile. He understood more than turnstiles and cashier cages. He had spotted something in me that others around me had not and he had called the shot on how I would react. Moe had seen my "no sale" sign when I hadn't known it was there myself.

The Commissioners carried out the wishes of the Mayor and the Governor. The fight was banned in Illinois—and in seven more cities before it found a place in Toronto the next month with George Chuvalo, the Canadian Heavyweight Champion, as the opponent. Terrell backed out. Since it seemed certain that I would soon be jailed or stripped of my title, his managers felt he could convert his paper WBA "title" into real gold without the risk of a fight with me. Their hope lasted only a year. I caught up with Terrell in Houston.

I would never have a professional fight in Chicago, once one of the greatest fight towns in the world. All through my youth I had longed for a title fight in that city, the center of my Golden Gloves amateur days. But maybe I did have one there, the most decisive one.

I had left Chicago without meeting Mayor Daley as Smith had planned, and I chalked it up as another city I would never be welcome in. But years later, when I flew into Montreal after winning the World Heavyweight Title from Foreman, there was a telegram waiting for me at the airport:

THE MAYOR OF CHICAGO WANTS TO BE THE FIRST TO CONGRATU-LATE YOU WHEN YOU ARRIVE IN AMERICA. ALL CHICAGO WELCOMES YOU. A PARADE TO CITY HALL IS PREPARED IN YOUR HONOR. THE CITY MEDAL OF MERIT AWAITS YOU.

Although there was a heavy rain when I landed at Chicago's Midway Airport, a crowd of city officials were there and a long convoy of cars took me to City Hall, where for the first time I met the man who's been Mayor of Chicago for twenty years. If he remembered how he helped outlaw me from boxing, he didn't let it stop him from putting a medal around my neck and saying to the crowd, "This is a great day and a historic day in the life of our great city. All of us watched you the other night. You proved a lot of people wrong."

Then he read his poem:

> Back to the city where it's pronounced "Zair"
> (As in "fair," "blare" and "His Honor, the Mare"),
> Returned the champion, Muhammad Ali,
> The self-proclaimed wonder, butterfly-bee.

Encircled by bodyguards, fans, pols and dolls,
Leaving no one to doubt that his presence enthralls,
From Midway, Ali sped to see Mayor Daley,
But the throng that awaited touched off a near melee.

Into City Hall, Ali strode with four hundred,
And even the "greatest" of champs may have wondered
If his fight against Foreman was really the test,
Or would getting to Daley be a tougher conquest?

But his phalanx protected, the crowd was deflected,
And he rose to the fifth floor, where Daley elected
To have Ali praised in his best poetry.
What follows was penned by "Spike" Hennessey:

Whereas, Ali always knew what the outcome would be.
He would move like a butterfly, sting like a bee.
He would outpoint his rival, but slug if he must
To put him away in the resiny dust . . ."

Now, therefore, I, Richard J. Daley, Mayor of the City,
Do proclaim for this champion, clever and witty,
Muhammad Ali his own special day
For receiving the honors he won the hard way.

I thanked the Mayor and said I was glad he found a word to rhyme with "witty" and I didn't mean "pretty." Everyone laughed, the world loves a winner.

The Mayor said, "Promise me you'll have a heavyweight title bout in Chicago. Chicago is a good place for a fight."

I said I'd agree if the proceeds went to help the Nation of Islam build a hospital dreamed of by the Honorable Elijah Muhammad.

The Mayor also assigned Pat Patterson, a city policeman, as my permanent bodyguard.

Chicago politics had changed, but there were those who stayed the same. Two days later, I received a letter from someone who had seen the event on television: "You, a draft-dodging nigger, gets a hero's welcome while there are thousands of Viet Nam Vets who are sightless or badly maimed. If there is really a God in heaven, one day you will be stood up against a wall and shot. Don't be so sure someone won't do it before your next fight—you black bastard!"

Nine years earlier the same letters had come in avalanches—only then they were not afraid to sign their names.

THE INDUCTION

I thought the letter was dead and buried, somewhere on a Houston street seven years ago. But I came across it when I was moving out of Cherry Hill, New Jersey, out of the old Spanish-style villa I had bought with the money I made from the first fight after my exile. I was going through stuff I had accumulated from my last three homes—my childhood home in Louisville, then Chicago and Philadelphia—to see what I wanted to keep, and what to throw away.

I found a faded red, white and blue jacket with KENTUCKY GOLDEN GLOVES CHAMPION on the back in pretty gold letters. I had walked all over Louisville wearing that jacket. I was fourteen years old, and it was the first big prize I had won. I threw the jacket into a box and opened the old chest of drawers where Belinda stored my papers. I pulled out a blue box, and a stack of letters spilled onto the floor.

Kneeling down to pick them up, I noticed the gold-and-green-trimmed letter from President Kwame Nkrumah of Ghana, the blue stationery from Premier Ahmed Ben Bella of Algeria, congratulations from President Charles de Gaulle of France, an invitation to Egypt from President Gamal Abdel Nasser, greetings from President François Duvalier of Haiti, King Faisal Abdel Aziz of Saudi Arabia, President Zulfikar Ali Bhutto of Pakistan, Prime Minister Jack Lynch of Ireland, and the long, plain white envelope I thought I'd thrown away. At first I was almost afraid to pick it up. I knew what it was and the memories it would bring back. I got a chilly feeling, and somehow it seemed as though the mailman had just delivered it, and the part of my life it represented was starting all over again.

I asked Belinda why she had put it there. "It belongs there," she insisted. "This is where I keep all the letters from heads of state."

Although I had gotten congratulations from all over the world after winning the Heavyweight Crown, at that time I was only the second American Heavyweight Champion who was never invited to the White House. Jack Johnson was the other. My only contact with an American President was this letter. It came on April Fool's Day, 1967, ten days after my title defense against Zora Folley. It read:

ORDER FOR TRANSFERRED MAN TO REPORT FOR INDUCTION

FROM: The President of the United States

TO: Mr. Cassius Marcellus Clay, Jr.
       AKA Muhammad Ali
       5962 Ardmore Street
       Houston, Texas 77021

Greetings:
    Having heretofore been ordered to report for induction by Local Board No. 47, State of Kentucky, Louisville, Kentucky, which is your Local Board of origin, and having been transferred upon your own request to Local Board No. 61, State of Texas, Houston, Texas, which is your Local Board of Transfer for delivery to an induction station, you will therefore report to the last named Local Board at 3rd Floor, 701 San Jacinto St., Houston, Texas 77022 on April 28, 1967, at 8:30 A.M.

Shortly after I get the letter I walk through downtown Chicago, and I find I'm not the only one who knows about it.

"Hey! Is that Cassius Clay? That looks like Cassius Clay!"

A group of American Legionnaires are coming out of a tavern on Michigan Avenue, and the lead man has his eyes on me.

"Yes, it's Cassius."

A man in a donkey cap lunges toward me for a better look. His buddies start screaming, "They gotcha! They gotcha!" "Sonofabitch! Thank God, they gotcha!" One waves a little American flag. Another

holds up a newspaper with its bold black headline: ARMY TELLS CLAY
—PUT UP OR SHUT UP!

They follow me for a while, but when I pass a city college, students
pour out, yelling, "Hell, no! Don't go! Hell, no! Don't go!" And in a
minute the corner is blocked with students and passers-by, shouting,
"Stand up to 'em! Stand up!" The old soldiers stand on the fringes for
a few minutes and then fade into the crowd.

When I leave for Houston on the twenty-seventh, I have to push
my way through a wall of journalists and travelers at the airport. One
of my lawyers, Chauncey Eskridge, who is flying with me, almost gets
lost in the commotion. People jam against me until I climb the board-
ing ramp and stand out on the platform.

"They want to hear your last words, Champ," Al Monroe, a
Chicago *Defender* editor shouts, and the other newsmen call out questions.

"You going to take that step?"

"Will you give up the title?"

"Don't you think it's your duty to defend your country?"

I wave back at them, but I don't answer.

I remember the color of the plane, a bright reddish-orange Braniff.
All of the passengers recognize me, and I sign autographs before getting
into my seat. Once we are in the air, the captain announces, "Ladies
and gentlemen, the Heavyweight Champion of the World is your
traveling companion. Have a delightful trip."

The first hour is smooth and I spend the time talking to Eskridge
and signing more autographs. Then suddenly we fly into some heavy
turbulence. We swoop and roll and bump, and the abrupt lifts and deep
drops send dining trays flying through the cabin. We think the plane
is out of control. Even the stewardesses look afraid. The captain jokes,
trying to soothe us over the intercom, but I don't hear much humor
in his voice. Eskridge has his head bowed in prayer, something I never
suspected he was acquainted with.

A woman across the aisle from me is praying out loud with a Bible
in her hand. When her eyes meet mine, she shrieks, "God is punishing
us because he's on this plane!" She strains against her seat belt and
points a shaky finger at me. "God is punishing us because we're helping
His enemy!" she screams. "Cassius Clay, you turned against the true
Christian God! God wants you off this plane! O forgive us, O Lord!"
She clutches her Bible. "Forgive us, Jesus! God is punishing us! God
wants you off this plane!"

The stewardess looks sympathetically at me as she rushes over to
comfort her. But I am in full agreement with the woman. God couldn't
want me off that plane half as much as I want to be off.

I check into the hotel in Houston at 7 P.M. I remember the exact time, because the clerk tells me, "I checked you in when you came here for your fights with Ernie Terrell and Cleveland Williams. It was seven o'clock both times. That's got to be a sign," he adds, shaking his head as if there's something ominous about it.

A near-sighted old woman approaches me as I walk across the lobby. She squints up through the thickest pair of glasses I've ever seen. "You really the man you look like?" I nod and she beams as though proud of her good eyesight. "I was in the Astrodome when you fought Army Terror that last time."

"You mean Ernie Terrell," I correct her gently.

"Army Terror," she says as though she hasn't heard me. "Now who you come to fight?" Before I can answer she continues, "Where your poem for this fight? I had trouble getting tickets last time. Where your poem for this fight? You help me this time."

I tell her she won't need a ticket for this fight, but she follows me as I walk to the elevator with the bellhop, expecting me to give her one.

It's a strange feeling coming back here. The same clerks, the same waitresses in the coffee shop, the same newsmen, photographers and reporters checking in, crowds in the lobby. The scene has the same uncertainty and tension of a major fight. There's a queasiness in the pit of my stomach, a feeling that hasn't left me since the flight.

"Thanks for the tickets to the Terrell fight," the bellhop says when we reach my room. "What you gonna do tomorrow?" he whispers, handing me the key to the same suite I had when I fought Terrell. "The Army's not so bad. You may not believe it, but I just got discharged. I didn't do too bad over there, if you know what I mean."

He holds out his discharge papers to autograph, and I sign my name and write "Peace" below it in big letters.

Once he's gone, I strip off my clothes and lie for a long time on the bed, just staring up at the ceiling. I remember the first time I fought in Houston. The Mayor changed Thomas Jefferson Street to Muhammad Ali Street in my honor.

After a while I glance at my watch and notice it's eight o'clock. In twelve hours I will be in the Induction Center, and afterwards they will quietly rename the street Thomas Jefferson and keep it that way.

I put on my sweat shirt and jeans, thinking I'll be more comfortable in the casual clothes I always wear when I'm training for a big fight, and go down to the dining room. I order the same dinner I always order the day before a fight: a prime rib steak, lettuce and tomato salad, a baked potato. Only when I finish do I notice the other diners. Some glance slyly toward me, whispering, and a few stare outright. When their eyes meet mine, they offer nervous smiles as though they themselves are being watched to see whose side they're on.

A reporter from the Houston newspaper appears as I get up to leave. "Is this the most decisive day of your life? Have you made your decision?"

"I already gave it," I say. "Don't you believe me?"

His answer will come back to me later at the Induction Center. "Yes," he says. "But those were just words. Words are not convincing. Acts are. How will you act?"

I turn away as the desk clerk pages me for a long-distance call from my mother. "People," she says, "have urged me to call you." I listen to her, knowing the pressure she's under at home in Louisville.

"G.G., do the right thing," she says. "If I were you, I would go ahead and take the step. If I were you, I would join the Army. Do you understand me, son?"

I assure her that I understand and tell her, "Bird, I love you. Whatever I do, Bird, remember, I love you." She starts crying and I say goodbye and hang up.

I go up to my room and try to watch television, but there's nothing I can keep my mind on. I turn on my tape recorder and listen to Sam Cooke, who was once my buddy. His music relaxes me a little, but not enough. I want to talk to people. It's 11:00 P.M. I go down and get a cab.

"Where to?"

"Just take me where the people are."

The driver lets me out in front of the Cinder Club, but instead of going in I stay out on the sidewalk, talking to a growing crowd of customers who have heard I'm there.

"Champ, you ready to join the Army?"

"Don't go, man, don't go."

I stand there talking and signing autographs until the owner of the club comes out and pleads, "The band's quit playing and everybody's coming out in the street, Champ. Come in or go away."

I decide to go, and he drives me to my hotel.

"I know you've given it a lot of thought, Champ," he says as we drive along. "But it really wouldn't be so bad to join the Army. They can make it real easy for you. Look at Joe Louis. He went. He got a good deal."

I nod. I remember seeing Louis once, coming through Chicago on his way to a five-hundred-dollar speaking engagement in Germany. It was almost winter and he couldn't afford to buy any warm clothes, so I bought him some suits and overcoats. I gave him a thousand dollars and had him stay with me for a few days instead of going to Europe.

The next morning I wake up at 6 A.M. Down in the dining room, again I order the kind of food I eat before a fight. The waitress is the one who served me when I fought Terrell.

"You want the same?" she asks.

"You've got a good memory," I tell her.

"How many customers ask for five poached eggs, two whole-wheat toasts, two orange juices and a glass of ice water?" She laughs and goes to get my order.

Across from me is a group of businessmen. Their name tags say they're from Kentucky. They looked up with a jolt when I came in, but now they sit with their heads buried in their morning papers. They seem more edgy than me.

A thin nervous little man couldn't pretend to eat like the others. He picked up his newspaper, circled one of the articles, walked past me, his nose in the air, dropped the paper in front of me and kept going. I read what was encircled: "The Kentucky State Senate Wednesday night approved a resolution asking heavyweight boxing champion Cassius Clay to enter the Armed Services immediately. The resolution said Clay's sudden aversion to fighting brings discredit to all loyal Kentuckians and to the names of thousands of men who gave their lives for their country during his lifetime."

I'm still eating when Eskridge comes over with Quinnon Hodges, an attorney from Houston, and Hayden Covington from New York. Covington was introduced to Herbert by Robert Arum, Main Bout's attorney, who knew of Covington's record with the Seventh-Day Adventists' cases and who also knew Herbert was looking for lawyers experienced in draft cases. Herbert made an appointment for all of us to meet with his father.

I had filed for draft exemption as a conscientious objector, telling the government that as a minister in the Nation of Islam ". . . to bear arms or kill is against my religion. And I conscientiously object to any combat military service that involves the participation in any war in which the lives of human beings are being taken." The claim was rejected in Louisville, and Covington took the case to the Kentucky Appeal Board. He based my appeal on religious grounds, and the fact that blacks were not represented on the Selective Service Boards that judged me. In a special hearing, Circuit Court Judge Lawrence Grauman determined that my beliefs were sincere, and recommended that my claim be upheld.

A few days later South Carolina Democratic Representative L. Mendel Rivers told the Veterans of Foreign Wars, "If the theologian of Black Muslim power, Cassius Clay, is deferred by the board in Louisville, you watch what happens in Washington. . . . We are going to do something if that board takes your boy and leaves him [Clay] home to double-talk."

Covington convinced me to move to Houston. His sister, he said, was married to Selective Service Director General Lewis B. Hershey, and we hoped I could get a better deal in Texas. But if the deal I got in Houston was better because my lawyer's sister was married to the draft boss, I hate to think what might have happened elsewhere.

It was two weeks before the Houston Board turned down my appeal. Covington called me in Chicago. "It looks like trouble, Champ," he told me. "General Hershey has just predicted that you won't be deferred. This isn't like any case I've had before. Joe Namath can get off to play football and George Hamilton gets out because he's going with the President's daughter, but you're different. They want to make an example out of you."

Eskridge looks at his watch. "How much time left?"

"It's seven forty-five," Hodges says. "We're due there at eight-thirty."

"Let's get the hell out of here. If you're half an hour late, they want to put you in jail."

I let them move out and I stay to pay the waitress. She has seen all of my fights.

"I'm so glad you've decided not to buck the Army," she says thankfully.

"How do you know that?" I ask, slightly surprised.

"By the way you're dressed," she says. "You're wearing casual clothes. Those going to join always come in casual clothes, because there's a bus waiting for you right after the examination, and you wouldn't want to ruin a dress suit on a bus. When they see you in casual clothes, they'll know you're ready to go. You're doing the right thing, and I'm glad. You'll like camp life."

I thank her and head for the elevator.

"Where are you going?" The lawyers try to grab me, but I run upstairs. I put on my best black mohair suit, white shirt, black necktie, and give my shoes a good brushing. I look in the mirror and everything checks out fine, like I'm going anywhere but to Viet Nam.

When I get downstairs I look for a cab with a black driver and call one over. The lawyers pile into the back while I sit up front with the driver.

"The courthouse!" Covington shouts. "We've got to be there at eight-thirty."

"Which courthouse?" the driver asks politely. "We've got two here."

"The one where they're drafting people. Try that one around the corner!"

But when the cab swings up to an old courthouse, there's not a soul around.

"If this is where they're drafting people," the driver says, "nobody's showing up today." He rocks with laughter. "The war's on and nobody's showing up."

Covington almost screams, "Then it must be the other building. Hurry up!"

The driver steps on the gas, still laughing. "Nobody's showing up for the war. Ain't that a bitch?"

He pulls up to a large stone building, the U.S. Customs House, 701 Jacinto Street, where everybody has shown up for the war. People waiting for my arrival have jammed the sidewalk. When they see our cab drive up, they wave picket signs and scream, "Muhammad Ali, don't go!" . . . "Muhammad Ali!"

The steps of buildings all along the street are filled with people and the windows crowded with peering faces.

Some students from Texas Southern University are marching with banners that read STAY HOME, MUHAMMAD ALI! Across the street in a blue denim jacket and jeans stands H. Rap Brown, holding up a clenched fist and surrounded by a group of young blacks shouting, "Hep! Hep! Don't take that step! Hep! Hep! Don't take that step!"

An elderly woman cuts through the crowd, grabs my hand and whispers, "Stand up, brother! We're with you! Stand up! Fight for us! Don't let us down!"

A band of long-haired hippies begin shouting, "We didn't go! You don't go! We didn't go! You don't go!"

Someone grabs my arm, and my lawyer says quietly, "It's the FBI. Go along." A group of policemen push the crowd back from the doors as I return Rap Brown's salute. I climb the steps and the people begin to clap and cheer. Newspapermen and photographers are wedging their way through and crying out, "Muhammad, give us the answer!" . . . "Are you going in?" . . . "What's your last word?" . . . "What will your stand be?"

When I get to the top of the steps I look back at all those people who have come to show me their support. Bundini, who has just arrived, spots "Miss Velvet Green." "There she is." He points across the street to a Chrysler parked near a fireplug. A white woman in a green outfit stands between two men, one of whom is her escort. The other is a chauffeur. "She couldn't miss this one." Bundini shakes his head. "This is the one she wouldn't miss for nothing in the world." He has named her "Miss Velvet Green" because whenever we see her she has on a green outfit, usually made of velvet.

She tiptoes to see over the crowd. Her escort, a tall, heavyset man, sees me first, nudges her and points in my direction. I catch the look in her eyes. I can tell she wants me to know she's there. Now she's satisfied.

Bundini mutters:

> Miss Velvet Green,
> The evilest bitch I ever seen . . .

She stands for only a short while, then her chauffeur opens the door and she gets back into the car.

The first time I ever saw Miss Velvet Green was in the Astrodome. A beautiful place to spill our blood and beat ourselves senseless. Gold upholstered chairs, rows of orange, green, brown, purple and yellow seats leading up to the roof, where I could see binoculars flashing. The traditionally white ropes around the ring were wrapped in blue. I felt like I did in Rome when I visited the Colosseum and stood in the middle of the arena where the guide said thousands of slaves hacked each other to pieces for the pleasure of the crowd. I had won, and I was climbing out of the ring after my bloody fifteen-round struggle with Terrell. Miss Velvet Green was one of the thirty thousand who came to see the fight in which I destroyed the World Boxing Authority's contention that there was another World Heavyweight Champion besides myself. I remember that night because half the crowd had been screaming for my defeat. Some were still shoving and pushing as we stood in the ring, waiting for the judges and referee to coordinate the slips.

Angelo and Bundini were starting to wedge their way to the dressing room when I reached out to keep them from pushing aside an elegantly dressed woman who was holding out a pad and pencil. As I took the pad and scrawled my name, I noticed that her face looked vaguely familiar.

"Were you here when I fought Cleveland Williams?" I asked.

"I come to all your fights," she replied evenly.

"Thanks, ma'am," I said. "I hope you keep coming."

"I will keep coming"—she folded the autograph away carefully—"until I see them take you out on a stretcher."

She said it so calmly and matter-of-fact that I wasn't sure I had heard right. "Why you want me beat?"

"God won't always let evil win!" She raised her voice. "I'm going to be there when they bust your face and stomp it in." Her voice was cracking. "If there is a God," she said as her escort pulled her away, "it's going to happen, and I want to be there."

Of all the things that have stayed with me from that night in the Astrodome, Miss Velvet Green's hatred hangs on the longest. Maybe because I wanted to talk to her and hear why she felt so bitter.

The headlines after the fight read: CASSIUS REVEALS HIS WICKED-NESS. IS MUHAMMAD THE MEANEST, MOST VICIOUS, MOST DEMENTED, UNSPORTSMANLIKE FIGHTER EVER TO ENTER THE RING? YES!!!! The New York *Post* reporter Milton Gross, who had seemed to be my only friend, wrote: "Boxing is a brutal business . . . but always, before Clay brought a sadistic streak to it, there was a community between fighters."

It's as though they thought that thirty thousand people came to the Astrodome to see my loving, tender side, to see how I treat women and children.

"What they're really bitter about," a prominent psychologist told me, "is that you won. You prevented your opponent from showing his vicious streak."

There is no way I can whip an opponent that will satisfy White America. If I whip one "tenderly," just tag him a time or two, they howl, "Ali's lost his punch!" If I pulverize him, they cry, "Ali's vicious!"

I hit Ernie Terrell until I knew he was out on his feet. His eyes were puffed, his nose bleeding, lips cut and swollen, but the referee egged us on. I knew that unless I held back he would be injured for life. It's against the rules, but I began to pull my punches. The crowd wanted more blood, and those against me hoped he could come up with a miraculous counterattack. But he was beaten and there was no point in pounding him any more. He had a family, sisters, brothers and parents, just like I had. Why should I maul him just to satisfy some of the screamers.

I've tried time after time to get boxing organizations all over the world to demand that fighters wear some kind of headgear. Football players need headgear, and hockey players need headgear. Don't boxers need some protection? There're too many deaths, too many injuries. And since promoters and sponsors refuse to cooperate, the only safety left is for the man who is doing the punching to lighten up when he sees his opponent in critical condition. I went out of my way not to hurt Terrell, but I was called a brute and a sadist.

"Why did you taunt him by asking him all night, 'What is my name?' " a Methodist minister asked me. "That was un-Christianlike, unkind and cruel."

"I wasn't just talking to Terrell," I told him. "I was talking to all those people who keep calling me Cassius Clay. They wouldn't call Sugar Ray Robinson, Jack Benny, Howard Cosell, or Edward G. Robinson by the old names they junked. Why do it to me?"

I wasn't angry with Ernie. I was angry at the people who were using him for what they wanted to do themselves. I wasn't whipping Ernie; I was whipping the WBA's fat-bellied, hairy-faced authorities who took my title. I had to let them see that any White Hope they sent to me would just get himself whipped even if he looked black. And if all I had to look forward to was a future behind bars for not going to Viet Nam, I was ready for that, too.

"RIGHT THIS WAY, Mr. Clay," says a man in a Navy officer's uniform.

I follow him into a large room, about half the size of a basketball court, where the recruits are standing in line. The officer motions for me to stand between a black boy and a tall, thin white boy. There are thirty draftees, but all eyes are on me as I take my place. I return their glances and notice that most of them seem uneasy. The white boy next to me is trembling. He seems very young, and his teeth are chattering. I speak to him, but he just nods his head nervously, afraid to look at me.

I remember standing there, silently, with a group of officers in front of us, sorting papers, checking lists and speaking in hushed tones. After what seems like a year, one comes over and explains the procedure: "First you will take a written test, then a physical examination, and then you will be called for induction. After that, you will line up outside for the bus to camp." He starts barking out roll call, pausing to scribble something beside the names of those who don't answer.

Three soldiers wearing arm bands are standing in the corners ignoring the roll call. Their attention is fixed on me.

A fat-faced aide, his uniform fitting him poorly, passes out forms for a written test while the commander tells us, "Awright, fellas, you got five minutes to answer the first ten questions."

We break into sections, and as I fill out my first sheet I sense someone looking over my shoulder. But when I glance back, the officer looks away.

"Awright, awright," the commander breaks in. "You got four minutes to finish the eight questions on the next sheet." When that's done, he shouts again, "Awright, fellas, get it together. Now do the twenty-five questions on the third page. Page three there, the one with the red X on top. You got fifteen minutes to do that."

We complete the written test and are ushered into another room to wait until they call us for our physicals.

"I'm going to call your names in groups of ten," the officer barks. "When you hear your name, you will follow the officer at your right. He'll take you to the examining room."

When my group is called I follow another officer into a large room furnished with eight canvas-covered cubicles, each one manned by a doctor.

"Strip down to shorts!" the officer shouts.

I strip down automatically. I'm used to working in shorts, but some of the others seem embarrassed and take their clothes off slowly.

One by one, we move toward the first booth, where one of the doctors is standing beside a table. His eyes light up when he sees me, as though this is what he's come to work for today.

"What's your name?" he asks.

"Muhammad Ali," I reply.

He frowns. "It's Cassius Clay." His jaws are set, and he holds his mouth tight as if to drive his point home with force.

I remain quiet.

"It's Cassius Clay," he repeats, "isn't it?"

"Well, it used to be, but—"

"It's still Cassius Clay," he cuts in. "That's who you're registered as. Put down 'Cassius Clay,'" he tells his assistant.

His aide, a short fellow with horn-rimmed glasses, makes a note on his pad and takes me aside to check my tonsils. I get a funny feeling that something bad is going to happen to me—like in Boston, where I was scheduled to fight Sonny Liston.

A few days before my second fight with Liston in Lewiston, Maine, I was sitting at the dinner table when suddenly I was struck by terrible pains and had to be rushed to the hospital. It felt like my intestine was pushing out through one of my testicles.

When I got to the hospital the doctors gave me a quick examination and told me I had a hernia, needed an operation immediately. It was more pain than I had ever had in my life.

"What's your name?" one of them asked me.

"My name is Muhammad Ali."

"No, that's not your real name," he said, slightly irritated. "What's your real name?"

"Muhammad Ali is my real name."

"Look here, now," he fumed. "I'm not going to send you up to the operating room until you tell me your legal name."

"I don't care what you do," I told him. "My name is Muhammad Ali, and I'll die right here before I answer to another name." It seemed like hot knives were cutting into my nerves, sweat pouring from every part of my body.

He walked away to consult another doctor who was standing in the room. "He insists on me calling him Muhammad Ali. He won't say 'Cassius Clay.' What should I do?"

The other doctor rubbed his chin, thinking for a second. They conferred until an older doctor spotted me and came over.

"What's wrong?" he asked.

When I told him, he called a nurse over and rushed me up to the operating room.

I KEEP MOVING through the routine checks, waiting for the crucial one.

"Jump up and down ten times," a doctor tells me. I follow his instructions, and he places a cold stethoscope on my chest and listens for a while. "You're okay," he says, motioning me along.

Another doctor wraps a band around my arm, blows it up, checks my pulse, looks at his gauge and makes a note on his pad. "All right." He grins and feels my muscles. "Those are some shoulders you have there. Who you gonna fight when you come out of the service?"

I go on to the next booth. The medic checks my eyes and ears. He pulls up my eyelids and peers into my eyes with a small flashlight. "Unh, huh," he says, inspecting my nose and ears. "Nothing wrong here. You'll be able to hear the bugle on the battlefield," he jokes. I look at him without smiling and move on.

"Gimme your papers," the next doctor snaps as I move into his stall. He's fidgeting and he speaks with a strong Southern drawl. "Take off your shorts . . . all the way down." He adjusts his glasses and appraises me like I'm the bull that came into the herd. "Up closer!" he snorts, leaning down to examine my penis. Of all the doctors I face, he is the most hateful. "He's checking for venereal disease or a hernia," an orderly tells me. The doctor jabs his hand into my testicles. He feels around with his thumb until he finds the spot he's looking for, and tells me to cough. "Again," he says. "So you don't want to go and fight for your country?" His hand is tight on my testicles and I say nothing. A chill creeps over my whole body, and I think of the days when castrations and lynchings were common in the South.

"Okay, give us some urine," the orderly says. "If it's all right, you won't hear nothing. If something's wrong, we'll let you know." He giggles.

I give up the urine.

"You can get dressed and go back to the reception room for lunch now," he tells me. "You'll be called for induction after you get finished."

I walk back and pick up one of the white boxes stacked on the counter and find a seat. I don't feel hungry, but I eat everything except the ham sandwich. After lunch some of the other draftees are a little more relaxed. They want to talk to me.

"Do you really think you coulda whipped Joe Louis?"

"Louis? He couldn't stand my jab. Too slow," I say, jabbing, dancing and shuffling.

Then one stringy-haired kid from North Houston looks at me seriously. "It's an honor to get drafted at the same time as you, Muhammad. I mean . . . well . . . I hope we're in the same camp."

I understand what he means and I throw a jab his way.

One boy who says he was born in Philadelphia asks, "If you go to jail, who will be the new World Champion?"

I look at him deadpan. "They'll pick up some dodo and prop him up as The Champion. They'll just make some straw champ and put him out there, but the people won't accept that."

Two others come over and whisper, "Are you going?" . . . "How can I keep from going?" . . . "What do your lawyers think about it?" . . . "What does your religious leader say?" . . . "Will they give you time out to fight?"

Some I don't answer. Some sound like plants.

I remember one boy sitting in a corner with tears in his eyes. He's being forced to leave his wife and four children. He doesn't want to go, but he's afraid not to go. All he wants from me is my autograph.

A short, red-haired white boy comes over. "It's something to see you in person. I've read so much about you in the papers."

"Like what?" I ask.

"Well, about your religion. You hate white people, don't you?"

I shake my head. "Do I act like I hate anybody?"

"No." He says nothing more.

An officer walks into the room and there is an uneasy shuffle as everyone tries to pull himself together. My name is third.

Someone whispers, "This is it! This is it!"

"Go left, turn down the hall and go to Room 1B," the officer says. "You'll be inducted into the United States Armed Forces! You'll be given further instructions when you get there."

The induction room had been used as a judge's chambers in earlier days and the floor was still covered with its original gold carpeting. A blond green-eyed officer, a little younger than myself, stands behind an oakwood rostrum with American flags on both sides. I'd see his name in the next day's newspapers: Lt. S. Steven Dunkley.

All eyes except Dunkley's are focused on me.

Without looking up from his papers, he orders, "The first four will line up in front and the next four will line up behind them."

We take our places, and I'm third from the left in the second row. I know that I'll be called next to the last to take the step.

A senior officer goes over to the lieutenant and whispers something in his ear. He looks up automatically, and when his eyes meet mine, I feel a knot rise in my throat.

The officers and orderlies had been chatting and joking when I entered, but now everything is quiet. A number of people I can't account for have stepped into the room, some wearing civilian clothes. The young officer at the podium clears his throat.

"Attention!"

We all straighten up somewhat, but the four in front are standing particularly erect. My palms are beginning to sweat.

Dunkley glances quickly around the room before reading his prepared statement. He's probably read it hundreds of times before, but now there is special emphasis in his voice. He tries to make sure that each word is clear: "You are about to be inducted into the Armed Forces of the United States, in the Army, the Navy, the Air Force or the Marine Corps, as indicated by the service announced following your name when called. You will take one step forward as your name and service are called and such step will constitute your induction into the Armed Forces indicated."

He pauses, and even though everyone else is watching me, it seems like he and I are the only ones in the room.

"Jason Adams—Army."

The first man steps across the line.

"John Allen—Navy."

He, too, steps forward.

By the time the first row is finished, my throat is dry and my head is starting to feel a little light.

"Leroy Bradlow—Army."

Cold beads of perspiration break out across my forehead, and I feel lonely.

"Luis Cerrato—Army."

The eyes of the senior officer are fixed firmly on me. A jumble of thoughts rush to my mind. I'm back in Chicago, sitting in the elaborately furnished suite of an Illinois politician, overlooking Lake Michigan.

A promoter in his plaid shirt and white pants was explaining that the World Heavyweight Champion can be guaranteed a gross of at least eighteen million dollars over the next three years.

I stopped listening, walked over to the window and looked out across the water.

"On a clear day, it seems like you can see all across America. We can make you even more famous in a uniform than you've been without it. Why don't you sign up?"

"The Champ is thinking it over," said the promoter. He put his arm on my shoulder. "I know you're worried, Champ, but the Colonel will be here any minute. One stroke of the pen takes all the worry off your mind."

"And when the Colonel comes . . . you don't mind referring to him as Colonel X for the time being, do you?" the politician asked. "I see they use X in your religion, too. So you should understand. We don't exactly want to make a big thing out of this."

"The Champ knows all about that," the promoter assured him.

"The Colonel will make you a member of the Guard in less than an hour," the politician continued. "And you'll be free. Just like a thousand other baseball, football and basketball players, the biggest names in sports."

"You come to camp a few days a year, and drill a couple of hours a day. You'll be assigned to the Colonel, so you won't have to worry about fighting. You keep the title and all the shit about being drafted means nothing."

"You hardly ever pick up a gun. Just do a few exhibitions here and there. It's perfect."

"Only if there's a real emergency, say, like an invasion. Are you ready?"

I sat back down on the velvet couch, but didn't answer.

The politician seemed irritated. "It took weeks to arrange this. You got no choice. Take it and enjoy life or go back to Louisville until they get your cell ready."

"Aw, don't put it that way," the promoter intervened.

"It's time to put it straight," the politician snapped angrily. "Let's face it, Champ. Every Congressman I know is screaming to get your ass in jail. There's not a Governor or Senator in the fifty states who'll stand up and say a word in your behalf.

"I'm giving you a way out. Snatch the rug out from under them. All you have to do is sign this application."

I was getting madder and madder, but before I could answer, the door opened and a tall gray-haired man with a trim military build came in. He was courteous, but in a hurry. He went immediately to the desk. "The papers are ready. I suppose everything is agreeable?"

"The Champ wants a little more time to think it over," the promoter said weakly.

"He's ready now," the politician shot back, "or he wouldn't have come up here."

"Are you ready, Mr. Ali?" the Colonel asked.

I shook my head.

"But you agreed before you came!" The politician slammed his fist on the desk.

"I agreed to come and hear you out," I said. "I agreed to listen because friends of mine, people I trust and respect, said I should hear your proposal. But I don't believe in putting on a uniform to back this war, no way. I don't want people to believe I'm for it, even a little. It's against my religious principles."

"It's not against your religion," the politician wailed, throwing his hands in the air. "You won't be the first Black Muslim to join the Army. I know lots of followers of the Honorable Elijah Muhammad and some of them are in the service right now. You know it, too. Who are you to judge whether the war is right or not?"

The Colonel stood there with a hurt expression in his eyes, as though my refusal was a personal rejection. "Is that your final answer?"

I started to speak, but the promoter cut in. "It's not his final answer. When he gets down to Houston and they call for him to take that step forward, he'll understand. Cassius's got good sense. Keep the deal open, Colonel. This ain't final." He extended his hand, but the Colonel just looked at him coldly. "If this thing gets out . . ." He turned grimly to the politician and then to me. "Well, the next time I see you, it'll either be in Viet Nam or in jail!"

I'M SWEATING. I look around. It seems like everyone in the entire Induction Center has crept into the room. For months I've drilled myself for this moment, but I still feel nervous. I hope no one notices my shoulders tremble.

My mind races back to the day when I was sitting on a bench at my first Golden Gloves competition, waiting for my turn to go into the ring. I was amazed at how big Chicago was compared to Louisville, and the prospect of facing unknown opponents from strange places overwhelmed me. An old battered-faced ex-pug called Punch Drunk Don was sweeping the floor behind me, and he noticed my knees knocking. He leaned down over my left ear and whispered, "Son, always confront the thing you fear."

But what do I fear now? Is it what I'll lose if they take my title? If I'm jailed or barred from the ring? Is it fear of losing the good, plush, glamorous life of a World Champion?

Before I had boarded the plane, Herbert and I went over the issue facing me. I was still concerned about the views of the Honorable Elijah Muhammad on the subject and what his teachings meant.

"His teachings symbolically stand for life in this dark, ignorant and confused world," Herbert explained. "Now that your eyes have been opened to the light, it's expected you'll see your own way. It will be your choice and your direction, and yours alone. Whatever that choice is, you've got to accept the outcome of your own decision. All the credit and all the blame will be yours. I'll not be standing there with you physically, because my presence is closely associated with that of my father's, but I'll be with you in heart and spirit as always. This decision you make will determine the future of your life, and the decision is neither my father's nor mine. It's yours and yours alone. All I can say is, may Allah be with you, and when Allah is with you, no one can defeat you."

Why am I resisting? My religion, of course, but what the politician told me in Chicago is true. I won't be barred from the Nation of Islam if I go into the Army. "Who are you to judge?" he had asked. All my life I've watched White America do the judging. But who is to judge now? Who is to say if this step I'm about to be asked to take is right or wrong? If not me, who else? I recall the words of the Messenger: "If you feel what you have decided to do is right, then be a man and stand up for it . . . Declare the truth and die for it."

The lieutenant has finished with the man on my left and everybody seems to brace himself. The room is still and the lieutenant looks at me intently. He knows that his general, his mayor and everybody in the Houston Induction Center is waiting for this moment. He draws himself up straight and tall.

Something is happening to me. It's as if my blood is changing. I feel fear draining from my body and a rush of anger taking its place.

I hear the politician again: "Who are you to judge?" But who is this white man, no older than me, appointed by another white man, all the way down from the white man in the White House? Who is he to tell me to go to Asia, Africa or anywhere else in the world to fight people who never threw a rock at me or America? Who is this descendant of the slave masters to order a descendant of slaves to fight other people in their own country?

Now I am anxious for him to call me. "Hurry up!" I say to myself. I'm looking straight into his eyes. There's a ripple of movement as some of the people in the room edge closer in anticipation.

"Cassius Clay—Army!"

The room is silent. I stand straight, unmoving. Out of the corner of my eye I see one of the white boys nodding his head at me, and thin smiles flickering across the faces of some of the blacks. It's as if they are secretly happy to see someone stand up against the power that is ordering them away from their homes and families.

The lieutenant stares at me a long while, then lowers his eyes. One of the recruits snickers and he looks up abruptly, his face beet-red, and orders all the other draftees out of the room. They shuffle out quickly, leaving me standing alone.

He calls out again: "Cassius Clay! Will you please step forward and be inducted into the Armed Forces of the United States?"

All is still. He looks around helplessly. Finally, a senior officer with a notebook full of papers walks to the podium and confers with him a few seconds before coming over to me. He appears to be in his late forties. His hair is streaked with gray and he has a very dignified manner.

"Er, Mr. Clay . . ." he begins. Then, catching himself, "Or Mr. Ali, as you prefer to be called."

"Yes, sir?"

"Would you please follow me to my office? I would like to speak privately with you for a few minutes, if you don't mind."

It's more of an order than a request, but his voice is soft and he speaks politely. I follow him to a pale green room with pictures of Army generals on the walls. He motions me to a chair, but I prefer to stand. He pulls some papers from his notebook and suddenly drops his politeness, getting straight to the point.

"Perhaps you don't realize the gravity of the act you've just committed. Or maybe you do. But it is my duty to point out to you that if this should be your final decision, you will face criminal charges and your penalty could be five years in prison and ten thousand dollars fine. It's the same for you as it would be for any other offender in a similar case. I don't know what influenced you to act this way, but I am authorized to give you an opportunity to reconsider your position. Selective Service regulations require us to give you a second chance."

"Thank you, sir, but I don't need it."

"It is required"—he never stops talking or looking at his notes—"that you go back into the induction room, stand before the podium and receive the call again."

"Sir, why should I go back out there and waste everybody's time—"

"It's the procedure," he cuts in. "I can't tell you what to do or not to do, but we must follow procedure."

I follow him back into the room, and notice that new faces have appeared. More military personnel, a stenographer and a number of men in civilian clothes, who, I learn later, are FBI agents.

A private hands me a note. "This is from your lawyer."

It's a copy of a letter from U.S. Attorney Morton Sussman.

> I am authorized to advise you that we are willing to enter into an agreement. If you will submit your client for induction, we will be willing to keep him here in the Houston area until all of your civil remedies are exhausted. Otherwise, he will be under criminal indictment. . . .

I crumple it up and stuff it into my pocket. One of the men in civilian clothes who has been watching me now turns and walks out the door. The green-eyed officer is still standing behind the rostrum, ready to read the induction statement. This time I'm closer to him. He's less than an arm's-reach away. I can see drops of sweat on his forehead.

"Mr. Cassius Clay," he begins again, "you will please step forward and be inducted into the United States Army."

Again I don't move.

"Cassius Clay—Army," he repeats. He stands in silence, as though he expects me to make a last-minute change. Finally, with hands shaking, he gives me a form to fill out. "Would you please sign this statement and give your reasons for refusing induction?" His voice is trembling.

I sign quickly and walk out into the hallway. The captain who originally ordered me to the room comes over. "Mr. Clay," he says with a tone of respect that surprises me, "I'll escort you downstairs."

When we reach the bottom of the steps, the television cameramen who had been held up by the guards focus their lights on us, while a platoon of military police scuffle to keep them behind a rope that blocks the end of the corridor.

"Muhammad," a reporter yells, "did you take the step? Are you in the Army?"

"Can we just have a minute, Champ?" another shouts. "What did you do? Can you just tell us yes or no?"

I keep walking with the captain, who leads me to a room where my lawyers are waiting. "You are free to go now," he tells us. "You will be contacted later by the United States Attorney's office."

I step outside and a huge crowd of press people rush toward me, pushing and shoving each other and snapping away at me with their cameras. Writers from two French newspapers and one from London throw me a barrage of questions, but I feel too full to say anything. Covington gives them copies of a statement I wrote for them before I left Chicago. In it I cite my ministry and my personal convictions as reasons for refusing to take the step, adding that "I strongly object to the fact that so many newspapers have given the American public and the world the impression that I have only two alternatives in taking this stand—either I go to jail or go into the Army. There is another alternative, and that is justice."

By the time I get to the bottom of the front steps, the news breaks. Everyone is shouting and cheering. Some girls from Texas Southern run over to me, crying, "We're glad you didn't go!" A black boy standing next to H. Rap Brown shouts out, "You don't go, so I won't go!"

I feel a sense of relief and freedom. For the first time in weeks I start to relax. I remember the words of the reporter at the hotel: "How will you act?" Now it's over, and I've come through it. I feel better than when I beat the eight-to-ten odds and won the World Heavyweight Title from Liston.

Eskridge pushes me to a cab waiting at the corner.

"You headin' for jail. You headin' straight for jail." I turn and an old white woman is standing behind me, waving a miniature American flag. "You goin' straight to jail. You ain't no champ no more. You ain't never gonna be champ no more. You get down on your knees and beg forgiveness from God!" she shouts in a raspy tone.

I start to answer her, but Covington pulls me inside the cab.

She comes over to my window. "My son's in Viet Nam, and you no better'n he is. He's there fightin' and you here safe. I hope you rot in jail. I hope they throw away the key."

The judge who later hears my case reflects the same sentiment. I receive a maximum sentence of five years in prison and ten thousand dollars fine. The prosecuting attorney argues, "Judge, we cannot let this man get loose, because if he gets by, all black people will want to be Muslims and get out for the same reasons."

Four years later in June of 1970, the Supreme Court unanimously reverses that decision, 8–0, but now this is the biggest victory of my life. I've won something that's worth whatever price I have to pay. It gives me a good feeling to look at the crowd as we pull off. Seeing people smiling makes me feel that I've spoken for them as well as myself. Deep down, they didn't want the World Heavyweight Champion to give in, and in the days ahead their strength and spirit will keep me going. Even when it looks like I'll go to jail and never fight again.

"They can take away the television cameras, the bright lights, the money, and ban you from the ring," an old man tells me when I get back to Chicago, "but they can't destroy your victory. You have taken a stand for the world and now you are the people's champion."

Bertrand Russell writes to assure me: "The air will change. I sense it."

The World Boxing Authority doesn't take nearly as long as the Government to pass judgment on me. As soon as I get back to my hotel room, I hear a radio announcement that the WBA has stripped me of my title again and that they will hold an elimination tournament to determine my successor. The WBA took action against me back in 1965. And on April 28, 1967, the New York Boxing Commission is the first to take my license. This time it will take me more than seven years to get it back.

In the morning the hotel lobby is crowded with people who have come to see me off. When I get to the airport, passengers break from the ticket counters and come over to shake my hand. A lean white Southerner comes up as I'm about to board my flight. He has three little boys and he wants them to meet me.

"I'm from Mississippi," he says, pushing the boys forward for an autograph, "and I like a man who speaks his piece. I'll tell you frankly, I don't know many Negroes. I've never liked Negroes. I'm gonna tell you right now I voted for Eastland, and go along with Maddox, but I admire you. I want my sons to be just like you when they get big."

I look surprised, and he quickly corrects himself.

"Oh, I don't believe in your religion. But whether they be in the Klan, or Baptists, or Catholics, or Republicans, I want them to stand up for what they believe in, like you do."

I give his children autographs and shake their hands, but I don't take his hand when he holds it out. I don't believe in shaking the hand of an opponent until I've defeated him.

When I fly out of Houston, I'm flying into an exile that will eat up what boxing experts regard as "the best years of a fighter's life." What savings I have will soon be gone and still there will be the expenses of maintaining a family and paying alimony, and the huge expense of carrying my case up to the Supreme Court.

Through it all, Herbert and I work closer together than ever, with nearly all of his time going into finding new ways for me to bring in revenue and supervising my court fight. Whenever a promoter sees the possibility of a fight for me, I cooperate but for some strange reason at the last minute the deals fall apart. I learn later that every move I make is monitored by the FBI, including phone calls—a practice which causes my lawyers to seek to have my case thrown out because of the illegal wiretap, but this fails.

In some ways, most of my exile years turn out as Chicago *Sun-Times* columnist Bill Gleason summed up: "In 1967 and beyond, through the days of Lyndon B. Johnson and into the early days of the Nixon Administration, the white race finally had a cause they could vindicate as just. Here was an avowed Black racist who said he would not fight in the war for reasons of his own. The crowd roared for the blood of Ali."

"There is an unanimity of feeling in White America that he should go to prison," Robert Marcus of the Chicago *Tribune* said. And I was "intolerable to a large segment of White America," according to Steve Caddy of the New York *Times*.

But I remember what happened a few days after I had come out and stood on the Federal steps in Houston. Mrs. Florence Beaumont, a Texas housewife who had supported my stand against the draft, died after she set her gasoline-soaked body aflame on the steps of the Federal Building in La Puente, California, in imitation of the immolation of a nun in Saigon who protested the war. Her husband, George, wrote me: "Florence and I often talked about you. Your sacrifice and dedication inspired her. She wanted to follow you in spirit."

I was shocked and moved; I had never seen myself as influencing anyone, I had only acted to uphold my own convictions.

But letters from all over the world are pouring into *Muhammad Speaks*, where I share an office with Herbert. One morning I receive a telegram from Jim Brown, the football hero of the Cleveland Browns, asking me to meet with a group of prominent black athletes who want to question me on my draft stand. Of all the pressure on me to conform, none has yet come from black people, who have mostly been opposed to my going to Viet Nam. The press reports that the black athletes have been called to persuade me to "support the government."

I fly into Cleveland wondering why a group of black athletes, who have never assembled for anything other than sports, want to see me. Outside the place where we are to meet, thousands of people who'd heard I was coming mill around, shouting, "Muhammad Ali is free!" ... "Muhammad Ali is free!" ... "Don't go!" and trying to push their way into the building.

Inside are some of the leading athletes of the country, including Kareem Abdul Jabbar, then Lew Alcindor of UCLA; Bill Russell, then player coach of the Boston Celtics; Sid Williams and Walter Beach of the Cleveland Browns; Curtis McClinton of the Kansas City Chiefs; Bobby Mitchell and Jim Shorter of the Washington Redskins; Willie Davis of the Green Bay Packers; Gale Sayers of the Chicago Bears. But very few have anything to say. I talk and they listen. And when it's over, most of them seem confused as to why they're there in the first place. Brown announces to the press that they have finally found me "sincere in my beliefs."

My main livelihood is coming from my appearances at colleges, black and white, and in a way it's worth being banned from boxing; otherwise, I would not have met some of the most attractive, alert and intelligent groups I have been associated with. On every campus, support for me is high. When I visit one college where the list of "undesirable subversives," as compiled by the House Un-American Activities Committee, is tacked on the bulletin board, a student has underlined my name and tells me proudly, "See, you're number one on the list." Even though I'm on top because my name starts with "A," the students make me feel good about it.

But the questions keep coming up: Am I really sincere about standing up to jail? Will I back down when all my appeals are over and lost? Will I really serve the jail term?

Even in exile I'm surrounded by people. I've never spent a night in jail. Could I accept the confinement? It is this thinking that causes me to make a move to test myself, even in a small way. The chance comes when a motorcycle policeman follows me down a Miami street and pulls me over to the side.

"Are you Muhammad Ali?"

"Yes, sir. I am, sir."

"There's a warrant out for your arrest." He explains that they've been looking for me for an old traffic violation for a year. "Follow me," he says.

And I follow him into what will eventually turn out to be a 10-day sentence in the Miami Dade County Jail. It comes two weeks before my Champburger restaurants are to open in Miami, a business venture Herbert has brought in so that I could earn revenue while being banned.

Accompanied by Chauncey Eskridge, I walk in to surrender myself to the county jail. They're surprised to see me. I'm fingerprinted and given some prison clothes, and before I'm assigned to my cell a short red-faced official says, "Since you gave yourself up on your own, we won't treat you like a common criminal. We'll let you choose your own work detail. Either laundry, the yard, the shop or the cafeteria."

I choose the cafeteria because an old convict in Chicago once told me it's the best place for a new prisoner, and I follow the guard to my cell. It's the size of four ordinary bedrooms, except there's no furniture —just steel bunks covered with plastic mattresses and flimsy sheets and old army blankets. In the corner, a face bowl and toilet. When I walk in, the door slams behind me and locks. I put my hands on the bars, look down the hall. The strangest feeling comes over me. I remind myself it's only for a few days.

"It's Muhammad Ali, The Champ! Hey!" Inmates in my own cell and the ones across the way begin jumping off their bunks, shouting, "Champ, what you doing here? Muhammad Ali, welcome home!" My cellmates huddle around me, ask me about the fights I had, the fights I hope to have. "I bet if you were Jack Dempsey or Gene Fullmer or Rocky Marciano," one prisoner says, "they'd let you off for that little rap." Another one cries, "If he wasn't black, he wouldn't be here!" I never tell them exactly why I've come.

When the lights go out, I lie on my bed, but I can't sleep. I think half the night about the people on the outside, about places I've been, but what I miss most is my wife and my daughter Maryum. I think of what would happen to them if my appeal is lost and I'm forced to live this way five years. The thought gnaws on me until I drift off.

I wake up with a guard banging his stick across the bars: "Rise and shine! Report for work!" He sees I'm a newcomer and explains, "Pick up your uniform in the laundry and report for work in the kitchen."

I go to the kitchen and do what I'm told. One of the cooks, a tall, thin black prisoner in his mid-thirties, comes up and welcomes me in Arabic. When I recognize his greeting, he apologizes and says, "I'm not a Muslim, but I studied a lot about it. A lot of prisoners joined since they been here. Can you take this for five years, brother?"

"If I have to," I tell him.

He shakes his head. "But you don't have to. That's the hard part, you don't have to. Just by changing your mind, you can be out from under." He winks.

A dishwasher approaches me and says, "You get a taste of this for five years and I bet you'll love to go to the Army, the Army'll seem like heaven. I'll trade the Army any day for jail."

In the corner a slim man in his forties who's been staring at me finally catches my eye and nods his head. "How you doing?" he asks in a soft, intimate tone.

"Okay, okay," I tell him, and go back to my work.

Ten minutes later I look up and he's still staring at me. "Are you married?" he asks. I tell him I am. "I bet you really miss your wife," he says, moving closer, "especially at nights. You can come to my cell awhile and talk." When I frown, he adds hastily, "No one is going to overpower the World Heavyweight Champion." He laughs softly. "Just when you're lonesome, come on up to my cell, that's all." But something about the coldness of my look makes him back away, and he shrugs his shoulders, gives up.

Before I finish work, the man who'd given me the Muslim greeting nudges me: "You may as well take advantage of being in the kitchen. This is how you do when the guards aren't watching." He picks out four chicken legs, wraps them in a napkin, stuffs them in my pocket so they don't bulge. "Take 'em back to your cell, hide 'em under your pillow," he says. "Just something to tide us over till the next morning. See you later."

After dinner we sit in our cells and talk. There's a debate going on over the radio about whether Dade Jail should allow all prisoners a Christmas amnesty. "Everyone should get out for Christmas except that draft-dodger," one woman is telling the moderator. "The only way they should let him out is send him to Viet Nam." "Muslims don't celebrate Christmas," a man calls in. "Keep him there!" It's known all over Miami that I'm one of the prisoners.

I remember on the sixth day a new guard coming into the cafeteria, pulling us over to the side. "We need somebody to take food to the men on the second tier," he says, "and to the ones on 'Death Row.'" Then, not waiting for volunteers, he looks over and points: "You come here, and you and you." He gives me an alternative. Second tier or "Death Row"?

"'Death Row,'" I say.

He loads me up with a trayful of food, points to a special group of cell blocks. These are the safety cells, what the prisoners call "Death Row." I follow his directions and come to cell blocks where the odor of urine and feces is so strong I want to hold my nose. I bend down and push the food through an opening at the bottom of the door. The cells are small, dirty. Worse than cages for animals and there are no windows. I try to speak to the prisoners. Most look weak and listless, their skin faded and washed out. Tears come to my eyes.

The first man recogizes me: "Well, I'll be goddamned! They got the World Heavyweight Champion serving me dinner. The world must be ready to come to an end." He knocks on the cell and arouses the next Death Row prisoner. "It's The Champ, Muhammad Ali. He's the waiter here."

"Jesus Christ, what the hell you laughing about?" the prisoner in the next cell growls. "What's so funny?"

" 'Cause I'm not dead yet," he says. "The only ones that can't find something funny in the world is the dead. That right, Muhammad?"

Other Death Row prisoners begin to call out: "Hey, Champ!" . . . "Come this way, Champ!"

I rush down and come up again and again bringing more food. An old man who's been on "Death Row" two and a half years awaiting trial says, "If I ever get out, I want a ticket to your next fight with Frazier. You think you can whip Frazier?"

I tell him I will.

"I made a mistake," he says, "and I'm paying for it. I killed a man by accident but if the State kills me it won't be an accident. It'll be deliberate murder."

He tells me he killed the man out of frustration, the same feeling everybody gets, and somehow this makes him more human, just like anyone else. I promise him if he ever gets out I'll whip Frazier for him.

In the morning the guard is banging on the bars: "The judge has declared a Christmas amnesty! A Christmas amnesty!" A yell and a roar goes up through the cell blocks. Some begin chanting Christmas carols.

"Does it cover me?" I ask.

He looks down the sheet and finally grins. "You on it too, Champ. The judge had a hard time getting you off. Threats on his life, threats against his family because they wanted you to stay in jail."

He opens my cell, takes me to a room where the little red-faced man pulls out a cashbox and hands me two dollar bills. "You're free now," the man says. I'm halfway down the hall and out of the building when a prisoner rushes up: "You dropped your money." I tell him to keep it.

I never knew the smell of fresh air was so good. I start walking and somehow I don't want to stop. I look at the faces of people on the streets and I can't get enough of seeing them. I look at the cars passing by, the grass, the trees, the birds. I see children and I hear their voices come up to me: "Hey! Champ!" . . . "That's Muhammad Ali." They run over, ask for autographs, and I sign. When I get to the hotel, I strip down and lay on the bed. I prop my head up on a pillow for the first time in a week. I want to sleep.

I feel as though I've been gone a long time. The phone rings. It's a lawyer I had known in Philadelphia and who has followed my case. "The way is still open," he says. "Champ, it's still open for you to make an agreement."

I say, *"No,"* and I hear myself repeating in my mind what I had said at a special hearing of my case in court:

"I know you would give me no trouble at all if I was the kind of conscientious objector who can go into the armed services and do boxing exhibitions on Army posts or in Viet Nam or travel the country at the expense of the Government, live an easy life and be guaranteed that I won't have to get out in the mud and fight and shoot. But if I could do this, I wouldn't have raised all this stir in court and on the streets. I wouldn't have given up the millions I know I will have to give up by not going to Viet Nam.

"I know my image with the American public is completely ruined because of the stand I take. If I could do otherwise I wouldn't even jeopardize my life by walking in the streets of America, especially in the South with no bodyguard.

"I do it only because I mean it. I will not participate in this war."

GOD BLESS THE CHILD

The clock radio woke me with Billie Holiday singing "God Bless the Child That's Got His Own." I rolled over on my back, thinking what a coincidence—some kind of omen. Here I have an appointment today to see Sonji, the only woman in the world that sings that song like Billie. My former wife, Sonji. I hadn't seen her since our day in divorce court four years ago, when we looked at each other like two angry strangers whose cars had collided in a freak accident. But something of her must have stayed with me, and I suppose something of me had to be still with her.

There was a heavy sleetlike rain falling over Lake Michigan as I walked the fourteen miles to her apartment across from the South Shore Country Club. I wanted to keep my muscles limbered up. I'd been in exile now for more than three years, and was still looking for that day when maybe I would be allowed to go back into the ring. Most of what I earned now came from the college lectures or the sale of some of the things I'd bought—like my first house in South Shore—with those "millions" the newspapers said I made during those thirty-nine professional fights. Actually, I had taken over a house on the South Side which Herbert had bought and lavishly furnished. With my manager as best man, Belinda and I were married in that house, and any income tha. came to me during my exile, and which made it possible for me to survive, originated from enterprises conceived by Herbert.

Sonji had agreed that we could meet and go over some of the little odds and ends that still tied us. And what to do about the remainder of the $150,000 alimony on which I could no longer afford to make payments. I suppose there were some good aspects to being barred from the ring. It had already made me more reflective and curious about the past. Since the Olympics in 1960, the whirling pace at which I'd lived had eased down, especially after I stood at the Houston Induction Center and refused to take the "one step forward." Now I was awaiting court verdicts which most prophets said would certainly send me to jail for five years. For that I was ready every waking morning. But was I ready to hear about my life from the woman who had first lived it with me?

In spite of all the charges and countercharges hurled at each other through the newspapers, she was still the first woman I had loved and who had put my religious faith and creed to the final test. And not since our divorce had I sat down with her to talk face to face. What kind of life did we have? What had really happened between us? Who had been right, who was wrong? What had living with me been like for her? How much had gone unsaid? Maybe she could say now what she had never said before . . . maybe I could listen as I had never done. Maybe I could tell the truth, too. I'll tell her that her side of the story will go in my autobiography exactly as she sees it.

When I got off the elevator my heart was pounding as though I was about to enter the ring against some unpredictable opponent. But when she opened the door her eyes were bright, and she had the quickest, friendliest smile.

After we'd gone over all the odds and ends, I asked her if we could talk about our life together. We sat down near a window overlooking the lake.

"Look," I said, "we'll start at the point where we first met. And we'll find out what each of us expected out of love, and let the chips fall where they may."

She thought for a while, then went and got a pack of cigarettes (a habit she'd broken when we first met). She had on a flaming-red corduroy leotard, and her small body had a way of surprising you when you looked at the hips. Everything in perfect proportion. If she'd gained a pound, I couldn't tell.

"Well," I said, getting comfortable, "as I see it, this is the way our relationship started . . . After my first trip to Africa, after I came back to Chicago, I was staying at Roberts Motel on 67th and South Park. My room was 101—and the time was about 7:30 P.M. when Herbert Muhammad called me from a restaurant nearby. He said there was a young woman who wanted to meet me, and that he would bring her over in about ten minutes. Sure enough, in ten minutes he knocked on my door, but you weren't with him. I said, 'Where's the girl you wanted me to meet?' He said, 'Right across the street, waiting.' So I put on my shoes and went across the street to the restaurant. There were about twenty-nine or thirty people there, but I knew you the minute I saw you. Up until that moment, you were the prettiest girl I ever saw. Your big, pretty black eyes had a shine in them. Your hair was cut short. A beautiful coffee-brown complexion. About five feet three and a half inches tall. About a hundred and twenty-five pounds—"

"I didn't weigh that much."

I ignored her interruptions and went on, "Usually that's too small for me, I'm six-three and I like tall, healthy women, but there was something about you that made me overlook all of that. You remember when Herbert introduced you to me as Sonji Roi? He said you were a friend of Dixon the tailor. He told you my name was Muhammad Ali, and I said, 'Let's have some ice cream.' "

"You're not telling it exactly right."

"What ain't right?"

"Because . . . that's not exactly the way it went."

"All right, you tell it. Start all over. How did we meet?"

"Well . . ." she paused to think. "You were in the motel room, all right enough. But Herbert did bring me there to introduce me. Soon as you saw me, you jumped up and you said, 'I swear to God, Herbert, you know what I was doing? I was laying across the bed praying to Allah for a wife, and here she comes through the door. Here she comes with the Messenger's son, so she's gotta be the one.' That's exactly what you said. And you came over to me and said, 'Girl, will you marry me?' "

"Just that quick? I said it that quick?"

"Just that quick."

"And then what did we do? Go ahead—it's better for you to tell it, you remember the little details."

"You call a marriage proposal a little detail? Anyway, then you said, 'Wait a minute, let me put on some clothes and let's go across the street and have some ice cream.' I said, 'All right, but I can't stay too long.' I was on my way to prepare for a picnic."

"That's right. The next day was July fourth."

"And you started telling me about the Fourth of July, not knowing that I had promised to take my son to a picnic that day."

"I remember—I made you cancel it."

"Yes. You said, 'What they gonna serve at the picnic? Hog?' You started right in attacking the barbecue, telling me how bad it was for my health, and turned my stomach against my date. That's what made me say, 'Well, maybe I won't go.' And when I got ready to light a cigarette, you grabbed the package. You told me if I squeezed all the nicotine out of the cigarettes into a glass and drank it, I would die instantly, and could I imagine what I'm doing to myself over a period of time? That's why I quit smoking that same day. And then we went across the street to that little restaurant. Drank tea. And then you started telling me more about the cigarettes and the pork, and . . . Don't you remember?"

"Yeah, now I remember. Hold it now . . . and then . . . Herbert had to leave. He said, 'Ali, could you step over here with me for a minute?' And we excused ourselves from you. Went in the washroom. He told me you had been waiting to meet me ever since you saw my picture on the cover of *Sports Illustrated*. The picture where I was in England with the London Bridge or the Tower in the background. Right?"

"Uh-huh."

"And you said you heard I always called myself 'The Greatest,' and you saw yourself as the greatest. So Herbert said, 'Watch out for her.' I told him you were the kind I would like to marry. His eyes got big and he looked at me and he said, 'Man, please, please, whatever you do, don't marry her! Don't even dream of marrying her. It will not work. She's not your type. Too hip. Too fast. I only brought her here to meet you. Not marry. Just treat her like a lady. Have a nice time, but don't think serious.' I told him okay, but in my heart I had decided to marry you as quick as possible. From the first sight I had decided to marry you. So after he left you said, 'I'm hungry. Are you?' I wasn't hungry, but I said, 'Yes, I'm a little hungry, too.' You said, 'I know a nice Chinese restaurant . . . let's go there.' I said come on, and we went. This was a pretty warm night. I can see you now. You had on a pair of tight blue jeans with a red-striped, long-sleeved sweater jacket. And when you got up I noticed that you had a beautiful little shape and a slight twist in your hips when you walked past me. I was more convinced that I was going to marry you."

"I couldn't believe it. That you really felt like that. It didn't seem possible."

"Remember? We went to the parking lot across the street and got my car. A long black limousine. You liked it, 'cause you said, 'Oh, this is pretty.' And I said, 'Thank you.' We went to the little Chinese restaurant and you ordered chop suey. I had a roast beef sandwich. And you asked me, 'Do you like chop suey?' I told you yeah, but I didn't want any because I was on a diet, getting ready for my second Sonny Liston fight. And you said, 'Okay. I understand.' But the reason I didn't eat the chop suey is because I'd heard they mix it with pork. We finished eating about eleven and left the restaurant. I was thinking to myself, Where are we going now? I want her to go with me to my motel ... So I said, 'I'm expecting a phone call at twelve o'clock.' That was a lie, but I wanted to be alone with you for a while. I was surprised but glad when you said, 'If the call isn't that important, you may as well come see my apartment.' After I heard that, the call was no longer important. Isn't that the way it went?"

"Well, okay, but not quite ... When we finished eating, we were with the chauffeur in the limousine and so you had him drive us up and down, all around the city, and then, when he brought us back to the hotel for your so-called phone call, you told him you didn't need him any more and you sent him home and we left the limousine and got in the red Cadillac."

"Oh, yeah."

"And rode around and played records."

"Right. Right."

"And then that's when you took me by to cancel my date."

"You canceled your date, and then we rode around in the red Cadillac before going to your apartment. You lived at 71st and Cregier, on the South Side. A big half-block-long building and about a half-block wide. You lived on the third floor. No elevators, so we had to walk up. When I went in, I noticed it was real neat and clean. The walls were snow-white. Red carpet all over the floors. Not much furniture, though."

"My furniture hadn't come yet."

"Not having furniture ain't no big thing."

"Just tell it straight. Don't make me look like I didn't have anything ... like I was hard up and barely scraping by. Don't ..."

"Just wait, now, and let me finish. I remember you told me you had ordered special-built furniture. Anyway, the carpet was thick and red and soft. You had one bedroom, a big living room and a nice kitchenette. I peeked in the bedroom, and was it big. Plush. With a wide king-size bed and a black Chinese dresser. I was staring at the dresser because I'd never seen so much face cream, cologne, powder, perfume ... and that's when you disappeared in the bathroom. You stuck your head out and said, 'Have a seat.' I said, 'Where?' There were no chairs, so I guess you meant for me to sit on the bed or floor. I took the bed. You spent such a long time in the bathroom, I said to myself, 'What in the world could she be doing in there?' Then out you came. Wow. You were ready. You really startled me."

"Do you have to go into all that?"

"I can see you now. You came out in a negligee. A red see-through negligee. It was about twelve-thirty. Then you turned on some soft music. We lay there on the bed and we talked for about an hour and you talked me into staying all night. So I got comfortable and I didn't leave your apartment until about eight the next morning."

"That was years ago. Why you still pop your fingers? You told me then, though, that you never wanted me to leave you. And when we awoke you took me straight to your motel and checked me into the room right next to you, Room 102. You said we would never be apart, never no more."

"And from then on I kept my word. That afternoon I ordered some lunch and laid around the room watching TV. Thinking about you."

"That was the afternoon you came over to my room and washed my hair."

"Me? I washed your hair?"

"Right. It was a holiday. Everybody was out picnicking and we were in love. The way you touched my head, I never thought a prize-fighter could have such a tender touch. Why'd you do it?"

"Well, I did notice beautiful black hair under your wig that hadn't been combed for a while. You were scratching it, so I said, 'Let me wash out the dandruff.' So I washed your hair and everything. And about six o'clock that evening I told you I wanted you to go with me to Louisville to meet my mama and daddy."

"I still couldn't believe it. All so sudden . . . so sudden."

"I told you we'd get married in a couple of weeks, and until then I was making you my wife, in my own way. I didn't see why I needed no white man to give me permission. So I just said, 'You are my wife.' And after about five or six days there in Chicago, we went to meet some of my kinpeople."

"But that Sunday you told me you wanted me to go to the Temple. It was my first time to go inside a mosque of the Nation of Islam. You had to go ahead of me 'cause you had to go to the Messenger's house first. So you had one of the Messenger's grandsons take me to the Temple."

"Yeah, I remember."

"I was worried over what to wear. I had a big pink hat on and a pink dress. I didn't know I was supposed to wear a scarf, but I got one from somewhere."

"You were supposed to pay attention to the sermon, not your clothes."

"And I met you afterwards and you wanted to leave town right away, but I had a job in the *Muhammad Speaks* newspaper office and you had to wait till I quit."

"Yeah, because you were two months back in rent."

"I was not!"

"Being behind in rent, that ain't no shame."

"Not on that apartment! I owed a girl friend some money, that was all."

"Well, you told me the rent on that apartment was behind."

"I didn't tell you that!"

"So I said let's pay up the rent. I said, 'Let's pay the rent up because we're going to leave.' And I paid the last rent."

"I wasn't behind, so don't you say that now, because I wasn't. I didn't . . . the only thing was I owed that girl some money and I gave it to her."

"Go ahead, tell the story. Don't get upset."

"The rest of the day you were explaining to me about how you couldn't go into bars and taverns and shows and telling me about different things you couldn't do. I didn't mind, I didn't have to do them. So we just stayed together. Mostly outdoors. And then we'd go back to the room and watch TV or something, and that Monday you came up to the newspaper office and wanted to find out who was going to pay me, 'cause I wanted to leave that day. What day was that?"

"About July the tenth, wasn't it?"

"Maybe. And I took our clothes I had in the cleaner's and put them in the car."

"We put them all in the trunk of the limousine."

"And that's when we headed out to Louisville."

"Just me and you . . ."

"And Big Jim, your chauffeur. The one who used to drive for the singer Lloyd Price."

"No. Big Jim had left me, remember? About July fifth I had three thousand dollars cash I had carried in my trunk, and when I woke up the next morning Big Jim was gone and the three thousand in the trunk was gone and we haven't heard of Big Jim up till today. No, someone else was with us . . . Howard Bingham! The photographer. He rode with us when I took you home to your apartment. Then Bingham caught a jet back to Los Angeles and we took the highway to Louisville. We got there that night and I took you by my house to meet my mother and father. I said, 'Here's the one who's going to be my wife.' Then my mother threw her arms around you. She took right to you."

"So did your father. They were nice. And she let me stay in her little room with the canopy bed."

"Yeah, you stayed in my mother's room. I felt wonderful all day."

"We fried chicken. And we went down in the basement and looked at all your scrapbooks. And the next morning we had to get out, on our way into Florida."

"We drove from Louisville to Miami, and I checked you in at the Hampton House Motel and went back to the house that the Louisville Sponsoring Group had leased for me during my training periods. And every day I would go over to the Hampton House. The people in Florida didn't know I had made up my mind that I was gonna marry. I wanted to keep everything quiet until we really got married according to the white man's law. So each day I came to see you, and you would go to a few of the Temple meetings in disguise, like you didn't know me, just to hear the Messenger's teachings. But the way you dressed and talked about going out at night I could see the teaching wasn't getting to you. And then I told you, 'You're gonna have to be my wife. Now, you know you're gonna have to wear long dresses, at least cover up your knees. And you're gonna have to quit using make-up, quit drinking and quit dancing and quit all your party and fun life. You're gonna have to quit.' You said, 'Well, I can learn to do it. But it's gonna take time.' Anyway, we stayed in Florida for a couple of weeks and then the Nation of Islam had a conference in Los Angeles. I had told Sam Saxon, the Muslim Captain in Miami, that I had actually married you, and he believed it. He said, 'But she's not a Muslim.' I said, 'She's gonna join.' He said, 'Well, you're all right if she's gonna join. Why don't you take her to hear the Messenger in Los Angeles.' So around four days before the conference, Sam Saxon and myself and you got in the car and left Miami and drove all the way to Los Angeles. We would check in the motels as Mr. and Mrs., and when we got to the conference they put you together with the other Muslim sisters. I introduced you as my wife and you had your scarf over your head. You had on a nice long yellow dress that day, remember?"

"Yes, you wanted me to wear a long dress."

"Well, it wasn't all that long, but at least it did reach a little below your knees."

"Had a hood on it."

"You looked like an angel. I was so proud of you. You went to the conference and did everything the sisters did. And after that we went back to the motel, drove around the city a little and headed back for Chicago."

"Then things started to get bad."

"Yeah, the arguments started. What kind of argument did we get into?"

"About religion."

"No, we got to arguing about . . . the skirt you put on after the conference. Why'd you go right back and put on one of your mini-skirts? I kept telling you, 'You can't be walking around in these short skirts. They should be down to your ankles.' "

"I didn't want to look like Old Mother Hubbard."

"But you could have at least wore them below your knees! You said, 'I just can't see that yet, and I'm just not gonna do it all of a sudden.' You remember saying that?"

"Something like that."

"We got to fighting, and I said, 'If you're gonna be my wife and be a Muslim, and you gonna be one, you can't be walking around in no short dresses! The wives of the other brothers will be pointing out that if Muhammad Ali's wife don't wear them, why should we?' And you said, 'Go to hell. Then I won't marry you. I ain't gonna wear them until I want to do it in my heart.' And by the time we got to Chicago we were so hot and angry, you sat in the back seat and left me in the front. We quit speaking and I took you to the house and let you out and I went back to my motel. But then I started thinking and thinking. I said, 'Well, after all, I love her and I got a lot of people thinking I'm married now.' It had been written up in the press that I was with my wife."

"They started taking our picture at the conference as man and wife."

"Yeah, people were saying, 'I saw him with his wife, but where were they married?' I didn't want to tell them 'Nowhere,' so I just said, 'I'm married.' But I thought to myself, I got it out now that I'm married, and in my heart I was and so were you. I'm gonna give her time. I know she loves me and I love her. Why should I fall out with her right now? It took a while to convert me. She can't see the Truth overnight. Neither could I. So I went back to the house. You were cleaning the place, washing woodwork. You always keep things clean. Always cleaning something. I said we'll go up to Indiana and get married. The Liston fight was coming up. We got married before the second Liston fight. Then I went into training. That's why we had to go to Florida."

"Now I look back on it, most of our married life was spent while you were training for Liston. What time did we have alone? Not even a honeymoon, 'cause you had to go right into training. So we went back to Florida and to the house the Louisville Group had for you. But at least I started cooking for you, 'cause you used to have the sisters cook for you and I wanted to change that. Then we flew up to Boston for the fight."

"We flew the first time, but the second time I took the bus. The red bus with Bundini and all the press writers. Remember, we took my big red bus up to Chicopee? Before that, well, we just lived like everybody else. You know, just get up, you'd cook breakfast, I'd go running. At first you didn't like it because I had you at the Hampton House at the beginning of that training . . ."

"You didn't want the fighters to even look at me. You scared Chris

Dundee to death 'cause he put his hand on my shoulder in a friendly gesture."

"A fighter don't like to have his woman always around the gym. I kept all the men at the cabin and I would go over to see you during the day. You had to be by yourself and you didn't go for that. It was hard for me to stay around you and stay in shape. You know I tried it a few nights. You stayed in the bedroom and I stayed in the living room, but in a couple of nights I would find myself sneaking over to your room. I had a tough time getting in shape. Isolation was too much for you. I'll say this, though, you're a natural trooper. We married August 14, 1964. So from the time we got married, it was eleven months to the next fight. The only interruption was the hernia."

"Well, it may have hurt the fight, but it helped us get in a few weeks of normal married life."

"Yeah, we got back to your apartment and fixed it up with the new furniture."

"That was nice."

"It was the first time I had real 'married life.' You cooked breakfast. I lounged around the house. The Messenger had placed Herbert in charge of developing and guiding *Muhammad Speaks*, and I'd run out to the newspaper office every day to confer with him. Other times I'd go somewhere or do something, then come home and watch TV or watch you cook. Or we might go out somewhere. Did we ever have any trouble? Like you getting on me 'cause I was always going out?"

"No, 'cause you never went anywhere, not without me. I don't know about the wife you got now, but you always wanted me to go with you. It wasn't that I insisted, you just wanted me. And I didn't have any trouble with all those fans and admirers swarming all over you. I would stand back and just let them go after you. And you would reach back and pull me up and say, 'This is my wife, y'all.' And that's how it went until the fire."

"That was a strange fire. Real strange."

"On a Sunday night, remember? We were out at a motel having dinner."

"I believe to this day somebody started it on purpose."

"I told you that."

"Didn't a thing in the other apartments burn bad. Just ours, and we on the second floor. This one started with us—in the middle floor."

"I know. We were sitting there in the Arabian Sands Motel having dinner when you got this phone call . . ."

"From John Ali, the secretary of the mosque."

"And he said the apartment's on fire. You thought it was a joke. I didn't believe it. But we rushed back and saw the apartment burning —fire engines, fire hoses for blocks all over the street. We parked on a side street and ran over. Remember what we saw on the ground?"

"What?"

"Two dolls you had bought for my Valentine Day gift. A boy doll and a little girl doll. And the boy doll was great big like you and the girl doll was real little like me. Someone had gone into our apartment and had thrown them to the ground—only the dolls."

"Yeah, Bundini was with us that night. He went inside and saved my championship belt. I couldn't stop him. Risking his life like that for a tin belt. The box it was in was burned bad, but the belt wasn't. Then we went up into the apartment and walked around on the two-by-four planks. The floors had been burned out. You missed some stuff and started crying. I told you this wasn't nothing but material stuff, we can get it all again, but you tried to save as much as you could and have it boxed up. I got mad and said, 'Ain't worth saving that old mess. We'll get some more.' But you said, 'No, I don't want to throw nothing away.' It was too late, though. I guess the suddenness of the whole thing really scared you. I'd never seen you so frightened."

"Only because the fire happened the night of the day Malcolm X was murdered. Because we had been in the Temple that Sunday and they interrupted the meeting and announced that Malcolm X had just been killed. I was afraid for you."

"For me? Why?"

"I was shook up. Malcolm X was the most talked-about Muslim at that time. The fire in our place just seemed too coincidental. Nobody knew where we were having dinner, and all of a sudden you get a phone call telling you your house is on fire. Who would know we were there unless you were being followed? It scared me. It really did. And the reporters coming around, asking you, 'Well, are you afraid?' As if they were building up to something . . . you know. I thought of all those strange people coming around . . . people who really liked Malcolm and may have felt by hurting the World Heavyweight Champion they would even up what happened to him. I was scared to death. And then the real serious arguments between us started."

"We didn't have no real bad arguments—just little debates, that's all."

"Call them debates if you want to. But there were certain things I questioned. It was only natural for me to discuss them with my husband, and . . ."

"You started asking me all kinds of questions about my religion."

"Well, certain things would happen and I would try to discuss them with you. I'm the kind that can't believe in anything just on blind faith, not even God. The arguments would come when I'd say something about the religious rules, or about the white devil, or . . . and you'd take it back and ask the heads of the temples, 'Why is my wife in doubt

about this or that?' You would never answer me yourself. You thought
the man should be the only one in the house who really knew what he
was talking about, so you would go and ask the Muslim officials, 'Why
does my wife think this way and why isn't it like this?' You couldn't
understand why little insignificant me would not just go along with the
program like the others and ask no questions."

"You wouldn't give me what I expected from a Muslim woman.
Not to be always ready to run out at night just for sport and play. Like
that night we quarreled in Miami when you wanted to go see the Jackie
Gleason show, or something."

"It wasn't Jackie Gleason. You thought you and Gleason were
such great pals, the way you had gone around shooting pool together,
but I knew better."

"Yeah, he came over to the gym and I took him to the black part
of Miami and we shot pool. Gleason was nice, but he tried to talk me
out of being a Muslim. Told me to think it over. Lemme see . . . Jerry
Lewis?"

"No, not Jerry Lewis."

"But it was some white celebrity."

"Johnny Mathis."

"Well, I didn't go for it."

"You forget, you had already told me I could go. But you got mad
when I started putting on some eye shadow."

"I don't remember that."

"You suddenly changed your mind about me going. You grabbed
a wet towel and started scrubbing my face, hard."

"Did I do that? I'm sorry. If I had known what I know now, we'd
still be married. You see, I was like a religious fanatic at first. I had just
gotten into the Faith in sixty-four, didn't know how to take it easy with
people and not try to force them to my belief. I didn't understand that
you had to treat people right and be an example and in time they'd see
your side. I acted like I thought every difference was a threat . . ."

"Maybe outside, to the public, you acted that way. But when
nobody was looking, when we had all doors closed, what did you and
I do?"

"Well, at home sometimes I would just let you put on your lipstick
and mini-skirts and let you walk around like that. Since you wanted to
do it. We got along all right doing that for a while, until we went to
Jamaica."

"When you helped Sugar Ray referee a fight or something in
Kingston?"

"Yeah, when you didn't wear the right clothes. That was shortly
after the fire."

"The only clothes I had was a few new suits you picked out for me. And there was this big, fabulous party for Ray Robinson on this huge estate. Everyone dressed so sophisticated. All the celebrities on the island were there, and everything. We started out so nice and friendly. Everybody was gay and having fun."

"So was I. Until I noticed your dress."

"How could you help noticing it? That orange knit suit. After all these years I still got it in the closet. A keepsake. You want to see it?"

"Never mind, never mind."

"Well, you bought the damn dress. You even helped me put it on. Then, when we got to the party, every time I stood up you'd snatch it down. 'Pull it down over your legs,' you said. Then people started laughing. They thought you were putting on an act. But I knew better. I was embarrassed and humiliated. I had figured since we weren't around religious people, it should be okay. When you had me around the Followers, I wore my special religious clothes. But you never acknowledged the fact that I had to live two lives. You kept me in two social gatherings all the time. One, like a religious cult. When I was around Muslims, I wore the clothes you dictated. Those long dresses. And I lowered my head, humble, spoke only when I was spoken to. The other was the world full of famous people, celebrities, and when I was around them I felt out of place acting like that. I felt if I'm gonna be in the world of the World Heavyweight Champion, I should look the part. Instead, you almost got into a brawl with Ray."

"You provoked it. You nearly caused me to beat up my idol. One more word and Ray Robinson and me would have tore at each other's throats . . ."

"So I'm there with this dress on and every time I stand up you're pulling it down. Movie actors, bank presidents, the Governor, Ray Robinson and all these other people drinking and eating and laughing, and I was embarrassed. So I got up and went out on the balcony. I was just sitting there crying. Then out you came. You saw a white man sitting there, too, and this got you. You snatched at me and said the way I dressed was 'lust for the devil's eyes.' And you snarled at the man and took me off the balcony, even though I'm not paying any attention to him. You said the man was gobbling up my legs with his eyes."

"I was vexed over that dress."

"But you bought that damn dress! You picked it! Then you snatch me right off the balcony and drag me straight through the living room, past the guests, past the movie stars, past the bank president, the opera star, past Ray Robinson and everybody. I'm crying and pulling away and you're jerking on me and yelling and you've forgotten everybody's looking. You're yelling and everything! You threw me in the bathroom, came in and slammed the door. I'm screaming and crying and you're trying to stretch my dress. And in trying to make my dress long, pulling and snatching on it, you tore it. You tore it bad. So now I'm nearly naked. I'm trying to break away and you're fighting me, pulling on my clothes, slapping me. Sugar Ray comes to the bathroom door and starts knocking on it. 'Let me in, man! Let me in . . .' He's yelling through the door like he thought you was killing me. 'Cut it out, Cassius! Stop it!' But you yelled back, 'Get away from that door, Ray!' "

"I did?"

"That's exactly what you did. And Sugar Ray said, 'What the hell going on in there?' And you said, 'This is my wife and this is my business. So get away from that damn door. You hear me?' I remember Ray said, 'I ain't going nowhere, man, until I know what's going on in there.' And you said, 'Listen, I'm gonna open this door in a second, and if you ain't gone, I'm gonna whip you good. You ain't nothing but a middleweight, so go on, mind your own business. You hear me?' I could hear people asking Sugar Ray to bust down the door and rescue me, but Ray was quiet for a while. Then I heard him going away and some of the people followed him. Ray had backed down. And when you finally let me out of the bathroom, I couldn't look in the face of a soul in that room. I went straight for the car. Then you got in and drove me back to the hotel. I was so hurt, so embarrassed, that I kept crying and telling you I was through. I said, 'When I get back to Miami, I'm going home. I don't want to see you as long as I live. I can't have this. I can't go through this no more.' When we got home, I was so exhausted I fell asleep and slept until noon the next day. When I got up, things were quiet, and like a flipped coin you were acting nice and sweet and considerate again. But I was still shocked, so when you started back into training, I slipped away, got on a plane."

"Yeah, well, I saw it coming. I felt something was going through your mind. You had gotten so quiet. Even in the gym I had the uneasy feeling you'd be gone when I got home. And sure enough, just a note on the pillow. Where'd you go?"

"Chicago. When you found out where I was, you called me up and talked eighty-eight dollars' worth. It was in all the Miami newspapers. Walter Winchell had it in his column that the Clays are fighting, or something. You kept calling me and running up these big phone bills. Well, I loved you, so I just went back again. But that kept happening, and every time I'd come back you'd promise not to do me like that again."

"And you'd promise to try harder to obey my religious code. But instead of you compromising, you had me compromising. On the phone, after we'd quarrel, you'd say, 'Can I wear just a little bit of lipstick?' To get you back I'd say, 'Well, just a little.' And once back, you'd say, 'Can I keep my red mini-skirt? Just one?' And I'd say, 'Well, yeah,' I wanted you back so bad. Your sister Lintoy was staying with us. I had hoped she would tell me where you hid out when you'd run off. But Lintoy never told me a thing. I remember you left for three days and I checked every hotel in Miami and Miami Beach. I was miserable. Why couldn't you go along? Why couldn't you?"

"I don't know. God knows I loved you and I needed you and I was proud to be wife of the World Heavyweight Champion. I liked the way you'd tell the world how pretty I was—'even prettier than me,' you'd say. I knew women considered you a prize catch."

"All you had to do was wear the right clothes and observe—"

"I know! I know! I got letters from women all around the world. Some agreed with me. Some were shocked and surprised that I didn't wear the dresses. Some of my close girl friends would come up and say, 'Baby, I'd wear a fisherman's net under a deep-sea diver's suit, with a Ku Klux Klan sheet and a monk's frock, if I had a husband that rich and handsome and famous, and he dug me wearing it.' "

"Good advice."

"They didn't understand. It wasn't the form of the thing. But simply to tell me 'believe' or 'not to do' something—that's different, even though I always want to obey my husband and I'll do anything to make him happy. Having a Messenger of God over him . . . this thing of having someone else above my own man, as his leader and teacher . . . I could never accept making another man happy, outside of my husband. I wanted no man to tell my husband what to make me do. I wanted only my husband to be the final word. You understand me?"

"There is where you were wrong. The Messenger ain't never told me, you know that. He don't never tell nobody, not even his children . . . ain't nobody that big."

"But, you see, I didn't know where the orders were coming from. On one hand you tell me what Elijah Muhammad don't like, and then on the other hand you go into the stores and help me pick the kind of short dresses Cassius Clay liked. And then tell me, 'Don't wear it because the Messenger says no.' But you picked them, paid for them, ordered some more. This is what kept me so confused. At night I would cry and ask myself, 'Whose woman am I?' And this is why you used to make me feel so bad all the time. I wanted to be one man's woman. I wanted you to be my hero, my god. Whoever you wanted to worship, let it be. But let you be the only man that I worshiped. And you took this away from me by steady trying to make me look up to somebody else, somebody above you. I only wanted to see you as being big. I didn't want to worship nobody else, because a woman pours everything she's got into her man. There's no leader, no king, no god, no nobody else she thinks more of than her man. You wanted to take this kind of love from me and make me give it to some other man. Well, I rebelled against that."

"You had nothing to lose by going my way."

"Maybe, but I was trying my best to please you. I'll tell you again
... when you would buy me things to wear to the Temple, I felt proud
to wear them because you had picked them. It was for you. But I
couldn't stand to hear you constantly say what your leader wanted of
me. Why? Because you were the only leader I was willing to acknowledge in our house. In our lives. That's why I wanted so much for us
to take a trip alone somewhere. Around the world. Like the one we had
planned after the second Liston fight. There was those letters from
Gamal Abdel Nasser, Kwame Nkrumah in Ghana, the Aga Khan in
Pakistan, Sukarno in Indonesia—all inviting you to come over and you
said you were coming. It didn't have to be that, but just go somewhere
and be together and explore new things together, just to get to know
each other. You understand? You were not to fight any more that year.
So we were going to leave for a trip around the world."

"And maybe if it had come off, we would be married to this day."

"I don't know. We dreamed about it and planned for it, but I felt
somehow it wasn't ever for us to be alone. Somehow it would be
prevented. In the Liston fight camp I was almost happy, even though
I was secluded, because I knew it was gonna be all over soon as you
knocked out Liston."

"But you acted nervous when I was training for Liston. Were you
afraid he'd whip me?"

"I was afraid because I had seen this Liston and the way he looked
at you. I saw him once looking at me after someone had told him I was
your wife. Like I was plunder. A winner-take-all look. The way he looks
at men and the way he looks at women—it's different, but more
frightening. I never saw him fight, but I had seen what's inside him.
All they would talk about around camp was how this man's hands were
the size of hams, and I knew you had already been hurt in sparring.
When we got in the room alone, you would hold your ribs."

"Jimmy Ellis did that. I had my mind on you, and I let Ellis catch
me with a right hand to the ribs. I had boxed eight rounds my last
training day. When Ellis hit me, I stopped short, and he said, 'What's
wrong, Champ?' I pretended to be bored. I said, 'Oh, I'm already
sharp. If I train any more, I'm burned out. I'm through for today.' So
I took a shower and tried to rub that pain out. I went back to my room
and rubbed with alcohol and wintergreen. There was a real painful and
raw feeling in my left rib cage. It made me cry out when I pushed it.
So I was just gambling and hoping that by convalescing for the next
three-four days it would wear off. But it stayed sore and it got sorer.
And on the night of the fight it hurt right in that spot."

"They said you could have postponed the fight."

"No. I already had one postponement because of the hernia. Now the tickets were all sold out. The world's press was there. Liston in shape, me in shape, postponement . . . too much of a setback for too many people. No one knew about my rib but you and Herbert and Angelo. Not even Ellis."

"You worried about that Liston fight so much."

"Well, all the rumors about Malcolm X's vengeance. And the only way Malcolm's people could be satisfied was to get to me. How could I fight under those conditions? Bulletproof shields protecting the newspaper writers. The pocketbooks of the women patrons being searched for guns. And when I looked at that crowd around the ring, that big, dark crowd, it was on my mind that somebody might be out there aiming a rifle at me. But above all, the added pressure that you and me were about to split."

"What do you mean? I knew nothing of us breaking up. I didn't have no idea about any of that. It wasn't me who put that pressure on you."

"That quarrel we had the night before the fight. I told you after Liston, you were either gonna do right, obey my religious rules, or you would just have to leave."

"You didn't tell me that."

"I didn't? Well, that's what I was thinking. After this fight, I said, this will be it. I said to myself, 'I'm in love with her. We love each other deeply, physically, socially. Everything's wonderful. But by us believing so different and not getting along, not being spiritually compatible, we should split.' "

"You never said anything like that."

"I knew after you left I'd need time to get you out of my system. So I said, I'm gonna do nothing until I whip Liston because then I would worry and long for you. I'd never be able to train."

"You kept all that inside you?"

"I had to whip Sonny Liston first. I didn't want to lose to Liston and lose to you, too. That would have been too much loss. I told myself, I gotta come out of this fight lookin' good. I got to keep my heavyweight title so I can still be The Champ while I try to find me another woman."

"You were that cold about it?"

"I had to be. If I find the boxing world laughing at me because Liston won, and me faced with the fact I had to quit my wife, although I loved her, I might have finally jumped out a window or something. But if I could still have the championship with the world honoring me, with people saying, 'Awwww, he whipped Liston,' with everybody coming around, all the women, all the cameras . . . well, I reasoned this might cancel part of the pain of knowing that I'm gonna have to break off with you. 'Cause you never wanted to leave me, and never intended to. You would say, remember . . . 'I want to stay with you and have a baby boy.' But I was demanding, 'You make a move now or that's it.' And right after that fight, though I had won, though I was being hailed and celebrated, I was really heartbroken because I knew the next morning . . . I knew I'd break with you. I had to. I woke up next morning covered with more sweat than I had during the entire fight and looked at you sleeping beside me. No movie star I had ever seen on screen or television or in person looked so good. It would take my breath away just looking at you. Even if, as people told me, you'd had a life almost like a Billie Holiday, you had the face and body and eyes —and sometimes the ways—of an angel. But I knew you would never really embrace my religion. And if I stayed with you, I would keep calling you back, letting you back on your own grounds, and each time you'd make the grounds steeper. So I held you all that night after I beat Liston until you went sound asleep and the thought of what I had to do made me shake like a leaf, like I was about to commit murder or something. I wondered if I could go through with it when I awoke in the morning. I prayed to God to give me strength—and looking at you lying there sleeping, I almost couldn't.''

"I didn't know you were being so deliberate about it. I remember when I woke up that morning you kissing me so hard. But I should have known, even though you said everything was all right."

"Would you expect me to give up all my convictions to keep the love of a woman?"

"Why not? A woman will give up more than that for the man she loves."

"And a woman who had broke her promise to abide by the rules and regulations of my religious faith? That would be like giving up God for a woman who broke her promise to—"

"You the World Heavyweight Champion. Don't you know God breaks more promises than any woman you'll ever meet? What promise did God ever keep? Especially to a poor nigger like you?"

"Hold it! That kind of talk always ended in fights. Still a face like an angel and the devil's tongue. If you had wanted me so badly, you would have tried harder. But you were spoiled, pretty woman. Spoiled easy and early."

"Not spoiled. You know I never had the life of no shielded angel. Everybody told you. I had a child when I was thirteen years old—"

"I wanted to adopt him."

"—and it took me out of school for good. My father and mother split early and my mother made her living in night clubs singing and dancing. But she gave me love. All I knew about my father was that he was a cook who gambled a lot and got killed in a card game. We had seen him so seldom my sister and I didn't even shed a tear when we got the news. My mother gave us love. Spoiled?"

"What do you call what I was giving you?"

"I'm not saying you didn't give me that in your way. Some people didn't understand either why I didn't just 'go along.' 'Why worry, just take the money and go along,' they'd say. 'Take the mink coats, the Cadillacs, the good life, why worry about him?' Why couldn't I do it? I don't know . . . when my mother died she was thirty-six and I was fifteen. I wasn't sure she died a natural death or was murdered, but after that I was on my own. I went to work in bunny clubs and winning beauty contests, modeling . . ."

"I knew. They told me all about that."

"Then did they tell you I had this dream of a knight in armor, some strong incorruptible man who'd come along and take me out of all of it? And he'd be strong and straight and he'd be his own master. Yet I wanted you so much."

"I told you, if you had wanted me so much, you would have tried harder."

"I did try. How could I stand by seeing you act like a tiger in the ring and out of it your knees trembling before some religious superstition, like a man who believes in ghosts?"

"What're you calling superstition?"

"I call it all superstition. You can't prove any of it, World Heavyweight Champion. Anyway, I asked you to question it. Remember, I said you don't have to answer my questions, just ask yourself the questions. Just ask yourself the questions, and in the quiet dead of night, answer. Don't even whisper your answer out loud. Just to yourself. You World Heavyweight Champion M.F. . . ."

"Well . . . the arguments we had were always religious . . . that was our difference . . ."

"I don't know . . . maybe the difference was deeper."

We sat quiet awhile and just looked at the rain pouring down into Lake Michigan. All of those eleven months came back to me in a way that made the boxing, the running, the gymwork, the press conferences, the talks on television, the draft board, even being stripped of the title, seem small, insignificant compared to what was inside our lives. This was the first woman I'd loved and wanted and this would be the last time I would see her. I had come here to close this chapter of my life and put it truthfully on the records, the way she and I saw it together. Her side of the story along with my own.

"You're going to put all this in the book?" she asked.

"Yeah. Just like you said it. Is that the way you saw it?"

"That's the way it was, Heavyweight Champion."

We were quiet again until the tape recorder stopped and we talked of current things, of my chances for another fight, my long exile, of back alimony due, of assorted things spoken with a naked frankness hitherto unknown, of my happiness with Belinda, my wife, Maryum, my child . . . and then her friends, and her own entourage, began to file into her apartment, seeking her attention. She was to open a singing engagement in a South Side night club. She said her first song would be "God Bless the Child That's Got His Own."

THE MESSAGE IS NOT
FOR THE COWARD

"**M**aybe the difference was, as Sonji said, "much deeper," not only in my separation from her but from White Christian America. Maybe I had completely underestimated the depth of the hostility and prejudice against those of us who were followers of the Honorable Elijah Muhammad. Yet I felt something was wrong. The true story was not being told as I knew it.

If the reaction of the ordinary working people in the streets had been as outraged as much of the press reported it was, I wouldn't have been safe walking around, even with bodyguards.

Even though I felt I could withstand any personal attack, I hadn't wanted to be the "Jack Johnson" of my time. But the outrage against my becoming a Muslim touched off a public upheaval that went far beyond the ranks of athletes and boxing promoters.

Al Monroe, a *Defender* writer, declared: "In fact, it's greater than that which met Jack Johnson. It later succeeded in driving Jack Johnson out of America, and this one has caused the world heavyweight champion to be banned from fighting in his own country and barred from leaving it."

William F. Buckley, Jr., pleaded for "someone to succeed in knocking sense into Clay's head before he's done damaging the sport."

Jimmy Breslin described me as a "Muslim and a bedbug."

Jimmy Cannon stated that boxing was better off being run by the Mafia than by the Black Muslims.

"The heavyweight champion is the symbol of masculinity and youth of America," one columnist wrote. "If so, it has now descended into the darkest dungeons of hell, into the worse worms of race hate and degradation, worse than when it was controlled by . . . gangsters . . . [who] were sweet angels compared to the people who control Muhammad Ali."

Nothing could have been further from the truth, and in the days ahead many of these writers would reverse themselves—although much of the prejudice they inspired still remains.

"When my father refers to white people as 'devils,' Herbert had explained to me years ago, "he means those who've oppressed us, lynched us, kept us segregated in ghettos. What my father meant is that white people have made themselves devils by enslaving and oppressing the black man and by subjugating and exploiting colored people all over the world. But a man's skin color is not what makes the 'devil.' A man with white skin is no better or worse than any other person."

I'd always had in my camp and in my entourage both white and black personnel, and there had never been any pressure upon me to eliminate any because he was white or black.

"Then what is a devil?" I asked Herbert.

"A devil is one who truly leads people from Allah. A devil is a mental attitude born out of false pride and self-exalting lies . . . one who goes against the natural order of creation and creates an adversary in the minds of the people against the Creator and His laws. And sets up its false ideas in the minds of the people instead of truth, and worship for the Creator, Sustainer of the Universe. The Holy Quran teaches us: 'No Associate has He.'

"The history of the white man in Europe and America shows that their minds have been ruled by the devil . . . in their actions and their deeds toward other peoples, even toward themselves. And God has the power to destroy the devil without destroying the people.

"To destroy the devil, we must destroy that with which we associate with Allah . . . be it wealth, power or fame, etc. This is why the Muslims are constantly saying Allah is the Greatest. Even worshiping yourself or being proud of being a great boxer, if you think this greatness comes from you alone, you have created an associate with Allah in your mind. So never forget to thank Allah for your greatness and always remember that Allah is the Greatest. This is better for you, if you but understand."

As to the charges that the Nation of Islam was a "hate sect," Herbert had pointed out that "Muslims in America do not hate anybody. But the history of oppressed people shows they must learn to appreciate themselves, to have confidence in themselves, to love themselves. The White Establishment, whether in slavery days or modern days, had taught us to hate ourselves. The image of everything positive in this country has been a white image, and blacks have been taught to feel ashamed and inferior. Everything black was bad—our hair, our looks, our lips, everything about ourselves.

"My father teaches that we must have pride and respect for ourselves. It's not color that we fight against. It's inferior conditions, inferior opportunities. Whites who treat us with respect are not looked upon as devils, not by my father."

Years later, I realized how Herbert had forecast the future policy of the Nation of Islam in America. When Supreme Minister Wallace D. Muhammad succeeded his father as spiritual leader, one of his first decisions was to open the ranks of the Nation of Islam to whites as well as blacks as long as they were willing to live by the rules of the Holy Quran. My earlier contacts with Minister Wallace had convinced me that he was especially talented and deeply concerned with improving the plight of the black man in our country. But it was not until he assumed leadership of the Nation that I discovered how much a part of the people he remained and how he placed the advancement and welfare of his people above all else. A strong believer in physical fitness, Minister Wallace, like his brother Herbert, had once studied to be a boxer; he had never quite forgotten the art, and he put himself through rigorous programs of physical fitness each day.

After I regained my World Heavyweight Title from Foreman, I had the unique experience of getting into the ring with this great spiritual leader, the Supreme Minister of the Nation of Islam, to help him in his physical conditioning, just as he'd helped me in my spiritual conditioning. We sparred through several furious rounds. Much to my surprise, he was fast and quick, as aggressive as Henry Armstrong, with a powerful left hook that reminded me of Joe Frazier.

Most of the people writing about me date my membership in the Nation of Islam from three days after my championship fight with Sonny Liston, but actually my announcement in Miami, after I'd won the championship, was just a formality. I became a follower of the Honorable Elijah Muhammad years earlier than that. And just as I had kept my disappointment over my Olympic Gold Medal to myself, I decided not to say anything about my separation from Christianity until I thought the time was ripe. Even so, because of my association with Malcolm X, Captain Samuels of the Florida mosque and other Muslims I had met, there was steady probing as to where I stood. When I finally went to Chicago to confer with Herbert and attend my first large Muslim meeting, cars of newspapermen followed me throughout the city. I raced them up and down the Outer Drive.

It was in 1959 when I first found out that there were Muslims in America under the leadership of the Honorable Elijah Muhammad. I was rushing to get inside a skating rink on 13th and Broadway in Louisville when I noticed a young black man waving a newspaper and crying, *"Muhammad Speaks! Read it! Muhammad Speaks!"* Ordinarily, I pass up newspaper sellers, but for some reason I bought the paper from him and put it in my back pocket and went on inside the rink. It was only when I was changing pants the next day that I thought about looking at it.

I don't remember the details of what I read, but I can still feel the powerful way it impressed me. It was speaking out boldly against the injustice and oppression of black people, saying things that I had thought and felt, but had no one to talk to about.

There was a drawing by a man I later came to know—Eugene Majied, one of the best illustrators in America. It was a cartoon of a slave who has converted to Islam and is praying with his hands open in the Muslim manner: "Oh, Allah! Oh, Allah!" A white slave master comes up behind him with an upraised whip: "Boy, who are you praying to?" The slave quickly hides his Islamic guise, bows his head and says, "Boss, I was praying to Jesus. Jesus Christ, our Lord and Saviour, Jesus Christ." The slave master lowers his whip and walks away, satisfied, saying, "All right, you keep praying to Jesus!"

The cartoon aroused my curiosity in a way no religious statement had ever done before. Why didn't the slave master want the slave to pray to Allah? Why to Jesus?

Until then I thought that the only real religion in the world was Christianity. I had been baptized a Baptist when I was nine years old, taught the Ten Commandments and Brotherly Love, but since I had never seen it practiced anywhere, it was easy for me to examine something different.

The next morning I took the paper to my teacher, Miss Lake. "What does it mean?" I asked her. "What do you think of this?"

She handled it gingerly and said, "I'll read it later and tell you what I think."

I never saw the paper again, and in a few days I forgot all about it. I was too busy boxing, skating, riding my bicycle and scooter, looking for girls, running up and down the streets with the gang. In fact, it wasn't until I turned professional and was training in Miami for a fight with Donnie Fleeman in 1961 that I passed a Muslim temple in session. A Muslim brother was standing outside on the sidewalk "fishing," as he called it, for new recruits. He followed me a little way down the street trying to persuade me to go in, if "only for a little while."

By then I had heard about Muslims from some of the fighters: their discipline, their restrictions, their beliefs, and it all sounded too strict for me. I was impatient to get going, but the brother was persuasive, and finally, in order to get rid of him, I said, "Well, I'll go in for a minute. Only a minute."

When I got inside, I found myself sitting among black people who were listening to the minister talking about the liberation of black people, about the one divine leader who could unify all black people, about black people regaining their identity. I stayed through the lecture.

What I had heard matched my own feelings, my desires and ambitions for the achievement of freedom and equality for my people, a driving force that had been inside me all my life. My brother Rudy saw Islam as clearly as I did and became a registered follower of the Honorable Elijah Muhammad even before me. Soon after I accepted Islam, Mr. Muhammad gave me the name Muhammad Ali, which means "one who is worthy of praise."

When I finally made it known that I was a Muslim, almost every educated friend, associate and prominent person I knew, black as well as white, was horrified. Sugar Ray Robinson warned me that my career would be wrecked if I became a "Black Muslim." Jackie Gleason urged me to "reconsider the step" he heard I was about to take. "Don't let yourself be used," he said. I thanked him for his advice, but I told him the main ones I didn't want to be used by were the enemies of black people, those who help oppress and subordinate them.

I can understand some of those warnings, because now that I look back on those days in 1959, and on into the early sixties, the hysteria and hostility against "Black Muslims," followers of Mr. Muhammad, was all over this country. The Muslims were portrayed as a "race hate sect," and although they were plainly a peaceful people, who carried no weapons and kept to themselves, they were looked upon as the most fearful enemy of white people in the world—the blacks who planned revenge for all the lynchings, murders, killings, discrimination inflicted for centuries by whites.

It was easy to whip up prejudice against Black Muslims in those days, and to some extent even now. Muhammad's mosques were being invaded by police in city after city, especially in the South. In Monroe,

Louisiana, Muslims were beaten and dragged from the mosques to jails; in Los Angeles the mosque was attacked by police under the pretense they were searching for weapons and ammunition, and unarmed Muslims were killed in cold blood. Muslims selling *Muhammad Speaks* on the streets in many communities did so at the risk of their lives.

Most of the middle-class blacks had been turned almost totally against us. "Why do you want to join something like that?" a black president of a black college once asked me. "Look where you are. You're likable and attractive. You can make millions of dollars. This will only block and cripple you, and one day you're bound to regret it."

I was being told that Orthodox Muslims all over the world, whether in Pakistan, Saudi Arabia, Indonesia, Turkey, Tunisia, disowned the followers of the Honorable Elijah Muhammad and would not accept them. Then, when I traveled to almost every Muslim country and was welcomed enthusiastically and saw other American Muslims receive the same welcome, I wondered why those who opposed me joining the Muslims would tell such a total lie.

The more I learned of the teachings and programs of Mr. Elijah Muhammad, the more I was convinced I was on the right track. What I learned came mostly from Herbert Muhammad, whose guidance, his father had advised me, I could accept with the full confidence that it represented his own thinking. Herbert was deeply devoted to his father, and the love and confidence between them was unshakable and everlasting. He taught me the basic concepts of Islam as we traveled together, lived together and sat together at his father's table.

In those days I regularly read the teachings of Muhammad, and I remember one message that seemed as though it was written especially for me:

Of this grief you and I must suffer, all of these burdens we must bear. It is beyond comprehension that the American Government—Mistress of the Seas, Lord of the Air, Conqueror of Outer Space, Squire of the Land, Prowler of the deep Bottom of the Oceans—is unable to defend us from assault and murder on the streets of these concrete jungles. . . .

The lynchers live right next door, down the street, up the alley, yet they are not brought to justice. What sane man can deny that it is now time that you and I take counsel among ourselves to the end of finding justice for ourselves.

When you stand up and speak a word in behalf of your own people, you are classified as a troublemaker, you are classified as a Communist, as a race-hater, as everything but good.

If God has revealed to me the truth of this race of people and yourself and I tell you of it and that is the truth, then don't say that I am teaching race hatred, just say I teach the truth.

The message I bring is not for the cowards. Those of you who follow me must be ready to withstand the barbs and insults of those who come to investigate, pry and claim that our ultimate aim is to undermine the American way of life. We have no such intentions and our critics know it.

How ironic it is that the very people who charge us with disturbing the status quo themselves go around raping, lynching, denying citizens the right to vote and talking in the Halls of Congress to call you and me everything from a beast to an amoral entity.

I have no alternative than to tell you that there is not any life beyond the grave. There is no justice in the sweet bye and bye. Immortality is NOW, HERE. We are the blessed of God and we must exert every means to protect ourselves.

"What my father meant by 'Life beyond the Grave,' Herbert, who is regarded as one of the best interpreters of Mr. Muhammad said, "is that there is no hope for coming into life beyond the grave. You must come into life here in Allah's Truth. Life in Allah's Truth is the beginning of Eternal Life. How we progress in this life will determine our station in the Hereafter. A believer must hope for life here. If life is to be beyond the grave, it must come into existence here. Allah is often forgiving, most merciful," Herbert quoted the Quran.

Of age-old predictions and prophecies, Herbert pointed out, "We must understand that when Reformers and Servants of God predict future events, calamities and disasters that are coming upon the people, and when we feel these predictions are long overdue, we are not to take these predictions as being untrue. What the Warners saw were Forecasts from God. They were warnings for the people, and when the people changed their ways then the Forecasts were averted due to their change."

In spite of the hostility and opposition, membership in the Nation of Islam has expanded so much that there is not one major city in America without a Mosque of Islam, and *Muhammad Speaks* has the largest circulation of any black publication in the world, with more than one million copies each issue. As strong and prosperous as we had become, I knew for a long time that one of Mr. Muhammad's dreams was to establish a major hospital and medical center in the black community in Chicago, and that he needed a much larger complex of buildings to house the overcrowded mosque and school. I let him know that I would do whatever I could to help. His staff searched all over Chicago for the right property and finally found one that was available.

The Greek Orthodox Church had built a modern temple and school complex in a neighborhood that had suddenly become all-black. The Greeks wanted to move again to a white area and were willing to sell it to the Nation of Islam for four million dollars.

Although Muslim business assets totaled more than seventy-five million dollars at the time, and the Nation of Islam is one of the most stable organizations in America, there was not a single bank that would underwrite the mortgage. It was then that Herbert (the chief business assistant for his father) was sent to look for financial aid in other countries.

While a number of Arab countries contributed to the Messenger's Hospital Fund, including Kuwait, Saudi Arabia, Bahrain, Qatar, Abu Dhabi, only Libya's President Muammar el-Qaddafi agreed to make the loan to buy the new mosque. But somehow a snag developed, and Herbert flew to Tripoli to talk with the President and work things out.

Qaddafi had made it known that he would like to meet me, and I expected an invitation. It came, along with invitations from other Middle East chiefs of state, shortly after I had knocked out the German Heavyweight Champion, Jergen Blin, in Zurich.

This was to be my first trip out of the country since the Supreme Court decision forced the State Department to return my passport. It was also my first time out of America since I had lost the decision to Frazier, a fight seen by more people around the world than any other sporting event in history, and in a few weeks I would find out just what the fight had meant.

I went to Tripoli with John Ali, the Muslim scholar and former National Secretary of Muhammad's Mosque of Islam, who would brief me on President Qaddafi's programs and plans. Qaddafi had seized power from King Idris I in 1969, and we flew into Libya at a time following his announced plans for unity, and his militant call to unite the Arabs. He was one of the first Arab leaders to take control of foreign oil rights, and there were threats that Libya might be invaded to stop him.

At the airport our plane was surrounded by soldiers. When we walked down the ramp, we were met by a crowd chanting, "Ali! Ali! Muhammad Ali! Ali!" Even the soldiers smiled and asked for my autograph. They drove us not to the old King's Palace, where I thought we'd meet the new leader, but to a building that looked like an Army barracks, and took us into a plain waiting room while a deputy went to tell the President we'd arrived.

It was here that I first met President Idi Amin of Uganda, also waiting for an audience with Qaddafi. Amin was a former prizefighter, and he laughed and flexed his muscles. He wanted me to come to Uganda, and he whispered confidentially that Qaddafi was the "best of the Arab leaders" and that Qaddafi was backing his new regime all the way.

Suddenly a deputy opened the door and there was the President, dressed in a tan fatigue uniform, a wide black belt around his waist and one silver medal on his chest. He gave me a warm Muslim embrace and stood back looking at me, smiling. He is close to my height, with a thin, handsome face. Even though we're the same age, he looks much older; not aged, but simply with the strong face of an older, very experienced man. When we sat down, I kept looking at him. There was something familiar about that face.

Prizefighters are known to have phenomenal memories for faces, maybe because our trade demands that we keep our eyes fixed, studying the face of the opponent. I knew I'd seen the President somewhere before. But I couldn't remember where. He had never been in America, and this was my first time in Libya.

"I've been wanting to meet you for a long time," the President was saying.

I jumped up: "I met you before, in London, Mr. President! In my dressing room, after the Cooper fight!"

"I was waiting for an autograph," he said. "But you were surrounded by so many people, you told me to wait."

It all came back. This was the bright-eyed Arab student in my dressing room, and even then he had seemed much older than the other college boys.

"I told you to wait," I said. "But when I looked around, you were gone."

"I had to go." The President laughed. "I was in school. I was not supposed to be out that night. I had slipped out to see you fight, but I wanted to get back before they found out. I got back before my classmates saw me. The older boys had gone to the fight rooting for Cooper. I enjoyed hearing them tell me how the fight came out. In fact, I enjoyed your fight the rest of the night."

A lieutenant with some signs written in Arabic came in and they exchanged quick words. When he was gone, the President turned to me apologetically and said, "We're in the process of changing the street names and the names of prominent buildings from those the Italians left to those in our own Arabic tongue, things that should have been done years ago." He told me that he had followed all my fights, and he spoke of the great disappointment in the Muslim world, especially in Libya, when I lost to Frazier. "In fact, it was a day of mourning in our country," he said.

I would hear the same thing when I went to Kuwait, Saudi Arabia, Indonesia, Malaysia, Egypt. I would hear it from Pakistanis, South Koreans, Thais, Indians, Burmese, working people who had been given the day off to listen to the fight over the radio. Wherever I went on this tour, they talked about my fight with Frazier.

"If we fight again," I assured Qaddafi, "those who left in tears last time will go away rejoicing. I promise."

As we sat and talked over tea and cakes, I found the President amazingly well-informed on the struggle of black people in America. He spoke warmly about what the black people in America had achieved, despite "American arrogance, the white superiority complex."

He told me about the long, bloody struggle of his people against foreign rule, which for centuries had skimmed off the wealth of the country, kept its people in poverty. And since oil was their most treasured resource, it was necessary, he said, "that the profit come back to the Libyan people."

Finally, I brought up the fact of the loan which had been promised to the Nation of Islam, and he spoke frankly of the opposition to it in his own administration. But he said Herbert had given him a good answer as to why he should go forward with the loan. It had been reported that the Libyan ambassador in Washington had been so opposed to the loan being made to a black American group that he held it up in the Riggs Bank and flew to Libya to persuade the President to withdraw it.

Qaddafi said that he was standing firm on making the loan. It would be the first time any nation in the world, including the United States, had made such a major loan to a black group in America. "If Christianity can spend millions to help Christianize the Middle East, why can't we spend something to bring Islam to the Americans?" he said. "I've taken some of the money we had allocated to the Army and set it aside for this loan to the American blacks. The loan will go through."

Before I got back to America it had gone through and the complex had become a part of Muhammad's Mosque of Islam, the largest Islamic mosque in the Western Hemisphere and one of the ten largest religious complexes in America.

When it leaked out that I had seen the Libyan President, I was swarmed by reporters, few of whom could get an audience with the young leader because of the hostility of the Western press. They wanted me to compare Qaddafi with the late Gamal Adbel Nasser, whom I had spent days with on my first trip to Africa.

Although there was a difference between them in age and in the emphasis they put on religion, in their determination to give their people a better life and throw off all foreign control, they were like twins. "The black people in America are emerging as one of the great people in the Western World," President Nasser had told me. "They are a highly talented people, becoming better educated and trained and more conscious than any minority group in the West. I believe, as your leader, Muhammad, believes, that there is no power on earth that can prevent black Americans from winning their freedom."

When I joined Mr. Muhammad, I became one of eight hundred million people all over the world. I came not only because it is a religion I believe in and understand, but also because I believe in the work and programs of the Honorable Elijah Muhammad and now in his successor, the Supreme Minister Wallace D. Muhammad. And I came at a time when to be a Muslim was equivalent to being an outlaw more dangerous than a Jesse James.

One prominent lawyer, Truman Gibson, formerly the attorney for the powerful Jim Norris group that controlled boxing during the days of Joe Louis, had a different opinion: "At the time Muhammad Ali became world champion," he said, "if Ali had not been a Muslim or a member of a strong black organization, the chances of the heavyweight title remaining outside the influence and direction of the crime syndicate would have been slim. The Black Muslim entry into the heavyweight picture finally broke the gangsters' backs. It was the one organization that the Mafia will hesitate a long time before trying to take over."

Years later I realized how prophetic Gibson's statement was. The New York *Times* ran an FBI transcript of a phone conversation between Mafia leaders who were trying to decide whether they should kill Matthew Shumate, a Muslim brother in Newark. Matthew, in self-defense, had beat the son of a prominent Mafia chief so severely that he had to be hospitalized for six months. The fight had taken place on a construction gang, where Matthew was foreman and had been attacked by the youth, who resented his orders. The tapped phones revealed that the Mafia had considered various ways of killing Shumate, a quiet, hard-working brother who always attended my fights. They discussed killing him either by knife, by beating or by pistol, but could never get the approval from the top Mafia boss, Carlo Gambino. The FBI said the Mafia feared it might ignite an all-out war between the "Black Muslims" and the Syndicate families in the Elizabeth area. They thought the Muslims would get the best of it.

The truth of the matter is that my becoming a member of the Nation of Islam had nothing to do with escaping the Syndicate domination that hung over boxing in the days before I came on the scene. It only had to do with my own belief that the program of the Muslims offerred the best opportunity for the achievement of freedom for my people.

At the time that I joined the ranks of the Nation of Islam and kept it undercover for fear of hostility and discrimination, I had no idea that in less than ten years' time the supression and fear, officially and unofficially, of "Black Muslims" would be turned around. I did know that the atmosphere would change. But I couldn't know then that by 1975 many officials in states where Muslims had suffered most would proclaim days and weeks honoring Mr. Muhammad and the Nation of Islam. And these would include the Mayor of Washington, D.C.; the Mayor of Detroit and the Governor of Michigan; the Mayor of Kansas City and the Governor of Kansas; the Mayors of Inkster, Michigan, of Gary, Indiana, of Chicago, Atlanta, Berkeley, Oakland, Newark, Los Angeles; the Governors of Illinois, Massachusetts, New Jersey, New York. Even the President of the United States would send an official representative to the funeral of Mr. Muhammad. The citizens of the black community, from the richest to the poorest, signed petitions supporting the cause of the Muslims. It became the largest, wealthiest and strongest black organization in the history of America.

The Honorable Elijah Muhammad lived to see that he had brought about a change in America's attitude toward "Black Muslims," and an even greater acceptance is forecast for the future. But many times I've found myself reflecting back on the big bold headlines in the papers when I announced that I had turned to Islam—ALI ADMITS HE'S BLACK MUSLIM, as though I had committed a criminal offense—in a nation that boasted about its "religious freedom." There has been a change in this, and I thank Allah that perhaps in some small way what I have done and exemplified has helped the people of my country see my religion as it really is.

OLD FRIENDS
AND DINOSAURS

King Levinsky, in his prizefight prime, must have been a good-looking man. Even if he sometimes acted like that character Lennie I saw in *Of Mice and Men,* there was something sort of soulful and human about him.

He was in Wolfie's restaurant one morning when I came in from doing roadwork for the Oscar Bonavena fight, trying to keep up his end of an argument going on near the pastry counter. When he saw me, he said, "Cash! You tell 'em, Cassius. Tell 'em I'm right."

"What about?" I said, slumping into a chair, avoiding his eyes. A young fighter doesn't like to look in the face of a scarred, punch-drunk member of the tribe. He might see his own future.

"They ask me why you always win. I tell 'em because you know all about losing." He paused for me to answer. "You understand, Cassius? You understand how it feels to lose? That helps you keep winning." His voice was a husky whisper.

I meant to say nothing, but I heard someone laugh. We were the only ones in there who knew about losing in the ring. And nobody else had the right to laugh. I got up and put my arms around the King's big shoulders and announced in a loud voice, "Ladies and gentlemen. You know who this is? The King. King Levinsky. In his day, one of the strongest. One of the greatest. King Levinsky!"

I kept it up until the customers, the waitresses, busboys and the kitchen staff applauded, and only then did I look directly at his face. There was a glow in it and his eyes were soft.

"You know what it is to lose out there, Cash?"

His voice was even lower now, but one of the customers heard him and shot back: "The Champ ain't never lost! He ain't like you!" He was saying it as though he thought the point would flatter me.

The King was looking at me; some doubt was creeping in on our kinship. "Cash, how it feel to lose?"

"Naked," I said, "and cold."

"Naked and cold," he repeated in triumph. "The worse way you can feel. They cut you off from the goddamn world. Nobody's with the sucker who loses."

He had moved a chair away from my table and the whole room had stopped to watch him. He put his hands to his head as though shutting off noise in a crowded stadium, bobbing and weaving, chased by some super-strong opponent.

"It's not the blows, is it, Cash?"

I shook my head. "Not just the blows."

"The blows, they rim you out. Ribs. Heart. Lungs. Stomach. Kidney. But it's all them witnesses. Everybody watching you. They make you split to pieces, like a goddamn plate-glass window hitting the sidewalk." He was reenacting the last fight he'd had in Chicago Stadium. "You sinking down to the floor, bleeding, and they roar *him* on. They roar *him* on. He's turned into a lion and they *cheer* the lion on . . ."

I got up and pulled him back to the table, and we drank juice and talked quietly while he took out his wallet and showed me photos of him in the company of Jack Benny, Robert F. Kennedy, Jackie Gleason.

"I never really understood losing," he said wistfully. "I lost. But I never really understood it. You did. You know . . ." He stopped as he noticed some of the customers looking at him as though he was from the circus, smiling at his thick speech. He just stared back at them awhile. Then his eyes brightened. "Cash. What . . . what the Beatle say when he came to the gym?"

I had to search back. On their first trip to America the Beatles had come down to watch me train for Liston. Half the hip section of

Miami had followed them in, including the King.

"All them people. Screaming and acting nuts." The King was laughing. "And you asked that skinny one . . ."

"John Lennon?"

"You asked him"—he closed his eyes to see it better—"you asked him if this was the way people act when a star gets big. And what did he say, Cash?"

Then I remembered. "He said, 'Champ, the bigger you get, the more unreality you have to face. The more real you get, the more unreal they get.' "

The King and I laughed as we relived that day in 1963 when four young guys walked in, sloppy clothes, white T-shirts, long hair, and asked me if I was sure I'd whip Liston.

"He falls in eight," I told them, and recited a poem I made up. All four got into the ring and we sparred around and pretended they were boxers. They stretched out on the canvas like they'd been knocked out and posed for a picture with me standing over them. The caption to read: CASSIUS SMASHES BEATLES.

We'd kept up with each other after that, and the last I heard from Lennon was the day he wanted to auction off my bloody boxing shorts —the ones I'd worn in the Henry Cooper fight. I'd given them as a souvenir to Michael Abdul Malik, a black militant from Trinidad, who exchanged them for all the hair on Lennon's and his wife Yoko's head. The hair and the bloody trunks were auctioned off to raise money to fight for world peace. I never knew how much my trunks brought, but Lennon said he was glad to see Henry Cooper's blood used for a good cause.

When the King and I got up to go, he looked at some of the spectators who'd been rudest to him and raised himself up to his full grizzly-bear height. "Yes, I'm punchy!" he said evenly. "Yes, I'm punchy." And as they quieted down, "But what's your excuse?" Then he turned to wink at me, saying, "The bigger you get, the more unreality you have to face."

We went our separate ways and I've never seen him since. But I felt some kind of blood-knot between the battered old fighter and myself, the young "undefeated." I was ashamed of the fact that in the ten years I had trained on Miami Beach, I had mostly avoided him, which was as much my loss as his. Levinsky, the loser, understood the qualification of a champion better than many fighters who had held the title. And when I got back to my hotel I started thinking about an evening I'd spent with Floyd Patterson.

I had not seen Floyd since our fight in Las Vegas, but when I came across an article he'd written for a national magazine, saying some honest things about the "loser," the admiration I'd had for him during my amateur days returned and I accepted an invitation to go out to his farm.

"The losing fighter loses more than just his pride in the fight," Patterson had said in the article. "He loses part of his future. He's a step closer to the slum he came from." Then, turning his attention to me, "I'm sure that before each fight Cassius Clay also goes through the mental torture and doubt. He knows how happy thousands of Americans would be if he got beaten bad, and maybe that's why Clay has to say, 'I'm the greatest. I'm the greatest.' He wants people to say, 'You're not,' and then he's forced to meet the challenge. Put himself in a do-or-die frame of mind. Go a little crazy, maybe, crazy with some ferocious fear. So far it has worked for him. What he will be like if he loses, I do not know."

So Floyd wants to know how I'd take a loss, I thought, as I flew out to his place in New York. He greeted me warmly and introduced me to his family. It had been a long time since I had been with a competitor, free from the artificial "hate" promoters and the press use to divide two opponents, and we began to discover and like each other.

We lounged around, talking about the future—his fight plans, my possible jail sentence—and I told him I'd read what he'd written about "losers." "I know the feeling," I said.

He surprised me with his sudden coldness. "You don't know what you're talking about."

"I do," I told him.

But he turned away. "You've been lucky. You've never lost," he said with what I thought was a touch of regret.

His chilliness caught me by surprise. Plainly, the bitterness of our fight in Vegas had not been washed far enough down the drain so that we could become buddies. "I've been on the brink," I said. "Man, I've looked down in that pit. I know."

"But as an amateur," he said spitefully. "You don't know until someone knocks you down from the top."

For a quick second I had the impression he was still in that ring in Las Vegas. How could I explain to him what drove me on to whip him so thoroughly and totally? What I was doing in the ring with Patterson that night in Vegas was directly related to what had been going on outside the ring. The rage and uproar over me becoming a Muslim was still at a fever pitch.

Looking at Floyd now, quiet and happy here at home with his wife and children, I felt he still didn't understand what happened that night and I wanted to tell him. I wanted to say, "Floyd, when I became a Muslim, you announced in all the papers you were out to 'bring the title back to America.' You said this was the main reason you wanted to beat me. It was then that I said, 'What do you mean, bring it back to America? It's already in America!' Floyd, I'm the Heavyweight Champion of the World, and I'm an American. I stand for the people, the black people, the poor people, the poor people in ghettos, both black and white.

"When you were Champion, Floyd, whenever you took a picture you'd either be picking up a little white boy or hugging a little white girl, which was all right, but I never saw you pick up little black children and pose with them. You came from the black, the poor, the oppressed, the denied, but you always catered to the whites, the privileged. Even then, I kept my peace until you made the statement that you wanted to bring the title back to America. You let the whites goad you into attacking me because I'd become a follower of the Honorable Elijah Muhammad, this black man who preached unity and progress, who had taken thousands of hopeless dope addicts off the streets and changed their lives, gave them purpose and programs. What he wanted was freedom, justice and equality for black people. You told the white press you'd never call me by my Muslim name, Muhammad Ali. You said, 'I'm gonna call him Cassius Clay, because that's the way he was born.'

"Then I said I was gonna give you a whipping. I said, 'I'm gonna give you a whipping until you call me Muhammad Ali.' I challenged you. I said, 'If you whip me, I'll go and join the Catholic Church, and if I whip you, you come and join the Honorable Elijah Muhammad and be a Muslim.' You never answered me on that. All the white press was backing you, all the Catholics, all the white Protestants. And even though Sonny Liston had destroyed you twice, they revived you just so you could get to me. The only reason they gave you a chance at a title fight was they wanted to see you perform a miracle. They wanted to see a nice Catholic boy defeat a Black Muslim.

"You told them Elijah Muhammad was taking all my money, which was untrue, because actually I was borrowing money from the Nation of Islam. They hadn't taken a quarter from me. You said when I lost the title the Muslims would drop me like a hot potato, so I wanted to take all this out on you, but not really on you—on your white supporters.

"And when the fight was on, whenever you'd get in a blow the crowd would roar: 'Ooooooohhh! Aaaaaaahhh!" But whenever I'd throw blows on you, things were quiet. So for thirteen rounds, things were mostly very quiet, because I was doing the whipping. I didn't see myself fighting you, Floyd. I didn't see myself hitting Floyd Patterson. I was fighting the white reporters behind you, the Jimmy Cannons, and the white celebrities, the Frank Sinatras, the Jim Bishops, the Arch Wards, the Dick Youngs, and when it was over they talked about how

cruel I was. I don't regret what I did. The trouble was, they wanted
to see something cruel happen to me.

"But it's not true when they say I carried you, that I could have
knocked you out, gotten you out of your misery. That's not true.
Although I didn't really press the fight until after the eighth round, I
never saw a time when I felt you were going to fall. I hit you so many
times my hands were in pain and I could hardly move them, but you
wouldn't fall. You kept taking it. You stood in there and kept taking
it. You took everything I threw and you still had punches to throw back
at me. You were good. You had guts and heart. You were greater than
those egging you on.

"Like the next morning when you went to see Frank Sinatra, what
did he do? When you went to see him to apologize for the poor
showing? You went up to his room and he turned his back on you and
hardly spoke to you, and you came out with tears in your eyes. But it
was not you that I was trying to beat and knock out. It was those
backing you. I was talking back to them. I was saying, 'I am America.
Only, I'm the part you won't recognize. But get used to me. Black,
confident, cocky; my name, not yours; my religion, not yours; my goals
my own—get used to me! I can make it without your approval! I won't
let you beat me and I won't let your Negro beat me!' "

But I couldn't explain it to him, so I let the chance go by.

The rest of the evening was quiet and friendly, but less real. When
I was a boy, boxing in Louisville, Floyd was my idol. My ears were right
up on an old radio in 1956 when he knocked out Archie Moore and
became the youngest boxer in history to win the championship, and I
spun around and shouted and shadowboxed half the night in the
kitchen. And when he visited the Olympic Village in Rome I wouldn't
let him out of my sight. He had been the Olympic Champion in 1952
and I was following in his footsteps. My dream was someday to have
him as a friend, a close buddy, and since it looked like I would never
fight again, it seemed now was the time to try. But too much had
happened, I suppose, in between the dreams.

Flying back to Philadelphia that night, I thought of Patterson's
mood and of those amateur fights I had lost. A true champion can never
forget a real defeat. It's like losing a good and lovely woman. It drives
you crazy until you really learn why. Perhaps Patterson had never
learned the "why."

It was the other way around with me. I'd had my baptism, my
heartbreak losses, and each defeat had only convinced me that I could
avoid defeat.

I remember the cold winter night in 1958, in the hallway of the
Chicago Stadium. I was walking alone. I had just been beaten by Kent

Green, a talented black southpaw. I could hear the crowd roaring as the finals went on, but I was out of it. Fighters, trainers and handlers were pushing by me, some on their way to the arena, some coming back to the dressing room, and now and then I'd get a pat on the back:

"Tough luck, Cassius."

"You gave him hell, though. You gave him hell."

"Good fight, Cassius. Good fight."

"You got nothing to be 'shamed of, kid. Nothing to be 'shamed of!"

All of which made it worse. I went on down the hall feeling lonely and wanting some kind of real companionship. I'd always loved company and there were a good many heavyweights from cities all over the Midwest, some I'd wanted to buddy around with.

Then I saw this old trainer out of St. Louis, Reverend Williams. (He had earned the "Reverend" part of his name because he did a little preaching on Sundays.) The Reverend handled nothing but heavyweights, which was odd because he was forever praising the talents of lightweights over heavyweights. Heavyweights he always referred to as "those dinosaurs." "Get in the ring and kick that goddamn dinosaur's ass" would be his usual instructions to his fighters. I saw myself as a "dinosaur" in size, but in execution and style I was aiming to be like the lightweights.

When he first saw me, the Reverend asked if I'd heard the joke. He had an old joke he used to bring down some heavyweight he thought was getting "too big." He would tell of this heavyweight, an ancient dinosaur who terrified all other animals in the jungle until he ran into a little four-legged dog-sized runt who wouldn't run.

"This runt just stood there looking up at this great big dinosaur," the Reverend would say. " 'Why ain't you running scared like the other animals?' this dinosaur asked."

At this point the Reverend would look around as though someone was supposed to answer.

"Then this little old four-legged runt spoke up and said, 'Because I ain't scared of your ass.'

" 'How come?'

" 'Because,' the little runt said, lighting up a big cigar, 'in a few million years your ass is gonna be extinct.'

" 'What about your ass?' the dinosaur asked.

" 'As for me, I'm gonna grow up to be a horse.' " And the Reverend would fall out laughing, and I'd laugh, too, though he'd told it fifty times to my own knowledge.

But this night I didn't laugh. I asked him the whereabouts of some of the heavyweights.

"Heavyweights," he said, going back to his handwraps. "Heavy-weights don't hibernate together."

"What you mean, hibernate?" I asked.

"Run together, hide out together, sleep together, buddy together . . . dinosaurs don't do that." He dismissed it as though there was something immoral about it.

"What's wrong with it?"

"It's against nature," he said. Then, more softly as he saw me get angry, "Everybody got buddies, I know. But not dinosaurs. The dino-saur's different. He's got his own satellites. His own crowd. Like each kite got its own tail. Oh, now and then a dinosaur might bump into another on the street. In a hotel lobby, or somewhere. But dinosaurs go it alone."

"Birds of a feather flock together," I said stubbornly. "Tigers go with tigers. Elephants follow elephants."

The Reverend shook his head. "But birds of prey don't flock together, and dinosaurs are demons of prey." He went back to his handwraps.

I sat down on a bench nearby while other fighters streamed out of the dressing room, headed for the arenas. The heavyweights just nodded and kept going. The welters, bantams, lights fooled around, friendly.

The Reverend was watching me out of the corner of his eye and came over and sat down beside me. "You a light-heavy now," he said. "But you got real dinosaur blood. You gonna be a big one, a champ. But you can't be buddies with heavyweights. Listen," he said, and leaned close to my ear as though to give me a great secret, "when dinosaurs see one another, they just size each other up for the kill. All they trained to do is tear each other to pieces. They know a day'll come when they'll have to go out there in that high-noon sunshine with all the world watching and destroy each other. They can't be buddies. Only one can be king. You ever heard of Joe Louis buddying around with Ezzard Charles? Jim Braddock and Buddy Baer? What dinosaur did Jack Dempsey buddy with? Go all the way back to John L. Heavy-weights walk alone, boy. Sure, big-ass football players, basketball, even hockey players pal around together, like fags. But not heavies. They come to your gym to steal your style, not as friends but as cannibals."

One of his own dinosaurs came out of the dressing room ready to go into the arena, and the Reverend straightened up to go. But he bent down once more to whisper, "Don't take no dinosaur for no friend."

Then he took his own dinosaur on off to the arena. He had only added to my loneliness and made me resolve never to be defeated again.

• • •

Many times since that night in 1958 I've thought of Williams' words, that heavyweights never buddy together. Especially when less than a year later I found myself going from gym to gym like the gunfighter in a cowboy movie, tracking down the big-name heavyweights, the Johanssons, Moores, Pattersons, Johnsons, asking if I could be their sparring partner. What I really wanted was to test them out. To see if my guns were better and faster. That way I developed a distinct advantage over the fighters in my age group. Many had to overcome a sort of ring-shyness, a reluctance to get into the thick of the fray. I believed in going directly to the O.K. Corral to try out my guns.

But I had another drive that was maybe even greater than my need to show off my guns. Why couldn't two men with common backgrounds, similar work conditions, same aspirations, and certainly the same day-to-day problems with promoters, managers, the public . . . why with so much in common could there be so few friends among us? The wish for a buddy among my own weight class never left me.

It was on my mind one morning in August, in the midst of my three-and-a-half-year exile, as I stood in front of a Philadelphia motel waiting to be picked up by Joe Frazier. I had called Joe and told him I was working on my autobiography. Naturally he was a part of it and his outlook should be included. He surprised me by agreeing so quick and friendly-like. Maybe because I hadn't fought in nearly three years and maybe because it looked as though I would never fight again, but I admired Frazier. And of all the people in my profession I would like to have had as a friend, he was the one. He was a fighter of the new breed. Not as outspoken as I was, but he could never qualify as an Uncle Tom.

He had an appointment in New York which matched with one I had. He said we could drive up and talk on the way. I would put the conversation on tape and include it in the book.

Shortly after twelve noon, he drove up in his gold-colored Cadillac with the sun roof. The grille and half the hood were smashed in like an accordion, but the car ran fine.

He smirked as he saw me marveling at the results of his recent accident. "It's still better than that junk you got."

He was dressed in his lemon-yellow cowboy outfit: yellow shirt, tan Texas hat, brown boots, yellow striped pants. I got in and we set out for New York. Perhaps the longest ride two undefeated contending heavyweights ever took with each other. He sat sideways in the seat, like he was riding a horse sidesaddle, so that his left hand could spin the steering wheel with a touch.

"Cut your tape on," he said after we'd gotten to the highway. "Let's rap."

I flicked on the tape, and as we moved out toward New York, this is the way things went that August day, 1970 . . .

ALI *(after nearly ten minutes' silence):* How long this take?

FRAZIER: We'll be there by five.

ALI: Hope so. I got an appointment at five.

FRAZIER: What you complaining about? I was supposed to be there at three. *(sour)* Fooled around waiting for you.

ALI *(long pause):* How's your leg? The one you broke in Vegas?

FRAZIER: I'll be all right. 'Nother two, three weeks from now, be able to get back in the ring. Got my weight down good, man. Look.

ALI: Yeah, you look good.

FRAZIER: Believe me, I ain't fat.

ALI: But you like me; you gain weight easy, don't you?

FRAZIER: Too easy. Well, that come from eating all that good food the wives cook.

ALI: All that good cooking.

FRAZIER: You sit home when you laid up . . . in the house most of the time . . .

ALI: Yeah, getting that late trim, then going to sleep. That's what gets you.

FRAZIER: Yeah. Gets you fat right away.

ALI: So eat unsweetened grapefruits, man.

FRAZIER: Unsweetened?

ALI: Yeah. Get you about five, six grapefruits in the box. Keep 'em cold. You wear a sweat suit?

FRAZIER: I gotta. I gotta bring my weight down. If I didn't do that, man, I'd be weighing about two-ten, two-twelve.

ALI: How much you weigh when you fight?

FRAZIER: Two-oh-four.

ALI: Sweat pants. That'll bring your legs down. Say, you see that cop —keeps looking over here.

FRAZIER: Yeah, man.

ALI: Wow! There's another policeman—right over there. Why they looking at us? They must be thinking, "Joe Frazier, Muhammad Ali? Why was them niggers together? What was them niggers doing?"

FRAZIER *(laughs):* They think we out here scheming.

ALI: You got good days ahead, man. You gotta fight Bobby Foster. That's gonna be some good money. People say, "Well, Foster's fast. He hits hard; he don't get hit easy; his arms are long; he's got a jab." With all that build-up, you whip him easy. That'll be a easy payday and you still ain't hurting the Heavyweight Division. You still got them heavyweights left.

FRAZIER: Yeah, yeah!

ALI: You still got Mac Foster coming up; he gonna be a million-dollar gate. You got George Foreman, that be a million-dollar gate. And by the time that gets ripe, they gonna be a couple more of them, see? So you got it made, if you just play it cool. And in the meantime, you can be getting some action and some big money. I wonder why Bobby Foster agreed to it.

FRAZIER: Well, you dig, Bob getting old. Must don't give a damn.

ALI: He wants to get his last good payday, too.

FRAZIER: Right, right.

ALI: You ain't really scared of Bob Foster?

FRAZIER: In no way. He lost to every heavy he fought. Zora Folley, Terrell, Jones—all beat him. I'd wreck him.

ALI: But tell the truth, now, man. If you fought me, wouldn't you be scared?

FRAZIER: No, man. Honest to God.

ALI: You really wouldn't be scared?

FRAZIER: No kinda way!

ALI: I mean my fast left jab, and the way I dance?

FRAZIER: Noooooo! I'd get close to you. They talk about how fast you is, moving away. But you gonna find out how fast I am moving *in.*

ALI: You remember that time you came to see me fight Zora Folley? You was on your way up. You wanted to learn from me.

FRAZIER: We all have a time for learning.

ALI: You believe you know enough *now* to fight me?

FRAZIER: Hell, yes! Maybe even if I didn't know enough, I would never turn you down. Any man that turn a man down in his profession, he's less than a man.

ALI: Not necessarily. I mean, the man could just be wise and biding his time. But like, if you ducked me now, you'd think "I'm less than a man," 'cause you The Champ and you supposed to be ready. But what I'm saying is, do you think you could decision me, or do you really think you could stop me before fifteen?

FRAZIER: Sure I think I could stop you before fifteen.

ALI: You really do?

FRAZIER: I really do. You see, the kinda stuff I'm gonna put on you, man, you ain't had to dig yet. You ain't never seen this before. You understand?

ALI: It's impossible for you to get away from my jab. Impossible!

FRAZIER: See, them other cats out there let you have your own way. Just like they let me have my way—

ALI: You take your way!

FRAZIER: I take my way, right. But they let you have your way. They let you jump around the ring, and dance and all that—

ALI: You couldn't stop me from jumping around the ring and dancing. What you gonna do?

FRAZIER: I'd get right dead on you! Every time you breathe, you be breathing right down on my head.

ALI: You be tired after five, six rounds of scuffling.

FRAZIER: You be tired trying to get away, too. Running and jabbing and ducking and dodging . . . you be tired, too.

ALI: I know what's happening. You just hate to admit that you can't whip me 'cause you The Champ.

FRAZIER: No, no, no, no—

ALI: Really, I done retired. If I came back . . .

FRAZIER: I'm retired, too. Until you come back. *(Pauses for red light)*

ALI *(leans out window to wave at cluster of black people peering into car):* Hey, you two foxes out there on the corner! Better watch it!

GIRL *(recognizing):* Hi, Champ! Howya doing?

ALI: You recognize me?

GIRL *(peering):* Who that with you?

ALI: That's Joe Frazier.

MAN *(comes up):* What the hell you two doing together?

ALI: We gonna get it on in the alley! We going right up here in the alley!

MAN: That's all right! Right on!

ALI *(as car starts off):* So you tell the world that you saw me and Joe Frazier! The real Champ and the ex-Champ.

WOMAN: When you gonna box him, Frazier?

FRAZIER *(leans out window):* I might just whip his ass right now, here in the car!

ALI *(to the world at large):* This Joe Frazier and Muhammad Ali driving to New York.

FRAZIER: He said something I couldn't hear.

ALI: He said, "Awww, man. What y'all doing together?" *(Laughs, turns to Joe)* No, seriously, man, you really think you can whip me? You know, somebody told me you was glad I'm not allowed to fight. Murray Worner—you know, the guy who staged that fake Marciano fight? He said you didn't dare get in the ring with me.

FRAZIER: No, man. No! Look. I wish it was in my power to give you a license. I would give you my own license if they'd let me fight you. That's how bad I want you.

ALI *(sighs):* Maybe we two could get together and get the fight on. Just show up on a street corner arguing until the people demand we be allowed to settle it. Damn the Governors, the Boxing Commissioners, the Mayors, the politicians, the Legion, the White Citizens Councils, the KKK . . . the people want it!

FRAZIER: I'm telling ya! They ain't gonna see nothing in their life like this fight. 'Cause you ain't afraid of me, and I ain't afraid of you. You understand?

ALI *(long pause):* But I really believe you afraid of me.

FRAZIER *(long pause):* No, I sure ain't.

ALI: I really believe that after I get in good shape, and after I get trim . . . You had Quarry and Ellis talking about how they wasn't gonna run and the press played it up.

FRAZIER: So in other words you gonna run a little bit, too, huh?

ALI: I'm gonna dance and move like Sugar Ray. It's impossible for you to whip a heavyweight Sugar Ray with your style, man.

FRAZIER: I been up against real race horses out there. But I whip 'em down to a slow trot. I put quicksand under their feet.

ALI: I gotta admit you good, but I'm the fastest. Fastest in the history of the whole world.

FRAZIER: Maybe, maybe moving away. But I'm the fastest moving in.

ALI: Had Ellis worked with you, like he did me, sticking and moving and standing on his toes, he'd've won. But you scared Ellis.

FRAZIER: It was a different fight, man, a different kinda fight altogether. You always had Ellis chasing you. You understand? But me, I'm chasing *him.* See, he ain't never had nobody chase him. So this a different kinda thing. Just like you; you ain't had nobody know how to go after you—

ALI: Karl Mildenberger was after me; Liston, Henry Cooper, Chuvalo was after me—

FRAZIER: They too slow!

ALI: Let me tell you the way I would have whipped you, man. Now, in the first place, you don't have no jab.

FRAZIER *(aghast, almost stops the car):* I don't have a jab?

ALI: Keep driving! Watch it! No, you don't have no jab.

FRAZIER: Man, I'd tear your head off with a jab! I'd hit you with a jab like a machine gun.

ALI: Naw, man. You don't have no footwork. You don't dance.

FRAZIER: Listen! Some guys get the wrong impression about what's happening out there. When I'm stepping into a man's jab, I'm not gonna step in with my head. I'm gonna step in with these hands. In front of me, see? And if your jab extend out to hit me, I got my hand here to catch it. Then mine can hit you. It's easy as that.

ALI *(disdainfully):* I throw 'em a little too quick for you to block.

FRAZIER *(shakes head ruefully):* I'd like to get this thing together.

ALI: I sure would like to get it on, too. 'Cause I got something for you, Joe. And why you always talk about you gonna come out smokin'?

FRAZIER: That's what I do! Ain't nobody that could put that smoke out. They slow down the fire a bit, but when that fire's gone, that smoke still right there.

ALI: Naw, man. I wrote a poem on you. Went like this:

> Joe's gonna come out smokin',
> And I ain't gonna be jokin'.
> I'll be peckin' and pokin',
> Pourin' water on his smokin'
> This might shock and amaze ya,
> But I'll retire Joe Frazier!

FRAZIER *(after pause):* Yeah? Smoke still smokin'. It's still smokin'. *(Both laugh)* I had my eye on you a long time. Remember when I used to call you up when you were about to fight Liston the first time? You'd say, "Come on. Keep training. I'm gonna help make you rich," and stuff like that. I listened to it, you know. Thought about it. By talking to you on the telephone—you know, you wouldn't let me get a word in edgewise—I made myself a promise.

I said, "I'm gonna fight on; I'm gonna train on, and one of these days I'm gonna straighten him out!"

ALI: Look, I'm a little too experienced for you, Joe.

FRAZIER: I admit, you some kind of inspiration for me, more'n anybody I ever come in contact with. Every time I see you running off at the mouth, you know what I said? I just said to myself, "Well, Joe, look. This guy can back up what he says. You gotta do just a little more." When I go on the road, I run a little harder. 'Cause I know I wanna be able to meet you one of these days. You know what I mean? I'd tell myself, the only way I know I can meet Cassius Clay is to keep winning, and keep knocking these cats out, you know? I had to get to you. Now here I am. They should allow you to fight, you know what I mean? Taking your license away like they did wasn't justice. Fighting was your way of making a living for the family, like me. With a family like yours, you know, you gotta have enough to support them right. Believe what you wanna believe in. I'm a hundred percent with you on that. You got a whole lot of people out there believe worse than you. If they give you a license, I'd fight you anytime, anyplace. But I'd prefer it should be here in the United States.

ALI: Right. I want it in a big stadium or something.

FRAZIER: I don't think we should flee the country to fight. This your home.

ALI: Look, Joe. Let me be frank with you. What you must realize is what you have riding against you if you ever fought me: you'd fight the two-time National Golden Gloves Champion—

FRAZIER: Hold it!

ALI: Let me finish!

FRAZIER: Now, hold it! You are two-time Champ, but what about me?

ALI: You wasn't no Golden Gloves Champion.

FRAZIER: You kidding?

ALI: Not Golden Gloves. What you ever win? The New York title?

FRAZIER: I won the New York title, right. And then I won it here in the East for '62, '63 and '64.

ALI (contemptuously): Local titles. I know you an Olympic Champion like me, but here's what you must realize. I'm a two-time National AAU Champion.

FRAZIER: What's more, I was a heavyweight.

ALI: I defeated—

FRAZIER: You was light-heavy!

ALI: No, I was heavyweight!

FRAZIER: You won in the Light-Heavy Division, man. I was always heavy. I used to weigh about two-thirty when I was about fifteen, sixteen years old. I went in the gym to lose weight. That's when I went in and found out I had a punch. You know, they had like seventeen heavyweights in the gym when I started. I ran 'em all out. I used to tote them steers when I worked in a kosher slaughterhouse. Then I'd come to the gym and chase everybody out of there—

ALI: Your running-out days are over. Here's what you must realize. I fought Sonny Liston twice, when he was at his best. Then I beat Fast Floyd Patterson. I beat the Champion of Germany, Mildenberger. All these title defenses. Henry Cooper, Brian London . . .

FRAZIER: What you want me to do?

ALI: And I fought Zora Folley, Cleveland Williams . . .

FRAZIER: Which one you want me to fight?

ALI: But let me tell you who you have beaten. You have beaten two men. You've beaten fellows that would not have ranked with me. Ellis was my sparring partner. See, you got your biggest thing on my sparring partner. So you must realize that I'm rougher than my sparring partner, so you gonna be in trouble when you meet me.

FRAZIER: I don't look at it that way. As long as a man got two hands and he in that top position, he can—

ALI: And another thing about you—

FRAZIER: Let me finish! If a contender's in the top ten, he got to be good. And they don't put you there, you gotta win your way up there. Work your way, fight your way. Now, these guys you name coming out in your time, you whipped them. I can't help that. They not around no more. I whip the guys who come around in my time.

ALI: You ever realize I got too much weight over you? See, I'm two-fifteen in shape.

FRAZIER *(thoughtfully):* That is a lot of weight to try to move around against a man like me, about two-oh-four.

ALI: I told you, if Ellis could have fought all the rounds like he did the first two—

FRAZIER: How could he, with all that pressure on him?

ALI: I can keep it up for fifteen rounds.

FRAZIER: Me too. Me too. *(Sighs)* That's the thing about it that gonna make this thing good. You see, you don't get tired. And I don't know what tired is myself. I'm just like a deer. I ain't even got a gall bladder. I run all day long, don't never stop. You ever see a deer?

ALI: Yeah. You know, I named my opponents, and you ain't no "deer." Patterson "The Rabbit," Liston "The Bear." And I name you "The Turtle."

FRAZIER: That's all right.

ALI: Joe Frazier, The Turtle . . .

FRAZIER: Slow but steady. You so fast, why you let them have Marciano whip you?

ALI: You mean in that phony computer fight? You *know* that was fake. Whites want to see Marciano go down as the greatest heavyweight of all time. When he wasn't. Leaving off myself and you, who you think would be the best two to fight the all-time title?

FRAZIER: Oh, like Joe Louis and Jack Johnson.

ALI: That's who I think.

FRAZIER: Well, I mean, really, guys like Dempsey, Marciano, Tunney can fight, but they no comparison to the black man. In ring power, I mean. You got one or two white guys that may really fight. Nobody's overlooking any good fighter. But they no comparison in power to the best black fighter. He got more.

ALI: Right.

FRAZIER: That's why blacks hold the title so long. They can't get a white guy in there edgewise, no kinda way. They tried to get one past Sonny, tried to get one past Floyd Patterson. They tried to get one past me, but I believe the next man gonna whip me'll be a black man . . .

ALI: He will be black, and I will be the one, if I get back.

FRAZIER: Well, I hope you do get back. But, man, you ain't gonna do no whipping. Not on me. I hope there'll be no hard feelings.

ALI: You mean after that showdown? Wherever it comes—

FRAZIER: Will you please let me talk . . . now?

ALI: Well, we're two champions and both of us can't talk at once. And we just gonna have to be equal. I can't let you outtalk me.

FRAZIER: You done expressed your feelings. Let me express mine. Now, you right about no hard feelings. All the fellows I destroy, I don't have no hard feelings. After I whip your ass, I'll buy you some ice cream. *(Sees Ali about to cut in)* Let me talk! You finished now? Let me talk. I got no hard feelings with you here or no other place.

But when we get in the ring, you on your own.

ALI: You be on your own, too.

FRAZIER: That's the only way I know how to be.

ALI: And if we can't get along, let's get it on.

FRAZIER: We'll get it on. Ain't no doubt about that. Because once that bell rings . . . See, you get out there and try to psych them guys. Me, I'm different. I'm the greatest psych artist ever put on earth. You outpsych Houdini easier than me—

ALI: Just for that smarty remark, I'm gonna make a prediction. I'm gonna tell you what would happen if I ever fought you.

FRAZIER: Be careful now, be careful. Don't get carried away.

ALI: I want this to go on record. I'm gonna lay out the blueprint of the first five rounds—

FRAZIER: Who say—

ALI: Let me talk! Then you say what you gonna do. Now, the first round —*Dong!* I'm coming out but ain't gonna do nothing. Just gonna show you off as being a amateur. I'm not gonna throw one punch. I'm gonna dance and I'm gonna hold my guard down beside my hips. And I'm gonna dance and move like I did with Floyd Patterson. And you won't even get in one punch. I'm gonna let you win that round. Then, second round—*Dong!* I'm coming out fast, but I'm not gonna shoot nothing but left jabs. And my right hand is gonna be down by my side. Not even gonna hold my right hand up for protection. Nothing but left jabs, nothing but left jabs, nothing but left jabs . . . the third round—*Dong!* I'm coming out. I'm putting the footwork together and I'm putting the jabs together and I'm putting the right crosses together and the left hooks—

FRAZIER *(explodes):* Shit! According to you, you done won the fight already—

ALI: And I'm not gonna miss a left jab that round. Maybe with one or two I might graze you. But all those jabs gonna be solid jabs. That night at the ticket booth, I want the people to pick up the program, and it be written out—round by round what I'm gonna do. Like when you read a menu for a eight-course meal. When you go to a restaurant, or if you go to a show, or when you go to one of your rock shows. Nothing will be printed on the card that night but the formula of how I'm gonna fight you. And after that fifth round—

FRAZIER *(can't stand it any longer):* Wait, wait—

ALI: You say what you gonna say when I'm through. Lemme finish getting in mine . . . don't be getting scared.

FRAZIER: Man, *scared?*

ALI: Yeah. Now, in the fifth round—

FRAZIER *(angry):* This fight has got to come off! It's coming off!

ALI: Listen, the fifth round—

FRAZIER: Why go further? You done beat me up already.

ALI: Naw, I haven't knocked you out. The fourth round I'm gonna tie you up.

FRAZIER: Who say it's gonna last that long?

ALI: Then the fifth round—

FRAZIER: How you gonna do all that?

ALI: I'm gonna right-cross you. And I'm gonna be teaching and talking to you. Telling you the history of your life.

FRAZIER: Awww, man, you done won the whole thing.

ALI: And after that fifth round I'll invent new punches. Now what do you have to say?

FRAZIER *(after long silence):* You done beat up everybody in the whole ring, plus the referee. Now, where I'm gonna be at when you be doing all these things? Counting my fingers?

ALI: You be trying to throw everything, and it ain't gonna land.

FRAZIER: Clay, it ain't gonna be that way.

ALI *(shrugs):* You have a right to say that. I have a right to say what I wanna say.

FRAZIER: All right, now. I'm gonna tell you what I feel about it. You gonna run for about, maybe, two. Then the sixth round, that would be your end—

ALI: No! Listen, don't you try any predicting.

FRAZIER: I'm telling you!

ALI: Be sure you can back it up! Your behind will be mine in round nine!

FRAZIER: Ohhh, now I see. You done gone past six. When we get to round four, ain't gonna be no more. That gonna be it. You be wore out.

ALI: I know how you psyched Ellis. *(Laughs)* You came on the Ed Sullivan show burning all that energy, just a day before the fight.

FRAZIER: Yeah.

ALI: That psyched Ellis. You know that? You come on cool enough, Joe, singing that song: "Oooooooohhhhhhh, baby,

OOOOOOOHHHHHHH, baby, I love you." It was live, wasn't it?

FRAZIER: Yeah.

ALI: That shook Ellis up. Here he sees you ain't worried. You cool and sharp out there singing when you shoulda been worried.

FRAZIER: Singing is just like a training thing. Know what I mean? I work up that kind of sweat, singing or training. Singing was just another routine, training . . . I'd get ready like that for you, 'cause you good. You can punch from either hand. But I don't think you got too much of a hook.

ALI: Oh no?

FRAZIER: No hook at all. You got a good right hand. I see that, but you can't hook, 'cause your arm's out too long. A man can't hook so much if his hand's long. Now, take me, I'm made for a hook for one big simple reason. My left arm is in a L. See? You didn't know that, huh? It's natural. It won't straighten out. This as far as I can stretch that hand out here, see? And I just come in like this. *(Takes hand off wheel and hooks)* It's automatically a hook. Just turn 'em right over. Instead of having to draw all the way back, I just turn it over. *(He demonstrates)*

ALI *(brushes it off)*: I got the answer to your hook. I lean backwards and move—

FRAZIER: But I hook to the body first. I get the head another time.

ALI: Man, you ain't gonna get the body. 'Cause soon as you start working the body, I'm gonna shoot for your head—quick! If you close to hitting my body with your short arms, I'm gonna WHIP! WHIP! WHIP! WHIP! Right on you. You won't get my body 'less you in a clinch, or trying to hold me.

FRAZIER: I ain't never held on to a man outta twenty-six fights.

ALI: If you relying on a knockout, you gonna be in trouble. You be losing round after round after round. And onliest way you gonna get me is to knock me out, and you will not do that!

FRAZIER: Oh, you gonna have to go.

ALI: You must think my being inactive for three long years slowed me down a little—

FRAZIER: Look! You ain't hurt a bit! I don't want no excuses. Ain't nothing wrong with you. Not a thing. You just had a little rest; that's good for you. Don't come up with that—"I been out of action for a while, it slowed me up." That rest made you more stronger.

ALI: That's what you'd tell people?

FRAZIER: That's the truth, and I know it.

ALI: Look. Let's be realistic. Suppose I'm never allowed to fight. But still I want to keep my body fit and sharp. Now, you needs a good fast man to keep you sharp because you go through so many sparring partners. Wouldn't you like to have the type sparring partner that could rumble with you four and five good rounds a day until you got enough? I mean, where you don't have to keep changing 'em 'cause they can't stand up to you?

FRAZIER: That's good . . .

ALI: I mean, wouldn't you like to have a good sparring partner that could tag you? And you can tag him, and he ain't gonna quit on you? I need a job.

FRAZIER: You don't need no goddamn job.

ALI: Don't tell nobody; it's between us, but I do. How much you pay?

FRAZIER: How much you want?

ALI: Couple hundred a week. That means eight hundred by the end of the month.

FRAZIER: Shit! You want a whole lot.

ALI: Well, if things get where I think I ain't gonna be allowed to fight any more, if it ever gets obvious that I'm through fighting, I'd want to go on and spar with you. But if we were ever gonna fight, I wouldn't do it 'cause it would hurt the gate. Like people seeing me beat you around the gym, or you beat me around the gym, or we get too friendly and kill a gate. But if I ever get—

FRAZIER: First, I like to know, who is gonna be the "sparring partner"?

ALI: Me! I'll be your sparring partner. I'm not fighting. I just said . . .

FRAZIER: Sound like you want to be the main event.

ALI: No. You heard what I was saying.

FRAZIER: I heard you!

ALI: If I get—

FRAZIER: I heard what you said, but to hear you switch it around like *I* would be the sparring partner . . .

ALI: Well, we get a big special gym. And I'm just gonna be your traveling sparring partner. If they won't let me fight no more, and won't give me a license, and—

FRAZIER: Okay.

ALI: Right. And we have our own rumbles every day. And then people will be able to look at sparring sessions and tell who would have won if we'd ever fought. Right?

FRAZIER: Well, that's good, too.

ALI: That's all I'm saying.

FRAZIER: All right.

ALI: Would they try to put me outta the gym if I show you up?

FRAZIER: I own the gym. I wanna keep you sharp in case you get your license back. I don't want no excuse. I'll make sure you get a personal key from me.

ALI: When you start training?

FRAZIER: Another month.

ALI: I want the press there. You're not scared, are you?

FRAZIER: No, man. Not a bit.

ALI: 'Cause I'm determined to get to you whether it's in the ring, Yankee Stadium, the Spectrum, Coliseum, Astrodome, in the alley or wherever. It's got to be said that I got to you. And you gonna have your chance to see what you can do.

FRAZIER: Remember, I ain't never been whipped either.

ALI *(suddenly):* Say, slow up, slow up! You gonna get a ticket driving this fast. *(Laughs)* Wouldn't that be something, you get a ticket and I'm riding with you? I'd say I jumped into your car and Joe Frazier got scared and drove like crazy. Make news all over the world. Now look, Joe. I got something else I wanna tell you. Some advice. I already learned this. All fighters when they come into money, first thing they do is get 'em a couple of nice cars. Ain't nothing wrong with it. I had raggedy cars all my life, and you had raggedy cars all your life.

FRAZIER: Yeah, yeah.

ALI: And when you get some money, you want something new.

FRAZIER: Right.

ALI: I know how you feel. Always keep you one good Cadillac. It ain't that expensive. Take the first real money you get, tie up a house. A good house for your wife and your babies.

FRAZIER: Yeah.

ALI: So if you get crippled, you got a place to sleep.

FRAZIER: Yeah.

ALI: When I started out, I put my money in things I didn't need: diesel buses, one like a Greyhound. Got my name painted on it. And LISTON WILL FALL IN EIGHT. For publicity. It helped, but I really didn't need no twelve-thousand-dollar bus. Then I ordered two limousines, cost fourteen thousand apiece. I really didn't need 'em. I wanted to be seen showing off in a limousine. You get used to one thing and you'll say, "Hell! I want something different." You see a long silver limousine with two phones in the back and you'll say, "Man. I got to have this." I'm telling you what I did. Everybody got little weaknesses. What's yours?

FRAZIER: My car. But I like to have it built the way I want it.

ALI: Ain't nothing wrong with that. Got something else to tell ya. More advice.

FRAZIER: Yeah?

ALI: Your motorcycle. Get off that damn motorcycle. I know you like it, so keep it. But ride it two A.M. in the morning. Maybe five A.M. in the morning. Ride it around the park. Don't be in no everyday traffic, darting in and out on the expressway ... ZIP-ZIP, BRRRR-BRRR . . . a quick takeoff, showing off like you do.

FRAZIER: You got nerve to accuse *me* of showing off!

ALI: Look, man, one fall, splint one knee, one smash, and there goes millions of dollars. All for that little old fifteen-hundred-dollar motorcycle? Now, I'm just like you. I love motorcycles. But think about your daughter, your children, your bones. And just think about millions of people wanting to watch you fight, all over the world. Two and three million dollars at one gate.

FRAZIER: Yeah.

ALI: You had a motorcycle accident once, like I did. That was a warning, man. Let that motorcycle alone. Motorcycles is for wild people. Please, do it for me. I know you love it and you gonna ride it no matter what anybody say, but ride that motorcycle at two in the morning, when ain't no traffic. I seen the way you do at a stoplight, challenging anybody to a race: BRUUUUM-BRUUUUM, then SKEEE-EEE-EEEEEE off you go and GGGGGGGGGG-GGGGGGGGG. It starts getting good to you, man, then you go taking chances. Look, man, President Nixon don't even dare walk the street, 'cause it's too much at stake. See, you ain't "Joe Frazier" no more, just a little unknown boy in the meat house. I'm not "Cassius Clay" no more, just a little ole boy running around Louisville making fifteen dollars a week working for Catholic nuns. See, everybody in the world know the name "Joe Frazier." Think about what I'm saying.

FRAZIER: I'm thinking.

ALI: Think: China, Japan, Africa, Georgia, Alabama, Cleveland, all the

TV, radio announcers know Joe Frazier. And what you riding on? Your motorcycle can mess up all that. All you got to do now is put on a suit and walk down the street, and somebody say, "Joe Frazier." The Hell's Angels may be roaring down the street, but the people ignore 'em and say, "Damn them. Where's Joe Frazier?" So right now you don't need to be a showoff.

FRAZIER: Sound like you got experience.

ALI: Awww, man. Why you think I'm telling you the truth like this?

FRAZIER: You steady trying to get that bike from me.

ALI: No. If you like your bike, keep your bike—in the garage or something. Every now and then you might want to start your motor and you might say, "I'm going to the store." Take your time, you know. Watch yourself. Look, seventy-five miles per hour, no faster. One blowout, a locked rim'll throw you, anything. Even forty's too fast to fall on.

FRAZIER: Thirty's too goddamn fast to fall on. I fell doing about thirty miles, man, and got all the bark tore off my ass.

ALI: Yeah?

FRAZIER: See down there? My leg twisted in.

ALI (shudders): That be awful if something like that happened now, before I get a chance to whip you in the ring. If that happened, you know what you ought to do? Get a gun and shoot yourself. Picture yourself up in a hospital and it's all in the news . . . "Joe Frazier leg broke in motorcycle spill. Ali-Frazier fight canceled. Ten-billion-dollar gate was predicted." And then the doctor comes into your room and says, "Sorry, Joe. No more."

FRAZIER (visualizes it, shakes his head): "We got to operate."

ALI: Yessir. "We have to take that leg off, Joe, and there'll be a lifetime limp in the other one." Joe, man, you'd look at yourself and say, "I'm a fool."

FRAZIER: Booo-hoo, booooo-hoo . . .

ALI: You ain't taking this serious. I'm trying to help you.

FRAZIER: Go ahead, go ahead.

ALI: Take that motorcycle and say, "Motorcycle, you a curse to me, man, you a curse. I got shows to do, I got foxes to see, I got too much at stake. And if I ever ride you, it's gonna be at four A.M. in the morning."

FRAZIER (sighs): That sure was a lesson to me.

ALI: And I'll tell you something else . . . Floyd Patterson was a real champion the way he carried hisself.

FRAZIER: Patterson? He didn't impress me no way. I could whip him with no legs.

ALI: *Slow up, man!* We coming near New York. *Slow up!*

FRAZIER *(peering ahead):* There's a hole wide enough for this Caddy. Let's get right on in there, come on, baby. Come on! What was you saying?

ALI: Slow up!

FRAZIER: Before you said that . . .

ALI: I was telling you some things that I know was right. Archie Moore was a real champion. So was Sugar Ray. Now you are known for being the best in the world. Now, here's what you gotta do. You gotta dress accordingly. When a person see Joe Frazier, they should be looking at somebody more important than the President of the United States. Like you were the President of the World. Nixon only runs the country. Now, what you got on is pretty for the stage, but it's not as pretty as a black suit.

FRAZIER: I'm casual and lounging now.

ALI: I seen pimps dress like this. They gonna look at you and respect you, but not like they would if you dressed up in a double-breasted suit with a vest, like you worth four, five million.

FRAZIER: I stay cleaner than the Board of Health, man.

ALI: But like children and kids wear pink suits and white shoes, and racetrack jackets, like sometimes I notice you do. You a Southerner like me and we Southerners dress like that . . . like some of your friends who sing with you. But notice the hipper dudes. Notice how they dress. Get a cat just like I did, to put some clothes together for you. And then say, "Man, what should I wear? What's best with this? What's the latest shirt? What's the latest ties?" And the darker your clothes look, you look more sophisticated. You look real dignified. Right now I'm dressed like a Senator would be dressed. Like the way Floyd Patterson carries hisself, the way he dresses. He's quiet, the way I wish I could be. I talk a lot. He act like The Champion. Ever seen Patterson, the way he talks? Real dignified?

FRAZIER: I told you, I don't want to be no Patterson no kind of way.

ALI: Right now you really don't have no image yet. You haven't been on too many TV interviews, and you haven't held the title long enough since you won it from Ellis.

FRAZIER *(gently):* No, I "defended" it against Ellis.

ALI: Say it that way if you want. You knew you was the best and you proved it. Like Terrell was Champ once. But after I whipped him, WBA had to say, "All right, *now* what we gonna do?" They give me back my title, see? That's what I'm talking about. You think about how you gonna do. Best thing you ever said was, "Look. I'm gonna fight. I ain't in no politics." Why get caught in something you ain't in and talk about something you don't have to talk about no way? You ain't obligated to nothing. You say, "I'm here to fight; I'm The Champion and that's it." But I didn't dig it that way, see. I saw Negroes getting lynched, and I saw Negroes off with white women when they got rich or famous, and poor black people going hungry. I had the title, but just because I had cars, was living easy, was on Johnny Carson and Merv Griffin, didn't keep me from seeing my people out there catching hell and I wanted to get out there and stand up and talk to 'em, even on the garbage cans. I like to go 'round people and talk to 'em.

FRAZIER: I do the same thing.

ALI: That makes me strong, when I help somebody. So after I got my title, after I got where I was, I just said, "The hell with Uncle Tom-ing." If you check it out, George Foreman is not a hero with black people just because he waved the American flag at the Olympics. George Foreman carried that flag 'cause he was a brainwashed black super-patriot. But John Carlos and Tommie Smith, they held up their arms in the sky; their image will go down in history! They stood tall with that black glove salute! Carlos, he's at my house now. I want you to meet him.

FRAZIER: Yeah? When?

ALI: Let me finish. I got other tips I want to give you. I ain't envious of you, as you know!

FRAZIER: Go on.

ALI: I was a Muslim, I still am. I stayed with the Faith, and I didn't hate nobody. I ain't never preached no violence but I couldn't take that Army step. That's when they finally got me in a corner. So I just said:

> Clean out my cell,
> And take my tail to jail,
> 'Cause better to be in jail fed,
> Than to be in Viet Nam, dead.

So anyway, I like what I'm doing. I was happy to see Ellis get his thing; I was happy to see you get yours, and I'm happy to see you win the whole thing. But I was glad you whipped Ellis. I helped

Ellis get everything he got, and he ain't mentioned my name nowhere.

FRAZIER *(quietly):* Well, that's the kinda guy we called a Tom. Lets everyone else talk for him.

ALI: So I was glad to see you whip Ellis.

FRAZIER *(thoughtfully):* Of all the guys I fought, I was special glad I whipped three guys. Ellis was one. Buster Mathis was another one.

ALI: Buster?

FRAZIER: He was a singing "Yes, ma'am" type Uncle Tom. Everything he hear the white boss say, you know, he try to repeat it. Mathis was a big, dumb, ignorant fellow.

ALI: How long ago you fought him?

FRAZIER: In '68.

ALI *(also thoughtfully):* I was in a Muslim meeting in Hartford, Connecticut, when it happened, teaching and preaching. Somebody come in and said: "Frazier just stopped Mathis!" I'd just got through lecturing and they announced the news. He put something on ya for a while, though, didn't he?

FRAZIER: Didn't do a thing to me.

ALI: He hurt ya, didn't he? First few rounds—

FRAZIER: Clay. I give Mathis one round. I think it was the sixth or seventh round. Them other rounds he was out there dancing, getting hisself tired, like you gonna do. That's the way you gonna do.

ALI: I got some news for you. You never met nothing like you gonna meet me, Joe Frazier.

FRAZIER: Well, I agree with that. I hope not.

ALI: Joe Frazier, you just the Olympic kid who got a break 'cause I stepped aside.

FRAZIER: I was gonna take my break if you didn't step aside.

ALI: You was gonna take it?

FRAZIER: Yes, I was. Gonna smash you right dead on your ashcan.

ALI: My ashcan?

FRAZIER: Yessir. And then you gonna ask, "What happen'?"

ALI: I was gonna ask you why you ain't got no modesty. Wait—what time you got now, Joe? How soon we be in New York?

FRAZIER: Going on four now. I think another half-hour. Yeah, we'll make it.

ALI: Good, I gotta be there by five. So . . . Look! Slow down here. No kidding, Joe. Police are really out here. We too near New York now, you won't hardly get away from 'em, Joe. No kidding. They'll get ya out here.

FRAZIER: Not if I see 'em first . . .

ALI: You ain't gonna get there no quicker.

FRAZIER: I know I ain't, but if I see 'em first, they can forget it. They gotta catch me.

ALI: What if they slapped you?

FRAZIER: No—now, wait a minute. They ain't gotta do all that just to write me a ticket.

ALI: What would you do if the police slapped you? Can you street-fight if you had to?

FRAZIER: Man, *what?*

ALI: Can you street-fight?

FRAZIER: Man, I kill a monkey in the street.

ALI: Think you can whip me in the street?

FRAZIER: Anywhere, man. *(A plane is coming into Newark Airport, almost parallel with the car)* Hey, there's a plane landing over there. Let's see how fast this car can go.

ALI *(shakes his head):* I don't trust 'em, though, man. I don't like airplanes, period. But I think if I was in it, right beside the pilot, and he show me how the motor work, explain things to me, about turbulence, and I could run the motor on the ground awhile and listen to it, then I'd feel safe. If he could tell me if a motor conked out, how far you could glide . . .

FRAZIER: That's one thing that Big Otis could do. *(Sighs)* There was a singing ass lost to the world.

ALI: Otis Redding?

FRAZIER: They found his body strapped to the seat. Remember?

ALI *(testy):* He'd fly anything. Otis fooled around with that little ole plane even when he knew the battery's bad.

FRAZIER: Me, I like driving.

ALI: All fighters like to drive. Joe Louis loved to drive. Jack Johnson drove everywhere. Jack Dempsey, Ezzard Charles, Sugar Ray likes to drive, Emile Griffith, Eddie Machen, Terrell—prizefighters like to feel the wheel in their fists and a motor underfoot. You just like me.

FRAZIER: Yeah. *(long quiet)* One difference between you and me, though. You make a little more noise, that's all. Me, I'm more the quiet type. You understand. You raise a whole bunch of hell all the time. They got to know you there. But me, I just slip around. Peep around, ease on in. If they don't know I'm there, they know I'm on my way there. Yessir. *(Blows horn)* All right, now, you over there! Hang on that Chrysler, buddy! Why, you four-eye fool!

ALI: The way you talk to white folks, ever have any trouble in the South, Joe?

FRAZIER: You mean after I become Champ?

ALI: Before.

FRAZIER: I whipped some ass—you always gotta do that. One of 'em called me a nigger and I called him a cracker and he didn't like it. Followed me all over town until night came. Then, when I get to the right spot, I let him catch up. Gawwd A'mighty! Remind me of my old Ziggy fight.

ALI: Ziggy? Who's Ziggy?

FRAZIER: Dave Sieglewicz—Texas. Remember the one I fought just before I fought Folley?

ALI: Oh, yeah. How long did that last?

FRAZIER: Not quite a minute . . . wasn't a round.

ALI: Was he scared?

FRAZIER: Yeah, he was scared. He started turning four, five different colors. I said, "What color is he, anyway?" He went through white, orange, pink, red . . . I said, "Wonder what color he gonna be." When we got in the ring, he mess around and touch me somehow, and goddamn! When he touched me, I think he got me a little mad. So I reached all the way back home. I went *home* and got me a hook on him—

ALI: Wow, no wonder you wear out sparring partners. *(Leans out to guard as Frazier pulls up into tollbooth)* THIS IS JOE FRAZIER THE NEW CHAMPION AND I AM MUHAMMAD ALI THE OLD CHAMPION! THIS IS JOE FRAZIER.

VOICE: Oh, I saw you on the Mike Douglas show. *(to Joe)* I saw him on the Mike Douglas show.

JOE: What about me? What about *me?*

ALI: Seriously, this is Joe Frazier, the new Champion.

FRAZIER: You saw *him?* What about me? I was there, too.

VOICE: I saw you on the Mike Douglas show, Mr. Ali.

FRAZIER *(chuckles as car pulls out):* He's still talking about you. Stop fidgeting, I'll slow down from here. I heard your wife's expecting. When she due?

ALI: In four, five months. When's yours due?

FRAZIER: Middle of August. Tell you what I'm gonna do. I'm gonna name my baby, if he's a boy, Joseph Clay Frazier, Jr. How 'bout that?

ALI: Wow! You really gonna lay that on him?

FRAZIER: Joseph Clay Frazier, Jr.!

ALI: OOOOOOOHHHHH WOW! That baby gonna be a bad little dude! *(Both laugh)* Look here, Joe. *(Pulls up shirt, shows stomach)* Three years off, I don't look too bad, do I, Joe?

FRAZIER: Naw. Ain't bad at all. *(Starts singing one of his songs)* How 'bout that for style?

ALI: You ever heard me sing? What you think of my singing?

FRAZIER: You can't sing a little bit.

ALI: I was a hit on Broadway! You never heard my Mighty Whitey song?

FRAZIER: Sheeeeeiiiiiitt!

ALI *(singing):* *When the night has come, and the land is dark, and the moon is the only light we'll see—*

FRAZIER: Hold that right there! Hold it!

ALI: You can't sing that good.

FRAZIER: Listen. *(Sings in a throaty, husky voice)* *When the night has come, and the land is dark, and the moon is the only light we'll see . . .*

ALI: Naw, man. You can't sing.

FRAZIER: *I won't cry—*

ALI: *I won't cry, no, I woooonnntt . . .* Sing on! Sing . . .

FRAZIER *(admiring):* You are a singing ass! *(Joins in, both sing in unison)* *Just as long as you stand, stand by me.*

ALI: So, darling! *(Music comes on car radio)* How you making it as a singer?

FRAZIER: Good, I love it. See, I make like thirty thousand in less than about four, five weeks just singing. The Latin Casino was thirteen thousand dollars. Vegas was what? Can't think what the hell it was, but it was good money, I know that much. Money I haven't even touched yet. I ain't had a chance to go pick it up . . .

ALI: Awww, you ain't got that kind of money, man. Wow, you carry that much dough in your wallet?

FRAZIER: Four, five hundred. Need some?

ALI: How about a hundred? I may stay overnight.

FRAZIER: Yeah, okay.

ALI: Pay you next week. *(Looks at the hundred-dollar bill)* I owe Joe Frazier a hundred dollars. Never thought the day would come when I'd owe Joe Frazier one hundred dollars. Hey, look over there.

FRAZIER *(leans out to yell at woman toll-taker):* Hello, honey. How you doing today? *(Woman looks coldly and turns away)*

ALI *(aside to Joe):* She's evil. When you get them evil ones, they start acting like that. Don't tell them who you are. 'Cause they quick to tell ya, "Well, so what?"

FRAZIER: I was trying to be nice . . .

ALI: What you think about Sonny Hopkins? You remember his baddest song?

FRAZIER: Yeah. You ever heard that tape I made out in Philly? Go like this:

> *Every time I come to Philadelphia*
> *I listen to*
> *Station WHAT.*
> *I dig the mighty burner,*
> *Make no mistake-a jake-a.*
> *Gimme Muhammad Ali!*

ALI: Did ya?

FRAZIER: Then he comes back with your voice saying, "Gimme Joe Frazier." *(Sings along with radio as music comes on again)*

> *You got to give a little,*
> *Take a little . . .*

ALI: That yours?

FRAZIER: No. That the Dells singing. Hear the song we sing last night? "Truly Loving Me?" That's my tune, man.

ALI: You only wrote two songs.

FRAZIER: I wrote more'n that. I got, like, several tunes of my own. I got something called "Knockout Drops," man. A beautiful tune. Girls go crazy over it. I say:

Baby, my loveeiinng is like TNT.
Anything come greater 'n TNT is me.

ALI: Hey, listen to this song. I'm getting ready a record called "It's All Over Now, Mighty Whitey." Oscar Brown's.

FRAZIER: I heard part of it, you sang back there.

ALI *(singing):*

We see you looking cruel with your cold blue eyes.
You think we just your fools, thinking you are wise.
We see you waddling in your greed,
While we are down here in dying need.
But it's all over now, Mighty Whitey,
It's all over now.

You had us in your lock, tight as any cage.
Mighty Whitey, Mighty Whitey!
And now you acting shocked 'cause we in a rage,
Us on the bottom, with you on top.
That's a game that we aim to stop.
'Cause it's all over now, Mighty Whitey,
It's all over now.

We can't bear no more. We don't care no more.
We won't scare no more . . .
Just as sure as we are black.
Till our roles are reversed, and the last are first,
And our color is no longer our curse,
You can do your worst,
We are not turning ba—a—a—c—k!
Call out your National Guard,
Call your police. P O L I C E . . .
Tell 'em to come down hard, it ain't gonna be no
     peace.
If you expecting us to Uncle-Tom,
You might as well go on drop your bomb.
'Cause it's all over now, Mighty Whitey,
It's all over now.

(Lets it soak in) If you got a band you could sing it. Well, if you could sing it, I would give it to you.

FRAZIER: What you mean if I could sing it? I like that.

ALI: You couldn't sing it 'cause it'd be a little too rough. Right now it wouldn't be good . . . little too bold for you. It's perfect for me, 'cause I ain't got a damn thing to lose.

FRAZIER: *It's all over now, Mighty Whitey, it's all over now . . .*

ALI: Let your top back so I can see better, Joe. *Wow, damn!* Look at that fox out there . . . *(Leans out of car)* HEY! I'M MUHAMMAD ALI. JOE FRAZIER AND MUHAMMAD ALI . . . COME ON OVER HERE! I've always loved New York. This is our city, Joe; the world is right here.

FRAZIER: I'll stop over here, let you out.

ALI: We don't wanna be seen too much together, you know.

FRAZIER: Yeah. They'll think we're buddies. That'll be bad for the gate.

ALI: Yeah. Ain't nobody gonna pay nothing to see two buddies.

With that, I reached down and flicked off the tape.

"All this is going in my book, you know," I said.

"Just don't change a damn thing," Joe shot back.

We were on West 52nd Street, and Frazier pulled over to the curb and slammed on the brakes. I climbed out. As autograph seekers came up, a little guy chewing a cigar recognized me. Joe just sat in the car looking. In a few minutes a man was handing me a card, saying, "My nephew talks about you all the time."

People were stopping on the sidewalk, looking, doing double takes, nudging each other. Although I'd been out of the news for nearly three years, a group of teenage hippies came running down from a show, crying, "Hey, Champ! Wait up, Champ! Wait up!" A man in a red sports coat with a poodle waved to some people behind him. "Hurry up! It's Muhammad Ali." Some showgirls broke from across the street: "O-O-O-O-O-WOW, O-O-O-O-O-O-WOW, it's him!" Then I was surrounded . . . they were throwing questions:

"When you gonna fight again?"

"You're the best in my book, Champ."

"When you coming back?"

"How 'bout the fight with Frazier?"

"What about Frazier . . . can you take Frazier?"

Frazier hadn't gotten out. I pointed to the wrinkled Cadillac. "Folks, that's World Heavyweight Champion Joe Frazier! Right there. Ask him. Joe Frazier!"

One or two people grinned like I'd included them in a secret put-on. I cried out louder, "JOE FRAZIER! THIS IS JOE FRAZIER!"

The guy with the poodle took his dog over to sniff around Joe, then gave his expert judgment. "Frazier? That ain't Frazier." Something about his self-righteous ignorance made even Frazier smile.

A few weeks ago I'd walked up around 42nd Street and, just for fun, whenever the crowd that followed asked, "What're you doing now, Champ? What're you doing?" I'd yell back, "I'm looking for Frazier. Anybody seen Frazier? I'm out to whip that chump, I mean 'champ,' "

and they'd laugh. And when I stood on the corner, they poured out of
stores, shows from across the street, until it took seven policemen to
clear the corner, and they were shouting:

"You're the real Champ!"

"Fight Frazier!"

"Make them give you a license!"

Now I put on the same act: "Where's Frazier? I'll take him on
right here on the corner!" They roared. All this with the real Frazier
in the flesh a few feet away and they couldn't recognize him.

I could have convinced them, though. I wanted Frazier to get out
of the car and walk down through Times Square with me. There'd be
enough people who'd know. It would dawn on them that this was a rare
sight. If we could each take a corner—say, he'd take the north side and
I'd take the south—and we pretended we needed strait jackets to keep
us from killing each other, all Times Square would be blocked.

As I stood there, even though I could imagine the big money in
a Heavyweight Title struggle between Joe and me, I was convinced that
it would never come off.

I had announced I was retired so many times that Herbert threw
up his hands and said, "Will you stop saying you are retired! They have
retired you. You had nothing to do with it. Just stop talking about
retiring."

Frazier had talked about retiring if he couldn't meet me in the
ring. He acknowledged that the only way to become a champion is to
whip a champion. What he whipped in Jimmy Ellis was my sparring
partner.

But I would have liked something more, not just to be in the ring
with Frazier, tearing away at each other like Williams' dinosaurs
. . . True, fighting was all that I had ever done, but there was always
something in me that rebelled against it. Maybe it was because those
who profited most from it didn't think of fighters as human or intelligent. They saw us as made just for the entertainment of the rich. Just
for breaking each other's nose, bleeding and having the cuts patched
up and pushed back out in the ring, round after round while we're
killing each other for the crowd. And at least half the crowd was white.

Then there was this nightmarish image I always had of two slaves
in the ring. Like in the old slave days on the plantations, with two of
us big black slaves fighting, almost on the verge of annihilating each
other while the masters are smoking big cigars, screaming and urging
us on, looking for the blood.

Since being barred from the ring because of my stand against the
Viet Nam war, my mail included letters from ninety-seven countries.
I had exchanged greetings and correspondence with people like Ber-
trand Russell and Jean-Paul Sartre, and foreign heads of state, and I

had won recognition from the leading people in America and white and black students across the country. And even though I was not always conscious of it, I was slowly changing. Boxing was behind me. I wanted to be known as a freedom fighter but I still wanted comrades—close friends who did the same work I did, felt the same way I did, buddies equally as strong and dedicated who would fight alongside me for blacks. I wanted a buddy like Joe. Two of us dinosaurs who could mean something to thirty million blacks. Who could help them. Me and Joe Frazier, I thought, have got to get together. Because, while I picked at him and made fun of him in public, underneath I truly admired him. He had the heart of a black fighter. Maybe he wouldn't agree with me on a lot of things—like presidents and prime ministers, governors and mayors, who didn't agree with each other—but we could work together on a common program. Some common program like Freedom, Justice and Equality for black people. Maybe I was dreaming, but I couldn't help it. I thought how good it would be for Joe Frazier to come to my house, and me to his. What he said in the car about naming his child after me really touched me. It let me know that he had some admiration for me, too, underneath.

I wanted to say something as he stood there and the crowd gathered around. I wanted to say:

"Joe, we can ride around together, you and me. Go through the ghettos. We could walk and talk together, not forgetting our people because we both earn money and we live halfway decent. We could go to the old black people who work on dead-end jobs, drudgery . . . and have nobody young and strong to help them. People nobody knows, nobody wants. The black people who don't know where their next month's rent is coming from. We could get up in the morning preaching freedom and justice. I know both of us, deep down in our hearts, are sick and tired of seeing black people hungry, catching hell, being shot and killed.

"You and me can be buddies, Joe. I don't care what they do to me, jail me, shoot me, I don't care. I just want to go down in history that I didn't sell out or Uncle-Tom when I got famous. I didn't go off and marry someone white, with all those fine black girls out there . . . I didn't marry someone white and overlook them . . ."

Joe didn't talk as much as I did, but he was shrewd. His Cloverlay, Inc., stockholders may think he's their race horse, like my sponsors back in Louisville thought. They thought that buying my contract gave them control of my soul. Frazier, my buddy, he would understand that. He knew he had to go along with all that in order to get ahead, the way I did. He knew he wasn't free to go where he wanted, to say what he wanted about race, politics, religion, because the fight bosses wouldn't like it. He knew all that.

This was the kind of buddy I needed. One that would go down with me, walk the streets with me. Our families would know each other, our children would grow up together . . .

Then I looked up from the autographs to see if he was still there. I wanted to go over to him, get back in the car with him. He was standing at the edge of the crowd, his cowboy hat cocked on the side of his head. But a chilly feeling went through me when our eyes met. His look was that of a traveling gunfighter who had come into town to appraise the fastest gun. There was no envy or jealousy in his look, only a cold, methodical appraisal, for he knew that only when he had defeated me in the ring would the world really recognize him as The Champion. He nodded his head slowly and got back in the car. Whatever chance we had of being buddies, of being close, intimate friends, was gone.

DINOSAURS IN A PARK

If I was, as Chicago *Tribune's* sports editor Arch Ward described me, the "unpopular, undefeated heavyweight monster-in-exile," the only way out of exile was into head-on collision with the "popular, undefeated heavyweight monster, Joe Frazier."

Nearly four summers had passed since I was stripped of the Heavyweight Championship. I had seen promoters who were trying to end my exile turned down in thirty-eight states. And when the summer of '70 came, I faced the fact that not a promoter in America could get a fight for me legally. My lawyers would ask the Supreme Court to allow me to leave the country to work while my case was being appealed.

A growing number of prominent people and black organizations spoke out for my right to practice my profession until the final Court decision was handed down.

"Freedom on bail," said Michael Meltsner, a Columbia University law professor, to a Federal Court judge while trying to get a license for me to fight in New York, "implies the right of a defendant to pursue his normal occupation while awaiting court settlement of the case."

But the only prize strong enough to break through what one sports editor described as the "most far-reaching boycott against a performer in American history" is the potential gate that an Ali-Frazier fight might bring. There was a chance it could happen, but it was only a chance and a slim one.

To this day I meet people from Philadelphia who swear they saw Frazier and me in a bloody street brawl about to tear each other's head off, free of charge. And they swear they've got thousands of witnesses who'll back up the story that we needed armed policemen to keep us apart and stop us from wrecking each other.

The top Chicago *Sun-Times* sports reporter, the late Wendell Smith, gave this version that he "scooped"—the "inside" story of how "boxing promoters around the world turned a sickly gray when they heard what almost happened between the belligerent warriors in a public park picnic area where everyone gets in on the cuff":

> Ali and Frazier came very near putting on the $10 million fight for nothing, absolutely free, in a Philadelphia park.
> It seemed that Muhammad, an irritating needler, became highly critical of Frazier's prowess on a Philadelphia talk show. . . . Frazier promptly and angrily dared him to repeat those remarks in a face-to-face confrontation in a Philadelphia gymnasium where both occasionally train. . . . Muhammad quickly accepted the invitation. . . . So did thousands of other citizens interested in a fight between the champion and the ex-champion. . . . The gym was too small to hold all the potential spectators and the police told the fighters to take their anger . . . to a nearby commons known as Fairmount. Frazier did a retreat upon the advice of his managers. . . .

The story spread all over the country—in fact, the world—and until now has stood up as the authentic version of the confrontation that I was supposed to have had with Frazier in his gym. I know how it got started, especially since I was the one who started it.

It was during the time when I was expecting another year of exile, when hopes of ever boxing again were at their lowest, and when attempts by discouraged promoters to get me a license had slowed down to a halt.

The American Legion, the Veterans of Foreign Wars and White Citizens Councils had announced they would boycott and shut down any arena that dared to let me fight. And now the story circulating among fight backers was that "even if the unpatriotic slacker is given a chance to practice his trade again, no one would show up."

My biggest income then was coming from college appearances,

usually arranged by Richard Fulton in New York. And in crisscrossing the country, I met all kinds of people, and regardless of what the newspapers said, I felt their support. I believed it when they said they were with me in my right to fight and opposed to the jail sentence hanging over my head.

To keep the promoters fighting for me, I had to prove to them that people were willing to pay money to see "a loud-mouthed, unpatriotic braggart" beaten. Then there was a chance some promoter could break through the resistance.

Now my time is running out. The Supreme Court decision on my jail sentence is due to come down any time. My lawyers believe my chance of escaping jail is not good, and although I publicly say that I am unconcerned about ever fighting again, deep down I want the chance to come back, to knock the pretenders off the throne, to prove that I could do what Joe Louis, Rocky Marciano, Ezzard Charles, Jack Dempsey and all the great fighters could not do—come back into the ring after a long layoff and beat the best fighters the world could put up against me.

I remember one evening falling to sleep while thinking about another boxing promotion for me that has been turned down in Seattle because of boycott threats from the American Legion. I wonder if there is any other force with more strength than the organization that opposed me, and I think of the people in the streets who want to see me win, and the people who want to see me whipped. All of them together want the same thing: to see me in the ring against a powerful opponent. And the most powerful of this day is the World Heavyweight Champion, Joe Frazier.

Inside Joe's own group, Cloverlay, Inc., the Philadelphia corporation with which he is under contract, Arthur C. Kaufmann, one of its strongest members and formerly the executive director of Gimbels, has declared he would resign rather than let Joe fight me: "It's time for good Americans to stand up and be counted," he's reported as saying in the Philadelphia *Evening Bulletin.* "If Clay wants to fight, let him fight the Viet Cong. I've got friends whose sons have gone over there. Until Clay serves his time or is inducted in the Army, I don't want Joe Frazier in the ring with him. Joe Louis and Gene Tunney served. Now Clay has 'taken the veil' of a Black Muslim Minister. Well, Frazier is a symbol to America and I don't want that jeopardized."

I get up the next morning and run nearly three miles around Organdy Park, just as though I have a fight in front of me. I have an idea and I'm so excited that when I get home I rest only long enough to allow Joe to get to Yank Durham's house, where I know he'll be that morning.

I dial and Yank answers the phone.

"Yank, tell me the truth," I say. "Are you and Joe trying to duck out of fighting me? Tell me the truth!"

"Are you crazy?"

"Then why don't you and Joe talk up the fight against me? Why aren't you talking it up?"

"You know why, fool. They won't give you no license. They saving you for jail, and nobody ever heard of a World Heavyweight Title fight in the penitentiary, that's why!"

"But if the people want to see me and Joe fight real bad, if we show them how bad the people want it . . ."

"What you have in mind, Cassius?"

"Where's Joe? Put Joe on the phone."

"Joe, come over here. Cassius wants to talk to you."

"Joe, what time you training today?"

"Four o'clock, why?"

"Where?"

"In my own gym, 22nd and Columbia. Why?"

"Because you and me are gonna fight each other at four o'clock. You and me."

Joe is silent for a while, but then I feel it through the phone that he's caught what I'm after. "You mean just a jive? Just to stir up things? Just sort of a show? Yeah! Your people hold on to you, mine hold on to me, and we play like we want to get at each other?"

"Yeah. Now look, Joe. I'm going to call all the disc jockeys, and all the TV announcers, all the newspapers. I'm gonna tell them you dared me to come to your gym, you dig?"

"Go ahead."

"I'm gonna tell them you said you'd knock me out if I dare come inside your gym. They know me. I don't take no dare. I'll tell 'em all I'm going in your gym to get in the ring and settle our argument at four o'clock. I want people to come out and witness how I would slaughter you if we ever had a real fight, you dig?"

"If you put it like that, nobody with any sense would believe it. Especially me."

"Never mind that, Joe. They think we two dumb, crazy niggers who hate each other enough to do anything. They think we don't get along. Everybody in the world wants to see us fight. Not just here, but all over the world. This is the fight they want, and nobody can stop it, Joe. I get mail from everywhere. They want to know who's the best between you and me."

"Yeah. I get mail like that, too."

"Then how can they stop what the world wants?"

"Put your ass in jail."

"That's what I'm telling the press. I got to get to you in the gym today at four o'clock before I go to jail. I want to whip you good before I go to jail. 'I gave them hell, and they've cleaned out my cell. But before I go, I'm gonna get Smokin' Joe.' That's my latest poem."

"I got a poem for you, but it don't go that way."

"You got to admit, Joe, you ain't in my class when it comes to writing poems."

"Shhhiiiiit! Bud Collins says Robert Frost went to his grave with a smile on his face. Your poems didn't threaten him at all."

"Now listen, Joe. My career is over. No promoter can get me a fight. But I won't be able to eat or sleep in jail knowing I'd left you out here unwhipped. Money or no money. I'm gonna say this to all the disc jockeys and all the announcers on the TV stations. Come out to the gym at four o'clock and see me whip Joe Frazier, you dig?"

Joe is getting the swing of it. "Yeah!" he shoots back. "Damn the ten-million-dollar gate. Damn the fight of the century. Damn the title. This town's not big enough for two bad niggers like us. One of us got to go, and it's gonna be Clay! One of us got to leave town and it's got to be tonight!"

"That's right, Joe. We'll tell the press we've got to get this fight on. We don't care if it ain't gonna be in Madison Square Garden. We don't care if they won't let us fight in the Houston Astrodome or on the Polo Grounds. We getting it on right here in your gym at four o'clock."

"Tell 'em to call me, and I'll confirm it." Joe is warming up to the idea. "I'll say, 'Clay had no business moving to Philadelphia, anyway. This nigger should have stayed in Louisville, where he was born. We ain't waiting!' I'll be at the gym. We might not even need gloves. We might fight bare knuckles like in the old days. No headgear. Slug it out, bone to bone, blood to blood! Goodbye, fool!"

I dial every radio announcer and disc jockey in Philadelphia and some in New Jersey. I call the Philadelphia *Inquirer* and TV stations. I remember to call the popular black disc jockey Sonny Hopkins, The Mighty Burner, who tells me he'll keep up the calling and call every announcer he knows for miles around.

I'm almost screaming at them now on the phone: "Joe dared me to come to his gym and fight him. I'm going to be there at four o'clock and we gonna fight till one of us drops! I'm tired of waiting for promoters to get this fight on. I can't wait. If you don't believe it, call Joe Frazier! You be there! Tell your listeners to be there! See me whip Frazier, free of charge!"

In minutes my own phone is ringing. Reporters ask if it's really true. Local reporters at first, then Los Angeles, Washington and, before I leave for the gym, Paris and London.

"Who started it?" an AP man asks. "Who's responsible?"

"You fighting Frazier in Frazier's gym?" UPI wants to know.

"Yes!" I answer. "You caught me just in time. I'm on my way out the door now. See you at the gym."

"Are you in shape?" another asks.

"Don't worry about my shape! This is dog-eat-dog, life-or-death!"

It's almost three-thirty. A few friends have dropped in and are as excited as I am. I dress in my blue-jean "freedom suit," red-and-white-checked shirt and my big heavy brogans, and we all go outside. The disc jockeys had put the news on the air instantly. A crowd of photographers has gathered and fifty cars are lined up outside my house.

My neighbors are jumping into their cars to follow us. The pharmacist from the drugstore on the corner drives up with some pills he says will give me "dynamite energy." He closes down for the day. The filling station manager has locked the pumps and all his crew is coming along.

We sit in my car and turn on the radio, the news flashing from one station to another:

"Muhammad Ali and Joe Frazier—a showdown at Joe's gym at four o'clock!"

"Joe's finally dared Muhammad to fight in his gym!"

"Joe says he'll knock Muhammad out inside four rounds!"

"This is the big Philadelphia showdown, folks! The great fight has come to Philly! Free! All free, if you get there early!"

Before we pull off, police on motorcycles drive up. One black policeman says he wants the honor of "escorting" me over to Joe's gym, in case I get lost. Squad cars with sirens on form in front of us, and with a caravan of fifty cars behind us, we drive to Frazier's gym. People run after the car, knock on the window and hold up their fingers in a victory sign.

Two reporters are perched on top of a truck with walkie-talkies, relaying to their stations every detail of the ride as though it's an army on the way to an invasion.

I stick my head out the window and yell to the crowd:

> I don't need no Coliseum,
> I'm whippin' Joe in his own gym!
> Come one, come all,
> See Frazier fall!

But we stop nearly ten blocks from Joe's gym, and the policemen in front walk back to my car and say, "We can't go any further. The street is blocked from here on."

I look ahead, and as far as I can see there are cars jamming the blocks all the way down to Frazier's gym.

"The only way to get there is to walk," the black officer says. "The cars have been pulling up around the gym for two hours now."

If I had any fear that Frazier might not cooperate, it's all gone now. Joe has obviously been telling reporters the things we have agreed on—only his version favors him to win.

Walking only makes the crowd bigger, and the excitement increases. People are looking out the windows and yelling:

"Ali's going to meet Frazier!"

"There's Ali! On his way to fight in Frazier's gym!"

"The showdown!"

"A fight! A fight!"

Now I know how Wyatt Earp felt walking down Main Street in Dodge City, on his way to get his man. And each yard I'm picking up more people. I pass a butcher who's closing his shop and yelling, "Wait for me! Wait for me!" He pushes his way through the crowd to get near me for an autograph.

I feel the greatest surge of hope and strength since the day I walked out of the Induction Center.

Even though what I'm going to do now is not real, never have I had such a reception from the people, not even in my biggest clashes with Liston, Terrell, Patterson.

We get to the door of the gym. The crowd is packed so thick behind me that police with German shepherds have been called in. The dogs are snapping at the crowd to push them back.

"Where's Joe Frazier! I want Joe Frazier!" I begin hammering my fists against the door. "Open up, Joe! I know you're in there! Open up and face me like a man! You ain't no Champ! I'm the real Champ! Open up, Joe!"

And the crowd picks up my call and starts screaming:

"Open the door, Joe!"

"Face him, Joe! Face him!"

Someone opens the door—I believe it was Yank Durham—and ducks out of the way as the shoving crowd pushes in, past even me. The police have to help us get inside by raising their nightsticks and threatening, "Get back! Let him in! Get back, now!"

Joe is over near the ring, sitting on the stool, testing a glove on his left hand as though he's going to use it on me. I feel good. Joe's going along with it. I will always love him for that. He doesn't have to. He's on top and I'm on the bottom. He's the recognized Champion; I'm the outlaw.

Maybe it's his fierce pride that makes him do it. Whatever Joe is, he's up from the earth. He'll never be satisfied with a title he thinks has been bestowed upon him by the Establishment . . .

I start stripping off my blue-jean jacket and screaming loud enough for those outside to hear, "I'm sick and tired of hearing people call Joe Frazier The Champ! There can't be two Champions! Who's the real Champion?" I ask the crowd jammed around the window.

Some yell back, "You are! You are!" Some shout, "Joe Frazier! Joe Frazier's The Champ!"

Joe gets up and comes toward me. "I'm gonna shut your mouth once and for all. You come here to Philadelphia to take over my town! Now you come to take over my gym! If I don't put a stop to it, you'll be trying to take over my wife! Let's get it on! I don't need no gloves!"

He throws the glove down.

There's a heavy frown on Yank's face. He's shaking his head as though he regrets agreeing to the whole thing.

"I'm ready, too!" I shout.

I move as though I'm going to jump on Joe, but my friends hold me back easily. Joe's people are holding on to him as though he's straining to get at me.

Suddenly the crowd outside is breaking in through the police line, streaming into the gym, threatening to wreck the place. Three black policemen beat their way over to me. The biggest puts his hands on my shoulders, breathing heavily, and speaks in a low whispering tone as though he has a crucial task to carry out. "You under arrest, Muhammad," he says, wiping sweat off his forehead with his sleeve. "You under arrest."

Joe is close enough to hear, and he cuts in, "What the hell you arresting him for!"

"We're going to have to lock him up if he don't get out of here."

"What's the charge?" I ask.

Frazier pushes his snub nose up to the policeman's face. "I invited him. He's my guest until I whip his ass!"

"He's obstructing traffic," the policeman says as politely as he can under the circumstances. "Ten blocks down, the traffic is blocked. No one can get in or out. The chief says to stop this thing and bring you in."

By now some of the words are overheard by the spectators and they begin shouting in a menacing way, "Let him alone! Let him alone! You can't arrest Ali!"

I see actual fear come into the policeman's eyes, and he wipes his forehead again and says, "We don't want trouble, but you've got the streets blocked. It's getting to be worse. If you want to fight, why don't you go out to a public place. You both prizefighters, and ain't no law against you sparring. But do it in a public place."

I look over at Joe and stage-whisper, "I like the idea of going to the park. How about you?"

"Be better here in the gym, but I can whip you in the park just as good."

The police are relieved. They put their hats back on, turn around and begin to beat their way back outside.

Joe and I keep yelling at each other, shaking fists at each other, both being held back by friends, and when we're jammed together I say to him, "Joe, we're gonna make a lot of money if this fight ever comes off. We're gonna make them white folks pay and pay good for it. We got them fooled. They think we'll kill each other."

Joe has risen to the occasion. He shouts, "I ain't waiting for no park. I want to whip his ass right here, on the spot!"

He stomps his feet and moves to get his gloves, but now three white members of a firm that helps Yank raise money for fights come into the gym, their clothes disheveled, their hair wild, sweat pouring off their faces. The first is a heavyset man in a brown business suit, his white shirt hanging out of his pants, who throws himself between Joe and me. He is one of the main investors.

"Please, Joe," the man pleads. "He's just egging you on. He's trying to build publicity for himself. Don't you understand? He just wants to get that jail rap off his back and he's using you. He's using you, Joe. Don't fight him in the park!"

Joe pushes him away. "I don't care what you say. People won't believe I'm The Champion until I whip his ass! I don't care what you say!"

Another firm member speaks with more control: "If you want to fight Muhammad, we'll get a fight for you in the Spectrum. We'll get the finest stadium in America, but don't go out in the park with him. Please! We'll get a fight for you in the best arena in Philadelphia."

"He ain't got no license," Joe answers.

"We'll get him a license!"

"Look, we can pass a law that will give Muhammad a license," the other says. "We'll pass a special law just for Ali, but don't go out in the park with him! Please, Joe!"

"They just don't want to see you and me getting it on!" I shout.

Joe begins pushing against his advisers.

The black policeman has come back to talk to me. "Leave the gym. For God's sake, if you gonna box, let's get out of here. They're wrecking the stores and offices out there. The neighborhood is in an uproar. Cars are parked all over everywhere. Please! Let's go to the park."

"You coming, Joe?" I yell. "What about it, Joe!"

But the firm members are clinging to his arm. "Joe, don't fight him free. Only for money, Joe. Don't fight him free!" They begin whispering in his ear, something I can't hear, and I see Joe's eyes turn away from mine.

I'm afraid I'm losing him, and I shout, "Joe! Don't act like no Uncle Tom! Don't let those white folks tell you what to do! We been waiting too long! They don't mean what they say! They ain't gonna pass no law to let me fight. They're jiving! They ain't for real. We don't need the white man's permission to fight! Half the people in Philadelphia out there, waiting for us. To hell with the money! Don't act like no Uncle Tom!"

"I ain't no Uncle Tom," Joe snaps at me.

His eyes are blazing and I know suddenly now that the pretense is gone and this is no put-on. Joe has always been a little slow in making out whether or not I'm serious or putting on, knowing whether he's in on the joke or the joke is on him.

"I ain't no Uncle Tom!" Joe is saying.

I wink at him to show I understand and agree. Then, "Let's go to the park. I'm ready! You ready, Joe?"

He looks grim for a second, but there's something in the air and he yells, "Let's get it on!" He jerks himself away. "Come on! I'm gonna show you something!"

They reach out again, but he pushes them aside roughly. Another one shouts, "Joe! There are millions to be made by fighting Muhammad! You'll both be injured! You'll ruin everything! Once you start, you can't stop! He's crazy! Clay's crazy!"

"Let him loose!" I yell. "For the last time, Joe, you gonna let this white man tell you what to do?"

Joe pushes away and goes to get his shorts and boxing bag. He's with me. Now only Yank can hold him back and he's suddenly disappeared.

But as soon as we get outside, a white policeman breaks through the crowd, escorting a tall, bony Catholic priest who holds his hands up and cries out, "Don't let them do it! They're mad! They don't know what they're doing!" The crowd actually quiets down and he goes on in a scolding voice: "You people, instead of egging this on, you should be stopping him! If they kill each other, their blood will be on your hands. Do you want blood on your hands?"

Nobody does. There's a lull. I see he's having an effect on the crowd, and he goes on preaching brotherhood and love they neighbor.

I cut in, "Reverend, the only blood that's gonna be spilled is Frazier's. I'm not gonna hurt him. I'm gonna whip his behind like I'm his daddy!"

The crowd laughs and the police begin shoving me past the priest.

One black policeman with captain's bars and another in a sergeant's uniform take me by the arm, pushing the crowd away from me.

A woman shouts, "Muhammad! Where you going? Where they taking you?"

I shout back, "To the park! We're gonna get it on in the park! We're gonna settle this thing in the park!"

People in the crowd start yelling at each other, "Ali and Frazier in the park! In the park!" They scramble, they run, they jump, they push ahead of us, leap into cars, try to back out or drive ahead, but it's impossible for anyone to get out. I'm stuck there, jammed, packed into the crowd.

Then I see a tall black horse stepping his way through, coming over to me, a white policeman on his back. The policeman cries out, "Jump up on the horse! Jump up!"

He reaches down and lifts me up on the horse, which easily picks its way through the crowd and down the streets.

I look down. A crippled boy was being shielded by an old man, pointing up at me. "That's him up on that horse," he says. "He's up on that horse." I reach down, pick up the boy, give him a hug and kiss, and let him ride the horse's rump for a few yards before handing him down to the old man. The crowd roars.

It's one of the hottest days of the year. Sweat is pouring off everybody. Horns are blowing. Another helicopter has joined the one that followed me here, and I can see the co-pilot looking down at me through binoculars.

By now, school is letting out and children are running down the streets to see what's going on, books under their arms. They wave and yell and join the slow march to the park. People on their porches wave as we go by.

It's like a holiday. It's like a Fourth of July picnic. Everybody laughing, shouting, screaming, slapping each other on the back, talking about the sight they're about to see. An Ali-Frazier fight! Knock-down, drag-out!

Then we turn into the park and I see a huge circle of cars around a small opening. I jump off the horse, go into the fieldhouse recreation room—into the kids' playroom, actually—and put on my boxing trunks. I want to make it all look real until the end.

I go back out through the crowd and climb on top of somebody's car. The police hand me a megaphone, and I say, "This is my home and I'm coming back to fight in it. I'm coming to get my title back! Who's the real Champion?"

They scream back, "You are!" . . . "Where's Joe Frazier? Where's Joe?"

"He's coming. He's coming!" I tell them.

But Joe was not coming. I later learned that Yank had pleaded with him to stop, that we had made our point. In one hour, more than twenty thousand people had come to see a Joe Frazier–Ali showdown. I wondered what a real promotion in a real stadium would've brought if we'd been allowed to fight.

Yank had persuaded Joe to get in a police car and leave. Now that I look back on it, I understand why he did it. It couldn't have been carried out. Joe and I could no more have put on a mock fight than two starving lions could pretend to let the other have all the meat. We both had too much pride and confidence to let the other pass a single blow without trying to match it with a better one.

The crowd had refused to go home, had lingered on, waiting for Joe to show up. Then slowly they had thinned out until the park was empty. But the stories of my "bloody street fight" with Joe hung around and grew bigger and bigger and spread to places I never expected to hear from. It was that evening that I got the first call from Georgia: "People down here'd do anything to get you in the ring against Frazier," Georgia State Senator Leroy Johnson said. "I'm trying to get you a license to fight in Atlanta. I've already talked to Herbert and you'll be hearing from us."

The hoax had aroused the only group of promoters who had what it took to open the ring to me again. Although I ended up fighting Quarry first, then Bonavena, it was the hoax that had forced the real thing: The Fight between Joe Frazier and Muhammad Ali.

• • •

RUMBLINGS FROM
THE GRAVE

We were to be two dinosaurs, as the Reverend Williams, the old Golden Gloves trainer, called heavyweights, scheduled to tear each other to shreds before the eyes of a half-billion other animals watching TV while machines counted the money.

Joe Frazier's camp thought this was the best of all times to take me on. "Hit the tiger when they first let him out of the cage." Don Warner, one of Frazier's sparring partners, described the talk in Frazier's camp. "That's what his lawyers and trainers advise Frazier. Take Clay while his legs still stiff and his reflexes rusty."

The attraction of that forty-million-dollar gate encouraged Florida's Governor Claude Kirk to announce his sanction of an Ali-Frazier fight for Tampa. My manager had been in close touch with the negotiations, and I flew down to Miami. But before my plane landed, Governor Kirk had backed down, saying, "Clay would not be welcome here."

Chris tried to explain the Governor's actions. "No politician likes to do an about-face in public unless his political life is at stake. Some awful pressure came from somewhere."

He read me part of a Detroit *Free Press* column by its sports editor, Joe Falls:

> Approving a fight for Clay would appear to the public to be approving of his way of life, and this includes draft evasion and this is a difficult thing for anyone to do, especially a public figure . . . the public sentiment against him seems so strong that no one wants to take the responsibility for sanctioning a fight for him. . . .

"He's talking about the fight they had set up in Detroit and Governor Milliken backed down," Chris was saying. "Everyone thought it was for real, until the public—"

"It's not the public," I said. "It's never been the public, not the mainstream of the people. I travel all the time. Wherever I go, whether the Deep South like Alabama or Louisiana, or from Maine to California, since the day I left the Draft Board, people, white, black, Catholic, Protestant, Jewish, welcome me, crowd around me, tell me they're with me. It's been like that all these years. In airports, train stations, bus depots, in small towns and little old gas stations, people recognize me, they come out and bring their children to meet me. They tell me how ashamed they are about what's happening to me.

"I've spoken in ninety colleges, Yale, Harvard, MIT, Princeton, Columbia, Purdue, Colgate and little unknown colleges like Alcorn, Bethune-Cookman, Miles, and they ask who's barring me from boxing. On every campus, every street, they come out for me like I'm the Pied Piper. There's more places calling for me than I can keep up with. It's not from the public . . ."

"Then it's political, from somewhere big," he persisted. "It'll take something just as big or bigger to beat it. Like the offer from the Astrodome."

He was referring to the only proposal which, on its face, might have ended my exile—but one I couldn't accept. The offer had come from the Houston Astrodome's owner and builder, Judge Fred Hofheinz, and it had been kept from the press.

I had gotten to know the Judge through my fights in Houston against Cleveland Williams and Ernie Terrell and through the friendly tours he took me on to see his famous Astrodome apartments, especially his own gold-and-green rooms, with priceless art, and those of his lifelong friend, President Lyndon B. Johnson.

After my conviction on the draft issue, the Judge said he was surprised not only at the conviction but at what he considered the weakness of my defense. He offered to throw the full weight of his immense political and financial powers behind a drive for my acquittal. He felt sure he could get it. And in return for his help he wanted an exclusive five-year boxing contract, mainly against opponents selected by a new team and for a percentage of my purse which was much like that taken by the Louisville millionaires.

Whether by signing over to the Astrodome owner I could have saved myself these years of exile, I'll never know. I could never go back to the old white domination, and Herbert's spiritual, business and religious outlook matched mine as a brother. To be independent was part of what I was fighting for.

That morning when I left Dundee's office I went to the airport to meet Chauncey Eskridge, who was my representative in a suit being filed against me. He was early and we had time to stop by Dr. Pacheco's office. I wanted to get the results of an extensive medical examination his staff had given me. Pacheco was looking over the x-rays when we got there.

"How long you think it'll be before you get a decision on Ali's draft case?" he asked Eskridge.

"I estimate at least another year," I remember Eskridge answering, a date that turned out to be almost exact.

Pacheco looked up from the x-rays and spoke of his surprise over the fact that Supreme Court Justice Hugo L. Black had just turned down Eskridge's petition to allow me to go across the border to Toronto for eighteen hours to fight Frazier. "What was in it?" he asked.

Eskridge said the petition pointed out that my income had been depleted because of legal fees; that I would put up $100,000 cash bond before going; that I would travel to Toronto by car and that the Justice Department could staff the automobile with as many marshals or agents as they considered necessary to assure my return; that we would put in escrow 70 percent of the total purse of more than one million; and that I had never failed to make an appearance in a Federal court since I had been indicted.

Eskridge turned the medical office into a law office. He started citing cases where convicted white performers had been allowed to travel all over the world to practice their trade while they appealed their convictions. He cited the case of Abbie Hoffman, whom a Federal judge had just granted the right to go to Cuba for twenty-six days while he was in a situation similar to mine, appealing his five-year jail sentence.

"Strange. What could they be afraid of?" Pacheco wondered. "It's like a conspiracy to keep him inactive until it's too late."

"How's his health?" my lawyer asked.

"Health's excellent," Pacheco said, folding up the report. "But the prime years of an athlete are short. Very short."

"How long you think he's got?" Eskridge asked. And when he saw Pacheco hesitate, he added, "Lay it on the line."

"I don't know." Pacheco turned to me. "I've been with you for nearly all of your professional fights, since you were nineteen, I've worked with hundreds of other fighters, Willie Pastrano, Luis Rodriquez, Florentino Fernandez, Sugar Ramos and Jose Napoles, but I've had less to do for you than any of them. The simple reason—you seldom get hurt. Medically speaking, you've got the soundest physique, the best exterior of any fighter I know. No one would know you were a fighter. When they first see you, they'd think you're an athlete because of the way you're built, but they'd think some non-contact sport, swimming, basketball, gymnastics. When I first saw you in the gym, I said this guy's magnificent. He's doing everything exactly the opposite of what the pros tell him to do. He's dropping his hands down, he's leaning back. I could see that you were going to be fantastic. You were the only guy I've ever seen in the gym with a dedication stronger than his sex drive.

"Now, here you are in 1970, after a hundred and fifty fights, amateur and professional, and you've never even had a tooth knocked out. But time takes a toll more irrevocable than a brutal beating. The body wears, changes, even more when it's not active. It ages. Reflexes slow down and they go. No one can tell how long a fighter's got, not when you deal with a super-athlete. We can examine the body but not the psyche, and that's where the real thing is locked."

"How long do you think?"

"Well, he's been nearly four years out of the ring," the doctor said. "If he were suddenly free to fight two months from now, it would be a miracle if he still had those quick reflexes. But if they keep him in exile much longer . . . well, I'll be frank. There's never been an athlete to lay off three years and come back in equal form. Certainly not a boxer. But if it takes another year, you ought to forget it. Think of another trade. It takes punishment to get in condition. Punishment from sparring partners, from the bags, from running the road. And when they're in a real fight, no boxer escapes punishment entirely."

I was holding some x-rays up to the light and barely listening, but it took all my control to answer cheerfully with a rhyme—something like:

> *In the ring I can stay*
> *Until I'm old and gray*
> *Because I know how to hit*
> *And dance away . . .*

They laughed and we turned to jokes until I walked out of the office with my lawyer to discuss the pending suit, a chore in which I had suddenly lost all interest. My head was ringing like somebody had hit it. All I could think was that minutes ago I was completely adjusted to my jail sentence and resigned to the fact that I might never enter the ring again. But to be told I was on the brink of something irreversible was a shock. Another trade? Truthfully, not since the first day I put on a pair of gloves had I ever thought about another trade. I had found the life I wanted to live.

I saw a cab barreling down and hailed it. I told Chauncey to catch another: I had urgent business that I had forgotten about; I could do the deposition some other time and would call him.

In a flash I had remembered that over at Angelo's Fifth Street Gym, Bundini and Angelo were training a solid new heavyweight prospect, Jeff Merritt.

When I got there, I took the long flight of stairs from the street to the gym above the drugstore. I ran into Bundini at the door. He stood back, eyes wide in surprise, then grinned as though he had sent for me.

"Where's Angelo?" I asked.

"Downstairs. Want me to get him?"

"Find the bags I left here. My shoes, shorts, trunks."

He followed me to the dressing room. I caught a glimpse of Merritt in the ring, shadowboxing, tall and rangy, his jabs stiff and short.

"That's my new baby," Bundini said as he saw me glance up. "Since you been gone I had to have a new baby and he's a good one. I got a livin' alligator, eats anything that moves. A half-starved alligator, guaranteed to eat up lions, tigers, elephants and fat, overweight ex-Heavyweight Champs."

I quickly got into my boxing togs and laced up my shoes. Bundini was getting out my rope.

"I won't need that," I said. "Jeff needs a sparring partner. I'm going to help you get him in shape for a few rounds."

Bundini dropped the bags and came over. "Champ, look. Me and you's friends. I'd do anything you say. But Jeff's in top shape; you in no shape. I just thought you wanted to loosen up like a normal person would. It's hard for a half-starved alligator to bite easy."

Now I was dressed. I began wrapping my hands; and Bundini knew nothing would turn me around.

"Jeff might not wanna do it," he said. "He got respect for you."

"Sure," I said. I had two thousand dollars in my pocket from a lecture I had given at Yale. I handed Bundini half of it. "Tell him here's a thousand dollars if he shakes up Muhammad Ali."

Bundini understood. "Good goddamn. You want a *High Noon* showdown—Wyatt Earp versus Jessie James." He went over and pulled Jeff aside.

Angelo came up, frowning. "This is crazy. This don't make no sense. You're out of your mind."

I finished taping as he talked.

"Look, do roadwork first. Be human. Limber up. You haven't been in a gym in a year. Ain't boxed anybody. Nobody walks in off the streets and gets inside a ring." Then he stopped. "You ain't listening."

I was listening to something inside my head. I knew I had not boxed seriously for years and that I was twenty pounds overweight. But I had to test myself. What had I lost? Could I get it back? I had to know, even if I was beaten to a bloody pulp in the process.

Bundini walked over to us. "The only one who can beat Muhammad Ali is Cassius Clay."

"Did you do what I told you?" I asked.

Bundini nodded. "He took you up on it."

Then he reached back and let out the war cry from our early days together:

> *Float like a butterfly*
> *Sting like a bee*
> *Rumble young man, Rumble*
> *W-a-a-a-a-a-a-a-a-a-a!*

I went out to the ring. Four prospective "boxing bankers" interested in Merritt had come in to watch him but, surprisingly, a lot of other spectators had almost filled the gym up, as though some ESP grapevine had told them Muhammad Ali was back and going against Merritt, whose last six straight knockouts had taken place right here in Miami Beach.

The bell rang and Merritt moved out directly into my path, not with a lunge or rush, but with a smooth feinting motion. His left flicked out and I could see his range was long and his defense good.

I moved back, shifted and danced lightly, giving him body fakes, none of which he fell for. His left kept flicking out. He was a talented pro, taller than me and four years younger.

I always take the measure of a man's movements, reach, speed, even before taking advantage of whatever openings I see. The only one-round knockout in my record is with Sonny Liston and I attribute it to the fact that I had already calculated and timed his motions in an earlier fight.

Before the end of the first round Merritt had decided on his attack. His left began raining in on me from long range, and he would follow up with a crushing right cross. In a second I had been backed into the ropes and he was unleashing a furious combination of lefts and rights that jarred my bones, even though I caught most on my arms and leaned away from them. It was easy to understand why no fighter could go the distance with him.

But when the bell rang I had taken his measurements. If my coordination and reflexes were all right, I should be able to thread the needle and tailor a suit to fit him.

Angelo came over to whisper, "Ain't that enough? You don't need to prove anything, not here in the gym."

I called Bundini over and said, "You tell your man it's two thousand dollars if he shakes me up. Two grand, cash. You got the money."

Bundini jumped back like his ear was burning, bowed low to the ground as though acknowledging orders from a Japanese general, and went back and whispered to his man. Merritt nodded, went over to the rosin box and pawed his feet, tested the non-skid and returned to his corner. He had a calmness about him, like an experienced hangman testing his rope. A real pro. I started thinking of the time Floyd Patterson offered to pay any sparring partner a thousand dollars if he could shake him up, and Angelo sent Turnbow in; Turnbow knocked Patterson flat on his back and collected the money. I knew Jeff was thinking about it, too.

When the bell rang for the second round, he came out throwing bombs. Where he had been throwing hand grenades before, now he was shelling with fifty-millimeter cannon and I knew he wouldn't stop. He had analyzed me, too, and judged that his main chance for a strike was total saturation. And he had the ammunition to unload. His chin was tucked between his powerful sloping shoulders and his drive was relentless. I knew he wouldn't tire.

Under this kind of shelling, a fighter can lose his sense of time, have the illusion that time is standing still, and a split second will seem like a minute. When he calls on his muscles to make decisions, automatic decisions, packaged by years of training and experience, if the reflexes are still there, he may make it in the split second. But if his mind and muscles have slowed, the illusion takes over and the decision comes too late.

I was calling for my right to counterattack over his fast left, using my right almost like a jab, but faster. Like a baseball player who steals bases by watching the telltale movements of the pitcher, I had his movements so cataloged and timed that I knew the meaning of the slight twitch that would involuntarily appear in his throat when he was about to unleash the bomb. Then I would cut over his blow. I began beating him to the punch again and again until the blood began to flow from his mouth. One series of combinations stunned him and he began to wobble. His prospective backers jumped up, crying, "Stop it! Stop it!" The timekeeper began banging the bell and Merritt sank slowly into Bundini's arms.

Bundini pulled his man over to the side and I shadowboxed another round, then went back to the dressing room, put on my clothes and headed for the airport.

Standing in the doorway, Bundini smiled his mysterious smile and murmured, "Nobody can beat Muhammad Ali but Cassius Clay."

When I boarded the plane for Philadelphia I still had my two thousand dollars.

I had found out what I needed to know. But what the doctor said about another year of inactivity was probably true. I could not shake the depressing thought that still, after all the excitement Frazier and I had created in Philly, no promoters could get me permission to fight in America or permission to leave and fight outside of it.

On the surface I made it appear that I was resigned to exile. "Cassius is totally indifferent as to whether he'll fight anymore," an interviewer from the Chicago *Courier* wrote. "He's content to wait until the Courts decide." But quietly and away from the headlines of the press, Herbert was testing every opening and probing for a chance to challenge the boycott. If he had been successful, the first Ali-Frazier fight would have taken place in Tokyo, not New York. He had flown to Japan to meet with Akira Jin, a senior boxing promoter, who had proposed an Ali-Frazier fight. But Yank considered Frazier "still too green" to fight me, was slow making up his mind, and by the time they agreed to it my passport had been lifted.

But Herbert had established valuable contacts for the future, particularly in meeting Yoshio Kou, Jin's assistant, who soon emerged as one of Japan's most imaginative promoters. When my exile ended, Herbert would work out plans in Tokyo with Kou and young Akri Hida for me to fight hard-hitting MacArthur Foster, whose only handicap —in addition to the fact that he had me to contend with—was that he was named after General Douglas MacArthur, and not a soul in Tokyo was pulling for him. Still, it was the fight that led to the staging of World Heavyweight Title matches in the Far East.

Where once I looked forward to every new possibility with a thick-skinned hope, now I was convinced that I would just have to trust Allah's will and, if I was lucky, I could become a minister for the Honorable Elijah Muhammad. But when a telephone call came from someone who had the means to end my exile, I almost missed it.

One morning in late July, Belinda, who I had just brought back from her monthly prenatal examination, answered the phone and said, "It's that guy from Georgia."

It was Senator Johnson. He had already called Herbert, and he started off with what he thought would be thrilling news: "Champ, we can get you a boxing license in Atlanta."

I cut in on him. "They've tried it in Georgia before."

"In Georgia, but not in Atlanta." Johnson has a slow drawl and always speaks of Atlanta and Georgia as though they're two different nations.

My manager had been contacted by a team of black and white politicians and "boxing bankers" under the name of House of Sports, Inc., who said they had gotten an agreement from Frazier's camp that he would fight me if I got a license. Johnson was its chief.

"Just a license is no guarantee," I told him.

The Governor of Mississippi had given me a boxing license for Jackson, then snatched it back. Herbert had sent Major Coxon, a friend of mine from Camden, New Jersey, and Kilroy down there—Mississippi was one of the few states that didn't belong to the World Boxing Association—to try to get what promoters were unable to get out of more liberal states. To my surprise, they came back with a bona fide boxing license, approved by the Governor of Mississippi and the Mayor of Jackson.

Herbert had suggested that in return for a boxing license, he would allow the gate receipts from the seventeen-thousand-seat arena in Jackson to be turned over to the Salvation Army.

I thought everything was in order until an announcement came over the radio that the Mississippi officials had denied they ever issued such a license, even though we had it in our possession. Telephone calls came in from lawyers encouraging me to sue the state, but I told them no. If I started suing every state that backed down on allowing me to fight, I'd have to take on the country.

Others tried. Howard Cosell, who along with a number of distinguished Americans had appealed to leading officials to help lift the ban against me, had brought up the matter to Vice-President Spiro Agnew. Cosell said he was surprised at Agnew's bitter opposition to any move that might help me regain my right to fight.

Colonel Hubert Julian, the Black Eagle of Harlem, had made an appointment for the Muslims' National Secretary, John Ali, and New York Minister, Louis Farrakan, to meet with a Pentagon official, L. Howard Bennett, to see what could be done in my situation. "We feel it's wrong that he should have to suffer and give up his profession," Bennett said. "As far as I'm concerned, he's a genuine conscientious objector and should be so treated. Other than that, the best we could do would be to give him a non-combat position where he could serve as a morale builder for others, but I know he's already rejected that."

Now Johnson, sounding unworried, unhurried, went on. "We've

got the money, we've got the arena, and now the Mayor wants to see you."

"Forget it," I answered. Then I sensed his deep disappointment and tried to explain. "This is your first try, and you would pick the toughest in the world. It's not your fault. Let it alone."

"Well, we hate to see you sit in Philly, go stale until you go to jail," he said softly. "Maybe my partners can explain it better. They'll be calling you."

But his partners had already called and I had refused them. I could think of nothing in Georgia that could prevent a repeat of what had happened in South Carolina.

A week before, I had flown down to Charleston to stage a charity boxing exhibition promoted by a young black South Carolinian, Reggie Barrett. Only when they had shown me their contracts for the County Hall, the approval of the City Council, the license and the rental taken care of, did I go down on the day of the event.

When I got to County Hall and saw the long lines of patrons at the ticket window, even though this was only an exhibition, my feet felt lighter. Then, as I came close to the window, I saw the clerk was not selling tickets, but refunding money. He waved me away without recognizing who I was: "Go on back home! City Council's called it all off. Y'all go home."

When I found Reggie, he was in tears. "The Council stood up until they got a call from Congressman L. Mendel Rivers. He's 'Mr. South Carolina,' head of the Arms Appropriations Committee. He said they were making him the laughing stock of Washington, D.C., by letting a draft-dodging black sonofabitch fight in his hometown. Even when my lawyers showed them I had solid grounds for a hundred-thousand-dollar damage suit if they backed out, the City Council revoked the agreement.

"He's the man in Congress the Pentagon depends on, and he was most upset it got this far. But stay as long as you want. Honest, most people here would welcome you, Ali."

He must have been right, for I stayed overnight in Charleston, with crowds of black and white youths following my every footstep. Yet in the morning I flew home exhausted. For days I refused even to answer the phone. I had resolved that Charleston and Jackson would be my last rejections, and if all that was left now was to serve the five-year jail term and forget boxing, I was prepared.

But every day the calls from Atlanta were coming, and each time Belinda would say, "It's that guy from Georgia." Since Herbert had urged me to look into the matter, I had second thoughts. Then one Monday morning I asked Belinda if she thought I should go back down

South to see what it was all about. Her face lit up and I knew she wanted me to go.

Herbert didn't go because he felt his presence would call too much attention to my religious affiliation and open up old hostilities.

The next day, on the way to the airport, Belinda gave me her doctor's report: a normal delivery was expected three months from then. Our last baby had been premature and lived no more than a few hours. We were careful on this pregnancy to follow the doctor's advice to the letter. I wanted to eliminate tensions and strains that might have caused the loss of my first son.

I kissed the place where the baby was growing in Belinda's body and boarded the plane. New life was coming into my house and it was thoughts of my unborn child, as I flew into Atlanta that morning, that made me review what assets I had now that my boxing career seemed about to end. They consisted of an $80,000 retirement fund, which I had established by deductions from my purses during my first six years as a professional, to accrue when I retired or reached age thirty-five. If forced to retire now, that income would be wiped out by what I owed: $250,000 in legal fees, the results of year after year of court struggles; nearly $40,000 in back taxes; $100,000 more in alimony owed to my first wife (a debt I was determined to pay out to the last cent) and a pile of everyday debts which seem to multiply mysteriously, especially when one is used to a comfortable life but no longer has the income to support it.

Pacheco's words came back to me. Although I had felt a sense of satisfaction sparring with Jeff, I knew that unless my exile ended soon, the tools of my trade would wither.

In this mood I met Johnson's committee of would-be promoters and fight backers who had come to the airport to greet me. What I felt, the hopelessness, must have been in my face, for Johnson threw his arms around me and whispered in his soft Southern way, "Give us a chance, Champ. We'll get it together. Stick it out."

"Where's the Mayor?" I asked. From dozens of past meetings with hopeful promoters I knew that unless the Mayor announced his support, the project would have a short life.

"He's waiting at the hotel," a tall, heavyset black man, introduced to me as Maynard Jackson, Vice-Mayor of Atlanta, answered.

They drove me to downtown Atlanta, took me up to a lavish lavender suite in a motel and introduced me to the other members of the committee: Mike Malitz, a third-generation closed-circuit genius who had helped form Main Bout, the company that televised my earlier fights; Harry Pepp, a white Atlanta millionaire, and his shrewd New York son-in-law, an attorney, Robert Kassel; Harold Conrad, who would act as Malitz's publicist; Jesse Hill, a black publisher and insurance company official credited with tiptoing past Governor Maddox's sleeping dogs with my license.

For what seemed hours I fraternized with this odd mixture of amateurs and professionals passing around champagne, martinis, hors d'oeuvres and slapping each other on the back as though they had pulled off the coup of the century. But I saw several of this smiling team sneaking looks at their watches, and I asked again, "Where's the Mayor?"

"On his way, on his way," Maynard answered.

Johnson pulled me over to a corner and tried to calm me. "The Mayor is coming," he said. "Not that he's anxious to come, but he'll be here, Champ, relax. We know as much about handling politics in Atlanta as you know about boxing in the ring. Ask Pepp."

Pepp, the thin, sandy-haired little merchant who looks as though he grew up underfed despite his family's wealth, pulled me away from Johnson and sat beside me on the sofa. "I know it looks like the same as what you've gone through before," he explained. "But there's something here missing in all the other packages promoters tried to put together. In Atlanta, there's black political power. The largest organized political power in the city is black."

Jesse Hill, a neat, wiry little man, founder of many black businesses in the South, sat on the other side of me. "We did something for the Mayor, now it's his turn to do something for us. We gave him the Mayor's post. We want the Muhammad Ali–Frazier fight in Atlanta."

"What about the Governor?" I asked.

"He'll bend with the politics, too, though he bends to some we don't bend to," Pepp said. "Johnson didn't get to be the first black State Senator in the Deep South since Reconstruction without knowing how to use political power. It's his job to work with Maddox. He's handled it well, or you wouldn't be in this room now."

Pepp would later show me a *Time* magazine article about Johnson, which said: "He delivered the vote that elected Sam Massell as Atlanta's Mayor. He even wields enough votes to intimidate Lester Maddox."

"His Honor the Mayor," someone said, and everyone stood.

A short, sun-tanned man with dark, oily hair came in and hesitated, looking around as though he wanted to make sure only the right people were there. He came directly to me, ignoring the introductions, and we shook hands.

"It's a privilege and an honor to be invited to meet you," I said. I was surprised to feel a hand so sweaty, the wettest hand I'd ever held. I understood why it took him so long to get here. I imagined he could hear the voices of his KKK constituents: "Mayor, you mean you going to shake hands with that un-American draft-dodging nigger? The Mayor of Atlanta going up to meet that 'Black Muslim'? What kind of mayor we got here?"

But the committee was all around him, laughing and joking, and after a few drinks Johnson had one arm wrapped around the Mayor, the other around the Vice-Mayor.

"Of course, Sam," I heard Johnson say, "House of Sports is going to contribute a good percentage of what we make off this to the Mayor's anti-dope campaign. In fact, you set the percentage."

Mayor Massell turned to me. "Well, I told you I welcome the fight. It's a clean, legal fight, and as long as it's that, I'm for it."

One of Johnson's aides came to the door and announced, "Press conference ready in the main banquet hall!"

We began moving toward the door—everybody except the Mayor, who turned to Johnson. "Well, Leroy, I've got a previous appointment. I'll be in my office if you want me."

His words took them by surprise. The room got very quiet. Young Kassel moved over to the Mayor, his lips tight, as though straining to control himself. "Your Honor, as you may recall, you gave us your word you would make a public statement in favor of this fight. The press is expecting it."

"If you need me, I'll be in my office." The Mayor was on his way.

"Look," Kassel said. "You know what Maddox's people will say if you don't show. They'll think you're quietly against us. They'll become bolder. The fight may never come off. This man's entire career is at stake here. It took a year to convince these investors to take a chance. This could all go down the drain. You gave us your word."

The others began to cut in and the room erupted with charges and arguments and shouting, and I could see the Mayor's dark face getting darker.

My whole future in the ring hung in the balance. Yet I felt sorrier for the Mayor than I did for the promoters. The same weariness and exhaustion I had felt coming back from Charleston came over me now. Why storm and bombard this lone Dixie Mayor when Mayors in New York, Chicago, Los Angeles, Detroit were just as fearful? As far as I could see, the promoters were out for what would profit them: the fight. The Mayor was out for what would profit him, and he saw no profit in being photographed publicly with Muhammad Ali in Atlanta, Georgia.

I sat quiet as long as I could, then I stepped between them. "Hold it, hold it, let me say something." They kept on talking, so I yelled, "Unless someone in the room wants to fight me for the floor!" They relaxed a little and laughed. "If the Mayor won't appear at the press conference, that's all right. I'll only be here a short while, he's got to live here all his life. As far as I'm concerned"—I was looking directly at him—"his word is good enough for me. He says he supports the fight. He doesn't have to be at any press conference."

A look of relief crossed the Mayor's face. "You know City Hall pretty well." Then he turned toward the door and said, "My Vice-Mayor will be there to represent me. If the press wants me to verify anything, I'll be in my office." He reached the door and turned back to say, "I have nothing against the fight as long as it's legal and a good portion of the money goes to the anti-drug program. Fair enough?"

Johnson pulled out one of his long, thin cigars and stuck it in the Mayor's breast pocket. With that, the promoters began to leave for the press conference, until they saw me headed in the direction of my own room.

"Hey! You're not going, Champ?"

I shook my head. "If the Mayor's not there, do you think I should be?" I asked Johnson.

I had a deep suspicion that this venture would go nowhere and that the Southern newsmen, who were getting a crack at me for the first time, would question me mainly on my attitude toward the draft, the flag, the Muslims, and would depict me as a beggar going from city to city and being cast out.

"I understand," Johnson said softly. "But please stay until I call you from downstairs."

I was back in my room, looking over the flight schedules to Phila-delphia, when he called. "Champ," he said, "this phone is right by the platform. We're ready to start. Just listen."

I lay back on the bed, holding the phone. I could hear Johnson addressing what sounded like a huge crowd. He was introducing the people supporting the fight, calling out their names—names that seemed to include every prominent black political, social and business figure in Atlanta, including Coretta King, Julian Bond and all the presidents of black colleges in the area. But when he began naming those who seemed to me ordinary people without titles, I hung up the phone and caught the elevator downstairs.

I felt ashamed to be hiding in my room when people were openly standing up for me. Whether the fight came off or not, I wanted to let them know I appreciated it.

When I walked into the hall, they began to applaud and shout, "Free The Champ! Free The Champ! Let The Champ fight in At-lanta!" In minutes the press conference turned into more of a revival, and the reporters forgot questions on my religion and the draft, and asked what the people wanted to know:

"Are you willing to fight Frazier in Atlanta?"

"Can a man get in shape in six weeks after he's been off for nearly four years?"

"How did you feel when you got a legal license in Atlanta?"

"Now what do you think of the South?"

Then one reporter from the Atlanta *Constitution* went to the phone and called the Mayor. The room quieted down until he got back.

"What did Massell say?" another reporter asked, his pad and pen ready.

"He's backing it up. He says we can quote him. He welcomes the fight."

A roar went up, and a New York reporter, who probably had been tipped off by the promoters, put in a call to Frazier's manager in Philadelphia. Again the room got quiet. After he had exchanged greetings with Yank, the reporter asked, "Mr. Durham, will you fight Muhammad Ali in Atlanta? Mr. Ali has a legal license." Then he turned to the room to report: "Yank says it's a lie. He doesn't believe Ali's got a license."

Jesse Hill stood up with my license, waving it in the air.

"The license is right here," the reporter told Yank. "I'm looking at it." Then he listened awhile and finally turned back to report: "Frazier's manager says it's a trick, but if it's real, if it's legal, Joe'll fight Ali in Atlanta."

Someone hollered, "We've got the Frazier-Ali fight in Atlanta!" They cheered while reporters ran out to file their stories.

For me it was like a New Year coming in. And although it turned out not to be the Frazier-Ali fight they had landed, they would have an Ali-Quarry fight. When it was impossible for me to fight, the Frazier camp had promised to sign with me whenever I got a license; now that it was possible they backed out to survey the situation, then claimed a "verbal agreement" to fight Bob Foster too binding to sidestep.

But the amateurs who had sprung me from exile held on to their license and went looking for a substitute. What they needed was a highly ranked, respectable opponent. Who could be more respectable in Georgia than a White Hope ranked as top contender in the World Heavyweight Division, Jerry Quarry? And Irish at that.

I remember talking to a reporter from the Atlanta *Journal* and asking, "What about Governor Maddox's reaction to all this?"

"We'll know in a minute," the reporter said. "We're going over to see the Governor now. His answer will be on TV in two hours."

When the hour came, I was in Paschal's Motel, waiting by the TV screen. The last time I had heard from Maddox was when he turned back my promoters in Macon: "I'll give Clay a license after he serves his term in the Army, or his term in jail. Then maybe I'll think about allowing him in Georgia."

Now he came on the screen. He was cool and calm and responded quietly to the reporter: "There has been a lot of controversy about this fellow Clay. When he rejected the draft, I'm sure it hurt him. He's paying for it. Well, we're all entitled to our mistakes. This is the way I see it. I see nothing wrong with him fighting here."

I had steeled myself to be on guard against false hopes, but I felt an excitement that stayed with me even on my flight back home to Philadelphia—even as I read a Chicago newspaper columnist, John Carmichael: "I advise Muhammad Ali to call it quits. He is an outcast, a fistic pariah. Maddox will never let him fight in Georgia."

But I had heard the Governor's own words, and I believed them —perhaps because I wanted to and perhaps because I was impressed by the power and the unity of those black and white people who wanted me.

I had not heard the Governor's last words on the subject, but the only question ringing in my ears on the way home was the one the reporter asked: Can a man get ready in six weeks after he's been away nearly four years?

RESURRECTION

So the Governor gave his word. But before the "bankers" put up the half-million, I test his word with a public exhibition in the heart of Atlanta. I want to go in a ring and wave my cape before the bulls —the Maddoxes, the White Citizens Councils, the Believers in the War.

Now I've waved it, and the bulls stood still. The exhibition is over and I'm on U.S. Highway 85, riding home to Philadelphia with Rahaman and Bundini. I stretch out on the back seat and try to sleep. I'm tired and feeling pain in every bone and nerve in my body. I made it through the last rounds by instinct, habit and will power. I'm quiet, and Bundini knows why.

"How did it go?" Rahaman, who came down too late to see the bout, is asking Bundini.

"Your brother cooked," Bundini says. "Your brother put the pot on the stove and he cooked."

He knows Rahaman wants to hear it all, but waits a few more miles before he begins: "I never seen nothing like it in my life. I been in crowds screaming for Elvis Presley and the Beatles. But when your brother walked down that aisle and got in the ring, I never heard no sound come from humans like what they gave your brother."

"How big's the place?" Rahaman asks.

"Morehouse College gym don't hold no more'n two thousand, but they sardine in five. Every kind of people they grow in Georgia: students and farmers, overalls and business suits, church people and long-haired hippies. I even look for some Klan clothes. It's a hundred-degree temperature inside. When they see Ali climb in the ring they're calling, 'The Champ! The Champ! The Champ!' Not just the rah-rah chant, but a spiritual kind of chant. Senator Johnson is trying to announce 'This historic occasion . . .' and 'Democracy in the Deep South . . .' but all they want to see is The Champ cook."

"They haven't seen him in a long, long time," Rahaman says.

"And I was in his corner the last time he was in Madison Square," Bundini goes on, "when most people wanted him beat because he had found out who he was and where he wasn't going."

"I know, I was there," Rahaman says.

"No, the time you thinking of wasn't the last time in Madison Square," Bundini corrects him. "I mean one time when he was in exile sitting in the audience to see the Ellis-Frazier fight. They were introducing the fighters in the audience and some of the crowd called for him to be introduced. But Harry Markson wanted to introduce him as Cassius Clay, not Muhammad Ali, and he walked out and some of the crowd booed. You remember that, Champ?"

I remember, but I don't answer.

"And we come from that low to this high," Bundini says, "where the people sound like they love him. Tonight they call him from the heart. We're standing in the corner and they're thundering in a way we ain't never heard before. He looks at me and I look at him and we're both crying."

"Were you crying, brother?" Rahaman turns to me. "Were you crying?"

"We both crying," Bundini goes on. "Tears coming down The Champ's cheeks. Angelo sees us crying and he pulls me out the corner and says, 'Don't act like that! You'll make him weak!'

"That hurt me. I say, 'Man, you don't understand. We're into blood. Blood is flowin'. Out of this The Champ can go out and beat man, beast or monster. Because blood is cryin' out to blood.'

"I say, 'He's bein' born again, Angelo. Let the blood of the people pour in on him. Let him cry. A baby being torn out of the womb, he got to cry.' I tell him, 'Cryin' like that makes him stronger, not weaker.

They out there cheerin' 'cause their blood is pourin' into somebody they love. Transfusion. It's got to make you cry.'

"A lot of people don't understand about champions. I didn't understand myself at first—not until I started working with one. One of the biggest names in boxing! When he was trying to make a comeback, all of his old handlers deserted him and he come to me and says, 'Fastblack.' That's what they called me in those days." Bundini laughs. "I was fast and black and they put it together, Fastblack. He said he wanted me to come work with him.

"I hadn't been around boxing much but I knew something about people and that man was in a bad way. All the bums were beating him. His arms were like banana peelings. His punches all tangled up like bubble gum chewed for four days and he said, 'I ain't got it back together yet, Fastblack, but I'm gonna get it.'

"And when he got hisself together it's down to the evening of the big return fight and it's time for him to take that rest before the fight. You know, Champ, like you always take? That last long sleep."

I smile to myself, but don't answer.

Bundini goes on. "And I'm in his house and his wife tells everybody to get out so The Champ can rest. But she sees me and her eyes light up and she says, 'Not you, Fastblack, you come here.' And she pulls me over to the door of the room where her husband is lying down. He sleeps naked like you do, Champ, and she says, 'You go in there and lie down with him.' "

"She said that?" Rahaman asks.

"I was green," Bundini says. "First time I'd been with a champ. No woman ever told me to get in bed with her husband before, and I didn't know what to make of it. 'Just lie in bed with him,' she says, and pushes the big chifforobe up against the door so nobody else can come in.

"He's lying there in the bed and I get in and lie next to him, and he cuddles up with my arms around him and goes to sleep. And the wife peeks in the door and sees me with my arms around her husband and says, 'That's good.' I'm learning. I'm in the lab.

"This business of going out to war, man-on-man, with the whole world watching is something you never get used to. It's new every time you do it. Like a blasting-off into outer space. Like a discovery of America. Like a birth. Like coming out of the womb for the first time.

"Here I am in bed with my arms around this pound-for-pound baddest dude in the world, who could chew nails and who must have been so tough when he was born he stood up and walked out of the womb by hisself. And he's like a child before the fight. Soaking up love. Love is what gives him strength. And his wife knows it. Now if I didn't know it too, I'd go lay a heavy bet on his opponent. I'd be saying, 'Who's this? This here's a faggot! This coward's gonna get his shaft beat off tonight.' But I know that ain't it.

"The night of the fight, when we get in the dressing room, he says, 'Fastblack, how's the crowd out there?' and I come back and say, 'They hangin' from the rafters.' Then he's walking down the aisle and I don't know he's changed. And when I try to help him up the steps he turns on me and says, 'Fastblack, what the hell's wrong with you? I don't need your goddamn help! I'm The Champ, man!' Then I understand. He's out of the womb, you see? He got to get born again, be a child again before a fight. But when he comes out of the womb, you have to feel sorry for that fool he's gonna fight.

"It's like that with Ali. Love is energy for him, too. He got to cry when he sees how the people love him. That's what I want Angelo to understand.

"So, then they brought out the lions, three hungry pros. Like the half-starved lions the Romans used to chew up Christians. Only this is for a 'Black Muslim.' Three powerful pros in top shape, each wearing headgear. But The Champ won't put on no headgear. I can't get him to put none on.''

"You shouldn't take chances like that," Rahaman calls back to me.

"They come at him full of fire and piss, throwing their bombs. Because all the TV and the newspapers are watching, and they want to get instant fame by knocking down The One and Only.

"And The Champ goes easy with them—don't try to hurt nobody, just spars nicely, scientifically, 'cause he knows if he was in shape he could hang 'em all.

"But he ain't been in the ring like this for years, and as the rounds go by and each fresh pro comes in he's getting tired and slow. His feet's dragging, and he's leaning against the ropes and holding on, worse than I ever seen him in my life.

"Now the same people who cheered him start booing, soft at first, then like a thousand foghorns. Booing 'cause he ain't showing them nothing.

"And one of the promoters who was to put up the Atlanta fight money comes over worried. I see he's thinking, 'Maybe we wasting money getting The Champ out of exile. Maybe he's too far gone.'

"And when The Champ comes back to his corner, I look at him and I say, 'What's the matter?' And he says, 'I'm tired! I'm tired, Bundini.' I grab him and put my head to his head and I look at him hard.

" 'You tired? You tired? We ain't been three and a half years waitin' for this night to get tired! Them's the same people out there that brought tears to your eyes a minute ago, cheerin' you like the return of the prodigal son.'

" 'What do they expect?' he says to me. 'This an exhibition.'

"Then I put my mouth in his ear and I say: 'This ain't no god-damn exhibition, nigger. This the Resurrection! Shorty ordered a Resurrection! Them people out there, they bringin' you back to life. The Government's ready to bury your ass underneath the jail. But they come to dig you out of the grave. Tired? When you spendin' them five years in jail you get tired. Not now, Champ, not now! Now's your Resurrection Day. Straighten up!

" 'Suppose when Shorty resurrected Jesus people saw him standin' around weak and tired and wobbly, no punch, no power? Shorty would say, "Send that fool back to the grave!" When people resurrect you, they put their own blood and flesh and bones in your body. You ain't suppose' to be weak 'cause they ain't weak.'

"Tears were back in his eyes. I know deep down in his guts he's tired, but I know the transfusion is coming in, coming in! Shorty's juggling the genes!

"They're booing 'cause they think if he love them like they love him, he would show 'em something. Like a woman whose man's in the bed tired and she thinks if the love was mutually strong he'd get up and shake some ass, tired or not.

"Then Harold Conrad, who's working with the ABC-TV crew there to film the fight, he comes over and tells Angelo that ABC-TV wants to stop filming 'cause The Champ looks bad. They ain't gonna buy this film for no *Wide World of Sports* if he's not showing them nothing. The Champ ain't showing nothing but a tired old overweight fighter.

" 'What they expect?' The Champ is asking me.

" 'They expect you to rumble!' I tell him. 'They expect you to rise and shine! Shuffle! Shoeshine 'em. They tellin' you to get in that ring and stop those suckers! They tellin' you they don't care if you don't go to Viet Nam, don't go in the Army, don't be a Christian, don't Uncle-Tom. They tellin' you to get in shape. This ain't no exhibition. This a Resurrection!'

"Then he went out them last rounds to meet the fastest, hungri-est, hardest of the pros, and lo and behold, he's like Shorty wanted him to be. He's dancing and shuffling! Shoeshining and shifting! His jabs slip out like a snake's tongue. He's circling and cutting the ring in half. And the people stand up on their feet and the gym got thunder inside, and I'm calling out to him:

" 'Dance! Dance, Champ! Dance!'

"He's throwing combinations like Shorty put a motor in his body, uppercuts, lefts and rights, whipping that sucker all over the ring!

"I'm calling to him: 'Dance, Champ! Dance for the little children in orphanages don't nobody want! Fight for them, Champ! You the boss! Dance for po' people with no jobs, who got rent to pay! Dance for 'em, Champ! Stick that sucker! Dance for them winos sleepin' in the gutter! For them people in hospitals who got TB, cancer, for them prisoners locked in jails and ain't got no bail! Dance for 'em, Champ! Dance for them dope addicts everybody's given up on! Dance for little pregnant girls who got no husbands! Dance for 'em, Champ! Fight for 'em!

" 'Whip them suckers for 'em! Shoeshine 'em, shoeshine 'em! Fight for them people needin' welfare, for old people who didn't get no pension checks! Dance for 'em! Go 'head, whip that sucker's ass! Have no mercy! Dance for them tired old whores out there hustlin'! For all them lonely people drinkin' in the taverns! In the pool halls! On the street corners! Dance for the sweepers, little people moppin' up airport floors, train stations, bus depots, gas stations! Fight for 'em, Champ! For the maids in hotels makin' up beds, cleanin' toilets! Whip them suckers! Shorty told them to resurrect you. Shorty told them to dig you up out of the grave! Ain't no Senators saved you, ain't no Governors saved you, ain't no President saved you! Ain't no bankers saved you! Them people out there saved you. Them people out there puttin' new blood in your veins! Stick that sucker in front of you! Stick him all night long! Can't nobody whip Muhammad Ali! Can't nobody whip Muhammad Ali but Cassius Clay, and he ain't here tonight! Dance, Champ, dance!' "

"O-o-o-o-o-o-o! I can see him cooking now." Rahaman laughs.

"And when the bell rings, the house roars so long the timekeeper has to ring the bell forty times before we can get The Champ back to his dressing room.

"But that's not the best of it," Bundini goes on. "The best came in the dressing room. I hear The Champ talking to my old street buddies from New York, Teddy and Pal. He says, 'Angelo's got the connection and the complexion, but Bundini makes me fight.' That's all he said.

"That was for me. It was the first time he ever give me my mojo back. I give it to him and he gives it back. I feel my body get younger. A man gets old quick when he don't get love. An unloved man is the endangered species. A man gets ulcers and brain damage when he ain't around love. What he said smoothed out the wrinkles in my body. A man minus love is a wrinkled man, but a beloved man is smooth.

"People who love you demand more from you than people who don't care 'bout you. That's why Sugar Ray would never even look into a friend's eyes when he was coming down the aisle to the ring. He put that hood over his head like a horse with blinders, he don't want to see nobody but his opponent.

"A man's got to be in good shape to live up to love. The Champ wasn't in shape, but Shorty called for the Resurrection and the people gave him the transfusion . . ."

Bundini turns and looks at me stretched out in the back seat. Rahaman has no more questions. We drive the rest of the way into Philly mostly in silence.

GYMS BEFORE
JUDGMENT

Herbert had worked out every detail of the Quarry contract, and it had been signed and sealed; the $200,000 purse is up in the bank; my new boxing license has been tested in Atlanta's Morehouse College gym, and now the promoters are counting on prayers, politics and profits to pull it off—mostly the latter. Yet I can't shake the feeling that somehow the same bad luck that has dogged my steps since the day I refused to be drafted will spring up again and cancel it all.

These are the days when I still hear the voice of the angry old white woman in Houston, outside the Armed Forces Examining and Entrance Station, waving her flag and yelling at me as I walk out of the building: "If you can't fight for this flag, you can't fight nowhere. Till you get down on your knees, kiss this flag and beg Jesus Christ and the White House to forgive you, you ain't The Champ no more. You ain't never gonna be no more Champ!"

And now that the day has come to announce my return, I'm

sleeping in the New York Hilton and trying not to hear Bundini hammering on the door: "Champ! Champ, wake up!"

"Stop shouting," I say.

"Wake up, Champ. They sent me to make sure you get there on time." He snatches off the cover.

"What time is 'on time'?" I roll over.

"The press conference at ten."

"What time is it now?"

"Ten."

I get back under the cover. "We leave at eleven. Let 'em wait."

Bundini widens his eyes like Mantan Moreland; then he starts laughing. It's the kind of answer he loves. "Now look-a-here! Look-a-here! You still Champ! Good God A'mighty, the real goddamn Champ! We back in business! Been some mean, lean years since we could make anybody wait. The Champ says, 'Let 'em wait!' "

He opens the door and goes down the hall shouting loud enough to wake the dead. "We back in business! The Second Coming of Muhammad! The Lamb coming to claim His own. The Champ says, 'Let 'em wait!' "

When I get to the lobby, the clerk has a message. It's from Jackie Robinson, and I go over to the phone booth and call him.

Since the day of my first fight in Madison Square Garden, when he came into my dressing room to welcome me, we've been friends. I liked his direct, blunt, black way of talking.

Since Jackie has for years been known as the "black man closest to Governor Rockefeller," my lawyer, Chauncey Eskridge, asked him to talk to the Governor about helping me regain my New York boxing license, which, as a Federal court decision said later, has been taken from me illegally.

"Champ." Jackie's voice comes over strong. "You still the greatest, next to me," and we laugh. "I've talked to the Governor," he says. "Not once, but again and again. All year!"

Knowing how hardheaded Jackie is when he goes after something, I can see him sitting across the desk, chin to chin with Rockefeller.

"Yesterday, I showed him where even in the Deep South, in Georgia where they fought a war to uphold White Supremacy, where they lynch people for not saluting the flag, they're going to give Muhammad Ali his right to fight. The people in New York would go for it, too, I told him."

"What did he say to that?" I am curious.

"He says a lot of people asked him about you. But he's scared to buck the White House. He says, 'Jackie, you know Cassius Clay is Nixon's pet peeve. Nixon hates his guts.' I told him he could get a lot of support in New York on the right of Ali to fight. But he won't move. He won't do anything to annoy Nixon."

"I thought a man with all that power and money would be independent."

"Not if you're chicken in the first place," Jackie says. "Some of the guys who work around him said he might do something if you would make speeches for the Governor and appear at rallies."

"I couldn't do that."

"I wouldn't want you to. One slave on Rockefeller's plantation is enough. I wouldn't want them to put shackles on you, too. I'm about to get out of this shit myself."

Although Jackie and I are miles apart on many issues, on other things I can identify with him in a way I seldom could with my early boxing idol, Ray Robinson. Outside the ring I had outgrown Sugar Ray. But not Jackie. Down to the final week of his life, he struggled, without losing his balance or his connection with the kind of people I come from.

"You might win your case in court anyway," he says. "Whatever you do, make sure that the fight comes off in Atlanta. Once you get in the ring, I'm not worried. Tell Eskridge I did my best."

I thank him, and feel something sinking inside my stomach.

Months later one of the Governor's aides approached my lawyer, asking me to sign a public letter of thanks to Governor Rockefeller for the fact that New York had finally granted me my license. The letter was to be used in his reelection campaign.

"How can we thank him when he refused to open his mouth?" Eskridge asked.

The Governor's people didn't know Jackie had kept us informed of his attitude.

The only public letter of thanks I could have signed would have named my manager, my own lawyer, the law professors at Columbia University and Ann Wagner, a lawyer for the Legal Defense Fund of the NAACP who spent all year digging up evidence to prove that the New York State Athletic Commission had granted boxing licenses to ninety fighters convicted of embezzlement, rape and murder, as well as fifteen convicted of crimes while in the service, and that the refusal to allow me a license while my case was under appeal was cruel and unusual punishment. It wrecked the State's defense that they had a long-established policy against granting a boxing license to anyone convicted of a felony who had not yet served his sentence.

• • •

BUT NOW Bundini and Angelo are tapping on the phone booth.

Bundini is indignant: "Champ, not even Jesus Christ would tarry like you on *His* Second Coming. He wouldn't keep *His* goddamn disciples waiting like you doing. Hurry up. Shorty don't give nobody no Third Coming, you know."

Angelo could never get over Bundini's irreverence. "At least you could call the Lord by His proper name," he says.

But talking with Jackie has reminded me of two stops I have to make. One to NBC, to cancel my appearance on the Johnny Carson show, the other to see Whitney Young of the National Urban League.

I tell Carson the Atlanta promoters want to let sleeping dogs lie; they think a national TV show might provoke a crusade against the fight. It was a wasted precaution, I find out later, since they launched an attack anyway.

"But if the fight comes off," Carson says, "would you and Quarry promise to give me your first appearance?"

"I will, but Quarry won't be able to make it." He laughs, and I can see they were beginning to believe it might come off.

I've lost the address of the Urban League, but Bundini, who is Jewish, remembers it's next door to the Women's Zionist Organization, and we walk over.

When I go in, the office staff, which I thought would be stiff and intellectual, surrounds me and cheers. Whitney Young comes from behind his desk, gives me the brotherhood hug and sits me on a couch. I thank him for the League's support, and Whitney talks of ways we might cooperate. He has spent years in Atlanta, and is willing to help coordinate the black and white leaders behind me.

"We can benefit mutually," he says.

"How so?"

"Well, we'll stand together, and hopefully some of our respectability will rub off on you, and some of your popularity and daring will rub off on us. Fair exchange?"

Afterwards we take a slow walk over to Sixth Avenue, to the hotel where hundreds of editors, reporters, photographers, publicists, fight people, TV crews are crowded into a small hall to witness what Bundini is describing as The Second Coming of Muhammad Ali: "Good Lord A'mighty, the Lamb's come back!"

The pre-fight press conference is the first I have faced since I fought Zora Folley at Madison Square Garden. Then the news was out that I was about to be called up for induction. Even before I reported to the Induction Center, some headlines read: CLAY PICKS JAIL OVER ARMY. CLAY INSULTS UNCLE SAM.

Almost all the columnists denounced my refusal to be drafted. Since the day I declared myself a Muslim, they called me "unworthy of wearing the crown of the World Heavyweight Champion" and looked eagerly for the day when some "Real American" would relieve this ungrateful "loud-mouth slacker" of the title.

Yet as they push me through to the front of the hall, I feel comfortable and at home, with no resentment. In fact, I detect a feeling of friendliness, here and there, even from some whose columns have hurt me most. From now on, most of them will stop trying to punish me for refusing to fight in Viet Nam or berate me because of my religion, though they will never treat me the way they would if I became a black Catholic or a black Christian Scientist. The public attitude toward the war will shift, and the vast majority will oppose it even stronger than I did.

But I have missed them, and they seemed to have missed me. I even missed the blow-to-blow word fights I was used to, especially with those who kept me under almost constant attack: Gene Ward and Dick Young of the New York *Daily News*, Jim Bishop, Jimmy Cannon, and Arch Ward of the Chicago *Tribune*, all of whom are now paying little attention to Jerry Quarry, but concentrating on me.

My passport is still revoked and my case is still pending before the Supreme Court. I am still barred from boxing in New York, but it's obvious that if the Atlanta fight comes off, things will change for me. Of all the shouting and excitement in that conference, which Dave Anderson of the New York *Times* describes later as "wild and hectic," nothing surprises me as much as a quiet request from Quarry.

We've gone through the charade of signing the already signed contract, and have begun to push our way out of the hall, when Quarry leans over and asks, courteously, "Champ, before you go, my wife would like to meet you."

I follow him through the crowd until a pretty, slightly built woman, dressed stylishly in brown suede, steps up and holds out her hand. "I thought Jerry was going to forget," she says. "I wanted to meet you for so long."

"I don't see how Jerry can get any training done with such a pretty wife. I hope you come around his camp." She blushes at my words.

"And this is my son, Jerry Lynn," Quarry is saying.

He is a well-built youngster who looks more like his mother than Jerry. He puts his hand into mine and I put my arms around him.

We move to the side of the room, and although reporters and photographers are still shouting questions, I'm conscious only of this little boy, looking up at me as though his father and I were the best of friends getting ready for a simple exercise in the gym. His hands are clinging to mine, and I feel disturbed in a way I can't explain even to myself. Then I realize I've been away from fighting too long.

Jerry won't be the first father I pulverize in front of his family:

there were the sons of Cleveland Williams, of George Chuvalo, Brian London, Zora Folley—and how many others?

Something Floyd Patterson said to me comes back: "Violence and hate are a part of a prizefighter's world. We fight, but we do not really hate down deep, although we try to pretend we hate when we are afraid of losing . . ."

I always try to build up immunity to my opponent's personality, at least until I defeat him. I create a special personality for him and invent, if I have to, motives for my attacks. That way I can fight better, even enjoy building it up.

But can I pretend hatred for a father whose little boy takes my hand in his, holds the fist that may smash his father's face or limit his father's future or ruin his reputation?

Someone brings a felt pen and I write my name on his hand, like a tattoo, and lift him in my arms as he laughs. He thinks the fight is only play-acting.

When I wanted to hold him most, and couldn't, was right after I had stopped Jerry. I caught a glimpse of him screaming his heart out. He had just seen his "friend" cut a gash above his father's eyes so deep that blood squirted out into the ringside. And, in the uproar, I wasn't able to console him as I had the children of other fighters. Like the son of Brian London, sitting at ringside with his mother when I smashed his father to the floor, almost in their laps. After I climbed down from the ring, I wouldn't go to my dressing room until I made my way over to where they were sitting. I had seen his mother's story in the London papers about how her husband's career worried her, and I was glad she accepted my consolations. And just so her son would not forget who and what his father really was, I picked him up and said, "Your father is a very brave man and most of his fights he wins and will win again. But more important than anything, he loves you. Don't you ever forget it." He nodded and smiled. With Zora Folley, I knew his wife and sweet children were home in Arizona watching the fight on TV. After he was counted out, I spoke into the mike Howard Cosell handed me and told Folley's wife, "Your husband's all right. He's in no trouble." I found out later she was glad to hear that, because all she could see was a crowd around him and someone giving him smelling salts.

I know what it can be to have a father decompose before your eyes. I never introduce my wife and children to an opponent, not until they're defeated.

As I STAND THERE I feel secure knowing I have never been defeated as a professional. Quarry has.

"How does it feel, Champ, after three years?" Two Germans who have been waiting for an interview break into our conversation. "Do you think you can get back into shape?"

"Sure he can!" Quarry's son says proudly before I can answer.

Then Bundini comes up. "We back in business! It's like old times! We flying to Miami. You ready?"

I'm ready—in a lot of ways. I have come out of a cocoon and something has changed inside me. The days ahead will never be exactly like "old times."

The contract calls for Quarry and me to spend the final two weeks training in Atlanta, but now he's on his way to California and I to Miami.

"See you in Atlanta," the Quarrys say, extending their hands.

I take only Jerry Lynn's, and I see confusion in Quarry's eyes. But like I've said, I never shake hands with an opponent until I've whipped him.

"Get ready for war!" Bundini's husky voice keeps booming as we go out on the streets, headed for the airport: PRETENDERS, GET OFF THE GODDAMN THRONE! THE LAMB'S COME TO CLAIM HIS OWN!

But I dream of Quarry and his son that night, and I wake up in a sweat.

We fly down to Miami Beach and end up in the Sea Gull, a small Orthodox Jewish hotel, sitting almost in the ocean, at the end of an isolated side street. Angelo explains, "You need a quiet, secluded place where people go to bed at night, where the food is kosher, where the lobby is not crowded with whores and hustlers." It has the kind of intimate friendliness I want that none of the plush places on the Beach can match. I make it my quarters, not just for the Quarry fight but for Bonavena and part of Frazier.

They give me Room 222 so I can walk up without waiting on the slow elevators—timed, the manager says, so as not to "jar the guests," all elderly and retired, except for the younger groups occasionally brought in by the rabbinical organizations.

I spread my sparring partners, Bundini, my father and Rahaman around in adjacent rooms. I draft singer Arthur Prysock's nephew, Paul, as the cook, whose chief job is to boil carrots, cabbage and peas, and prowl the butcher shops for the biggest kosher steaks on the Beach, steaks we often share with the visiting rabbis who stop in 222 on their way from meetings. They look at old fight films with us, countless snapshots of Bundini's son's bar mitzvah, and engage in long disputes with Bundini, whose religion has a slightly unorthodox twist.

The proprietor, a kind, elderly man, keeps apologizing for the sparseness of the quarters, not knowing I don't miss the swank hotels. The biggest and richest will later offer me ten thousand a week to use them as headquarters, but I can still remember not too long ago, when I first began training in Miami. Then no hotel on the Beach would accept black clients, whether they were Cassius Clay or Sarah Vaughn or the countless black travelers who were confined to the segregated George Washington Carver Hotel on the Miami side. I could only come over to Miami Beach to train, and at first even the drugstore under the Fifth Street Gym refused to allow blacks at the counter.

The day before I'm scheduled to leave for Atlanta, my last day to train for the Quarry fight, I'm in the gym and my sparring partner, Blue Lewis, is pounding my stomach like he would a medicine ball. I've been away from gyms for forty-two months, and Quarry will go for the body. Blue lets me know that a sledge hammer is coming; he telegraphs it, but I can't move.

Once I heard Jersey Joe Walcott and Joe Louis, who could knock down mules, talk of blows that had knocked them down, and Jersey Joe said, "When one comes out of the blue, you can get over it quick. No hangover. But the one you see coming, but still can't get away from, goes down on tape and you play it back at funny times. When you're dreaming. Or just walking down the street."

Now I see a blow like that coming. It starts out for the pit of my stomach, but suddenly curves and crashes into my ribs. The pain is like a terrible toothache shooting through bones, up the spine, up the back of my head. I hang there, my back against the ropes, while he sends telegrams of more to come crushing into my side. Then I slide slowly down the ropes to the canvas. On the way down, out of the corner of my eye, I see some startled faces, wide eyes, the crowd in the gym rushing up to the ring: "Is he hurt?" . . . "Is he faking?" . . . "Did you see that?"

I stretch out on the canvas and feel Bundini's arms lifting my shoulders, his mouth on my ear. "You sure make it look real, Champ." He is trying to laugh. "You all right?"

He's seen me go through this act a dozen times just to liven up the gym—but now he is not sure what it is. I know what it is.

I remember pulling myself slowly up by the ropes and winking at the crowd. Some of them wink back like they're in on the joke, and laugh. Somehow I finish the workout and even include a round of shadowboxing. Then Angelo pushes the crowd back from the ring and I follow him into the dressing room.

In the crowd is Arthur Burke, a lawyer who's waiting to take me over to Miami to file the deposition in the suit against me—the deposition I put off to test myself in Angelo's gym. Burke's never been around prizefighters before and he tries to follow me into the dressing room, but Angelo pushes everybody out. Only the closest members of the crew can come in. When the door shuts, they huddle around. They were quiet outside because reporters were looking. Now they scream:

"Why'd you do it? Why'd you let a sparring partner hit you like that?"

"My God! Somebody get the doctor!"

"If the rib's broke . . ."

"It's his way, The Champ's way." Bundini is resigned. "The way he gets in shape. He trains that way."

I see Blue sticking his long head through the door like a horse looking in the barn, as much pain and regret on his face as in my ribs. "I didn't know you weren't ready. You told me throw 'em in hard."

I shake my fist at his head. "If you didn't, I'd get another sparring partner."

Blue. I've known him since the Golden Gloves. No ordinary sparring partner, he's one of the hardest hitters, one of a number of little-known fighters who have almost no chance of becoming known because no manager will let a "name" fighter get in the ring with them. Although now and then someone makes a mistake. Like South America's Heavyweight Champion, Oscar Bonavena, will do when he takes Blue for a "soft touch," accepts a fight with him in Buenos Aires, is knocked down three times in four rounds before the referee "disqualifies" Blue—so Oscar can make more money in America.

When Blue leaves I step into the shower stall, but the pain comes down so hard I double over until Angelo steers me to the dressing table. "Doctor's on the way. Lie down, stretch out."

I try to get up, but the pain makes me close my eyes. When I open them, I see Dr. Pacheco bending down, feeling my side.

Chris is shaking his head. "If we postpone, God knows when we'll get this far again. We got to keep it out of the newspapers, too."

"You're making too much out of it," I say.

The doctor straightens up. "We can't tell a thing until we get the x-rays. The papers don't have to know. You don't have to tell them. The Champ's the one that's got to know."

"Quarry'll know before morning," Bundini says.

It's a strange thing about secrets in a fighter's camp. It's easy to keep the press from picking things up, but the spy systems inside camps are another matter. Quarry'll know all about the rib long before we face each other in the ring. In fact, he will tell me he counted on it.

"What's it all about?" Angelo walks around, shaking his head as though some deep supernatural mystery is at work. "The same thing happened before the second Liston fight. You let Jimmy Ellis smash you in the same spot two days before that fight, and we were scared to death. You don't even remember it."

I remember it, all right. Only a few months ago I talked to Liston about that blow. I ran into Sonny in the State Building in Sacramento. I was brought out there by Henry Winston, an Oakland promoter who thought he had enough pull with Governor Reagan to get me a boxing license. It was the first time I'd seen Liston since we fought that night in Lewiston, Maine. And though I didn't know it, it would be the last time we'd see each other.

We sat there on the bench, two "former" Champions, both banned in California, both trying to get the ban lifted so we could earn a living and both about to be turned down by the Governor. I was uneasy sitting there trying to think of something to say. It was the one time we'd ever been peaceful in each other's presence. We knew each other only from heavy crushing blows, violence, bitterness and all the hostility and insults that go to make up a "Big Fight." And even though we knew the hostility and hatred was concocted, it was still under our skin and took a long time to wash out.

I finally opened up by telling him how Jimmy Ellis almost broke my ribs a few days before our Lewiston fight. Sonny listened closely and his eyes lit up, like he was hearing the answer to an old riddle that had puzzled him for a long time.

"They came and told me about it," he said slowly. "It came in the gym like a hot tip on a horse. But I didn't believe it. I'd never known Ellis to hit that hard. If they'd said Blue Lewis, Cody Jones or Mel Turnbow, I would've believed it. But I thought it was one of your tricks." He shook his head sadly, like a gambler who's missed his turn to roll his own loaded dice. "If I had only believed! I wouldn't have to be here begging these bastards for no license." Then he gave me that cold, unblinking stare he used to send shivers down the spine of his weaker opponents. "And after I got through with you, you wouldn't be either. Had your ass back to Louisville for good. I could've shut your big mouth, once and for all."

When we parted, we said we'd see each other again, but in less than a year Sonny was found sitting alone on the sofa of his Las Vegas home—he had been dead for a week. Police reports said he died from an overdose of heroin, but Joe Louis, his closest friend, will tell me this is a lie, that Sonny had been murdered. "If heroin was in his veins, somebody other than Liston shot it in. Sonny never dealt with heroin," Joe said.

Whether the outcome of our last fight would have been the way Sonny imagined had he known of my bad rib, I have my doubts. But in the film of that fight you can see me come out at the bell dancing and circling with my right hand close to my side, protecting my rib.

The damage Ellis did was kept out of the news, but it had more to do with my quick knockout of Liston than anything mentioned in the "inside reports" of that fight. Including the crazy claim that the fight was "fixed." I figure the "fixed" cries must have come either from those who were so desperate to see me beaten that they were hurt even worse than Liston to see me win, or from those who know little about boxing, less of Liston and nothing about me.

Liston's managers wanted that title back and wanted it bad. The Heavyweight Title is where the money is—nowhere else. No fix in the world would bring Liston and his managers the kind of money that goes along with holding the title. And what fool would fix the championship fight to last less than two minutes? A fix would be rigged to look more like a contest.

I went into the ring that night knowing I couldn't take any chances on Liston's big fist pounding my bruised rib, and the first time I caught him making a motion to lunge in, I met him halfway with a short right cross that had all the speed and power I could put behind it. It hit his chin like an electric bolt. Even my worst critics admit I am the fastest heavyweight ever to enter the ring, and it's been said I can hit you before God gets the news.

Some cried "fix" because they didn't see that blow. Those around ringside who blinked their eyes missed it, and the controversy about that "invisible" blow never stopped. But some cameras caught it, and *Life* magazine had pictures showing that it had lifted Liston off his feet before he was dumped on the floor.

ON THE DRESSING TABLE I look up at the ceiling. The pain is making me dizzy, throbbing in my ribs, and I see the faces of people I've met and they seem to surround me—reporters, students, photographers, waitresses, mothers, airline hostesses, cabdrivers, hotel clerks, tourists, gas-station attendants, prostitutes, pimps, policemen, autograph seekers, all asking each other out loud questions they never ask me:

"How old is he now?"

"Can he win in a comeback?"

"Will he ever be in shape like he was before?"

"Fighters get old quick, don't they?"

I remember pulling myself up and getting dressed without answering Pacheco about the x-ray. He has sent Bundini to the drugstore with a prescription for something to kill the pain, and he keeps talking about the x-ray. "I know a radiologist who won't talk. A Cuban doctor who stays out of the news. I can set it up tonight, so nobody'll know. As late as twelve o'clock."

"If I feel pain later on, I'll call you," I say. I know in the end I will have the x-ray and all I'm doing is prolonging the agony because the results might mark the end of me and why rush into that? I slip a hot towel underneath my shirt, push my way through the reporters who're still hanging around and leave the gym. I have to go and file that deposition. Murray Worner is suing me for publicly calling the "computer fight," which he arranged and promoted, a fake. On my way to the car I think of the wild drive to Fort Lauderdale to see the man who helped me fake it—Rocky Marciano.

I was behind the wheel of the biggest car we could find and I drove on down to Fort Lauderdale with Jimmy Ellis, Angelo and Dr. Pacheco. I ran red lights, cut ahead of traffic, broke speed limits, because I didn't want to be late for Rocco Francis Marchingiano's funeral.

I wasn't sure of the exact location of the place, so I drove along until I saw this big, sprawling crowd. A mixed crowd, some in dark suits, evening gowns; some in bathing suits, shorts, sandals, gay shirts, beach robes. The ushers recognized me and got me up front to a pew just before the priest came in to say the Mass.

I saw his casket on the platform and I got the same chilly, unreal feeling I did that night in Louisville when I was fourteen, riding my motor scooter through the rain, and on somebody's car radio I heard the announcer over the roar of the crowd: "The winnah and still Champeen of the World, Rocky Marciano!" It seemed such a short time between the cry of that announcer and the voice of the priest saying the Mass and the crowd not roaring but quieter than any crowd Rocky had ever performed for.

They had already closed the bronze lid, but I could see through it like it's made of glass. I saw his wide face looking the way they fix dead faces, heavy and stiff and waxy. Not like Rocky and I had fixed it only a few weeks before, with all kinds of life and action, the face of a member of our trade after a terrible battle. I believe he would have liked it better to go out looking that way.

We have worked his face over with make-believe bruises, lumps and phony marks of pain and sweat. We have poured ketchup over his forehead to look like blood flowing from a cut eye, ketchup above his lip to make a nosebleed. We are filming what a South Miami promoter has gotten us to agree to fake, the so-called "Muhammad Ali–Rocky Marciano fight of the century." Part of a series of computer fights in a so-called elimination contest, matching up fighters of different generations who could never be matched.

"It's all bullshit!" Rocky, breathing heavy, takes off his gloves to rest after we fake another knockout for the computer. "The computer is bullshit! This ain't gonna be what no computer says. This fight will be rigged to come out the way it'll make the most money for the promoters—not us. You just watch, Champ. How'd we get in this shit in the first place?"

We got in it for the money. Which for me means $999.99, the only purse I have been allowed to earn "boxing" since I was stripped of my title. They have brought Rocky out of fourteen years of retirement for what will turn out to be the last "fight" of his life.

It comes at a time when Rocky is near his forty-sixth birthday and I'm near my twenty-sixth. He has gone into training to lose forty-five pounds in order to get into something that looks like shape. They fix him up with a toupee, set up a ring with a black background in the studio and put five cameras around us. The rounds are one minute each. And before we finish the faking, we do seventy of these one-minute plays where we pull punches, fake blows. My glove never hit his face, his glove never hit mine. I snake-lick jabs within a fraction of an inch from his eyes and he throws hooks that never touch their target. Grunt and groan and snarl and snort. They put sound effects behind each punch, and dub in an announcer giving the blow-by-blow description of the furious, frantic clash.

The promoter asks me if I can think of some ending, and I plan the one that is actually used: I show Rocky how to hit me and I fall as though it's real. We have seven different endings—some with me winning, some with Rocky winning. Some segments we fake so good they are left untouched by the editors. There is no computer telling us what to do.

And through all the fakery, something is happening between us. I feel closer to him than any white fighter in the trade. We talk "fighter's talk" in the way only friends can, blood talk, nitty-gritty talk. Our work is phony but our friendship has become real.

The Mass was over and the pallbearers lifted his casket. I followed them outside. Hundreds of tourists were waiting to get a look at Rocky and the Big Name celebrities who had flown in. All in all, it wasn't a sad funeral.

I remember a dignified middle-aged woman who I thought was one of the mourners. She brightened up when she caught sight of me and took out of her pocketbook a picture of her husband in an officer's uniform. "My husband is a Colonel in the Air Force in Viet Nam," she said. "Jack will be just delighted to know I met you and got your autograph." I had my doubts about Jack's "delight." The young ushers come up eager for me to sign the obituary, and two sun-tanned girls who looked like they had just gotten off the beach tried to borrow a pen from the mourners to get autographs.

Usually I give anyone an autograph, any time except a few hours before I go in the ring, but right then I felt I shouldn't. It seemed like it would make the dead not only gone, but worse, forgotten before he was even under the ground.

I shook them off and held my hands behind me, and they went after the Big Names who had no scruples about signing in the presence of the dead. I looked on and hoped Rocky was somewhere taking down their names so that whenever they joined him, he could whip them for upstaging him at his own funeral.

Sports historians who know Rocky and I spent so much time together always ask my opinion of the greatest of modern white fighters. What was Rocky like? He had once been a loyal admirer of Sonny Liston and had picked Liston to beat me. After I twice destroyed Sonny he became one of my staunchest supporters.

Rocky was quiet, peaceful, humble, not cocky or boastful. I can't stand heavyweights who talk too much. If you saw him on the streets you would probably pass him by. He liked to wear plain clothes: T-shirts, a golf hat, a pair of blue jeans and tennis shoes; not the kind they stuffed him in for his last performance.

Heavyweights have a way of smelling each other out like Great Danes when they first meet, and in the weeks we pretended violence Marciano took my measurements and I took his. Underneath his aging frame he still had the ghost of what he must have had in his prime.

Very few young people have seen Rocky in action. He defended his title only six times during the four years he held it. And his fame came mainly from wins over the once-retired thirty-seven-year-old Joe Louis, the twice-retired thirty-eight-year-old Joe Walcott, forty-two-year-old Archie Moore and the washed-up thirty-four-year-old Ezzard Charles. All great names, but way past the end of the game. How Marciano managed to escape fighting the young black heavyweights of his day and age is the same mystery that surrounds so many of the White Hopes of the past, like Dempsey, Tunney and Sharkey. This is not to take anything away from Marciano, who deserves his place as one of the best fighters of all time, to be ranked among the greatest of the great heavyweights, but I don't believe he would have survived if he had to fight as regularly as I did when I was Champion—taking on a top contender every few months, avoiding no one in the world.

I lay no blame on him for the outcome of our phony computer fight. He probably had no more knowledge of how it would be finally decided than I did. But as the fraud came near an end, it was plain that neither of us, both undefeated Heavyweight Champions, liked the idea of being dramatized as "defeated" by the other—especially in a fake fight—and we were both on edge. Tension crept in as we saw the end was not in our hands. One afternoon in a workout I unleashed a string of lightning-fast jabs that kept coming almost the entire round. Rocky was amazed and said it:

"I never seen a fighter with hands that fast."

Later he said, "If all this bullshit don't come out right, I'm gonna blast it to kingdom come. We'll get together on it."

I wasn't sure what he meant. Or whether he had any inkling of what the "ending" was to be. The "results" had been ballyhooed all over the world as a deep mystery—a great secret "more closely guarded than the gold in Fort Knox," as *Time* magazine said. It was to be shown on one, and only one, night to "850 movie houses and arenas in America and more around the world, after which all copies are to be destroyed and the master print given to the Library of Congress."

But two weeks before opening night Rocky's body was taken from an airplane that crashed in Newton, Iowa. He never lived to see how "all this bullshit" came out.

"There's no mystery about it at all." Arnold Davis laughed and poured himself a heavy drink.

Davis is the grizzled old Philadelphia *Inquirer* reporter I've known since I first moved there, and now and then I drop by his house to pick up batches of sports clippings he saves for me.

"After all, that computer is no fool. The computer knows who's who in the equation. Take you, a loud-mouth black racist who brags 'I'm the greatest! I'm the King!' You won't submit to White America's old image of black fighters, you won't even submit to White America's Army. You're barred from the ring, stripped of the title, and on the other hand here's the real White Hope, the undefeated World Heavyweight hero of post–Joe Louis days." He leaned back as though overwhelmed. "Every self-respecting made-in-America computer knows how to add that up. They killed you off but can't get rid of the ghost you left behind. And there is not a white fighter around to chase it away.

"You know what they want?" He leaned close, as though somebody might hear him. "They want your ass whipped in public, knocked down, ripped, stomped, clubbed, pulverized, and not just by anybody, but by a real Great White Hope. Not a chocolate White Hope like Frazier or some of the others, but a genuine White-to-the-bone Hope, and none's around." He looked sorrowful and then brightened up. "That's where the computer comes in.

"We need Marciano to club you into submission. They'll dig up the old heroes to say we had real red-blooded white men in those days that could handle niggers like this. A white ghost against a black ghost. Acted out in the half-naked flesh, with you participating. Fantasy—but a lot of people live on fantasy. The ending is supposed to be a mystery? To whom? Marciano will beat you bloody.

"And it will all sell like hell in South Africa, to say nothing of Indiana and Alabama." He downed his drink and offered me "one for the road," one he knew I would refuse. I thanked him for my batch of clips and left.

Later, at home, thumbing through some of them, I come across a summary of a computerized elimination tournament of the "16 greatest"—done by the same promoter directing the "superfight." In it, I'm beaten by Jim Jeffries, history's clumsiest, most slow-footed heavyweight. The one Jack Johnson knocked out in real life. In his turn Jack Johnson is whipped by John L. Sullivan, while Gene Tunney takes care of Joe Walcott. The computer shows that even Joe Louis would go down under the White Hopes of the good old days. The computer is unmerciful.

It left me ashamed of what I had been doing. I had gone all over the country promoting the series as fair and accurate, especially the Marciano-Ali show.

When it came on, I was sitting in a crowded Philadelphia movie house and saw myself on the ropes being destroyed by Marciano, in one of the "artistic" endings few actors could equal. But the people around me thought it was real. Some sat stone-still, some booed and yelled, some cried.

In England they knew my skills, and exhibitors called the promoter and asked to be sent another "ending" more in keeping with reality.

"You can't denounce or disavow this thing now," my Washington lawyer warned me when I told him what I wanted. "They'll sue you for everything you'll ever make. They'll say you're crying because you lost."

But the "loss" was not all there was to it—the time would come when I'd take real defeat and feel no shame or guilt about it. What disturbed me was what I saw and heard all around me from the people.

This had come at a time when I was in the deep-freeze part of my exile and there was no thaw in sight. I felt I had disappointed millions of people all over the world, people who had good reason to believe that when they saw me facing an opponent the result would not be a fix or trick but something real. Their faith in my openness and honesty had always made me feel good. And I looked around for a chance to make clear what the "superfight" was and what my role in it had been.

The chance came quicker than I had expected. I was on the Dick

Cavett show and the subject of the computer fight came up. I said something like:

"I want to say this in front of everybody while I am on nationwide TV. I did promote the computer fight as being fair and accurate and scientific but I was wrong and I apologize for it. I should have examined it closer before I told people that. The whole thing is a sham. It's made to take your money and fill up theaters all over the world and leave you thinking you have seen a real fight, which it's not. It's phony all the way. There's no machine that can take Joe Louis' record and Jack Dempsey's record and tell you what would have happened if they had fought each other one night in their prime. This is just a Hollywood fake."

Cavett had no idea what I was going to say. The "superfight" had just been bought by his network for *Wide World of Sports*. When we got off the air he gave me a little smirk. "You'll be hearing more about this, I believe."

I did. Murray Worner, the promoter, sued me for two million dollars. Losses, he said, suffered after I denounced the fight. Losses which he claimed included the refusal of Sugar Ray Robinson to go through with a lucrative agreement to film a computer fight in Europe against Marcel Cerdan, the great French fighter of another generation. Sugar Ray lost faith in the computer.

It's NEARLY three-thirty when we reach the street of the promoter's attorneys, Whitman, Wolfe & Glick, but before we go into the building there's so much pain in my body I hold up for a minute, go over to a Mexican tamale stand and pick up a cold drink. The owner and his friends crowd around. They say, "Hi Champ," and scramble around for something to be autographed, hats, caps, collars, shirttails, and I write and rest against the wagon, the towel under my shirt wet with sweat.

The lawsuit is something far away now and I feel I'm facing a fight inside my body much more real than what's upstairs in the lawyer's office. I hardly hear the questions when I get there. When it's finished, the promoter's lawyer is friendly, walks me to the door and says, "I know you're not a betting man, but I am. I'd bet a year's pay you beat Quarry but I wouldn't bet a dime on the chance of this fight going through." And at that moment, neither would I.

It's been advertised that I will appear that night at an ABC basketball game between the Floridians and the Virginians at Miami Beach's Civic Auditorium, and Dr. Pacheco says I could use a diversion to take my mind off the pain. When we get there, Rahaman and I, I try to sit where I won't be noticed. The usher takes me to a seat in the bleachers, but people spot me and pass on the word. A stream of thin-faced, blond Southern students keep coming up until the usher asks me to sit with the team's owner, where it's easier to block off the crowd.

The color guard is on the floor for the singing of "The Star-Spangled Banner" and all around me heads are turning my way, and I can read the faces: Is this "Black Muslim" going to salute the flag? Muslims don't sing the National Anthem, do they?

I stand up and sing until "home of the brave and land of the free" is finished and two young white boys edge up to me with their notebooks out. One asks, "Mr. Clay, how is it you don't have to go to jail?"

I look him over. There's really no hostility on his face, just curiosity. "Well," I say, and lean back a little, "I've got three hundred thousand dollars in the bank just for lawyers, and if you read the history books, they seldom put anyone with that kind of money in jail. Interview the people in jail. Find how many in there got fifty thousand dollars, or twenty thousand dollars, or ten. It's hard to put money in jail in this country."

They never look up, just keep scribbling away.

Then it's eleven o'clock and I motion to Rahaman, who's been waiting all evening for me to give the signal to leave. He gets the car and we drive across the bridge to pick up Pacheco. From there we go to the office of Dr. Carlos Llanes, a radiologist and orthopedic physician for the Miami Dolphins.

"How much you charging?" I ask, as though this is the issue.

"Well," he says good-naturedly, "if the rib's all right, just see that I get a ringside seat at the fight." He smiles. "If not, no charge, because you'll be unemployed for a long, long time."

A Cuban technician carefully processes the x-rays and takes us back to the waiting room.

"How long now?" I ask Llanes.

"Not long."

I sit there trying to overcome the feeling that I am doomed never to fight again, and that each time I come near a fight something will stop it.

I had even asked Dr. Rex Hillman, who had worked with prizefighters for twenty years and knew their psychology, if I was getting superstitious. "After all," he said, "you've been turned back seventy-two times, though you had a good contract each time. If a bride steps up to the church that many times and her groom fails to show up each time, I wouldn't say there was anything unnatural about her being suspicious. I'd be a little superstitious myself. But I'd still try for marriage number seventy-three."

The technician walks in. He takes us to where Dr. Llanes is

looking at my x-rays, and for a while nothing is said. Then the doctor asks me how much longer I have to train.

"I leave tomorrow for Atlanta," I tell him.

"What would it take to postpone the fight?"

A chill goes through me. "A broken rib that's about to jut through my skin. That's all. Otherwise I go on."

He's still looking at the pictures. "Can't you take a few weeks off?"

"For me this is it."

"Well, there's a bad bruise here"—he takes off his glasses and puts his finger on a spot on the x-rays where my rib cage is—"but at least nothing's broken. Maybe if you're careful . . . Don't get hit there any more, and don't forget my ticket."

When I get back to the hotel some of the rabbis who've heard I'm leaving surprise me with gifts and a going-away party in the lobby. They sing old songs and seem glad to see me back at work.

One of them has a story from the morning paper announcing that Quarry has already arrived in Atlanta. There is a front-page picture of Quarry and Audie Murphy, the WW II hero, shaking hands. To balance things off, I take pictures showing the rabbis wishing me luck.

I sleep sound that night, wake before the alarm goes off, and I'm out running on the golf course. Jimmy Ellis is out even earlier and has almost finished his course. My ribs still hurt, but knowing that nothing is broken makes it bearable.

Running is the source of my stamina. Early in my career I learned to run until I'm tired, then run more after that. The running I do before the fatigue and pain is just the introduction. The real conditioning begins when the pain comes in; then it's time to start pushing. And after that I count every mile as extra strength and stamina. The reserve tank. What counts in the ring is what you can do after you're tired.

Up ahead Ellis suddenly drops back. He has finished his five miles. Bundini, driving alongside him, stops the car, jumps out and catches him. "Look!" he shouts. "Go run with The Champ! For the last time. Run side by side with him like you did when you were boys. Do it for old times' sake! You two born and bred together! Do it for The Champ! He's coming back from a long journey. They had him almost in jail. Go up there and put your shoulders next to his. Give him the spirit. Put the holy ghost on him. Make it like old times!"

Ellis is almost exhausted, but he pulls up beside me and matches me stride for stride. He's still the skinny kid I met on the streets in Louisville twelve years ago. My teammate in a hundred tournaments. My sparring partner in all my major fights. We run shoulder to shoulder, and it lifts my spirit. At a fork in the road he wishes me luck and goes on his way.

When I get back to the hotel, we rush to pack and get ready for the flight to Atlanta. I'm making phone calls to Philadelphia when C.B. Atkins, one of Herbert's business aides, and Blue Lewis, my sparring partner, answer a knock at the door.

"Someone here with some packages for The Champ!" Blue yells over his shoulder. "Gift packages!"

He comes back with two boxes neatly wrapped in white tissue, tied with red and green ribbons, and tosses one to C.B. Then he reads out loud the lettering on top of his box.

"It says, 'To Cassius Clay from Georgia.' " He begins tearing it open.

"Who knew I wanted cake for breakfast? Get the knife."

Suddenly, yelling and cursing, he drops the package. Blood is dripping from his hands. The package is on the floor and the body of a little black chihuahua has rolled out, its head severed from its body. A message in the box reads: "We know how to handle black draft-dodging dogs in Georgia. Stay out of Atlanta!" A Confederate flag is the only signature.

In the other box is a rag doll in yellow boxer shorts and tiny boxing gloves. A rope is tied around its throat and the head is jerked to the side to show its neck is broken.

C.B. and Blue run down the hall to catch the messenger, but they come back alone.

The little dog's body is still warm, and we make the box a casket. But I keep the doll. Without the rope around its neck it will make a good toy for my three-year-old daughter. It's a well-made doll, a lot of care went into it, and it looks a little like me. Not as pretty, but a good resemblance.

When we land in Atlanta, it's right there in my lap.

THE SECOND COMING

We are on the edge of a little lake. The birds are beginning to gather in the trees, thousands of chattering dark birds. Senator Johnson has provided my crew with his own cottage, inside the city's limits but miles from its center. We leave the highway, make a sharp turn off a dirt road and suddenly we're in a clearing where Johnson's cottage sits near a little man-made lake. Tall trees around it shut off the other houses down the road and make the place seem secluded. It's unlike any place I've lived in when I trained, and that sells me on it.

The Senator is proud of his country home. He shows us through the house, which looks a lot like a private hunting lodge, with rooms and beds enough for half my crew. Then he takes us outside and up to the wall of fir and pine trees.

"This is the season when birds, tens of thousands, come in the evening and sleep in the trees, and they sleep sound. Won't wake up unless there's an awful lot of noise, then they light out in droves. Fly so close to the house, you can't see out the window." He laughs. "It reminds you of Alfred Hitchcock's *The Birds*. How you like it?"

Angelo wants me to reject the place. "We didn't come to study the birds and trees. The Champ is used to having people around. He thrives on people. Just a little privacy when he wants it, is all."

Johnson stands his ground. "Hardly anyone knows how to get here unless you give them the route. If you station a guard at the highway, they can check out any car before they turn in here."

"The Hyatt House'll pay us to stay there," Angelo persists. "We can have a whole floor."

Bundini backs him up. "This kind of place, you can get ambushed. We need the city."

But I know I need a change. True, I always thrive on city training, but I remember the feeling of exhaustion I had during the exhibition, and I need to concentrate on training and conditioning.

We're standing on the edge of the little lake.

"What do you think, Champ?" Johnson wants a decision.

"How'll we get food out here?" Angelo says. "We can't trust just anybody to prepare Muhammad's food."

"I'll send my sister," Johnson says. "My own sister."

So Lydian, sister of Senator Johnson, and her four children take over the household duties, and during the day cook for the boxing crew from the time we arrive until the day we leave.

It takes twenty minutes to get from this secluded spot to a rambling old stucco building put up during the Depression. They've converted it to a gym from a wrestling and roller-skating arena and arranged it so Jerry and I train at alternate hours. A ring has been rigged up with rubber hoses for ropes and a thick canvas cover over some steel plates on the floor, plates that jangle and clank when the boxers move around. Some of the sparring partners don't like it, say it's like a telegraph, the floor betrays every move they make. But I've been away from gyms and ropes and canvas so long, I like the sound.

I even like the pre-fight physical and weigh-in—partly because it puts me another step closer to the end of exile, but mainly because pre-fight physicals are important to me.

Most fighters see this routine as a nuisance; their physical condition has already been certified, and if they need more checking, it is done quietly in the locker room or the dressing room, not before a crowd second in size only to the main fight. They know the purpose is not the health of the fighter but the health of the box office, to let photographers take pictures and reporters write suspense stories to build up the showdown.

The doctors come searching the fighters for heart murmurs, high blood pressure and anything abnormal. I come in searching, too. My examination is more careful than the doctors'.

For this weigh-in, the stands are jammed with the oddest assortment of people from the Deep South: farmers who've driven in from the Georgia countryside, clerks, students from the numerous black and white colleges in the city and people who've flown in from New York and Miami. They spill down from the seats, block the aisle, crowd around the scales and put the police and ushers to work.

I strip down first, and Murray Goodman, our press secretary, makes a path for me up to the scales. I'm standing on them when Quarry comes through the crowd in his green-and-white robe, with his manager-father. Then I hear a commotion, and I look back over to Quarry's side. His face is flushed red, and he's shouting at the promoters. There's so much noise I can't make out what he's saying, but he's furious.

"Go see what's wrong," I tell Angelo, but before he comes back I hear what's wrong. Quarry is yelling, "I ain't goin' in the ring with no black doctors in my corner!" Now he's screaming at his father, who's trying to calm him down. "If that's what I've got to do, the fight's off!"

Only then do I notice the two doctors sent by the Atlanta State Commission. Both are black.

In my fourteen years of fighting, from the Chicago Stadium to Madison Square Garden to the Houston Astrodome to the Felt Forum, promoters have assigned only white doctors—even though most of the fighters are black or Latin or Asian. Now the first black doctors Quarry sees, he wants fired or he won't fight.

"Well, well, well!" I shout out over the noise. "We got soul doctors in the house for once! Welcome, brothers, welcome." I clap my hands and the crowd joins in.

One of the promoters, Harry Pepp, is whispering to Quarry, and he's quieting down.

"What happened, Angelo?" I ask.

"They told him he wouldn't have to accept black doctors," he says. "Quarry thinks a black doctor might find some excuse for stopping the fight and awarding the decision to you."

I remember looking at Quarry then, as though I'm seeing him for the first time. I resolve that if the fight comes off I will see to it that he needs a doctor—any doctor—bad. Some newsmen strongly criticized me for characterizing Quarry as a White Hope and bringing the "racial issue" into boxing, but they know the issue was there long before I was born. Who put it there and who keeps it there? I was seeing Quarry as just an ordinary, decent, fair boxer because of the nice people in his family, whom I'd met, but now I think, it's arrogant of him to act as though I need the aid of a doctor to whip him.

The doctors pronounce our pulses and hearts "normal," and the photographers, TV cameramen and the press secretary insist that we sit down at a little card table in front of the ring and pose together.

We sit on the same side of the table, a little apart, and the photographers keep calling: "Closer!" . . . "Get closer!" They push us together until Jerry's ear is almost at my cheek. And while the cameras are clicking away, I whisper into Jerry's ear, "This just between you and me, Jerry. I don't want a soul to hear it."

He jerks back and stares at me. His eyes are inches from mine.

"They can see us talking, but they can't read lips." Then I give it to him. "You're gonna get the worst damn whipping of your life. I'm gonna whip you till you're cherry-red. You insulted all those black doctors."

His face flushes and he tries to pull away, but the photographers are screaming: "Heads together!" . . . "Closer!"

"I'm the one who's gonna do the whipping," he murmurs.

"Jerry, I thought you were smart. I gave you credit for being a very intelligent, refined fighter. If you don't want black doctors who are here to help you, how you must hate black me who is here to harm you—and harm you I will."

The press secretary is shouting, "Give the fighters room! Give the fighters some room to breathe!" The TV people start a chant: "Stand up! Stand up! Make 'em stand up!"

We stand up side by side to do the old fist-on-chin routine. Jerry extends his arm to reach my chin, and I extend mine to reach his. Only, mine touches his chin easy because of my long reach and his comes only to my shoulder.

The photographers want more: "Heads together!" . . . "Closer!" And again Quarry's head comes close to mine.

I've noticed that Quarry is easily upset over details. Now I whisper, "You got on the wrong kind of shoes. That's a shame; look at your shoes."

He looks down at his feet in spite of himself. His shoes are ordinary dress shoes.

"Look at mine," I say. "Eight-pound brogans. Make my feet lighter when I get in the ring. Give me strength; make me faster. I just wanted to advise you for your next fight. This one forget about. The whipping you're about to get will be awful. Here you got President Richard Nixon praying for you. Spiro Agnew betting on you. Governor Wallace right next-door watching you. And still—in the heart of the White South and on international TV—you're gonna get whipped. I'd hate to be in your shoes."

"You wait," Jerry blurts out. "You just wait till we get in the ring. Your ass can be had too, you know."

"Louder!" the press is shouting. "What you guys talking about?"
... "Somebody get a mike up there!"

But the pre-fight physical is over. The doctors have put away their
stethoscopes and arm pads and are writing up their reports on little blue
sheets. I know more about Quarry than they do. Quarry can be reached
not only by gloves but by words. I'm equipped with both.

When my crew jams into the station wagon with me to ride back
to the cottage, I take the little rag doll off the seat and hold it in my
lap. I'm uneasy again. While I could look into Quarry's eyes and sense
his uncertainty over the outcome of the fight, I wonder if he could
sense the deeper fear I have—not the outcome of the fight, but
whether the fight will come off at all.

It's not the occasional threats that are coming by phone and
through letters, or the rumors of "bombs" that the police are tracking
down. There's something about the faces in the crowds, faces that seem
confused, uncertain whether to applaud or boo. "Debates" about me
are aired on the radio and there is hysteria in the voices. Angelo believes
it's the tension and stress that always break out the closer the hour
comes to a big fight, but I think there's more to it than that.

I don't notice how much it's affecting those around me until one
day in the dressing room a sparring partner opens Bundini's suitcase
and discovers two Colt .45's.

Angelo is upset. "If they think we're carrying guns, they'll come
at us with guns."

"It's for The Champ's protection," Bundini says. "I see the eyes
of some of these people. You don't notice, but some of them hide back
in the crowd."

"Nobody's shooting anybody!" Angelo cries out.

Reggie Barrett argues back: "They shot John Kennedy, didn't
they? They shot Martin Luther. They shot Medgar Evers. They got
more reason to hate this man, Muhammad Ali, than they did King. At
least he was a Christian."

"What good would two guns do?" Angelo is persistent and I
support him.

The policemen assigned to guard us are angry, and warn us, "Guns
invite guns."

Bundini agrees to get rid of the .45's. He is never to bring them
inside the gym and never to have them around me again.

After the uproar over the guns, I remember lying on the bench
letting Luis Sarria, a former Cuban fighter who has become my chief
masseur, rub away more of the extra pounds. It's the day Angelo has
reserved for interviews with the foreign press, and Mario Widmar, a

Swiss editor from *Blic*, Switzerland's largest daily paper, wants to know: "What keeps you going? You're up at five, in bed by ten. You've got to want to break out of this and live normal. What keeps you going?"

"That short walk," I say. "From the dressing room to the ring. And all those faces out there waiting to see if I can come back to life, or if I'm dead forever. When I drop my robe off and answer the bell, people all over the world are watching. People who never saw me fight before but who heard what I said and what I did and what I am. They're asking, 'Is this the braggart who says he's the greatest? Is he all big talk? Or is there something real to him?' "

An English reporter I knew in London, Peter Wilson, hands me an AP dispatch and asks if I've read it.

"What's it about?" I'm lying on my stomach and I don't want to roll over.

"It'll be in the morning news, but I would like your comment for the English press before that."

"About what?"

"Well, Governor Maddox has declared he'll do everything he can to stop the fight."

The dressing room is quiet. The reporter reads from the dispatch: " 'Governor Maddox urges all Atlantans to boycott the fight of Clay and Quarry. He further urges all patriotic groups in the city to let promoters know how they feel about it. We shouldn't let him fight for money if he didn't fight for his country.' "

I reach out and take the dispatch. It goes on to report the "overwhelming" support all over the country being given to the Governor for his stand against the fight. Macon's Mayor, Ronnie Thompson, praised Maddox for his stand and sent a telegram to the Governor offering 100 percent support in efforts to keep me from fighting: THE DRAFT-DODGER, CLAY, SHOULD NOT BE ALLOWED TO ENJOY THE BENE- FITS FOR WHICH AMERICAN PATRIOTS HAVE DIED AND BLED.

For a long time there is silence in the locker room, with reporters drifting in and out. My first thought is, if the fight is canceled, I'll make a call to Belinda to tell her I'll be coming home to see my five-week-old daughters.

Then someone says, "Senator Johnson for Muhammad," and I pick up the phone.

"Ali." Johnson is quiet, calm. "I know you heard about Maddox, but don't get upset. Stop by the office on the way up to the house."

Outside, the black policemen who've been assigned to our group walk up and put their arms around me. "Champ, if you don't mind, we're going to double the guards around you."

Angelo is nervous; he's seen some police shove students who wanted autographs, and the response of some students who were pushed back almost touched off a fight. "There's no fence around Ali," he says. "There's no barrier. He takes to the people, people take to him."

We are on the sidewalk, and people who've been in regular attendance at the gym are gathering around. One holds up a headline from the Atlanta paper: GOVERNOR MADDOX DECLARES OCTOBER 26 TO BE A BLACK DAY OF MOURNING. URGES PATRIOTIC CITIZENS TO PROTEST.

The crowd follows us to the car, some putting their heads to the window and shouting, "What do you do if they stop the fight?"

"I go home," I say.

"If you can't have the fight here, where would you like to have it?"

"In the Governor's mansion!" I shout back.

We drive into the black community, to the law offices of Senator Johnson, who is waiting for us along with some of his partners. Johnson is standing near a blackboard, casually lighting his long cigar as though he's never seen the headlines.

"How are the ticket sales going?" somebody asks.

"Sold out," Johnson says. He writes a figure on the blackboard. "Closed-circuit tickets on the East Coast booked solid. Everybody wants to see this fight. Even those against it."

"Look, we didn't come here for bullshit," Angelo says. "We got a right to know. There's a change. The Governor has changed his mind. There're calls to stop the fight."

Johnson tries to dodge Angelo's question. He continues to talk of the great build-up, the interest in the fight that is now international. For the first time the Russians have a beam into Moscow by satellite. England. Germany. Japan. The lobbies of the hotels where the fight is to be shown are crowded already.

"You never answered the only question that matters," Angelo is saying. "What's the chance of the fight being stopped, even by injunction? There's a rumor that Maddox is going to court. That he got a case against the fight."

Johnson and his partners exchange looks, and Johnson pulls his chair closer to the table. "We had a close scare. But I think it's over."

"How close?" I ask.

"This close." Johnson is holding his fingers a fraction of an inch apart. "If Maddox had looked up the legal statutes about four weeks ago, he could have stopped the fight. The fight was illegal. There is an old city ordinance in Atlanta that's been on the books since Reconstruction days. The staging of boxing matches between a white fighter and a black fighter is illegal, something left over from the post-Civil War days."

"You didn't know that?" Angelo asks.

"The head of the City Athletic Commission discovered it and told Jesse Hill. We had to act quickly, so Maddox wouldn't know what we were doing. We control most of the votes in City Council, so we just passed an ordinance giving the Building and Athletic Commission the right to draw up rules for the Athletic Commission. We didn't specify any particular rules because that would have gotten in the paper. And today we wouldn't be here."

He pulled out a little book, *Rules and Regulations Governing All Boxing Contests in the City of Atlanta:* "Section 28 says no mixed bouts shall be permitted between white and black contestants in the City of Atlanta and said rules shall be binding and made a part of the agreement of all matchmakers and promoters.

"We got the Commission the right to delete that paragraph and they just did. Now the fight's legal."

Harry Pepp, the little spice merchant who put a fortune in the promotion, looks sick even now, just sitting there listening to the narrow escape. He seems to have the same awful feeling that I have, the premonition that somehow something will prevent me entering the ring again.

But Johnson is hopeful. "If Maddox tries to dig up something legal, he'll find the bone is gone."

"And illegal?" I ask.

"All kinds of rumors circulate," Jesse Hill, the insurance man, says. "Some started from this one."

He shows me a Chicago *Tribune* story from its sports editor, Gene Ward:

> Cassius Clay . . . is gone forever. There's no way he can recapture the past or return to his prime. Those sports writers and sportscasters who worshipped in his retinue are hailing his proposed comeback against Jerry Quarry in Atlanta as though it was a holy rebirth.
>
> I also used the past tense because I don't believe the Quarry fight will ever come off on October 26—or ever . . . I don't think it will be a veteran group who will block the Clay–Quarry fight. . . . I think it will be the great American public who puts the kiss of death on the fight and on Clay.

"Some people here might try anything, but they can't win," Hill says. "They want to stir the old KKK against us so they can say the fight's a threat to peace or likely to cause a riot. The next three days'll tell if anything's to go wrong."

The first thing I notice wrong is the phone.

It's after 12:30 P.M. and I remember picking it up after we got back from seeing *Soldier Blue*. The movie kept me up past the curfew I set when I train but I'd gone anyway, with Reggie Barrett, Bundini and my brother. We argued about it on the way back to the secluded little woods.

We forgot the keys and couldn't wake up the security guard; we knew he was inside because his car was outside, and we banged and shouted at the door but noise wouldn't wake him. Then finally I went around to the room where my father was sleeping and rapped on the window until he let us in.

I stomped through the living room in my eight-pound brogans past my whale-sized "security guard" sleeping on his cot. His belt cut his body in half like a rope on a sack and he shuddered every time he snored. It was time for him to leave, but he never woke up.

"Dreamin' about demons," Bundini said sympathetically. "Let me have the phone after you get through."

Bundini wanted to call his son in Tel Aviv, where he had been sent by his Brooklyn synagogue, and he wouldn't sleep until he heard the voice of "my blood" from the Holy Land.

I pick up the phone and try dialing Philadelphia before I know it's out of order. The hospital was to tell Belinda today if it's safe to take our newborn twins home. I try again. There's no dial tone. I haven't seen my babies in five weeks, and if anything's wrong I'll go back to Philadelphia. It's the only thing I know that would make me pull out of the fight.

"It's dead—you try it next."

"What time we running in the morning?" Bundini asks.

"Set the clock for four. They pick us up at five."

I'm not too worried, because the phone has gone out like this before. Sometimes calls come in but none can go out. It's usually fixed in a few minutes.

My wake-up system works this way: At 4 A.M. Belinda has two alarm clocks go off by her bed in Philadelphia. Then she calls me here. That way I can hear the news from home as well as get ready for roadwork. I'm sure the phone will be back on by 4 A.M. It's never stayed off that long.

I take off my jacket and heavy shoes, lie across the bed, my door open. Quarrels go on in the other rooms between Bundini and my father, my brother Rahaman and C.B. and Reggie Barrett. Clashes, loud and bitter, that come out of camp the closer we come to battle. They sound deadly to an outsider, but in the morning it's all over and everybody pushes for the same thing—to win.

When I can't sleep, I go to the mirror to see how the pounds have come off since I started training. I throw jabs at the face in the mirror until Bundini's in the doorway, grinning. "Quarry's ass is up for grabs, the body's ready! Turn it over to The Champ!"

I drop down on the bed and grab the phone.

"Forget the phone," Bundini says. "Shorty wants you to rest. Rest's the most powerful medicine in the world for a fighter. Sugar Ray taught me that."

He eases the door closed. I lie back, but I know the only thing that can rest me now is word from the hospital about my children. I see them all over again in the Women's Medical Hospital in Philly the way I saw them first.

My face was pressed against the glass. They looked so tiny. Needles in their veins, tubes for feeding, masks over their mouths. They didn't look like babies. They looked unreal.

"How much they weigh?" I asked the doctor, and I was afraid of the answer.

"Oh, a little over two pounds," he said.

"They're not breathing," I told him as though I'd discovered something he overlooked.

"Not regular, but every once in a while they take a breath deep enough for you to notice. See?"

I was shocked. How could anyone live on that? No wonder they were on the "critical" list. I turned around and faced the doctor. "I'd like to know the truth, Doctor. Have they got a chance?"

His eyes flickered a little bit and that frightened me even more. "They've got a chance. It's a chance."

"My last child was a boy that size," I explained. "He lived for half an hour."

The doctor understood. "But these are girls. Girls start out tougher and stronger. Boys start out fragile. Girls have a better chance to survive."

I remember feeling a twinge of guilt: I had prayed so hard for boys. I was lucky they were girls. Boys might not have made it.

They came while I was teaching boxing at Don Bragg's boys' camp near Atlantic City; I had met Bragg in Rome, where he won the 1960 Olympic Pole Vault Championship.

They had the same heartbeat, so the doctors hadn't expected twins. And they showed up three months ahead of time. Belinda named them Jamillah and Rasheda, after two children I had known in Egypt.

"How long before I'll know if they can make it?" I asked the doctor.

"If they get through the next forty-eight hours, that's a pretty good sign," he said. "So long as they get a little stronger each day. It may take weeks."

I said I had signed to fight Quarry, and the doctor, a fight fan, congratulated me on the end of my exile. Until I told him the fight was only six weeks off and I was thirty pounds overweight.

"I should be worrying about your health as well as your twins. The time is too short. You'll be below par."

Every day the promoters and trainers called from Miami for me to come down, but every day I put on the face mask and white gown and looked down at the twins and nothing could pull me away.

Senator Johnson called: "They're saying that you're afraid to fight a white fighter in a Southern city and you can't face the wrath of the patriotic public for your refusal to fight in Viet Nam."

Angelo called: "The papers are beginning to suspect there won't be a fight. What's holding you?"

I stayed until the morning they took the oxygen masks off, and although still in the incubator they breathed better and one gave a little kick. Their faces were getting pinkish, and the doctor smiled and said that was a good sign.

I DOZE OFF thinking about the twins. When I wake up, the house is quiet and my light is still on. Something outside has snapped me awake, and without knowing why I go to the window and look out. The porch light splashes over a wide spot on the grass and all around it's a dark sea.

I go to the kitchen to get the jar of carrot juice the cook leaves for me. I take a deep swig and walk with it up to the living room, stumble over shoes and gear and stand there in the dark identifying the different styles of snoring. My father down the hall—a deep hum. My brother in the side room—like a steam whistle. Bundini sleeps with his mouth open, snores like he's gargling his throat. Only the security guard's missing; he has gone home.

The temptation to pour a little carrot juice into Bundini's mouth is too great. He leaps up coughing and cursing until his eyes get used to the dark and he sees me leaning against the wall, laughing. "What's goin' on?"

"Time to get the gas!" I cry out. "Get up and get the gas!"

And he jumps for his pants and shoes. "Get the gas" is our code word for roadwork. Then he sees I'm still laughing. "What the hell you up to?" he says. "Why ain't you asleep?"

"What you think I'm gonna lay on Quarry?" I ask him.

"Lay that jab on him till he cries for mercy! Stick him, Champ, stick him!" He's shouting as though Quarry's right there in front of us.

I step out on the porch and start boxing lightly. I dance on the wooden slats jabbing, throwing combinations, enjoying a feeling I'd been denied for three years. I want to feel the thick grass under my feet, and I step off the porch and start jabbing my way up the incline toward the trees, whipping out punches and dancing.

I see Bundini's face behind the screen and his scowl has turned into a grin. "Lay it on him, Champ!" he's calling from the door. "Whip him for old times' sake. You the boss! This is Atlanta, Georgia, but you still the boss! Let 'em have it! Whip it to 'em! Champ—"

Then the first shot comes: *Pow!*

My back is to the lake and I hear something whoosh through the trees. I stop and whirl around in time to hear the second *Pow!* and see a flash. I hear Bundini yelling, "Get down, Champ! Get down!" He's halfway out of the door when two more shots come in succession, and I throw myself on the ground as he reaches me. We crawl and scramble up to the porch and into the house.

Voices come out of the dark:

"You black sonofabitch!"

"Get out of Georgia!"

"You draft-dodging bastard!"

I hear three kinds of voices, one high-pitched, one nasal, the other deep and husky.

Then more shots ring out and in the flash I can make out three figures that seem to be moving around the rim of the lake.

Bundini has my head in a half nelson as though his arms can protect me. I hear my father cry out, "What's happening? What's going on?"

"They shootin', they trying to get your son!" Bundini says.

"They're trying to stop the fight," I tell my father.

"I told you we needed protection!" Bundini yells. "I told you!"

"Phone the police," my father is saying, and I reach for the phone. It's still out.

Reggie has woke up and is standing with us. "They know we ain't got shit to hit back with," he says. He flips off the porch light and looks out the window. "They know we ain't got a weapon. They wouldn't come if we did."

He looks around for something in the house for us to "fight with" but there's nothing there but an old Civil War sword Senator Johnson has on the wall.

"What they doin' now?" Bundini asks. "You see anything?"

Reggie cautions everybody to be quiet while he peers out into the dark. "Can't see. But they want to come closer, I know 'em."

He speaks from experience. Reggie is from a black family that's lived in South Carolina for four generations and been harassed and attacked in fights over property rights during the worst days of the Klan terror. He's considered our "authority" on mobs and lynchers.

Bundini suddenly leaves his post as my protector and gets down on his knees and pulls something out from under his sofa, a case that contains pistols and cartridges—the same two pistols he swore he had gotten rid of three days ago.

"Where the hell you goin'?" Reggie looks at him as he's pushing open the door. "What the hell you doin'?"

My father and brother grab at Bundini. Tears are in his eyes and he looks like a wild man. He steps out on the porch pointing the gun toward the clump of bushes and begins firing and screaming: "Here we are! Come on, you sonofabitches!"

He's shooting wild and my father yells out, "Get that fool inside, they'll kill him! Get him in here!" But Reggie goes out and comes back with one of the guns. He reloads it and hands it to Bundini, who fires until it's empty, screaming like a terror all the time: "Come on if you wanna die! Come on, we ready for you!"

Whether it's Bundini's shooting or his loud voice that touches off the birds I don't know, but the droves of sleeping birds that Senator Johnson told us were in the trees suddenly come alive and for a while the air is full of screeching and fluttering birds bouncing against the windows.

Reggie pulls Bundini back inside and we huddle there, listening for a long time to nothing at all but our breathing.

Now and then someone picks up the phone and tries to dial it. But mostly we sit there just listening. The night sounds outside seem loud, the crickets, the bugs and occasionally a flutter of a bird as it settles back down.

Then suddenly the phone is ringing. Reggie gets it and I ask him who it's for.

He turns his eyes to me. "They ask for you, Champ."

I take it gladly. Maybe Belinda is calling early, maybe somebody across the lake is inquiring what's going on. Maybe they'll come down here.

I have the phone to my ear and I hear a high-pitched nasal voice: "Nigger—if you don't leave Atlanta tomorrow, you gonna die."

"What you want?"

"You Viet Cong bastard! You draft-dodging bastard! We won't miss you next time. We won't miss you!"

Bundini reads the look in my eyes and grabs the phone. "You gonna die 'long with us, you bastard! You gonna die, too!"

I take the phone from him and hang up. In fifteen seconds it rings again:

"Listen, nigger, you go in that ring Monday night, you'll never get out. I'll die just to see you die! Ain't gonna be no fight in Atlanta."

I listen and say nothing. I'm used to looking for something in a person's voice to tell me more about him. Is this a bluff? Is it somebody drunk? Is it for real? Then I say, "What do you mean? I can't hear you."

"You hear me, you nigger bastard! You wait and see! We'll be waiting out here for you. Stick your head out the door and see what we mean!"

He hangs up and we're all quiet until Rahaman says, "Call the police."

But when we try, the phone is dead again. "I ain't staying here," Bundini says. "I ain't staying and let 'em come pick us off."

"They know we got guns," Reggie says. "They'll stay outside."

"What you gonna do, Champ?"

I remember standing up and walking over to the door. My heart is pounding as though I had stepped off a cliff and was suddenly snatched back. I go into the kitchen and pour another glass of carrot juice.

Rahaman is saying, "They want to kill us."

I know that more than killing me they want to scare me off. They want me out of town. They want to get the fight called off, the way more than seventy-two "almost completed" fights had been called off in the last three years, in city after city. This one is closer to coming off than any of the others. The old premonition that something will prevent me from ever entering the ring is back, but now I'm determined not to let it take over.

"Just let me alone for a while," I say to my crew. "Let me think a while."

I go to the kitchen cabinet and find some long-handled spoons that Johnson had imported from Siam and drum on the plastic counter. I feel calmer. Whatever happens in the ring with Quarry is almost incidental. This is where I have to win the fight—here, now.

"What you gonna do, Champ?" Bundini stands there, and tears are in his eyes. We used to laugh at the way Bundini cries so easy, but I'm not laughing now.

An old lawyer in Louisville, who used to help bail young black militants out of jail, once said, "I do not carry a gun and I'm not a man of violence, but many times I've been saved by the gun in the holster of my brother." Only a year before, a friend was driving me from Fayetteville, Arkansas, after a college lecture, where I had shared the platform with Floyd McKissick of CORE and Whitney Young of the Urban League. We were followed by a gang of cursing whites calling for the head of "that black bastard Cassius Clay, that draft-dodger," and moving up to side-swipe us off the road into a rock ravine. My friend pulled out a big Colt .45, began blasting away and calling, "Come on if you want to die, you sonofabitches! Come on if you want

MY OWN STORY   319

to die!" And suddenly they decided not to take a chance on dying and stepped on their accelerator and let us live.

Bundini is sitting on the kitchen stool looking at the ceiling as though he can see straight up to heaven. "Shorty," he says, "what's my mission? I don't mind dying, but I don't want to die before I know my mission." He pauses to give "Shorty" time to answer. Then, patiently explaining to anyone who will listen, "Shorty always lets me know."

Rahaman comes in and says, "We ought to get the police. What time do they get here?"

Barrett follows him. "What the hell's keeping that policeman? Tell that sonofabitch we need guns."

The policeman, Lieutenant Hudson, who is in charge of our security, is due in a half-hour. It's nearly five o'clock.

One thought keeps coming to my mind. In order to win I'll have to step into that arena and complete the fight. I'll give no excuses to anybody to call off the fight. "You don't do anything until I tell you," I say to Barrett, "and you won't say a thing. You put all this in the newspaper and it'll draw more nuts, and Maddox will say my presence is a nuisance. You'll wake all the sleeping dogs that want to get at our throats. They got nothing to rally around now. You won't say nothing until the fight's over."

"We need some guns." Bundini is stubborn.

"What would be the biggest thing we could do in Georgia?" I ask him.

"Get in the ring and whip the devil out of that sucker. Whip him in front of all the world!" Then he starts grinning because he knows he's answered the way I want him to.

A car horn outside is blowing and Reggie snatches open the door.

"Y'all ready, Champ? We got a station wagon all ready." It's Lieutenant Hudson of the Atlanta Police Department. This time he's got two assistants, armed to the teeth.

"We'll be ready in a minute," I say. "What road we take?"

He pulls out a map. "We may as well tell you now, Champ. I know you people don't want too many police around, but we've got inside information at headquarters there might be an attempt on your life." He raises his hand quickly as though to ease my fears. "We've got information that some elements—not characteristic of Atlanta, mind you—are going to try to disrupt the fight by attacking The Champ with firearms. That's why there'll be a new security force in the gym, out here and wherever you go from now on. We hope you don't mind."

Bundini and I look at each other.

"Now, for roadwork," the lieutenant continues, "we know you've been scheduled to run along Highway 85. It's been in the papers. But the Police Department wants you to change that. We'll take Highway

20 and we'll switch every day, if that's all right with you."

The phone rings and my father calls out, "It's for you."

It's Belinda. "The twins are home. The doctor thinks they'll make it."

I'm stretched out on the bed for the last rest. It's four hours before the fight, and the phone keeps ringing with good luck calls: Whitney Young, Martin Luther King's mother and his wife Coretta, Jack Lemmon, Anthony Quinn, Bill Cosby, Sidney Poitier, Marlon Brando, Henry Fonda . . . I try to doze off, but in the kitchen I hear the Reverend Jesse Jackson telling Bundini what he thinks the fight is all about.

Even though Jesse and I have different religious views, we're of the same generation. "A lot came out of our generation," I hear him say. "But a lot came out of the black generation before us, too."

"There was a lot of Toms," Bundini says.

"Tom was a circus," Jesse says. "Tom was a Chinaman's game whipped on the white man. Without Tom, we wouldn't be getting ready for this battle today. This ain't a fight. It's a war between two schools of thought. Whether he wants to or not, Quarry represents the establishment. Nothing shows the sickness in American society more than a prizefight between a White Hope and a black man. This fight is about democracy and how it is practiced by people like Maddox, Agnew, Wallace, Nixon, on the one hand, and by ordinary people, black and white, on the other. I'm glad to see it happening in Martin Luther King's hometown. He would have loved it this way."

PREVIOUS PAGE: Muhammad Ali, 12, at a gym in Louisville, Kentucky, at the beginning of his career. 1954. (Popperfoto/Getty Images)

LEFT: Muhammad Ali receives the gold medal for the light heavyweight class in the 1960 Olympic Games in Rome, Italy. (Thomas Hoepker/Magnum Photos)

ABOVE: Muhammad Ali fights Ken Norton in 1973 in San Diego, California. (Photofest)

ABOVE: Muhammad Ali flirts with Belinda Boyd in a bakery
shop. Belinda would later become Ali's second wife as
Khalilah Ali. Chicago, Illinois. 1966. (Thomas Hoepker/
Magnum Photos)

RIGHT: Out for the count. Muhammad Ali yawns while
babysitting two of his daughters, 9-month-old Laila (left)
and 2-year-old Hana (right). London, England. 1978.
(Frank Tewkesbury/Evening Standard/Getty Images)

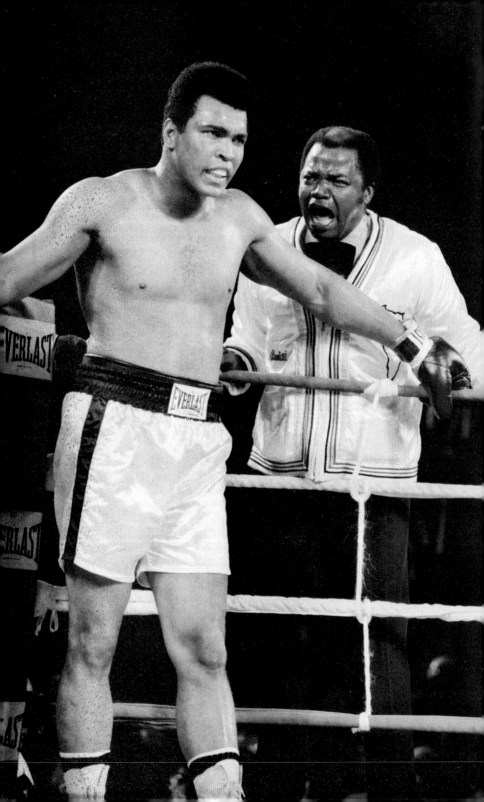

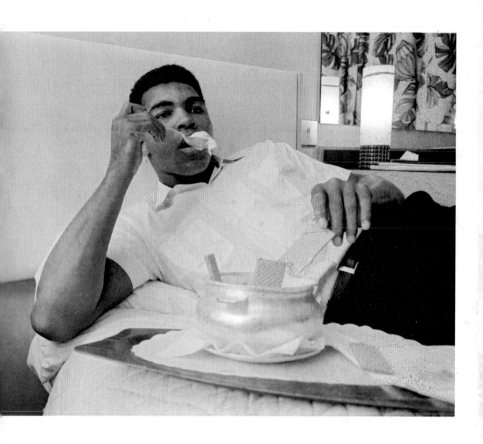

RIGHT: Muhammad Ali is hyped up by his famous cornerman, Drew Bundini Brown, before fighting undefeated World Heavyweight Champion George Foreman at "The Rumble in the Jungle." 1974. (A. Abbas/Magnum Photos)

ABOVE: After the fight against Brian London, Muhammad Ali rewards himself with a big bowl of ice cream. London was knocked out in the 3rd round after Ali landed 11 punches in 3 seconds. London, England. 1966. (Thomas Hoepker/Magnum Photos)

FOLLOWING PAGES: Muhammad Ali with his mother, Odessa, at "The Rumble in the Jungle," The World Heavyweight Boxing Championship in Zaire against George Foreman. 1974. (A. Abbas/Magnum Photos)

THE GOLDEN DREAM

I had planned to dedicate Quarry to Jack Johnson. To dress up like Johnson, come in the ring in a pearl-gray derby, striped black coat over my boxing shorts, announce to the Georgia audience that I was dedicating my first fight after exile to him, and say, "Jack, wherever you are, rest easy in your grave. This White Hope won't get away."

The idea came from watching old Jack Johnson films. Joe Jacobs, who has one of the largest boxing libraries in America, had brought them up to the camp, and for the first time I realized how remarkable he was and how much the whites hated him. I liked the way he fought and the way he talked—intelligent, clear, bold, not humble.

All I remembered about his life was that he married white women and he lay on his back and covered his eyes from the sun while they counted him out in a fix against Jess Willard.

When I saw the play *The Great White Hope*, I understood his life better. James Earl Jones, the actor, took me backstage. "Johnson, in his time, was as much a rebel as you in your time," he said.

Jones described how Johnson was hounded out of America on trumped-up charges because of the resentment whites had over a black World Heavyweight Champion—the real "Mr. America" spot—and a champion who was bold and arrogant and who broke all the taboos white racists held sacred. The only way they agreed to allow Johnson to reenter America without being thrown in jail was for him to give up his title, and the fix with Willard was the result.

Many times I've been asked if I'd ever thought of leaving America during my exile, when it was obvious that I would be welcomed in other countries and allowed to practice my trade. I admit the thought crossed my mind. Thousands of young people who opposed the war were doing it and finding a new life. The underground routes were easy to contact. However, for me it would mean being separated from my family and from my people, from the black culture I grew up with—and weighing it against that, I could not give it serious thought. I'd do better struggling it out right here at home.

Jones told me he had built his Jack Johnson concept around me and my life, but I told him I had been offered $400,000 to play Jack Johnson in a movie even when I was in exile, when I had no income, and I had turned it down. A black hero chasing white women was a role I didn't want to glorify. I thought a black male hero needed to glorify, in real life or on the screen, some of the black women who brought them and their brothers into the world.

Not that I have not known and met many good and fine women who are white, but it seemed to me that white women allow themselves to be used as the symbol of White Supremacy, and I thought it better to give all my attention to women of darker races, especially my own.

Wilt Chamberlain, who didn't like my stand, wrote in his book, "Muhammad Ali is a good friend of mine," and then went on to say that I didn't have "enough intelligence to string three sentences together," that the public tended to equate my "loquaciousness with intelligence," and that he preferred to date white girls because they were more intellectually "compatible" with him than black women.

I asked Wilt why, since his mama was black, his grandmama was black, his great-grandmama was black, and all his sisters were black— why all of a sudden he found black girls "incompatible." (Not that I ever knew of any black woman grieving over his absence.) I never got an answer, which didn't surprise me, as I had never heard of Wilt associating much with black men or women or doing anything worthwhile for blacks. In fact, the association he was most proud of was with Richard Nixon, who used him once as sort of a spear-carrier in his election campaign.

The most outstanding feature about Wilt was that he was the world's tallest Uncle Tom, which I always believed made him forever unable to cope with Bill Russell on or off the basketball court. Although Wilt might have been the tallest fellow athlete I didn't see eye-to-eye with, he was not the one I came closest to having a knock-down-drag-out fight with. This came when I flew down to Albuquerque, New Mexico, to speak at a banquet honoring the retiring World Light Heavyweight Champion, Bobby Foster. The entire state of New Mexico, from the Governor on down to the Mayors, was there to salute Bobby. They had flown in some of the leading entertainers, including Charlie Pride, Sly and the Family Stone. All went well until Foster overheard me sympathizing with a group of Indians as they depicted their plight in New Mexico, as oppressive as blacks had it in the ghettos. He broke into the conversation, screaming, "You can't talk that way in my hometown! Don't come here and talk that way! You'll never do this again to me!"

"What kind of Uncle Tom are you," I asked. "I came down here to honor you, but if you act like a fool, I'll whip you good."

Bobby lunged at me and drew back to throw a blow, but someone held him up. "I don't even want you here anyhow!" he screamed as they pulled him away.

Somehow, that evening, standing on the platform, I managed to pay Foster some glowing tributes. He'll never know, however, how close he came to getting a whipping far more severe than the one I gave him in Lake Tahoe.

I had never been able to take to black performers who turn their back upon their people as soon as they reach what they consider "having it made," which is one reason why I never followed up my earlier crush on Leslie Uggums. I had met Leslie shortly after my first fight with Sonny Liston, and I took her and her mother out for dinner. I was struck by her good looks, her energy and her wit. But when I took her home in a cab, on a route that took us through Harlem, she locked the doors and began speaking with such bitterness and hatred for the people, she seemed like an entirely different woman.

"Why?" I asked.

"Because they're so dirty and dangerous and filthy," she said. "I can't wait until we get away from here." Her beauty seemed to fade and she seemed just like an ordinary ugly woman thereafter. Her mother urged me to come see them again, but I never did.

When I told Angelo about my plan to come into the ring as Jack Johnson, he frowned. "You're no way like Jack Johnson. Why you always compare yourself with other fighters? You're not like Sugar Ray. You're not like Joe Louis."

"Who am I like?"

"You're like new. Something different, you're like yourself. They can't compare with you."

I turned to Bundini and for once he agreed with Angelo. I insisted on doing it anyway, but in the end, there wasn't enough time to carry out the plan.

Angelo kept telling me, "You're not like any of them old fighters."

I know better. Who I am is what those who came before me made it possible for me to be. Just ahead of me were some of the best fighters the world ever saw, like Joe Louis, Sugar Ray Robinson, Henry Armstrong, Archie Moore, Johnny Bratton, Kid Gavilan, Sandy Saddler, Jersey Joe Walcott, Ezzard Charles, Floyd Patterson, Chalky Wright, Jimmy Carter, and others who had new styles and powerful punches.

I used to hang around the gym and hear the pros talk about famous old fighters and their feats, and it sounded more exciting and daring to me than any tales of the Wild West: stories about Black Panther Harry Wills, Tiger Jack Fox, Panama Al Brown, Gorilla Jones, Deacon Tiger Flowers, Boston Tar Baby, Kid Chocolate, Joe Gans, Battling Siki, and others just as good who fought all across the country, almost always in places where the audience wanted to see them stomped. For a black fighter in those days, just to climb in the ring— as the films showed Jack Johnson doing, with crowds screaming for his "lynching"—was a brave deed.

Jersey Joe said to me once, "Sometimes it felt like I was in a KKK convention whipping the Grand Wizard while they were still putting up 'White Supremacy Forever' signs."

I hired Harry Wyle a few months before he died. Wyle, who had seen them all, almost since the days of Joe Gans, used to take black fighters from town to town, sleeping in cars because no hotel would house them, sending a white associate into restaurants to bring out food because no restaurant would serve them, training in church basements and coming into the stadiums shielding their water buckets from spit, with the audiences screaming, "Kill the coon! Kill the coon!" as they passed on their way up to the ring.

"Deacon Tiger Flowers was told by a squad of deputies in an Ohio town that if he dared to defeat his white opponent, he would never leave town alive," Wyle told me. "When he refused to promise to obey, they cursed him and tried to provoke him. But the Deacon, a real Baptist deacon in church on Sunday, always spoke soft and civil and kind and would not be provoked. So they let him go in the ring.

"He knocked his man cold in the third and walked back to his dressing room with the fans booing and the deputies following him. But the Deacon climbed out of a washroom window, made a freight train and got away, still in his boxing trunks."

McClure "Kit" Carson, who fought as a welterweight, and who was a trainer for Joe Louis, Eddie Perkins and other champions, told me why he believed so many black fighters became known as "knockout artists": "because it was too hard to win by a decision.

"I was fighting Bud Hamner in Harvey, Illinois, and beating him so bad that a white policeman in the audience hollered, 'Snowball!'—they called me 'Snowball' because I was black—'Don't knock him out! Don't knock him out, Snowball!'

"I leaned out of the ring and hollered back: 'If I don't knock him out, I can't win!' "

Then the whole audience picked it up: 'Snowball, don't knock him out! Don't knock him out!'

"But I needed the win and decked him for the count."

"There was no region fairer than any other," Dick Sadler, who developed George Foreman and who was once a brilliant boxer, said. "The South didn't allow black to fight white. The North was bad. The West was terrible and the East was disgraceful.

"In one place I had to cover my fighter's head with a wicker basket in between rounds to protect him from beer cans and bottles thrown when he was winning over a local white boy. It was hard for a black athlete to make a dollar in those days. We were totally barred from big, popular sports like baseball or football or basketball. Boxing was all."

Promoters used the excuse of keeping a white titleholder from fighting a good black challenger by saying, as Tex Rickard did when he helped Jack Dempsey avoid fighting black Harry Wills and paid Wills fifty-thousand dollars, "It will sell out the house, but it will cause a riot."

But as promoters became more interested in the benefits from a full house, more black fighters got title shots, until there came a period when they totally dominated the sport and only thinned out when basketball, baseball and football opened up to black athletes and they began to by-pass boxing for the better benefits in the organized sports.

Perhaps because I had been banned from boxing for all those years, and had faced opposition and hostility, I found myself thinking of the black fighters who had come before me, and in the evenings while I was waiting for sleep, I watched the old films and thought about how they lived and what they faced.

And when I looked back on their lives, I was inspired by the courage and confidence they must have had during the days when blacks were being lynched and jailed in the South for just bumping into a white man on the streets or talking back to a white policeman. Those black fighters climbed into the ring again and again, in towns where they were not allowed to stay overnight, or eat a meal, or attend a movie theater, and the record books show that in the majority of the fights they somehow came out the winner.

Governor Lester Maddox's attempt to inflame white people against me was weak compared to what the old black fighters faced when the Maddoxes were the majority. The more I thought about them, the more I wanted each of my fights dedicated to one of those fighters.

All through the Quarry bout, Bundini screamed from the corner, "Jack Johnson's ghost watching you! Ghost in the house!"

I wish I could have given Jack's ghost a little better show. When I stopped Quarry, the news flashed across the world that I had come back from where I left off. But I knew better. Before exile, I could go six rounds at the fastest pace without feeling it. It took only three rounds to get Quarry, but near the end I was tired. My jab was off target. My uppercuts were off. I saw openings I couldn't cash in on. I caught him with two solid rights that stunned him and opened a deep gash over his eye, but I was shocked that I felt tired and I wondered what would have happened if he could have lasted ten rounds.

When I appeared with him later on *Wide World of Sports*, he said only his cut eye spoiled his chances of showing what he could really do with me. I promised to give him a rematch. I always want my opponents to be satisfied that they've been well whipped.

QUARRY HAD TO WAIT almost two years before he got the chance to show "what he could really do with me." The rematch was set for Las Vegas: "The worst place in the world to train," Herbert had said. "If you're not in shape before you get there, you'll never get in shape while you're there."

The night of the fight, I discovered a crew of TV cameramen sitting in my dressing room, their gear already planted. Howard Cosell's crew.

Angelo was furious. "Nobody gets in unless they're invited and we didn't invite nobody!"

They were apologetic and got up to leave, but I said, "If they'll stay on the other side, maybe it's all right." They stayed quiet. Even so, there were nearly twenty people in the room—my team, arena officials, special reporters.

I was pulling off my eight-pound boots and peeling off my three pairs of thick wool socks when there was an outcry from Bundini: "Good God A'mighty! Where the boxing trunks? Where the shoes? The mouthpiece? The cup, the robe? We sending The Champ out to war stark-naked?"

Nobody had brought the boxing gear.

There's always a feud between Angelo and Bundini, and this touched off the worst of the year. Finally I said, "Cool it! We've got plenty of time. Mike Quarry and Foster fight first. They're not even on yet. The hotel's only a few blocks down, and we've got drivers."

The big policemen let Bundini squeeze out and Howard Cosell squeeze in to set up his interview.

Cosell, whom I have known since my first victory over Liston, is described by many of my friends as my "announcer opponent." But when I was barred from the ring, Cosell was one of my most persistent defenders. He had a commercial with a tag line that went: "If you don't believe Muhammad Ali is the champ, get in the ring with him."

While he was getting his crew set up, the bouncers moved back to let in Otis Taylor, the tall pass-catcher for the Kansas City Chiefs, and I told the room he was the "world's greatest football player."

Cosell said, "Taylor, tell him I'm the one that made you. Tell him I'm the one that discovered you."

The microphone was off, and Cosell asked confidentially, "If Quarry should happen to win tonight, what happens to your return match with Frazier?" Before I could answer, he continued, "Haven't you boxed yourself into a corner where you can't afford to lose not even a single fight? What happens if despite the odds, you should lose?"

I looked across the room and saw the cameramen raising their eyes and listening attentively. I decided to go another way. "If I lose, so much the better for you reporters of history, but worse for me. If you think Quarry will win, you're about to witness history. If I'm upset, you can tell your grandchildren you were there. You were on the scene the day Jerry Quarry upset Muhammad Ali."

There was more commotion at the door, and I saw the big bouncers bowing down and stumbling back in awe. Joe Louis was coming in. The Patriarch of Boxing. Louis, in a blazing-red sport coat, jaunty golf cap perched on top of his head—who worked for Caesars Palace as a permanent tourist attraction and had been helping with the publicity, along with Billy Conn, to create the "big fight" atmosphere. And while I trained, whenever he came to the gym the people would give him a standing ovation.

"Joe, one thing I got to know," I called out to him one afternoon. "Who you picking to win this fight?"

Joe knew why I was asking, and wouldn't answer. He came over and gave me a playful left hook on the jaw.

"Because if you're picking me," I went on, "I'm worried to death. Everyone you pick is the loser."

He smiled and threw another left hook.

"When I fought Liston the first time, you picked Liston; when I fought Liston the second time, you picked Liston; when I fought

Patterson, you picked Patterson; when I fought Chuvalo, you picked Chuvalo; when I fought Terrell, Cleveland Williams, Bonavena, you picked them."

"Well," Joe said, "if we go by that, Quarry's the next champion. Because tonight I'm picking you." He chuckled and sat down on the bench beside me.

Many times I've been thrown together with Joe, and at one time I thought we could become close friends. We never talked about boxing—women, clothes, business, money, but not boxing. Now, sitting here on the long bench, our backs propped up against the wall, waiting for a so-called "easy fight," I still couldn't shake my nervousness, and I was glad Joe was there. I felt a warm closeness and I said something I would never want the reporters to hear. "Joe, I'm nervous."

He looked at me and threw another left hook, only this time it went around my shoulder and he let his arm stay there.

"What does it mean?" I asked. "Were you ever nervous before a fight?"

Joe didn't answer for a while, but I saw his eyes had tightened as though he was remembering millions of jabs and right crosses, body punches and blocks, his days in the gym, and his way of functioning as a fighter. Then he said slowly, "Only when I felt something around me was wrong. You find out what's out of line, where the center of the thing is."

"Did the crowds bother you when they pulled against you?" I asked him.

"When I got on top and when I beat Schmeling, I felt they were always with me," he said. "Until I got old and tried a comeback."

"I know, but before then?"

"In the beginning it was like with you. In the beginning the blacks were with me, the whites against me. Then they all got behind me when they saw I wouldn't be beaten. It's going to get like that for you, too."

We were talking in hushed tones, the cameramen and reporters trying hard to hear us. Some were surprised at seeing such friendliness between Muhammad Ali and Joe Louis, two generations of black heavyweights: one quiet and noncommittal about most things, held up as a model, a "credit" to his race; the other, outspoken, aggressive, denounced as "the most unworthy representative" of the heavyweight crown in history. I sensed the newsmen wondering, What are they talking about?

Joe had been quoted as saying many bitter things about me, all repeated to me, and he may say them again, but at this moment I loved him deeply and I was glad his arm was on my shoulder. "It will never be that way for me," I said. "Not all pulling for me. Were your opponents ever afraid of you?" I asked him.

He nodded. "For a while nearly all them were scared. You at the point when they'll be scared of you, too. Like the fox and the lion my mother used to tell me about."

"Tell me," I said.

"The lion says to the fox, 'Brother Fox, most all the animals in the jungle—the deer, the antelope, the rabbits—all pay me a visit now and then. How come you never do? Why you so scared?' And this old fox says, 'I see footsteps going in your den, but I never see no footsteps come out.' " Joe laughed. "All those fighters go in the ring with you never come out with a victory. All 'cept Frazier."

"Frazier didn't beat me, the judges did that."

"Fighters get scared. But a scared fighter is a dangerous fighter, sometimes the most dangerous."

Bundini broke in with trunks and cups and the room suddenly came alive. The TV monitor on the table was turned on. The screams and roars from the crowd were deafening. Foster was climbing into the ring.

"How much time we got?" I called to Angelo.

"We got time. We got time." Angelo was digging into the bag for my shoes.

The bouncers let Joe DiMaggio in, and he came over to shake hands. "Go easy on our last White Hope," he said.

I couldn't tell if he was kidding or serious.

Mike Kaplin, the referee, broke in and yelled when he saw I was only beginning to dress. "Ain't much time," he cried, looking at his watch. "You go right after Foster. If it's a quick knockout . . ." He went over to Angelo. "Look, Quarry wants to flip a coin to see who gets what corner."

"What the hell for?" Angelo was busy with the shoelaces. "Muhammad will take any corner."

"But Quarry goes in first."

"So we'll take the corner Quarry is not in when we get there," Angelo said with exaggerated patience.

Mike looked around speechless for a while. He wanted some excuse to make his routine duties important. Then he turned to me. "Well then, let me recite to you the special boxing rules of Las Vegas, Muhammad," he said appealingly.

"I have been here before, Mike," I said.

He ran down the rules anyway, then finally started out the door and stopped for one last shot at me. "Muhammad, you sure you don't want to pick a corner? You've got the right to have first choice, you know."

"Corners don't win fights, Mike," I said, and turned to the monitor. Foster-Mike Quarry was in the third round.

"Who you pick?" someone asked.

"If it goes over five, Mike Quarry's got a chance," Angelo said.

I looked at young Mike dancing, his hands down in imitation of what he thought was my style, and I felt a twinge of sympathy for him.

"There goes the first White Hope," someone said.

I was thinking that Mike, just turned twenty, energetic, strong, talented, might get a decision, when Foster wrecked him with a knockout blow. Mike lay like he was dead.

"You on next! You on next!" somebody screamed in the door.

Angelo was lacing my shoes, and I was still tense. Things seemed disorganized—everybody scurrying about in each other's way.

I thought of what Louis had said: "Find out where the center of the thing is, what is out of line." I thought back quick over my roadwork and gymwork. I was glad I had forced myself to do extra roadwork, extra rounds on the bag, working constantly with fast, fresh sparring partners. That was done right.

Then I got ready to run down what I needed in the ring, what I wanted my handlers to do, and not to do. Angelo and Bundini have heard these instructions a hundred times, but I never go into the ring without telling them and I started in the quietest voice I could. "Now, Angelo, I always tell you: when I come back to my corner in between rounds, the first thing I want you to do is to hold open my trunks so I can take a deep breath."

"I understand." Angelo nodded as though hearing it for the first time.

Bundini was standing by, erect, holding my robe and towels.

"Then take out the mouthpiece, wash it right away. Wipe my face only if I need it. Put the mouthpiece back in before the buzzer goes off."

"I know, I know," Angelo said.

"And keep your face away from mine; don't breathe in my face. I don't want your breath in my face."

"Of course," Angelo said. "Of course."

I had learned a long time ago that people—even knowledgeable, experienced ones—look at things they are not participating in themselves like it's a movie, not quite real. I wanted to tell that to my cornermen. That out there the crowd was real, the stakes were real. There would be hard blows, and pain. Much pain. I hit and am hit, and the blows hurt, and draw blood. My blood.

It had come to me what was making me nervous. My cornermen were taking Quarry lightly. Like he was an untalented amateur. And

I know from experience that no professional fighter can take another fighter lightly. The only expected thing is that a fight is full of unexpected things. To take struggle lightly is a mistake I made once, hope I will never make again, or let anyone around me make. Out there, you can get a fractured skull, broken ribs, eyes injured, face cut, killed.

"When I come back from the round," I told them, "all I want you to do is to tell me if I won the round or if I lost it, don't tell me something that's not true. Don't be telling me I'm ahead if I'm not. If you do, I'll fire both of you. Somebody else will be in that corner next time. And, Bundini, don't shout so loud out there!"

Angelo jerked his head up, looking hurt. They didn't know if I was joking or angry. They'd heard every word before but what I felt was too deep to ignore. Angelo muttered back, "Anytime you want to fire me, you fire me." Both were shook up.

"It's time! You're on! It's time! You're on!"

I wrapped myself in the robe Bundini was holding, and I went out to meet Quarry. I was no longer nervous.

In an hour it's all over. In the seventh round I see Quarry dazed and defenseless against the ropes. I hit him with anything I throw, and he has no defense. I motion for Mike Kaplin to step in, *step in!*

Mike, whose regular job is dice table man at Caesars Palace, will apologize later for being slow. "No heavyweight in history ever asked the referee to come save his opponent from punishment," he explains. "You caught me by surprise."

They get Quarry out of the ring and back to his dressing room long before I reach mine. This time not even the bouncers and club-slinging police keep the crowd from pouring inside the dressing room, jamming me up against the wall.

The nearest reporter, Dick Young of the New York *Daily News,* is kneeling under the crowd, asking me the same question over and over again—something like: "Champ, were you surprised when Quarry tackled you like a football player in the first round? Lifted you up off your feet?"

I said no, but somehow it hadn't bothered me. It only told me how scared and desperate he was.

My breathing is regular. I don't feel tired at all.

"Was this one of your easiest fights?" Young is asking.

"I suppose so," I say. "I must be better than I thought I was."

"How good did you think you were?" he asks.

"The greatest!" Bundini shouts. "The Boss is back!"

I don't answer, but for the first time since my Second Coming, I know I've regained my stamina. My feeling for the ring space is back. What Sugar Ray said was right: "The only way for a fighter to get back in shape is to fight his way back."

"This is the last of the White Hopes," a British reporter says. "Would you rather see no more?"

"No," I answer, "we need all we can get. Find some more."

A reporter comes in from Quarry's room. "Quarry says he left his fight in the dressing room. When he saw his brother Mike lying on the floor, not knowing whether he was dead or alive, it took something out of him."

When I'm finally dressed and on my way out, a young woman comes up and tugs at my sleeve. We move a little way off from the crowd. "Someone ought to congratulate you," she says. "Poor Jerry. We wanted him to win so much."

"The Quarrys got nothing to be ashamed of," I say. "Jerry's a great fighter."

"You were lucky tonight," she says. "You had a lot to overcome."

"Well, Jerry wasn't at his best tonight. He wasn't as hard to overcome as I had expected."

"I didn't mean from Jerry. From me, from my dream. I'm very close to the Quarrys, and I dreamed about you every night before the fight."

"What about?"

"I dreamed about you for nine straight nights." She is speaking slowly, looking directly at me. "I dreamed I came up to your room and made love to you all night, every night, even the night before the fight, and when you got in the ring you were so weak he knocked you out in the third round." She stops for a minute. "If I had followed my dream, Jerry wouldn't be crying now in his room."

Now her eyes are streaming with tears. I take her arm and move her toward the elevator.

It was a golden dream she had. If Quarry had defeated me, he would have been hailed as the greatest White Hope in the history of boxing. He would be on the threshold of a million dollars; he would get more movie offers; and he would be a cinch to fight Frazier. He could run for Governor, backed by the Veterans of Foreign Wars, the American Legion, the White Citizens Councils and all those thankful that a noble Hope had come along to put this "unpatriotic loud-mouth black braggart" in his place.

As for his fan, I suppose greater love hath no woman than that she would lay down her virtue to guarantee a friend's victory. Whether it would have worked for Quarry, I'll never know, but I'm glad she didn't put it to the test.

I walk down the hall and pass by Quarry's room. The door is half open and inside I catch a glimpse of Jerry and Mike, heads down. I start to go in and console them, but then a woman comes to the door, sees me and closes it.

FOR THE VICTIMS

On the night of my first fight with Quarry, bomb threats had been made on my house in Philadelphia, and although the police were standing guard, Belinda moved in with a friend. Before I went in the ring, I spoke long-distance with the police captain. "Just some nuts in a last-ditch strike at you," he said, "now that you got a legal right to fight. Win your fight and you get what you want."

What I wanted most was a chance to spend some time with my twin girls. Outside an incubator, I had never seen them breathe. And all week after Quarry I stayed home, read telegrams and handled the offers for fights that were pouring in. But mostly, I played with my three daughters.

"I'm surrounded by four women," I told them. "The whole house full of fine foxes."

Every day I held them in my arms and watched them change before my eyes, a different look, a different sound, something different with their feet and hands. Once, when I was holding Jamillah, kissing her soft cheeks, I stuck out my tongue and she mistook it for a nipple and started sucking away on it. I was amazed. "Belinda, can you beat this? She thinks this is her mother's nipple!" I was kissing her all over and rubbing my nose against hers.

Now there'll be less time to spend with my family and I realize how precious these moments are. I thank Allah for blessing me with such a beautiful family and a loving wife. How does Belinda see her life with me? Once I heard her on the phone giving an interview with a reporter from a woman's magazine: "When I first met Muhammad in Chicago, I was thirteen years old, but I didn't really get to know him until three years later when I was working at the Muslim bakery . . . What really attracted me to him? Well, when he became a Muslim. My mother and father had come up from Jackson, Mississippi, and joined the Nation of Islam before I was born, so together with my two sisters and my brother, we were Muslims from birth . . .

"No, he didn't exactly propose to me. He just came to me one day and said, 'You're going to be my wife.' What could I say? He's the World Heavyweight Champion. You just don't argue with a man like that. But if I didn't feel I was compatible with him, I wouldn't have married him.

"I thought his fighting days were over. In fact, I didn't think the day would come when he'd get back in the ring. I was ready to sacrifice with his going to jail, but now that he's fighting again it's a different life, less time with the family. But I know he really loves me and the children and he wants more than anything else to keep us together . . .

"What do I do when he's not around? There's so much to do with three children. I take them to the zoo, to the museum, to school and back, and I cook for them every day. I study karate and I've been riding horses most of my life. I've got a lot of ribbons and trophies from competitions, and I plan to teach the kids how to ride . . .

"I want my children to get a good education, a good knowledge of themselves and a desire to help their people. I want my girls to be perfect Muslim wives, even better than me. Maryum wants to be a doctor and that's all right with me, but I still want her to be a wife. I don't want my daughters to go unmarried. I'd like them to get married at a young age, fulfill their careers, but also take care of their husbands . . .

"I'm really glad for Ali now, because I know how hard he's worked to get where he is and I know how much it means to him to fight again. But a couple of things I don't like. First, it's dangerous work. I hope someday he'll be able to go back into the ministry, under Supreme Minister Wallace D. Muhammad, teaching our brothers and sisters the truth of Islam. The worst thing of all is the leeches that come around. They take advantage of him because he's too kindhearted. That I hate, really, because I want to stand up and block it, but he won't let me. That's the worst part of it . . .

"The biggest thing I've learned from him is how to cope with pressure. How to live under pressure in the ring and out of it. He's a genius at that . . ."

The phone rings and Belinda goes to answer it. "The enemy's on the phone," she calls.

It's Yank Durham's big heavy voice. "Is it true what I hear? You know what I'm talking about!"

I knew exactly what he was talking about. It had leaked out that Herbert had worked out a contract for me to fight South American Champion Oscar Bonavena, even before the blood had dried over Quarry's eyes, and I had signed.

"Let Bonavena go!" Yank screamed. "You'll ruin everything! I'm out here building up The Big Fight for you and Joe. They talking about a forty-million-dollar gate. Five million for the fighters, the biggest prize in history, and you risk it on Bonavena!"

"If I can't take Bonavena, I'm not ready for Joe."

"Are you ready for five million? That's the name of the game! Back out of Bonavena!"

"I'm not in it just for the money, Yank. I've been fighting for seventeen years. A real champion don't duck anybody."

"Will you stop that Boy Scout shit! Listen, Bonavena will elbow you! Butt you with his head! Below the belt! Hit you behind the head! He don't care if he don't win! He just wants to leave you in bad shape!"

I knew Yank was thinking of how Bonavena fought Frazier twice and floored him twice. And when their last fight ended, Joe was so exhausted he collapsed in his dressing room.

Yank gave up. "I'm calling Herbert! It's useless talking to you!"

Herbert knew I needed to fight Bonavena to get back some of what I lost during exile. He and Yank had united on The Big Fight, with Yank turning over all negotiations to my manager, who could demand the heavy purse since people would be coming mainly to see me either whipped or victorious. Herbert was better at handling bidders like Madison Square Garden, Houston Astrodome, General Electric, the owners of the Dallas Cowboys, the owners of the New York Jets, and would come back with a contract. Frazier was going up and down the country swearing he'd never fight unless he got the lion's share, but behind the scenes our managers had agreed we split the purse fifty-fifty, whatever came. Yank had given me the impression that he would no longer duck me, that the road to the title was open.

"The only obstacle that might block the Frazier fight is the Supreme Court decision coming down against you," my lawyers were saying. "And the decision is due any day now." The only other obstacle was Bonavena, and I planned to remove that.

"What's the date of that fight?" Yank had asked.

"Sometime in December is all I remember."

I had forgotten the date was December 7, but those who wanted revenge for my refusal to be drafted showed they wouldn't forget me when the date got into the newspapers. Their phone calls reminded me: "You black draft-dodging traitor! You fight on Pearl Harbor Day and you won't live to collect the money!" . . . "They should put you in jail on December 7, not in the ring!" . . . "You're making a mockery of the day you helped disgrace!"

When I came into New York for the Bonavena fight, a Garden official read the messages to me: "If you allow that coward nigger to make money on December 7," one said, "those brave boys who lie entombed in the U.S.S. *Arizona* will turn over in their graves. Now you made December 7, 1970, a day of infamy along with December 7, 1941."

Harry Markson, the Garden's boxing director, seemed worried. "They threaten to boycott us unless we kill the fight." A New York State assemblyman had denounced the fight and demanded that Mayor Lindsay stop it as a "disgrace to the people of New York to allow a draft-dodger to perform—on the anniversary of the Japanese attack on Pearl Harbor."

A feature in *The Scrantonian* said: "The War Veterans should finish the job of destroying the Garden. Any place which harbors such an insult to those that died in Pearl Harbor—isn't worth keeping." And they wondered if "the Greedy Garden" would have "the nerve to play the National Anthem prior to the main event."

Joe Aquafreda, the Garden's security chief, told me that the arena had hired the most massive security force in its history. "We'll have a hundred police on the outside and one hundred fifty special police on the inside. We'll have twenty more mounted policemen covering the front and back. We've had fifteen bomb threats already. We'll search every seat again before December 7."

"Every seat in the house is sold out," Teddy Brenner said happily. "And it's still two weeks before the fight, not a ticket left."

Even so, for some strange reason, before the fight began, the Garden would "forget" to play the National Anthem.

Now all training and weighing-in and promoting is over, and I'm down to the last five hours before I leave my hotel room to go over to the Garden for this second fight after my exile.

"Champ, who we dedicate tonight to?" Bundini is asking, remembering that when I fought Quarry, I had planned to dedicate each fight to a prizefighter. "How about Bratton?"

I nod, and Bundini takes off his cap and places it above his heart. "Little Johnny Bratton, with the lion's heart and the lamb's bones, once the beauty of boxers, the fighters' fighter, now a jobless, punch-broken derelict on the streets of Chicago." Bratton is one of the people Bundini loved most in life. "Can I order the sign?" he says.

He phones across the street to the art shop for the glowing red sign to hold up in the ring, dedicating my fight with Bonavena to Bratton.

"Let's make him feel good," Bundini says when it comes. "For all the pain and punishment he took. For what he gave in the ring and for what he lost."

I look it over and like it, but in a few hours I will change my mind and dedicate this night to someone who has taken more pain and punishment than any prizefighter who ever lived, pain that was meant for people like me, and who has seen the world pass him by without notice.

Down to three hours before the fight, and my room is still crowded. I need to take my rest. I want the room cleared. There is one visitor left to come, and he will not come into a crowded room. Since early morning old friends and new ones, people who have waited three years to see me come back, neighbors I grew up with in Louisville, have been in and out of the room. I think of the mistake I made in Atlanta. Up until forty minutes before Quarry, I was standing in front of the Regency Hyatt, helping load friends on buses, giving passes to those without tickets, to all kinds of people, and entertaining those who came in to see me end my exile. And what they wanted most was so simple: a handshake, a touch, a word, a nod of recognition, an autograph, a hug. I wanted to give it to them, especially the people of Atlanta who broke down the bars for me, and I tried to get a ticket for everyone I promised one to. One little nine-year-old boy I told to wait outside the front door of the arena and I'd get him in. I was almost in my dressing room before I remembered. I went outside and there he was, waiting. "You took an awful chance," Herbert told me after the fight. "All that had to take something out of you."

So I want seclusion for Bonavena, but here it's three hours before fight time and my room is jammed. I look around and catch Angelo's eye. He had just read me a UPI story that predicts: "Bonavena is the best opponent Ali could select for the test to see how he might fare against Frazier. Everyone knew coming into the Quarry fight, Muhammad could go three rounds. What we wanted to find out was whether he could go more. . . ."

I give Angie the signal to clear the room. And slowly the people move toward the door.

I stop Dustin Hoffman and give him a hug. He had come down every day to watch me train. We had done roadwork together. I had been so impressed with his limp, clubfooted walk as "Rizzo" in *Midnight Cowboy*, I was surprised that he could run fast enough to keep up with me.

"Get some rest," he says. "I'll be out there at ringside."

Bud Collins of the Boston *Globe* is one of the last to go, and he stops to look at my watercolor drawings sitting up against a lampshade. In my early fights I used to spend the hours after roadwork and between gym and bedtime painting pictures. My father has more talent, but I had painted a series of oils and watercolors I call "Predictions Before a Fight." I had been giving them after each fight to the artist Leroy Neiman. Collins wants this one where I stand in the center of the ring, my arms up in victory, Bonavena's blood all over my white trunks and Bonavena stretched out flat on the canvas. A sign above us says, ROUND NINE.

I start to offer it, but I remember that Robert Lipsyte, of the New York *Times*, one of the most fair-minded writers and one who the Honorable Elijah Muhammad once granted a three-hour interview, woke me up this morning and offered two hundred dollars for it—an offer I refused, not because I wanted more, but because I planned to give it to him as a gift.

I tell Collins, "I'll give you my new poem with the prediction in it."

And I hand him the only copy of my poem about Bonavena:

It's been a long time since I put my predictions in rhythm and rhyme,
But it was Bonavena who started it all by getting out of line.
He has asked the Commission to waive the three-knockdown rule.
He must be crazy or maybe a fool.

He couldn't have been talking to some angel from heaven,
Now he has the nerve to predict I'll fall in eleven.
If this is his joke, it's at a bad time,
For being so rash, he'll fall in Round Nine.

I understand in Argentina, the officials plainly said,
They wanted little Oscar to shave his shaggy head.
When I start going upside his heavy mop,
Bonavena will yell, "STOP!

I'd rather go to the nearest barbershop."
Before Round Nine is out,
The referee will jump and shout,
"THAT'S ALL, FOLKS, this turkey is out!"

Bud laughs as he walks out the door, and Angelo continues to slowly move the crowd out until he sees Minister Jeremiah Shabazz shoving his way in. Angie looks to see if I want him stopped, but Jeremiah is bringing the only guest I want to see.

"He won't come if too many are in the room," Jeremiah says quietly. Minister of the Philadelphia Mosque, Jeremiah had served with the Honorable Elijah Muhammad for more than twenty years and will soon become one of the key national representatives of the Nation of Islam.

Finally, only Bundini, Reggie, Durham and some close friends are left. I walk Angelo to the door. He has an uneasy look on his face, puzzled that, as my friend and chief trainer, he is not to be kept inside this time. Jeremiah has told me the guest I'm waiting for will not talk in front of a white man.

"We due in the Garden in less than an hour," Angie warns.

"Call me when it's time," I tell him, and turn to Jeremiah. "Bring him up."

In a few minutes Jeremiah is back with a thin black man, medium height, in his late thirties, dressed in gray pants and an old Army jacket from his service in the Korean war. His face is full of strange frowns that stay in his brow as though he had once been deeply shocked and puzzled, and somehow the look froze forever in his face.

"This is Brother Judge Aaron," Jeremiah says. "He tells me he wrote you a dozen letters."

I remember the name "Judge" because it sounds like a title. I remember his letters in a shaky scribble, too hard for me to read.

"I get so many letters, Brother," I say.

"Tell him who told you to come," Jeremiah says to Aaron.

He sits down on my bed. "I saw Martin Luther King a week before he died. He told me I should see Muhammad Ali. He said you wouldn't let the world forget me."

"Give him the message," Jeremiah says.

"I'm the message. I'm the living message." The wrinkles are deep in his brow and there's a puzzled, confused look in his eyes.

And even before Jeremiah says it, a chill is going through me: "They cut his nuts out. They wanted him to be a warning."

Bundini comes to his feet and stares unbelievingly at the thin, quiet man. He shouts, his voice deep and husky, "Who could do a thing like that! Nobody could do that! I don't believe that shit! Nobody could do that!"

Aaron looks eye to eye with Bundini for a second, then slowly unbuttons his Army jacket and strips to the waist. Cut into the flesh across his chest are the letters KKK. Then he unbuttons his belt and lets his pants fall to the floor, steps out of his shorts.

"Good Gawd A'mighty! Good Gawd!" Bundini keeps saying.

Heavy scars cover Aaron's groin, and where testicles once were is a mesh of crude keloid scars that crisscross his crotch and cut across his penis.

Bundini slowly sinks back in his chair, tears streaming down his cheeks.

Now the name comes back to me. This is the Judge Aaron I first heard of when I read his story in the Muslim newspaper *Muhammad Speaks*, but I never thought he would live. I go over and sit beside him. His thin hands are trembling, and Bundini, his own hands shaking, lights a cigarette and puts it between Aaron's dry lips.

"Why you?" I ask. "Why pick you?"

Aaron inhales heavily, that look back in his eyes. "It could have been any black man that night, I guess," he says. "They had set out to get one. It was the time civil rights protests were everywhere. Martin Luther King was in Alabama. It was when all the marching and protesting was on. And that night I needed a loaf of bread to make sandwiches for work. I was going down Tarron City Road to the store, my girl friend with me, and this car drove up with seven white men in it and they started shouting at me, but I kept walking.

"Then one of them screamed out, 'Nigger, come over here!'

"'Who are you?' I asked. I couldn't see them very good until they began jumping out of the car and rushing over to me.

"'Nigger, we the police! Come with us!'"

Aaron inhales deeply and holds the smoke inside so long, it seems it will never come out.

"Look," I say. "You can stop if you want to."

He shakes his head. "I haven't had a chance to talk about it in a long time. I told my girl to go for help and she breaks out and runs, but they drag me to the car. They stuff me down on the back floor, and when I try to get up they beat me with a wrench until I almost pass out."

He takes a deeper drag and lets the smoke out slowly.

"They blindfold me. They ride me around for a while. Then they pull off the main highway. I could tell by the bumpy road. They were going up a side road and in about half an hour they stop the car and I hear the driver say, 'This is the place. Get that nigger up the road.'

"They get me out of the car and make me crawl on my hands and knees, kicking and cursing me as I try to crawl blindfolded in the direction they want me to go. When I get to the place, one of them snatches off the blindfold. I'm in an old farm shack and the man who drove the car is saying to me, 'Nigger . . . you one of them smart-aleck college niggers?' I say, 'No, sir,' and the other says, 'Nigger, you one of them loud-mouthed Martin Luther King niggers?' I say, 'Oh no, sir. No, sir.' I felt sick. I thought I was in the middle of a nightmare."

Someone in the hall is pounding on the door: "Ali! Ali! Open up!"

Bundini opens the door and shouts out, "Champ ain't ready yet! Champ's restin'! He ain't ready yet!" He comes back and sits beside Aaron.

"Go on," I say.

"Even then, I don't know what they want to do. But one they called Joe Pritchett kicks me and says, 'Nigger, take off your pants and lay down on your back.' 'Yessuh, he one of them smart-alecky civil rights niggers,' the one who was driving said. 'I can tell.'

"I told them I didn't know anything about civil rights. I don't know no sassy blacks. I don't even vote. I never been in no demonstration. They just laugh."

"Didn't you try to get away?" Bundini asks with pain in his voice.

Aaron looks surprised at the question. "I tried to get up and run for the door, but something struck me in the head that felt like a hammer. It was the butt of a gun. I get up again and they hit me again. Then I hear the leader shout, 'Hurry up! We wastin' time! Hurry up! We got to git five more niggers tonight! Hurry up with this nigger!' "

Someone outside is calling, "Ali! Ali! Time for the Garden! Time to go!" I motion for Bundini to throw the latch on the door.

"They knock me down and jump on me. They spread my legs apart and one of them holds one leg and another holds the other leg. Two others are holding each of my arms. 'You know what they do to cows and hogs in the country?' the leader asks. 'That's what we gonna do to you. That's how we handle loud-mouth uppity niggers. We gonna send you back with a message for all them young niggers. We want you to go and let 'em see what happened to you.'

"I tried to scream, but the heaviest man got down on his knees and pressed a crowbar across my throat. I was choking and trying to turn my head from side to side to get air. Then I hear the man on my neck say, 'If this nigger git loose, take this gun and blow his brains out.' 'Put the trademark on,' someone says, 'put the mark on.' Then the heavy one takes his knife and slashes the initials KKK across my chest."

Sweat is pouring down his face, although the room is cool. His eyes have a faraway look.

"Ali! Ali! It's time to go! Ali! Open up!" More voices, but I nod for Aaron to go on.

"Then the leader opened a package of razor blades. He gave half the blades to the man beside him, who drops down between my legs and looks back up at the leader. 'Do I take out one nut or two?'

"The leader shouts, 'Cut 'em both off! Makes no damned difference! Whack 'em off!'

"I strain every muscle in my body to break loose. I try to scream, but blood is in my throat and I'm choking. I feel someone's hot hands holding my privates and then I feel the cutting. I feel them slashing my groin and I feel the pain . . ."

Aaron gets up and starts pacing the room, sweat coming down his face as though he's living it all again.

"Ali! Ali!" Now I hear Angelo's voice outside. "ALI! Are you in there? We only got a few minutes! ALI!"

But even if it means the fight has to be canceled, I cannot answer the door. I've almost forgotten everything except this tortured black man walking up and down my room.

"They had their hands across my mouth, but the pain made my screams come through. When they had cut out what they wanted to, they stood up. They laughed and poured a jug of turpentine over the cuts. I was screaming and praying: 'Oh, God! Oh, God! Please have mercy, God!'

"When I said that, that must have sounded funny. The man on top began to laugh and the one holding my legs laughed and said, 'Nigger, do you like white women?' I said, 'No, sir. I don't like them.'

"He turned to the other and said, 'You hear this nigger? He says he don't like white women.' The other leans over and spits in my face and says, 'What white women ever done to you to make you not like them, nigger?' I thought I had said something wrong and I tried to change it: 'They ain't done nothin' to me, sir. No, sir. I like them all right.'

"Then the first one hit me with the butt of his gun. 'Nigger! What you mean you like white women!? What you mean by that?'

"Then I hear Pritchett yell, 'Hurry up! We ain't got all night here! Hurry up and finish him!'

" 'Nigger, you know what we cut out?' one of them shouts in my ear. I couldn't look down, but I know where the pain is coming from. 'He can't see,' the man holding the bar under my neck says.

" 'Well, tell him,' another said. 'We cut your black nuts out!'

"I cried out, 'Oh, God! Oh, God! Oh, God, where are you!'

"I remember looking up, seeing one man standing, his hands dripping with blood, my blood. He's holding the testicles like a trophy.

They all begin to shout and stomp and slap each other on the back and laugh until the leader calls them to attention: 'Gentlemen. Gentlemen. Let us stand together and unmask.'

"They line up and take off their hoods and this the first time I see their faces. They line up for some kind of ritual. Each one touches his forehead with the blood from my parts and pass it on to the next. The last one throws the testicles down in the dirt and they start stomping it and screaming at it and cursing it. Pritchett is saying, 'This one nigger won't never bring no mo' niggers in the world.' They're screaming and yelling at my testicles and had almost forgot me until one of them looked down and I must have been crying, because he said, 'Look! Look at this nigger crying!' and they came over to look at me, and Pritchett said, 'Git up, nigger. Git your clothes on!'

"I tried, but everything in my body felt like it had been cut or torn. 'Oh, God! I can't move! Oh, God, please help me move!' I just couldn't pull myself up.

"Then the leader says, 'Here, put his nuts in this Dixie cup,' and one of them kneeled down in the dirt, scooped up my parts in a paper container. They carried me out and dumped me into the trunk of the car and drove down near the creek. Then they pull me out of the trunk like a sack of fertilizer and the leader says, 'Show this Dixie cup to every smart-alecky nigger you see. Niggers like Martin Luther King and Reverend Shuttleworth. Wait! Now hold it! We got another message we want to put in that cup, ain't we, boys?'

"One of them found a piece of paper and he started writing something on it, but when they finished and Pritchett called for them all to sign it, nobody wanted to sign what was written. And finally Pritchett grabbed the paper and tore it up and pointed to me. 'This nigger and what's in that Dixie cup is all the message we need.' He turns to me. 'You go show 'em what happened to you! You hear? When the other young niggers see that, they know we mean business!'

"Then they kick me and I roll down the bank of the creek and into the shallow part of the water. I lay there until I hear their car fading off, then suddenly I hear it stopping, turning, coming back again. I believe they changed their minds and decided to finish me. I rolled under the water like I was drowned and I stayed with my head partly under the water and holding my breath until I heard the car move away again."

"ALI! ALI! ALI! You late! Bundini, is Muhammad in there?"

Bundini sticks his head out and shouts, "We be out in a minute." He comes back and asks Aaron, "How did you get away?"

"I don't know. I crawled somehow until I got to the highway. Cars and trucks pass me by. Some would slow down, see who I was and go on. It was the worst feeling. On the side of the road like a dying dog and everybody passing by. Then a car stopped and a man took me to the hospital. The doctor called the police . . ."

"Did they get those guys?" Bundini asks.

Aaron nods. "I identified them. They had a court trial, and most of them were given some time in jail. They been free a long time now. We all still lived in the same town. I moved away a few months ago because I couldn't find no work."

"Did you get medical help?" Jeremiah asks.

"Well, I'm a Korean war veteran. I go to the Veterans Hospital for medicine every month. They say I can't live without it."

For a while the room is silent. Even the pounding at the door has stopped.

"What do you want from me?" I finally ask.

"I don't know," he says quietly. "I wanted to see you. I just wanted to see all those kind people they wanted me to give the message to."

"ALI! ALI! IT'S LATE, ALI! TIME TO GO! ALI! TIME TO GO!"

I reach out and put my arms around his shoulders.

"I just didn't want to be left lying on the road . . ."

I hug him and his face lights up in a warm and beautiful way. And for a minute the confusion leaves him and I see what he must have looked like in all his innocence before they wrecked him.

He has been in my room less than an hour, but he has made me understand more of what I fight against and what I fight for and what I have come to mean to those who hate me most and to those who understood what I stand for. It is then I decide to change the dedication of this fight and all future fights over to "the unprotected people, to the victims."

And when I tell Bundini, he smiles. "Even Johnny Bratton would like that better," he says. "He was the victim."

Judge will go with us to the Garden. I walk him to the door and ask a question I'm curious about: "Who gave you the name 'Judge'?"

"My mother," he says.

"Did she ever tell you why?"

He nods slowly. "She said she wanted me to be fair to people. Give justice, she said. Be like a good judge. Justice."

"Justice," Minister Jeremiah says. "That's the greatest word there is, 'justice.'"

"No," Judge answers slowly. "My mother didn't say that. She said there was one word greater."

"What?" Jeremiah asks.

But the frowns are slowly coming back in his face and the puzzled look in his eyes. He is staring across the room and listening to the commotion outside my door.

"What?" Jeremiah persists.

"Mercy," Judge finally says.

Aaron made me think of all the people who support me. It's on my mind when I leave the hotel, and halfway to the Garden I decide to get out of the cab and ride the subway the rest of the distance. A crowd follows me to the employees' entrance and I invite them all in to see the fight as my guests.

When I get to the dressing room, the officials say this is the biggest gate in the Garden's history and thousands have been turned away, but Bundini was able to get Aaron a ringside seat near my corner, and I could see him.

When the bell rings, I come out prepared to put Bonavena away sooner than I had predicted. But early in the fight I realize I've underestimated him. I had taken him as a joke, but his awkward style, rugged strength give me trouble. My timing is off. I'm missing blows I should connect with. My right crosses go over his head and my jabs don't stop him. In the ninth, I go all out to take him out, but he weathers the storm and actually shakes me.

I box carefully the rest of the way, pile up points till the fifteenth and last round, when, as I learn later, his manager, Gil Clancey, seeing he's hopelessly behind, sends him out to score a knockout. Oscar comes out, head up, pushing his luck. Almost by instinct my left hook catches him coming in, a blow so hard it even jars my bones. Bonavena goes down and gets up, but I know he's through. His seconds throw in a white towel.

"Finish him off for Judge Aaron!" Bundini yells. "Take the wrinkles outta his face!"

He climbs to his feet for the third time, but I put him back down to end it. It's the first time in his career he's ever been counted out.

Of all that happened that night, the heavy blows I threw and had thrown at me, my prediction of when I'd knock Bonavena out backfiring, the screams and boos for and against me, nothing stayed in my mind as long as the face of that mutilated man looking up at my corner, round after round.

Three years out of action may have weakened me, but I knew my real strength came from all the Judge Aarons and their faith in me. And I knew I'd soon be stronger than I was before.

THE DINOSAURS MEET

Nineteen-seventy is almost over and it's beginning to look real. When the year began, I didn't think I'd ever work again. Now my twins are born, I've been licensed to fight in Georgia and New York, I stopped both Quarry and Bonavena, and I'm back in condition. Nothing can stop The Big Fight now—my fight with Joe Frazier is finally on.

All through December of 1970, Herbert sifts through offers from promoters, and every night he reports the latest bids: $400,000 from London, $600,000 from a Tokyo promoter; then $1,000,000 from the Houston Astrodome. Madison Square Garden fell away when the bidding reached $1,500,000; NBC had made an offer for $2,000,000. We talk over each bid and Herbert tells me, "We can do better."

Then a week comes when he calls and says, "It's a five-million-dollar purse to be split between you and Joe. I know I can get a higher one, but it may take weeks. If the Supreme Court decides not to send you to jail—"

"Take the two and a half million," I interrupt him.

"Now, you know you won't end up with two and a half million. That's the figure the newspapers will play up, but the Federal Government gets a million and a half off the top, before you even touch it. Then after the City of New York and the State of New York take out their taxes, you'll have about six hundred thousand dollars left. Then training expenses will run another two hundred thousand. You are looking at four hundred thousand." Herbert explains it carefully.

I was surprised at the amount and had a hard time believing it.

Herbert is right. Newspapers across the country, the covers of *Time* and *Life* magazines, TV and radio sportscasts all focus on the "$5 Million Fighters."

Even so, at the time that size purse is unbelievable. And the price range for my fight contracts is permanently changed.

"This must be the age of absurdity, or incredibility, if not insanity," Milton Gross writes when he hears about it. "The money is something out of a Hollywood extravaganza. Never before in the history of entertainment—have any performers ever been offered over $5 million for a one-shot thing."

Nobody believes that Herbert has pulled off such a fantastic deal until photostatic copies of the two $2,500,000 checks are printed in the newspapers.

"We had to get it," Herbert tells me. "This is the rarest event in sports history. Two undefeated Heavyweight Champions have never fought before, and it may never happen again. You're the best-known performer in the world; there's not a president, a king or movie star that can draw a crowd the way you can. Besides, you'll never know how much you could have made these last three years. A fighter's life is short. I got to try to get some of it back for you, and this is the way to get it."

Herbert's bargaining method, which he uses in every fight after my return, is just to state the price he's shooting at: based on his analysis of what the fight can draw, based on the history of the performers. "Then the first bidder that comes in with the cold cash and puts it in a Muhammad Ali bank account, that's the one we deal with," he says. "Pledges and promises don't count. At some point you have to stop listening to pledges. We got higher bids than five million, but Jack Kent Cooke and Jerry Perenchio put the money up in your name and Frazier's name."

Four years later, when the Boxing Writers Association finally acknowledges Herbert as 1974's Manager of the Year, he has outstripped other fight managers so far in promoting and getting big purses for their fighters, that Murray Goodman, boxing's greatest publicist, says, "Boxing needs a new category for a manager like Herbert Muhammad. He has created more million-dollar gates than all other managers combined. He knows the value of his fighter. He has made the best-known performer the best-paid performer in the world. He has enabled his fighter to earn an average of five million dollars per year after he returned to the ring from exile.

"When you're trying to protect your fighter," Herbert said, "you can't ignore the history of the prize-fight game. The ways they have of taking money that rightfully belongs to the fighters are so complicated and intricate, the only way to see that my fighter gets a fair share is to ask for a guaranty so large that even if they are stealing, it won't affect the fighter's purse much. I found the best way to protect my fighter is to have the promoters sign an agreement that there is no income other than what is stated in the contract, and if so, the fighter will have to get a negotiated percentage.

I already know Jack Kent Cooke, the owner of the Lakers basketball team and the Felt Forum, but I don't meet Jerry Perenchio until I go to the Garden to sign the contract. Jerry has the look of a mischievous boy, excited because he's beat out all the veteran boxing promoters. He has never promoted anything in boxing before and he sounds proud that his first try is so successful. He has only been associated with show business.

"This is the greatest event since I've been alive," he keeps saying. "It transcends boxing. It's phenomenal! I'll give it more build-up than the Normandy Invasion. It will be the greatest single grosser in the history of the world. The *Wall Street Journal* sees a potential gross of forty million dollars."

As he brags about how much he'll gross, I begin to feel maybe Joe and I had settled for too little, and during Toots Shor's press conference I holler to Frazier, "Joe, we've been taken!" I want to get together with him and do it over. But Joe and I are dinosaurs now, and the time when we could cooperate on anything except tearing each other apart for the undisputed World Heavyweight Title is gone. We don't even look at each other eye to eye. The time for that is gone, too.

I make it easy for Jerry to direct what Red Smith described as "the gaudiest promotion of all time." He'll merchandise every aspect of The Fight. Movies will be made, books written, souvenirs sold by the millions all over the world. Jerry's contract even gives him the trunks, shoes and gloves of both fighters. "If a movie studio can auction off Judy Garland's shoes, Gary Cooper's belt and Marilyn Monroe's dress, Muhammad's and Frazier's things should be worth something special," Perenchio says brightly. And one evening after I had selected my fighting outfit, one of Jerry's aides comes into my dressing room to remind me, "When the fight's over, all the clothes of the fighter become the property of the promoter. The gloves, the trunks, the shoes. It's all in the contract."

The contract calls for me to spend the ten days before the fight promoting it in New York. I love crowds and being surrounded by people, but the lobby of my hotel is so jammed and the crowds multiply so fast that I'm forced to escape to Miami for the last seven days. On my way to the airport, flocks of blacks, whites and Puerto Rican youngsters run across Manhattan after our limousine, catching up with us at stoplights, beating on the window, trying to twist the door open until I promise one, who has sprinted twenty blocks, tickets to the fight.

Angelo is shaken. "I've never seen New York like this!" he says.

We don't come back to New York until the day of the weigh-in. And when it's over, the crowd that has seeped through the guards and surrounded the stadium exits is so deep, they are afraid to let me go back to my hotel room. Teddy Brenner and Harry Markson, two Garden officials, take us up to the Garden Restaurant. "No police can control this crowd," they say. "You could get knocked down. Not on purpose; they just want to touch you, see you, hear you. Anything could happen."

"You've got to stay inside the Garden. We've got an apartment ready here," Markson says, and takes me to a room where there's a TV and a cot.

Angelo is afraid of it. "We got nine hours to go. Ali always lies quietly in bed for the last five or six hours before a fight. It's the only way he can rest."

But the Garden is more afraid of what might happen if I try to leave, and I agree to stay inside. All that day I'm locked up inside the Garden. But I can't rest on the cot. I lie awake until it's time to take the elevator down to the dressing room and put on the trunks, shoes and robe I have had designed specially for this fight.

When I get to the dressing room, Burt Lancaster is already set up there to film a documentary and hear my predictions. I am listening to some poems he has received urging me to win when I hear someone calling, "Rahaman is fighting! Rahaman is fighting!" I run out and stand behind the crowd on the ramp so I can see my brother in the ring against an English heavyweight, Dan McAlinden. But they pull me back to finish the documentary.

My brother is a beautiful artist and sculptor, with talent even greater than my father's. Of all his gifts, fighting's not one.

I move back to the dressing room. On the way I see Joe Louis. "Joe! Thank you for that prediction. I thank you for it."

Louis, as usual, has picked my opponent to win.

"The only thing Clay can do to win," Louis has said, "is to get back those three and a half years. And he can't do it. Four years ago he could have beat Joe, but not now."

"Come to my victory party," I tell him. "I'll make it the last time you'll pick against me. I was worried until I heard you were betting on Frazier."

"It ain't only Joe betting on Frazier," one of my trainers says as we go in the room. "All the old pros are picking Frazier—Archie Moore, Floyd Patterson, Jack Dempsey, Billy Conn, Jersey Joe Walcott. And all the writers think Frazier will win."

I feel even better. I have never lost a fight when the odds are against me.

Teddy Brenner yells, "You on next!" In a quiet recess of the dressing room Herbert and I confer and give thanks to Allah. We go over our battle plans for the last time.

Then I make the long walk behind my crew through the crowd that roars when I come into sight.

I climb into the ring and begin warming up, dancing in wider and wider circles. Accidentally on purpose, I touch Frazier's shoulders as he stands in his corner. For a split second we look at each other, eye to eye. I'm shaken, and when the bell rings I fight two fights: the fight that was in my mind—the fight I talked about—and the one I am in for fifteen rounds. And they are not exactly the same.

"No contest," I tell Bundini. "Have a sign made up, 'No Contest,' and carry it into the ring, with another sign saying, 'No Smoking,' and I'll carry a fire extinguisher in, 'cause Joe's always claiming he's coming out smokin'."

I had written more poems about Joe than any fighter I'd ever faced:

> I'm gonna come out smokin',
> And I won't be jokin'.
> I'm gonna be a peckin' and a pokin',
> Pouring water on his smokin'.
> It might shock you and amaze ya,
> But I'm gonna destroy Joe Frazier!

THE REAL FIGHT is on . . . I hear that familiar sound that comes up from the crowd when a fight starts, the eager roar of the crowd calling for blood. I've heard it since I was twelve, it sends chills through me each time it comes. I hear it now, and I know Frazier does, too. It will get in his blood and mine and drive us on to die out here if we have to.

Frazier moves directly at me. I expect it and I circle him, but he keeps coming in, his chin close to his chest, bobbing, weaving. A short jab that I'm surprised he has. It reaches me.

I strike back with a quick left and right and we clinch. I feel his strength. I step back. I shoot lefts and a right at his head. I jab, but my jabs are off target. He bobs under my right. He's boring in, relentless, determined. I'm watching for his hook, his heavy weapon. I shoot rights; most get to him but some go over his head.

He's coming in, swinging, and the people scream: "Joe! Joe! Come on, Joe!" His arms are like steel as he tears loose and explodes a hook in my side. I tie him up in the clinches. He's shooting for my body, but I tie him up. I snap lefts and rights to his head. Near the end of the first round, I'm trying to time his bobs and weaves, and get goin' stronger, the way I had planned it.

I'm talking to the press in my gym: I'm the real Champion! I've been waiting for three years, listening to all this talk about who is the real Champ! All you writers. Hear me! When it's all over, I'm gonna call all of you writers to the front. I'm going to say, Who's the real Champ? You underestimated me again! Forty-three out of forty-six of you picked Frazier. I told you he was a homemade Champion. I'm gonna have a good time for four or five rounds before I really get serious. I've been waiting for this. This time, write the truth. You all got good ringside seats. Tell the people what's happening! Tell it the way it is, not the way you want it to be with me knocked out. Tell it the way I fight it.

I'M THROUGH rounds two and three, both of which I win, and deep into four when suddenly I feel the first of the hard hooks explode against my jaw. So hard, I believe he caught me by accident. Bells ring in my head. I shoot back. I stab back, but he drives in again, bobs, weaves and comes under.

I try to hold him in the clinches, but he breaks through, his left hook whips into my ribs, whips down on my hips. I've never been hurt before in the hips, but when Frazier hits you, you feel it. He pins me against the ropes, and suddenly he leaps and a hook blasts my head. I fight him off till the bell ends the fourth.

When the bell rings for round five, I circle him. Frazier comes on, still relentless, harder and faster. How long can he keep it up? I shoot a left uppercut that should have stopped him. His head snaps back, but he ducks and bobs and weaves and pins me against the ropes.

My jabs bounce off his head, but he keeps coming. Why is he so confident? I can feel it. So confident that near the end of the fifth he drops both hands, jeers at me, dares me. I take the dare. I shoot straight rights to his head, sharp rights that wipe the jeer off his face.

When the bell rings, he walks back with a wobble. I shook him. But I'm feeling the effects of the blows he slashed into my ribs. I've never fought anyone with so much drive. I have a new respect for Joe. Sometimes his timing, his rhythm, is uncanny. He moves in, takes two and comes up. Even though I'm hitting him four blows to one, his hooks get to me more and more. I've got to do something about it. The sixth is coming up, I know I'm ahead on points, but already I know I'll need a miracle to end it in six.

I put my prediction on TV: the cameras were shooting me for the closed-circuit audience. I gave them a special message: my predictions of how the fight would end. I predicted the sixth round, gave it to them in a sealed envelope which they were to open only five minutes before the fight. I wanted it that way so there'd be no late betting on it. "Here I am, five minutes before the fight and predictin'. If I were a Patterson or Terrell or Chuvalo or any other fighter, I would be praying or shadowboxing at this time, but I'm putting it down on paper. I'm putting it on record for all to see." In the envelope were my words:

> It won't even be close!
> Joe will look like an amateur!
> And I will be the pro!
> I'm going to shuffle and jab and clinch and holler,
> And I'll have a good time for four or five rounds
> Before I really get serious.
> I predict Frazier will fall in Round Six!

JOE KNOWS what I predicted and he comes out fast, direct, hard. His head bobbing and weaving, his neck on a swivel. I jab and shoot straight rights at him. I hook him and he pushes me toward the corner. I lay back on the ropes again, and his left explodes against my hips, my ribs. Then he brings it up to my head and I seem paralyzed. I don't hit back. I lay on the ropes, and the crowd is booing . . . Joe has opened the round with a hook to my jaw that stuns me. Now he tries to move in for an uppercut. I shoot sharp jabs to his head and try to move him back, but he's pushing, driving like he's a tank. He's smashing at me on the ropes. His arms are short, stubby, and he can hit at close range with awful power. I try to move back, but he pins me against the ropes and he's throwing bombs. The crowd is up and screaming, "Joe! Joe! Come on, Joe!" They think he's close to a victory, and they've never seen me this way before. They're yelling, "Joe! Joe! Joe! Joe!" He's throwing punches and they're landing. Something has gone out of me; I feel tired and the fight is not half over. I know from experience that if I hold on, I will grow stronger. But the air in my lungs is hot, my arms are heavy. I look out at the crowd. I think how the world is watching. I've got to do what I said I would do.

I had forecast: I'm gonna say to Smokin' Joe, "Come on, Joe. Let's smoke!" I'm gonna reach him because my arms are longer. I'm faster and when I hit, it's gonna be devastating. It's gonna be sharp. His body punches ain't that bad. Body punches never really could kill anybody. I'm gonna say, "Come on, Joe. You can do better. Joe, you ain't smokin' at all."

BUT HE *is* smokin'. I think I take the seventh, but in the eighth, Joe drives on, moves on, pushes on, falls on, but keeps coming on. I jab him, straight sharp jabs. He moves me against the ropes. I give him light, sharp jabs. My weariness is greater now. I wonder if Joe Louis is right about those three and a half years. When I lay on the ropes, the crowd boos, and yells for Joe to take me out.

The bell rings. I go back to my corner. I've got to turn the fight around.

The ninth comes, and I feel my strength returning. When Joe comes in, I catch him with a sharp right. He staggers me with a hook, but I'm shooting straight rights to his head, and they're beginning to connect. All of a sudden, everything comes into focus. I'm not missing any more. He's bleeding from the left nostril. He staggers. I'm putting it together again! He's backing up! I land six, seven, eight straight solid rights to his head. There's a lump over his eye the size of a coffee cup, getting bigger and bigger with each blow I land. But he keeps coming in, keeps coming in, but now I'm ready for him. Everything I throw hits! When the round ends, he's bleeding above the eye, from his nose and mouth. But he won't go down. Now I know he'll die before he quits.

I told the fans, the crowd that came around the gym each day: "I'll come out and touch his nose with my fist." I stand up in the ring and demonstrate how I'll hold his head at a distance. I'll talk to him: "Let's get it on, Joe! I'm gonna whip you and all those white folks who are backing you. Boy, you in trouble tonight! Joe, you won't land a blow. So you set up a victory party? Duke Ellington's gonna play at your party, you say? NO! No! No! Not tonight, Joe! You won't have no victory party tonight. You'll be coming to my victory party. I'm gonna have a party for you when this is all over, Joe. In round ten, if you still in the ring, I'm gonna tag you and tame you like you was a pussy cat. You ain't the monster the press make you out to be. You'll see by round ten."

JOE IS on top of me and I feel his left hook against my jaw. I'm holding my hands up high, but he gets through. I shoot lefts and rights to his head, but he digs his fist into my ribs. His chin is on my chest. I know why he's moving with such force, why he's so fierce in this round. Yank Durham predicted that I would go in the tenth round. My back is against the ropes and he's pressing hard. The same exhaustion I felt earlier comes down on me. I'm missing again. The tight focus I had in the last round is gone. Still I catch him coming in with a straight left. I hook and throw a right, and it blunts him. And in the clinch for the first time, I feel his heavy breathing. The pace is killing me, but it's killing him, too.

The bell. The round is over, both of our predictions failed. I just manage a slight edge. But I've got five rounds to recover. I've done it before, I can do it now.

When he throws a punch at me, I'm gonna shake my head and say, "Man, you ain't landing a blow!" Then I'm gonna do a little shuffle and I'm gonna hit him—BAM! and say, "You know you don't stand a chance, sucker." I'm gonna clinch with him. I'm gonna have a ball. If the sucker's still crazy, I got a new punch, the Ali Ghetto Ripper. I'm gonna lay it on him in the eleventh. If it goes that far.

I COME out determined to win the eleventh, twelfth, thirteenth. And I want the remaining ones. Frazier is bobbing, weaving, more confident than ever. Suddenly he dips under my right and comes up with the hardest hook I've ever taken in my life. It flung me back across the ring. I'm almost out on my feet. My head is numb and I see him coming, but I jab and back off. There's water on the floor and I slip, but there's no count. I get back up, but in the next round he comes out again, throwing himself recklessly, taking blows that bounce off his head, off his chin, off his face. His mouth is bleeding. In the twelfth and thirteenth, I stay away and throw punches, long-range. They cut into his head, but he presses on, crowding me. He'll take three, four, five, six punches to get a solid shot at my body, at the hips, at the head. There's something about the way he comes in, bobbing, weaving, that throws me off. He's easy to hit; then he's not easy to hit. I've never fought anyone with a will so strong. He's human, I think, so it's got to be hurting him. His left eye is swollen. His right eye is cut. His lips are torn as though they are going to drop off. I'm throwing jabs and scoring, but he's still moving in. I get by the fourteenth. Just one more to go.

I walk down 146th and Broadway. Pedestrians forget where they are going and follow me. Traffic is blocked. People pour out into the streets, and I cry out, "Where's Joe Frazier! Where's the White Folks' Champion! When I git him in the ring, you'll see. There'll be no contest."

I've been building up this fight since I was in exile. It'll be the biggest fight in history. Greater than when David fought Goliath, greater than when Grant took Richmond, greater than when any two men ever fought each other on the planet Earth. I'll be whipping the people that took my title and gave it to him.

Red Smith says the build-up started long ago: "It goes back to the days when Clay's posturing and preening and rancid verse and self-praise began to make total strangers yearn to see him stopped with a fistful of knuckles. Frazier is the first candidate conceded a chance to accomplish this."

But Red is wrong if he thinks Frazier will be the victor. I'll close the book on all the fighters. If Joe Frazier whips me, I'm gonna crawl across the ring, and say, "Joe, if you whip me, you the real Champion of the World. I'm gonna crawl across the ring and look up at you and say, 'You the real Champ of the World.'"

THE GARDEN is on its feet. Only a few shout, "Ali! Ali! Ali! Ali!" But Frazier's supporters are confident and loud: "Joe! Come on, Joe! Knock him out, Joe! Knock him out, Joe!"

He's moving into range. I want to circle, jab and come through with a straight right. I see an opening. I move toward it, then I see him dip. He dips and leaps up with his left, almost from the floor. I see it coming. I think I can ride it back. But he has it timed to perfection. It explodes against my head and I don't remember going down. Only being down. Looking up and hearing the count, and knowing I had no business being down. I get up and take the count. The roars from the crowd are in my ear. "Joe! Joe! Joe! Joe! Joe Frazier!"

"That's the blow that did it, that blew out the candles," Bundini will tell me later.

I jab and tie him up, hold him off, keep him from following up. When the bell rings and before I go back to my corner, I see his face is a mass of blood and lumps, swollen, but so is mine. My jaw is swollen to the size of a melon. Halfway through the fight, Angelo thought it was broken. As I stand back in my corner and wait for the verdict, all my bones ache. My hips feel like they've been beaten by baseball bats.

"The winner by unanimous decision, undisputed World Heavy-weight Champion, Joe Frazier!"

People are pouring into the ring past the police. I move behind Bundini and Angelo to the steps until I feel somebody pulling my arm, making me turn around. Joe has come over to my corner. "You put up a great fight," he says. His face is so swollen I can hardly see his eyes, but I know he's looking at me.

"You The Champ," I say.

He seems to like that. It's the first time as a pro that I have to acknowledge another man over me. I had promised to crawl across the ring and say, "You a bad nigger."

Joe seems to read my mind. Blood is seeping from the cuts in his lips. "We don't do no crawling," he says. "You fought one helluva fight. You one bad nigger. We both bad niggers. We don't do no crawling."

People are pushing past me to get to shake hands with The Champion.

"How do you feel?" An announcer is pushing a microphone up to me, but I move past him. I don't tell him that my first feeling is relief. I'm glad it's over.

I don't remember how I got in the dressing room, but I remember lying stretched out on the rubbing table, Bundini taking my trunks and cup off, cutting my shoelaces, and in a second I'm naked on the table. All I feel is fatigue. I want to go home and see my children.

Angelo is screaming, "Don't let nobody in here! Nobody comes in!"

People are pushing at the door, trying to get in past the guards.

I hear a woman's voice pleading to get in. I see Diana Ross's thin arms reaching over the head of a policeman, waving at me, and I say, "Let her in. Let her in."

They allow her to slip through and she comes over, tears pouring down her face. "You The Champ. You won. You The Champ." And she kisses me.

"No, I'm not," I tell her. "I'm not The Champ no more, Diana."

"You did fine for somebody who's been out the ring so long." A voice I know very well is speaking and I look up. It's Bird. "You fought a good fight," she says, and I look at her and know she means it.

It is the first time my mother ever saw me take so much punishment in a fight. She holds my hand, and as soft and tender as she is, the touch of it hurts, and I wince and draw back.

The pain makes me close my eyes, my hands are swollen, my jaw feels heavy and numb, and I hear Dr. Pacheco: "You've got to get an x-ray."

They let my father in and I hear his voice cutting through: "We been robbed! They robbed you!"

"Well, I believe I won more rounds than he did," I tell him. "But I lost the decision. I never argued with a judge's decision. I won't start now."

"We goin' to the hospital," Angelo says, and I begin to put my clothes on.

A small man in a gray suit comes in and starts packing my trunks, my shoes and gloves, until Bundini screams, "What you doin' with that!"

"They belong to the promotion," the man says politely.

"They stay with The Champ! These his war clothes. They for his grandchildren."

The man looks surprised, then says patiently, "They belong to the promoter. It's in the contract. They're to be auctioned off. After all, people who put up five million dollars have a right to get some souvenirs of their own."

"The promotion got enough!" Bundini snaps. "They made millions. They got The Greatest beat for the first time. They got him bleedin', his jaw busted, his lips cut, his bones bruised. He fought his heart out tonight! He laid his life on the line. He wouldn't stop! He wouldn't quit! He gave his blood! What more you want!"

The man stares at Bundini for a second and examines the faces of everyone around to see who's on his side. Then he backs away, decides to go without what he came for.

When I get to the hospital, the x-rays show nothing broken. Bruised, but nothing broken. I find out later that Frazier goes to the hospital, too, but he lays there for weeks. When I leave the hospital, instead of the long ride home to Cherry Hill, I go back to my hotel. I'll leave tomorrow. I want to sleep all night and half the day. But when morning comes, newsmen gather in the hall, waiting to get in, and I wake up.

I hear Angie tell them, "Leave him alone. Let him rest. He's not takin' any pictures. He's not talkin' to anybody."

I motion for Angelo to come in the room. "Let 'em in," I say.

"They want to come in with TV cameras and lights," Angelo says. "They want it shown all over the world—you lying in bed, jaw swollen, eyes black. Yank Durham won't let them even talk to Frazier."

"That's Frazier," I say. "They know I always talk after a victory. Now I've got to talk after a loss. Let them hear how I lost. Let the people who believe in me see that I'm not crushed, that I've had a defeat just as they have defeats, that I'll get up and come back again, just like other people do."

I don't believe I really lost that fight. But I want people who believe in me see me take defeat. I remember Levinsky's words: "Cash, how it feel to lose?"

"Naked . . . cold," I told him.

"It's not the blows, is it, Cash?"

"Not just the blows."

"It's all them witnesses. Everybody watching you. You sinking . . . and they roar *him* on."

I get up. The dinosaurs will meet again—and again.

IT'S THE FIFTH DAY of training and I'm running on the road in the dark before sunrise, my sparring partners trailing behind me. I'm tired, but I'm pushing myself. My lungs burning, my head ringing, my boots heavier with each step. Ahead of me, in Zaire, Africa, is a fight I've got to win. The kind of fight I've been working for since I came out of exile, a title bout, the World Heavyweight Championship.

Only four months ago, in Madison Square Garden, I fought Frazier for the second time. I won it and evened up my score with him. But before I got in the ring, I'd won it out here on the road. Some people think a Heavyweight Championship fight is decided during the fifteen rounds the two fighters face each other under hot blazing lights, in front of thousands of screaming witnesses, and part of it is. But a prizefight is like a war: the real part is won or lost somewhere far away from witnesses, behind the lines, in the gym and out here on the road long before I dance under those lights. I've got another mile to go.

My heart is about to break through my chest, sweat is pouring off me. I want to stop but I've marked this as the day to test myself, to find out what kind of shape I'm in, how much work I have to do. Whenever I feel I want to stop, I look around and I see George Foreman running, coming up next to me. And I run a little harder. I've got a half-mile more to go and each yard is draining me, I'm running on my reserve tank now, but I know each step I take after I'm exhausted builds up special stamina and it's worth all the other running put together. I need something to push me on, to keep me from stopping, until I get to the farmer's stable up ahead, five miles from where I started. George is helping me. I fix my mind on him and I see him right on my heels. I push harder, he's catching up. It's hard for me to get my breath, I feel like I'm going to faint. He's starting to pull ahead of me. This is the spark I need. I keep pushing harder till I pull even with him. His sweat shirt's soaking wet and I hear him breathing fast and hard. My heart is pounding like it's going to explode, but I drive myself on. I glance over at him and he's throwing himself in the wind, going all out. My legs are heavy and tight with pain but I manage to drive, drive, drive till I pass him, Till he slowly fades away. I've won, but I'm not in shape. I've still got a long way to go. I'm gasping for breath. My throat's dry and I feel like I'm going to throw up. I want to fall on my face but I must stay up, keep walking, keep standing. I'm not there yet but I know I'm winning. I'm winning the fight on the road . . .

If there's any secret about my fights, it's how I prepare myself. During the first six years of my career the idea of being trained a long way from people, away from the crowd of the city, never crossed my mind. I knew I'd build my own gym sooner or later, but I never thought it would be up on a mountain or out in the woods. Most of my fighter's life I couldn't tolerate the kind of training camps old boxers like Sugar Ray Robinson, Jack Dempsey or Gene Tunney had somewhere in the country, in the hills. I had to have the city. I had to see people around. I loved the hotels and city gyms, where I could step outside and mingle with the crowds. I thought I'd go crazy if they took me away from the city.

When I fought Doug Jones, I trained right in Manhattan. When I fought Liston, I was living in the black ghetto in Miami, training in Miami Beach. For Henry Cooper, I was in London, right down at the Piccadilly Hotel. For Mac Foster, I trained near the center of Tokyo; for Mildenberger, it was Frankfort, Germany. For Cleveland Williams, I was at the Americana Hotel in Houston; for Patterson, it was the El Morocco in Las Vegas. For Jergen Blin, I trained in the heart of Zurich, near the big banks.

I'd have my breakfast with the people. After working out, I'd go to a hotel lobby, shake hands, hear what the talk was, sign autographs —even on the day of the fight. I loved the city, I loved city people.

Angelo, Bundini and Blood would warn me: "You're fighting tonight! This is the World Title fight! You shouldn't be out here signing autographs and shaking hands. Millions of dollars are at stake!"

But in the big cities I'd go out in the streets and talk to ordinary people, to those not working, wineheads, drifters. I'd sit on garbage cans, play ball in the alleys with children. It was in my blood to be around people while I was training. I didn't think I could ever go up in the mountains, look at trees, chop wood, run in the morning, sit around till training time, then sit around again and look at nothing but trees and mountains until dinnertime. I said I couldn't spend a week in a training camp like that, I'd rather be in jail.

But now I'm up in the hills training at the best fighter's camp in heavyweight history, and I'm more at home up here with my log cabins than I am in my house in Cherry Hill. What made me change? My first fight with Joe Frazier, the first time in my life as a fighter it was necessary for me to rest and recover and heal. Mark Kram, in *Sports Illustrated*, called the Frazier-Ali fight "one of the most destructive fights between big men" in history. It sent Joe to the hospital for nearly seven weeks, and it took some time before the swelling in my jaw went down and the soreness of my bones went away. I began to see what the old-timers were doing.

I bought land for my camp from a mink rancher named Bernard Pollak. It's on a ridge in the Poconos, thirty miles outside of Reading, Pennsylvania, on Highway 61, overlooking a valley covered with rolling fields, pine forests and fertile farmlands. I took a small cabin for myself, built a kitchen, a gymnasium, two bunkhouses for my crew, four cottages for guests and a stable and corral for horses. I call it "Fighter's Heaven," and I invite fighters from all over the world to come and train up here.

I remembered how Archie Moore had decorated the grounds in his San Diego camp with boulders named after fighters. And when Harvey Moyer, a construction expert, took me to an excavation site and showed me huge rocks left over from the Ice Age, I wanted to use them as symbols of former Champions. Moyer put his whole company to work moving them up the mountain and putting them around the edge of the camp. On each one I painted the name of a great fighter: a huge forty-ton boulder, I named Joe Louis; a big flat one is Rocky Marciano; the prize one, a rare twenty-ton lump of coal, is Jack Johnson; a rugged boulder, I call Jersey Joe Walcott; there's Archie Moore; Sugar Ray Robinson; Kid Gavilan.

Leroy Neiman painted a giant picture of me in boxing trunks on the wall of the gym, reaching from the floor almost to the ceiling. Belinda went down to Winston-Salem and brought back an old Rules of the Kitchen plaque, and my father copied it in huge, red letters, put it on the kitchen wall and signed it "Cassius M. Clay, Sr."

Now I've been hiking up hills, cutting down trees, chopping wood, just like the old fighters, and it's given me more confidence. I like the quiet of the night when at first I couldn't stand it. I still want people around, but I need only a few now. The training has changed, too. I'd strayed from the practice that got me the championship from Liston. I cheated a little here and there and it finally started to catch up with me. I got lazy.

Now, for this fight, I'm following my old plan of training. I sacrifice for my diet, watch my weight, run till I almost pass out. And then there's the sexual discipline. I've learned if a fighter works three or four weeks, say, without sex, without his wife, it's better for him. But most of the time a fighter is on and off while he's working. It's happened to me before many times. If a fighter can go six weeks, he'll pass through certain stages of conditioning. He'll be arrogant, he'll get rowdy. For the first week, it's tough. But if he can keep it up, he'll get to the point where he doesn't miss it. Then he starts getting stronger and in better shape. His timing, his eyesight, his rhythm, everything starts coming in. He's steady getting strength. He gets three or four winds and he runs longer. I believe the more time he spends without sex and keeps living right and training, the better shape he's in. He can go longer than the man who waits until the last ten days to shut off sex. Everything comes natural. The fighter who's gone six weeks, his bones are hard and strong. He's loaded with power. Then Mother Nature takes care of him by relaxing him at night with wet dreams. When that comes, you know you're really in shape. The next day after that you might feel a little weak, but it's a relaxed kind of weakness. The base is still there. Mother Nature just took care of the overflow.

How long does it take to prepare? Most Heavyweight Champions in the past have gone into training four to six months before a fight; some have prepared for a year. George started training four months before Zaire, but I'll only need about two months because I stay active, fighting every two or three months. I never really allow myself to get out of shape. Even when I'm at home, if I go to the grocery store or if I have a mile trip I walk it or run it. I eat the right foods, I don't drink, I don't smoke. I don't eat greasy foods, and since I'm a Muslim I don't eat pork, ham or bacon. I believe my diet makes me faster— and even my worst critics will admit that I am the fastest heavyweight in the history of boxing.

But I've been off four months since my second fight with Frazier, and I've picked up a little weight. I've been eating banana pudding and homemade ice cream, constantly nibbling on cookies and Sara Lee cakes, drinking all kinds of soda. Now I have to be extra conscious of my weight. I have to get the sugar out of my blood. All sugar is outlawed. I eat fresh vegetables, good lamb, veal, squab, fish, good kosher chicken, kosher beef. I drink nothing but distilled water and fruit juices. In the morning I have poached eggs, wheat toast and grapefruit or orange juice. I prefer unsweetened grapefruit because it keeps the fat off my stomach. All this makes me feel good mentally. It makes me know I've got the discipline I need. I'm in control of my own diet.

After I get my appetite under control I want sparring partners whose styles are similar to Foreman's.

I've been studying George ever since Herbert arranged for the match. I've got films of all his fights and I've studied his record, checking out his opponents, how he beat them. I look for a clue, a key that'll give me new insight when we meet up.

Angelo usually knows where to find the right fighters to train with. Whenever I fight, I want sparring partners who can help me work against my opponent's style so that when I get in the ring with him it won't be like the first time. When I fought Canadian George

Chuvalo, I found Cody Jones, a short sparring partner with a slow, slugging style; when I fought fast Floyd Patterson, Jimmy Ellis had the perfect style. For left-handed Carl Mildenberger of Germany, I found a southpaw; for Henry Cooper of London, I found a fighter who had a hard left hook and I learned to duck, to get that left hook in line.

For this fight I'll try to get three sparring partners, maybe Bossman Jones and two Philadelphia heavyweights—young, fast, smart Larry Holmes and Pennsylvania State Champ, big Roy Williams.

Even after we get everybody down to the camp, I'm still not ready to start training. I have to take a week just to get the thought in my mind that a fight's coming up. Going into this match is a business and I've got to take it seriously. Everything I've built for myself and my family depends on it. I have to think about George. I concentrate on him so much that I can feel his presence around me. I shadowbox with him.

Angelo, Bundini, Blood and I get together and make a system. I must have a plan when I'm in training and I try to follow it as close as possible. I have a time to run, time to get back to my cabin, time to eat, to rest, to go to the gymnasium. I must clock myself so I spend a certain time in the boxing ring, certain time jumping rope, certain time at the heavy bag. All these things must be worked out before I get down to business.

Now, after a week, I get up at five o'clock in the morning and run. I'm alone except for my trainers and sparring partners. It's still dark out. The only other living thing I see is a rabbit that races across the track in front of me. For the first three days I run a mile a day to get adjusted to the idea of running, to get the smell of the grass and the mountain air, to get the feel of the road, to build up my legs and ankles, to constantly jar my heart into condition. After that I start adding to it, a mile a day.

This is the key for me. My defense depends on my legs. When I've lost, it was because my legs gave out. I couldn't dance, I couldn't jump out of my opponent's range. I got hit. Now I run myself to exhaustion so that if I have to go to the fifteenth round with George I'll be ready. I'll be tired and winded, but I'll be used to working under that tiredness. I push myself on the road so that no matter how hard my fight is, I won't get as tired in the ring as I do out here running.

It takes time to run and build up my legs, build my stamina, lay off sex, eat the right foods, get up and strain myself. If I run only three miles and I'm not tired, then I figure that day didn't do me any good. I've got to add on another mile or two until I make myself tired. When I'm doing my exercises, I don't start counting till I start paining. And the minute I start paining, I keep pushing under that pain. Then the next day, after I rest, it might take twenty sit-ups instead of ten to give me a cramp. Later it might take thirty. But if I tried to do thirty the first day, I'd break my back. So it's conditioning.

After running I take a long walk and I think about what I have to do for the day. Training is tough and boresome; sometimes it helps to have something to think about and take my mind off the pain.

When I come back off the road around seven-thirty, I take a rest. Running and jogging stirs me up internally and mentally to the point where I've got to cool off. I'm tired but I'm wide awake. I rest but I can't sleep; I'm too jittery, too jumpy. I stay in my cabin for a while, watch television, read the papers or look at magazines. I bring my opponent into focus and I plan for the battle.

Around nine o'clock I have breakfast. I don't eat very much because I don't want too much on my stomach before my afternoon workout. Afterwards I sleep from about eleven till one-thirty. By two o'clock I'm in the gym.

Going in the gym means nothing if you don't have roadwork under your belt, so I never start working here till after I've had at least five days of running. These running periods give me enough energy to work three rounds on the speed bag, enough wind to jump rope four or five rounds, enough stamina to get in the ring and box hard for three or four rounds. I want to look good, even here, because people pour in by the hundreds. Now I see the crowd and I go to the training room, put on my socks, shoes and trunks, get my hands wrapped.

I train like I fight. Some fighters train in four- or five-minute rounds, but I break up my workout into three-minute rounds just like in a fight. I start with three rounds on the heavy bag, three rounds on the speed bag, three rounds on the jump rope. And between each round I take a one-minute rest because this is the way it's going to be in a fight. No shorter, no longer, exactly a minute. This means a lot when I'm working myself into condition. I can be really tired after the fourth or fifth round, but if I'm in shape all I need is one minute to get my wind back, to sit and breathe in and out as slow and as deep as possible. One minute will recuperate me. If I'm not in shape, I could have a five-minute rest after the first round and it would mean nothing. My heart, my pulse, my timing, internally, would be off; I'd be sore. But if I'm in shape, one minute will stimulate me and charge me up enough to come out strong and aggressive the last and fifteenth round.

When I'm in condition, I use that minute for thinking. I check out my opponent, look at him and see how he's feeling. I ask Angelo or Bundini if I'm winning. If they say yes, this makes me more confident; if they say the last round was close, this makes me fight harder the next round and be more cautious. That minute means a lot if you know how to take advantage of it.

I make up my own schedule every day. I've never had a trainer tell me what to do or how to fight. That stuff you see in the movies about a trainer with a cigar in his mouth shouting, "Come on, boy, let's run four miles today, don't stop, keep going," and one of the boys at the gym telling the fighter, "Jab, jab! Slow up and hit him, and next time I want you to throw two uppercuts with the right hand"—that's real amateurish. Just a hustling trainer who's got a fighter he's using like an animal, never mind what happens to him as long as he can make a few dollars with him, and he's so desperate and money-hungry he's trying to talk him into greatness. Champions aren't made in gyms. Champions are made from something they have deep inside them— a desire, a dream, a vision. They have to have last-minute stamina, they have to be a little faster, they have to have the skill and the will. But the will must be stronger than the skill. Many fighters have lost to less skillful opponents who had the will to win, who were determined to keep going.

Fighters are discoverers, they discover something about their opponents or about themselves that others don't know. No one can tell them how to fight and what to do. Maybe a good trainer might say, "I notice that every time you jab this fellow, he drops his right hand. Next time you jab him, notice it, and when you feel you see an opening, drop a hook over that right hand when he drops it. Hit him with a left jab to the body but fake him to the head first. Whenever you fake him one to the head, he throws his hands up to block it. He's open." Or, "You're jumping around too much. You have nine more rounds to go, this is just the first round. Slow down a little, pace yourself, move only if you have to because you'll tire yourself out." These are the things a trainer can do. Get the fighter up in the morning, be in the gym with the clean towels and the shower shoes, be there to put the mouthpiece on, take the headgear and the mouthpiece and the gloves off the second the fighter steps out of the ring because he's hot and frustrated. Bring him stuff to read, tell him where a good movie's playing, see that the proper food is ready on time. And be there at the gym in case the fighter's cut. Hire his sparring partners, pay them, see that they have transportation back and forth from the gym. All of this and more is the job of the trainer. But in the end, the fighter is on his own.

I move to the heavy bag for three rounds. This bag was designed to build up hitting power. I remember what an old trainer told me once. He said, "Always hit that heavy bag like you're trying to knock a hole right through it." The heavy bag weighs between a hundred and fifty and two hundred pounds, and it's about five feet tall. This is the most important part of the workout. The minute I hit it, I feel it knocking weight off me. It jars the weight off, tightens my stomach, trims my waistline, tightens up my muscles. It makes my wrists stronger, my fist, my knuckles. If I don't pound it when it comes back at me, I feel like I'm cheating. It makes me hit it. I push it out and let it come back and hit me in the stomach to toughen up my shoulders and arms.

The first few days I hit it, the bag feels like sandpaper. The heat and the friction will knock the skin off my knuckles, but I'll keep on hitting it. My knuckles will be tender and soon they'll be covered with dead skin. I'll keep working on the bag until this skin gets white and cracks. Then I'll tear it off and let my hands heal for a week before getting back on it. Old-timers like Jim Corbett and John L. Sullivan who fought with bare knuckles used to toughen up their hands like this.

In my last match with Joe Frazier I really needed it. When I fight a man like Joe it's hard on my hands. A lot of times I threw hard punches at his chin, and by the time the punch got there he moved a certain way and my hand struck him in the head. My knuckles came through the gloves pretty easy and I could feel the print of his skull. Joe takes a lot of punishment, and after knocking up against his hard head for nine or ten rounds my hands started to get sore. If I hadn't conditioned them on the heavy bag, I wouldn't have been able to hit hard enough to keep him off me.

After the heavy bag, I go right to the speed bag. This is the small bag that instantly snaps right back at me. The minute I hit it, it's right back. I hit it twice with each hand. Two shots with the left, two shots with the right. As fast as I can, two shots with the left, two shots with the right, again and again. It sharpens up my eyes, watching my hands go back and forth, and it builds up my arms. This is especially important for the Foreman fight. George throws bone-crushing punches, and my arms have got to be strong enough to withstand them for the whole fight so I can keep my guard up. They can't get tired and drop. If they do I'll be in trouble.

Next I take a few rounds jumping rope. This is good for my leg muscles, good for my wrists, constantly flipping that rope. It's good for my timing, and the jumping up and down builds up my heart. I start to get tired but I know I've got to do this so I won't be tired in the fight. So I won't be embarrassed and get beat.

I save my sparring for last, instead of doing it first like most prizefighters. I want to go in the ring tired. If I went in right away, I'd have all my stamina, my resistance wouldn't be low and I wouldn't be under any pressure. I want to be ready in case George lasts more than ten rounds. If he does, I may have to beat him on points and I'll need extra stamina to win.

I always make sure that my sparring partners are fresh. I make sure they do nothing but rest up and wait for me. We go at it strong and I'm twice as tired as they are. This forces me to liven up when they put the pressure on. It forces me to get them off of me. It forces me to dance and stay on my toes, to jab and get in, jab to the body and get out, hook to the head, tire them out fast. I'm tired mentally, too. This makes me think and react under pressure. It's equivalent to going into the tenth, eleventh, twelfth or thirteenth round of a fight. This way, when I beat my sparring partner to the punch after he comes in stronger, I have a good feeling because this man is fresh. I know that even after I've done all my other training and I'm tired, I can still go with this man, who is much fresher and has more energy than I have. I can still get to him, I can still take him.

In the ring with a sparring partner, I usually concentrate on defense. Right now I'm getting ready for George. I block punches. Slip away from him. Lay on the ropes. Let my man tire himself out. I only open up at the very end of my session. I know I can beat my sparring partner. I hired him so I can let him try to beat me while I figure out his style. And I do figure it out.

I'm tired and groggy, but I keep driving myself. My arms and legs are sore from working out and absorbing punches, but I know this is crucial. I look at my sparring partner and I see George's face. Now my eyes suddenly seem to clear up. I forget how tired I am. I can see blows coming at me before they even leave my sparring partner's chest. My left and my right are on target. I can hook, uppercut. I can do anything I want to do. My muscles do anything I tell them.

After the workout I take a shower, get a massage and take it easy until around five o'clock, when I have dinner. Then I sit around and talk, or read, or look at a movie until ten or eleven o'clock, when I go to bed.

By the time the fight is ten days away, I'll be through with most of my physical training. Now I concentrate on my mental conditioning. If my body isn't ready by then, it'll be too late. I'll follow my plans up until three days before the fight and then I'll start to loosen up and rest. Then I'll have to save up my energy so I'll be at my strongest when the bell rings. I want my mind and body working together. I'll be ready for anything George has to dish out. And I know what I throw will be too much for him to handle. That's the way a fighter prepares.

THE CONTRACT

After my victory over Joe Frazier, I feel the kind of peace that comes when a fighter has finally evened up an old score. I've wiped out the bad taste of both the Norton and Frazier defeats, and for the first time in my life I'm thinking about retirement, about a different kind of life with my family and children, away from camps, gyms, rings and press conferences.

I considered myself lucky to get Frazier in the ring. Herbert had held off signing for the second Frazier fight until Foreman made up his mind about accepting a four-million-five-hundred-thousand-dollar offer to fight me. Even when Herbert sent Atkins out to Oakland, California, to persuade Foreman to accept what would have then been the highest purse in boxing history, Foreman has refused to sign with any promoter. And Herbert only works with a promoter after the fight is signed. Madison Square Garden, Jerry Perenchio and United Artists are among several promoters offering millions for the Super Fight, but it will be a newcomer who comes in with the best offer.

I'm sitting on a pile of logs outside my mountainside gym in Deer Lake, Pennsylvania, and looking down at the cars rolling by on Highway 62, when I see a long black Cadillac turn into the little road that winds up the mountain to my camp.

Kilroy, my camp aide, is looking through his binoculars. "It's Don King," he says.

In a few minutes the Cadillac swings up, and out step two young fighters and King, dressed like he's on his way to an opera, with a brown tuxedo, ruffled shirt and bow tie. King is taller than I am, with a full, round stomach and foot-high hair that stands straight up on his head. He's a showman promoter and he talks like he's reading from a book.

He leads his two fighters, Jeff Merritt and Earnie Shavers, to the edge of the cliff overlooking the valley below and the Blue Ridge Mountains across the way. "My God!" he says. "Such a glorious site for a fighter to rest and heal, with the sweet balm of nature, those cruel blows which fate and Frazier deal out. After such a great victory in Madison Square, a great Champion deserves something to delight the eyes and rest the soul. Majestic mountains, evergreen trees, and such spaciousness to exalt your triumph!"

Sister Lana, my cook, recognizes him and yells, "We've got liver and onions, cabbage and beet soup! You want a plate?"

King backs away from the cliff. "It would delight me no end, dear, to taste food cooked by your sweet and tender hands, but please, go easy on the onions. Ali, now I need your attention for a while."

I am listening. I've known Don since the days when he was a gambler in Cleveland. He had left Kent State College to make a living in night clubs and the numbers. I hadn't seen him since he served four years in jail after a man he had a fistfight with died. He has astonished old hands in fight circles by picking up two poorly guided heavyweights —Jeff Merritt and Earnie Shavers—and pushing them both into the top ten in the world listings in less than six months. Now he's promoting the World Heavyweight Title fight between George Foreman and Ken Norton in Venezuela. With the help of my manager Herbert Muhammad, he became the first black to break into the tight white circle of major fight promoters.

"I was inspired by you," he tells me. "It came when I first saw your dramatic demonstration of marketable skills when I was Number 4819 in Cell 12, Row 12. They let us see your first 'Fight of the Century' against Frazier in '71, and it was then that I decided not to return to gambling, but to go into show business."

"Why'd you pick boxing?" Kilroy wants to know.

"My dear man, is there a difference?"

"You want to bring 'Candy' and Earnie here to train with me?" I ask.

"That's only part of what I want," he tells me, moving closer. "The other part is more important. With your manager as my guide, I come to bring you a shot at what Herbert knows has been unjustly denied you for two long years: a fight for the World Heavyweight Championship. I can sign George."

"Nobody can deliver George," Blood says. King wants our conversation to be private, but at the mention of George Foreman the camp comes alive, everybody crowding around.

"What makes you think that?" Booker Johnson, one of my camp assistants and formerly a manager himself, asks. "Because you black? George don't give a damn about black, blue, brown or white. All he wants is to keep the title, where the green is."

"Is that all you got to say?" I ask King.

I hide the feeling of hope that starts up in me. Am I finally to have a title fight before I retire?

"George has got to come in," King is saying. The biggest cash ever paid in the history of performers? Julius Caesar never paid his best gladiators half that much. Jesse James never performed for that much. No actor, dancer or singer in the history of the planet Earth ever got that much for a single performance."

"It's a trick," Blood says. "Nobody in his right mind would pay ten million dollars for a fight!"

"If you don't believe me, you can check it out with Herbert. He masterminded the whole play," King says.

Herbert had already called me from Chicago and told me he had a ten-million-dollar certified check from Jerry Perenchio for the Foreman fight and that Madison Square Garden was almost as good, but no one had signed George yet.

"I've got the proposal George has got to take," King says. "Now I must tell you what Brutus said to Cassius of Rome:

> 'There is a tide in the affairs of men,
> Which taken at the flood, leads on to fortunes;
> Omitted, all the voyage of their life
> Is bound in shallows and in miseries.' "

"Why you say that?" Blood asks.

"When I deliver Foreman, Ali must take full advantage of it, for it may be his last chance at a title fight. No other promoter can do it."

• • •

As I watch Don drive down the mountain, I wonder if he realizes that George doesn't want this fight. He's already turned down three offers. Like most Heavyweight Champions, he'd like to avoid any dangerous opponents until he's milked the title dry. George hasn't even defended it in his own country yet. He wants to wait until I get older and slower.

When King gets to Chicago, Herbert explains: "Muhammad signing first means nothing. Muhammad is the challenger. Naturally he's willing to fight The Champion. Go get George to sign the contract and you automatically got me. We offered a fight to George before we fought Frazier.

"I know that," King says. "One of George's aides wanted two hundred fifty thousand dollars under the table and a sixty-forty split on the nine million. That killed the deal. George has lost confidence in most of those around him, including Sadler, he tells me."

It's then that Herbert decides to call George direct and put the two of us together. "The only commitment that might count is one from George," Herbert tells King. He had sensed that Sadler was losing control over George long before the split came.

On February 10 I fly into Chicago, where Herbert has planned to set up a conference call from his house to George. Finally it comes through and George is on the phone. It's the first time I've ever sat with Herbert while he's maneuvering for a fight, and it feels strange.

"George says he's ready to take you on," Herbert whispers. "Challenge him!"

I grab the phone: "George, you think you got the nerve to get in the ring with me?"

"Anytime, anywhere, for the money," he snaps back.

"They're talking about ten million dollars. Let's make it history," I say. "Don King's coming out there with the contract. I've looked it over and it's all right. Let's get it on! If you're not scared."

"Scared of you? I only pray that I don't kill you!" he growls.

I put down the phone and tell Herbert, "He sounds shaky."

Herbert sends King out to see George, but weeks pass before he comes to my camp to report. "George wouldn't show up when I was supposed to meet him, so I had to track him down in a parking lot," he explains. "I told him I was sure he'd win. I told him he's eight years younger than you, punches harder, and can't lose. He had to feel assured that he's going to win or I couldn't have gotten him to sign for any price."

"What else?"

"I'll tell you frankly what I told him. I said, 'George, Ali is on his last legs right now. It would be better for you to knock him off and get credit than to watch someone else do it.' "

"Don't believe it, Ali," Blood interrupts him. "He'll just go back and tell George's camp the same thing."

"You want George to win?" someone asks.

King raises his eyes to heaven. "May the best man win. I confess, when I'm in Ali's camp, I want Ali to win. When I go over to George's camp, I want him to win. I'm trying to promote both fighters. How can I do otherwise?"

He wipes his forehead. "The fight game is the most thankless in the world. I bring in ten million dollars, and the fighters are suspicious. Make one false move and Herbert won't trust me. Stumble again, and George, who says he only trusts God, and suspects Him most of the time, will cancel out.

"All the other promoters are trying to sabotage this thing, and George is even more skeptical of me because I'm black. He thinks I'm fronting for the white boys. But I'm my own man. Henry Schwartz and Barry Bernstein realize that if they are going to try to stage big-money fights between black fighters, they have to have a black man in a real position of responsibility at Video Techniques. The real director of these fights is Herbert—only he never likes the limelight. But he calls all the shots. This is a new day."

"Awright, awright. Get down to business," Booker interrupts.

"I know that George is in financial trouble," King continues. "His divorce is going to cost him nearly a million when it's all over. Besides that, he's being sued by Barbra Streisand's manager, who's claiming he's got a piece of George.

"I told George that so many people are suing him, that even if his lawyer, Sargent Shriver, got elected President, all the Kennedys combined couldn't save him from bankruptcy. I made him understand that his only chance is to fight you."

"Is that what got it?" I ask.

"No," King says. "Not that."

"What got it?"

"I told him this is the biggest event in the history of sports. The Italian government wants to stage it in the old Colosseum in Rome where the gladiators fought.

"Then I told him we had a possibility of having it in Zaire, in the heart of Africa. In Zaire . . . two black champions returning to their ancestral homeland for the Heavyweight Title fight.

"We've got offers to do it in New York. United Artists is offering ten million to do it. The Cowboys want it in the Dallas Stadium. Frank Sinatra wants to sponsor it.

"I told George, wherever you fight, over a billion people will watch it. They will be the judge of who is 'The Greatest.' "

"I know that got him!" Bundini says.

"No! George was stubborn. He insisted he should be paid more than Ali. 'When I fought Joe Frazier,' he says, 'he was paid like a champion and I was paid like a challenger. Why should Ali get fifty percent? It belittles The Champion when a challenger gets equal pay.'

"I told him, 'Herbert won't let Ali get in the ring with you for less money. He knows Ali is the drawing card and he knows you can't make a million dollars fighting someone else, let alone five million.'

"That started to grab him." King smiles, remembering it. "We had walked almost all the way back to his hotel, and he still hadn't signed. I knew that this was my last chance and time was running out. So I got right down to the nitty-gritty.

"I said, 'George, you've modeled yourself after Sonny Liston, haven't you?'

" 'Well, yes,' he told me. 'I have. I'm built like Liston, but bigger.'

" 'Well, Muhammad stopped Liston twice . . .'

" 'That was when Liston was old,' George says. 'He don't deserve no credit for that. If Liston had been my age . . .'

I interrupted him. " 'George, you're the young Liston. You can show the world what Liston would have done to Ali in his prime. You can rewrite history.'

"George looked thoughtful. He loved Liston. He was impressed by Liston's brute force and power, and he has captured most of it and more.

" 'Besides,' I told him. 'Until you beat Muhammad Ali, the world will never recognize you as The Champion. As long as he's alive and fighting and you don't show the world who's the best, they'll look at Ali as the master.'

"I dropped that bomb on him and George was grim. 'All right,' he said. 'What's the deal? Tell the truth. If I find a single lie, I'm backing out.'

Sadler has turned the negotiations over to Herbert because he knows Herbert will get the best deal for both fighters.

"I told him, 'I'm committed to pay one hundred thousand dollars by February 15 to each fighter and another hundred thousand in ten days. Then Herbert wants an irrevocable letter of credit in his bank and your bank for two million, three hundred thousand at least ninety days before the fight. If Zaire comes through, I'll have the whole ten million up in thirty days. If any payment date is missed, you and Ali keep all previous money, including the two and a half million as 'liquidated damages,' and you're no longer obligated to fight. Then, to protect you, if Norton somehow beats you in Venezuela, the contract calls for you and Ali to fight for a million and a half each.'

"George picked up the contract and started reading. 'I've never done anything like this on my own before,' he said. 'Usually, Sadler or my lawyer or somebody advises me. But I'm going on your word that everything will go down like you say. Where's Ali's signature?'

" 'You The Champ,' I tell him. 'The challenger signs after the Champ.'

"George hesitated a long time, then signed.

" 'What took you so long?' I asked him.

" 'I thought you were joking. I wasn't sure,' he said.

" 'My way of joking is to tell the truth,' I answered him. 'That's the funniest joke in the world.' "

King laughs and shows me the contract which I know already has Herbert's approval. But for publicity purposes, they want my signature, too. I sign.

"I hope this sticks," I say.

King does make it stick, but I come close to unsticking it.

Looking back on the scramble to firm up the fight and all of Herbert's sifting through of bids from promoters in at least fourteen countries in Europe, Asia and Africa, one of the shakiest moments came not because of Foreman but because of me.

I saw a chance to fight Quarry before taking on Foreman. Fighting Quarry appealed to me because he was flying up and down the country crying that black fighters were "boycotting" him.

"I'd like to shut Quarry up once and for all!" I said when I met with Arum and Brenner in Herbert's New York apartment. King, who was solidly opposed to the Quarry fight, had stashed himself away in the bedroom so he could come out at the right time to counterattack.

"Look, the Foreman fight will never come off," Arum said. "The investors are backing out already. Go ahead and take this Quarry fight. It's a sure thing."

"Why go with Don King?" Brenner insisted. "Don't you know King is a gangster? A killer? We don't want this gangster in the business."

I picked up the pen to sign, but Bundini, who's been with me all morning, broke out in tears: "Champ, don't do it. Think of all the people in Africa you'd be letting down. Far as King being a gangster, it was gangsters that built Madison Square!"

Later I found out that an intermediate fight with Quarry would make the backers in Zaire pull out because they would be afraid I might get cut or butted by Quarry and force a cancellation of the title date.

It was Herbert who decided the issue by abruptly letting me know he was opposed to my signing.

I let Quarry go. He would keep on crying about being boycotted until he got a fight with Joe Frazier. They had to stop the fight to save his life.

A few weeks later I missed what I will always believe was an opportunity to inspire a fighter to win the World Heavyweight Championship from Foreman. I missed it by minutes.

It was in Caracas. I was there to see the title fight between George and Ken Norton. For the first time Herbert and I met Mandungu Bula, now foreign minister of Zaire, then assigned by President Mobutu Sese Seko to work out the details for the Zaire title fight. He and his assistant, Tshimpumpu Tshimpumpu, wanted to know if we were satisfied with the contract.

"There is one clause I don't like, and I want out," Herbert explained to Bula. "It's the one that obligates us to fight Foreman for a million and a half if he should lose to Norton. If Foreman loses tonight, there's no way we want to fight him. We want to meet the man with the title—whoever he is."

"Zaire is mainly interested in bringing Muhammad Ali to Africa for a title fight," Bula agreed. "We are only interested in Ali fighting whoever has the title."

Herbert's eyes lit up. "Suppose we change this to say that the winner of this fight here in Caracas—who will be the Heavyweight Champion—will take on Muhammad Ali in Zaire for the five million dollars?"

Bula frowned over the contract awhile, then said, "All right. We'll change it, and initial it right now."

It was an hour before the fight, and I thought it only fair to get the news to Ken Norton that he was guaranteed five million for his next fight if he won from Foreman.

Norton was the underdog, and I was supporting him. I grabbed a cab to his hotel and rushed up to Norton's room with the news. But it was too late. Norton had just left for the stadium.

I got to the fight in time to see a sluggish, uninspired Norton take a devastating battering from Foreman.

Hours after the fight, Norton heard what had been at stake: enough for him to retire a millionaire after that one fight. He broke down and cried.

I still think if he had known earlier, I would have fought Norton —not Foreman—in Zaire.

THE BOSSMAN COMES

Herbert had flown into Kinshasa weeks earlier with his wife and daughter, Antonia and Safiyyah, to meet with key Zaire officials and help the government plan to make the first World Heavyweight Title fight in Africa a historic event. He brought back an accurate picture of weather conditions, food and service facilities and had made last-minute alterations in the Letter of Credit, which guaranteed my purse.

"Zaire's the first country in history to sponsor a World Heavyweight Title fight," Herbert said. "If it comes off, other countries will follow."

After Zaire, Herbert will accept similar fights supported by the governments of Malaysia and the Philippines, with at least six other countries making offers.

The working-out of the twelve-million-dollar Letter of Credit to cover the purse of both George and myself, as well as other costs, had been the most crucial part of the agreement, as it had to be transferred through three banks on two continents before reaching my bank in Chicago, an agreement which almost collapsed several times.

Herbert had put through special improvements and safeguards for both George and myself. Both our camps had been concerned over the temperature, inasmuch as a part of Zaire is on the equator, but Herbert reported back that in the fall the weather was no worse than Houston or St. Louis in the summer.

He found that processing the fight had been so new to Zaire that when President Mobutu gave orders to Barclay's branch in Kinshasa to transfer the twelve million dollars, the bank manager was sure there was some mistake. He took off for the rest of the day, went swimming, almost missing Herbert's deadline for the transfer.

President Mobutu was furious and sent soldiers to the pool, arrested and jailed the bank manager, and only when the bank president of Barclay's in London flew down to Kinshasa to make amends did Mobutu agree to let the famous old English bank stay in Zaire.

"But the important thing," Herbert said when he returned, "the people are kind, courteous and highly intelligent. They've opened up their homes and hearts to put over the show, and most of all, they all know about you and support you. Just be in good condition when you get there."

I am in the last week of training in America. We will fly to Kinshasa on September 10, and the fight is now set for September 24. I wanted to go to Africa much earlier to get used to the climate, the people, the gym, the roads, the food, to get as comfortable and at ease as I am up here in the Pennsylvania mountains. I want to be almost ready to fight when I get off the plane.

Almost every afternoon after training I review George Foreman fight movies: his Olympic fight with the Russian, his tough, ten-round struggle with Spain's Jose Peralta, his slaughter of Joe "King" Roman, his murder of Joe Frazier, his destruction of Ken Norton. Now I've learned all I can from watching him on film and I'll learn more from a sparring partner coming fresh from George's camp.

Bossman Jones has sparred with George for weeks; he lives with him, buddies with him, studies him, and I expect him to show up any minute.

"Blood's bringing him back from the airport," Bundini says. "They ought to be here now."

I plan to take three sparring partners to Zaire: Larry Holmes, twenty-one years old, a tall and crafty boxer with sharp punches; Holmes has twelve straight knockouts on his record, no losses. Roy

Williams, Pennsylvania State Champion, an inch taller than me, a tough, rugged fighter with sledge-hammer fists. And maybe Bossman Jones, if he's right.

This afternoon the crowd in the gym are mostly people from around Pottsville, farmers and students who know they are seeing me off for the last time. The leader of a troop of Boy Scouts from Harrisburg puts a red scarf around my neck and says, "Bring back the championship for Harrisburg." I promise to bring it back. And a grizzled old contractor says, "Do it and we'll carve your name in them mountains like they did Jefferson and Washington at Mt. Rushmore."

Someone is shouting, "He's here! Bossman! He's here!"

Bundini spots him. "Got to talk right away, Bossman."

Only those who work close with me, like Kilroy, C.B., Booker, Harold, Angie, are allowed in. They hustle Bossman into the dressing room and close the door as though he's a CIA agent. They prop him up on the training table.

"All right, Bossman. We been waiting," Bundini says. "You the last sparring partner to work with George. Ali can give you a thousand-dollar-a-week job throughout the fight, plus all the food you can eat, and a round-trip ticket back to California. Now, let's have it."

I'm pulling off my sweat shirt and Sarria is wiping me down with a towel. Bossman is cool. "Where is the good bunk I'm supposed to have? And I need a car to get around up in these mountains." Bossman knows he's in a good bargaining position. He overlooks nothing.

"It's taken care of," Kilroy answers. "You know that's all taken care of."

Bundini is impatient. "Now, go ahead. You know what we want. You slept, ate, fought with George for six weeks. Tell us about him firsthand."

Bossman rubs his heavy black eyebrows and strokes the goatee that gives him a devilish look. He speaks quietly. "Y'all want me to tell you the truth?"

"Naturally," Bundini says.

"Tell us, Bossman," the others begin to prod him.

I raise my hand. "Let him alone. Let Bossman take his time. He's just not sure where to start."

"What about Foreman?" Blood asks.

Bossman scratches a bald spot on the top of his head. "You know, I been boxing fifteen years. A hundred fights. I'm a light-heavy, but I handle the heavies. They all call me in for a big fight. Quarry did. Foreman did. Patterson, Liston . . . just like George did."

"We don't want your life history," Bundini says. "Tell us what we asked you."

"Is Foreman training hard?" Booker asks.

"He trains every day," Bossman says. "He don't like to publicize it, but not a day goes by that he don't dig in, getting ready for Ali."

"How much roadwork does he do? Does he do as much as Ali?"

Bossman shrugs. His shoulders are so heavy they make him look hunchbacked. He crosses his thin legs, and like a professor before a classroom he's pleased that his students are giving him so much attention. "George's roadwork is different from Ali's," he says. "I've run alongside both. Ali, he runs on the road down the valley. George runs up the mountains."

"What you mean, Bossman?" Bundini growls. "Ain't nobody but goats run up mountains."

"George Foreman does." Bossman stands his ground. "He runs up hills and mountains. I don't know how he does it. I never seen nobody like George."

"Mountains this steep?" Bundini asks.

"Steeper," Bossman says. "He knows he's never had to go fifteen rounds before, and he knows Ali could do it. So he's getting in condition to go fifteen rounds."

"How does he handle his sparring partners in the gym?" Angelo asks. "Does he bang 'em around?"

"Only now and then. Most times he trains like Ali, on defense, strict defense."

"But he's a slugger, not a boxer," Angelo says. "He doesn't box like Ali. Ali's the best boxer of all times."

Bossman nods his head. "That's what I tell everybody, too, but Ali can't count on George not boxing. George gives the impression that he's a big dumb brute, but George can box. He's never had to box because he tags you and then he goes for the quick kill. He don't give you no chance to get your breath."

"He's a dirty fighter," Angelo says. "I saw how he hit King Roman almost on the floor. He'll hit you when you're down."

"George plays to win. You say it's foul, but George walks home with the money. The people accept George as a brute, and they come to see him knock somebody out. George got the guns to do it. I see guys, fighters who could stun you, who could knock you out, but George is the first one I been in the ring with I know can kill you. He may never kill nobody, and I hope he never does, but he's got the power to kill, and he knows it."

"Look," Bundini interrupts him. "We didn't pay you to come here and build up George. George got weaknesses. You bound to have found some weaknesses in all the time you trained with him. What about his women? A big strong stud like that."

Bossman looks far away and shakes his head. "I ain't seen nothin' like it."

"Ahhhhhhhh, ha!" Bundini grins. "Tell us like it is."

"He can go months without a woman," Bossman says.

"You lying no-good bastard!" Bundini shouts.

Bossman looks sad. "I never seen it in a prizefighter, but George he won't touch a woman, I do believe he's got some sissy in him, won't even talk to a woman when he's training."

"What does he talk about?" Blood asks.

"Money is all," Bossman replies. "All he talks about is making even more money when he takes over Ali's place in the eyes of the people—"

"Look here, Bossman," Blood says. "We want to know where your loyalty is. We can't have no double agents in Muhammad's camp. All your talk is how great George is."

"You asked me to speak the truth," Bossman answers.

"Then tell the truth," Blood cuts back. "If George and Muhammad fight tomorrow, who would win?"

The room is still. All eyes are on Bossman. He takes his time . . .

"Go ahead before we run you out of here," Bundini warns.

"You know I trained with Muhammad, and I trained with George. I took punches from both. Ali hits hard. But George hits harder. Muhammad's left jab used to be the sharpest thing next to a razor blade, quicker than a snake's tongue, but his left ain't what it once was. It's good, but . . ."

"You say that in front of Muhammad?" Kilroy is amazed. "You say that?"

My trainers rise up, but Bossman will not back down. "Ali's jab ain't what it used to be. Muhammad's getting old. Let's face it, and I'll tell you why . . ."

I raise my hand as they move to push him out of the room. "Let him talk."

"Muhammad is the best boxer alive," Bossman says. "I believe it. But in order to beat George, he's got to get his left jab back. In order to get his left jab back, he's got to leave women alone. He can't train with sex on his mind."

Bundini, on the verge of throwing Bossman out of the room, does an about-face and takes off his cap in reverence. "Shorty must have sent you, brother, with those divine words of wisdom."

"Against George, Ali can't have sex up until the last week of the fight and expect to get back all the strength he lost in two months' time. If he has sex down to the last week, he'll never get that snap back in his jabs."

Bundini is beaming.

"Let's face it," Bossman goes on. "Every time a fighter has sex when he's training, that's a setback. He has to start all over. He can say to himself, 'Well, I'm gonna stop next week,' but you can't get back what you lost. George is young. He ain't interested in the glamorous life, or having ten women a night. He don't want to do nothing but wipe out Muhammad."

"Does he have any secret punches? Does he have any punches that he's working on?" someone asks.

"George has one punch which ain't no secret," Bossman says. "He calls it the 'anywhere' punch, because anywhere it hits you, it breaks something inside you, a muscle, a bone, a shoulder, a finger, a rib. He starts it out like this." Bossman draws back to imitate George. "He starts out like it's going to be a hook, but ends up like a slider. He ain't aiming nowhere, just anywhere. It's his best punch." Bossman sits back down.

My dressing room is quiet. I have my clothes on, and I sit down beside Bossman on the table. "Bossman, all you say sounds nice for people who never been in the ring, but let's talk fighter to fighter. Fighters know what to talk about."

Bossman nods.

"Take your size arms. Stretch 'em out. With your reach, do you sometimes get to him?"

Bossman looks uncomfortable.

"Look up. He's askin' you a question," Blood says.

Bossman looks uneasy; he mutters in a low voice for my ears only. "The sparring partners know better than to hit him. Once you hit him, he'll tear your head off. He don't pay enough for that. No, I never hit him." Bossman looks down at the floor.

"But if you wanted to, could you reach him?" I ask.

Bossman will not answer directly. "George likes to get you on the ropes, and go to work on you. Ali, you can't lay on the ropes the way you do and expect to beat this man. You can't gamble on ropes. You got to outbox him, move, dance, move, the way you do when you're at your best. The thing you got in your favor at your age is you know how to pace yourself. George may not know how to do that, but he knows how to corner a man on the ropes. He can lift you up off your feet with one punch. If you lay on the ropes, and rest, he's gonna break your ribs. He'll hit you on your way down or on your way up. By the time the referee gets there, you might be beat to death. His most killing punch is a kidney punch. That's the only part of your body you can't tighten up. You do a thousand and one sit-ups but you can't do nothing about that kidney.

"George wants to win this fight bad. He wants to be accepted by the world as the real Heavyweight Champion. It's killing him. It's eating him up to have the title, and have them still call Muhammad Ali the People's Champion."

The room is quiet again. We know Bossman is speaking what he believes.

"I hear all of what you said," Bundini says. "I see you been brainwashed. I agree with Blood, I want to know where your loyalty is. We can't have no double agent in Muhammad's camp."

"You ask me to speak the truth," Bossman says quietly.

"Then tell the truth now. If George and Muhammad were to fight tomorrow, who would you pick to win? Who'd you bet on?"

Bossman is cornered, and he knows it.

I first met Bossman in Atlanta, where he was a sparring partner for Jerry Quarry. Quarry used him because he could imitate my style. They call Bossman "The Chameleon." And though he's undersized for a heavy, he's always been rated in the top ten light-heavies. I heard that Quarry asked him the same kind of question, when I was about to fight Quarry in Atlanta and when he told Quarry to his face, "Muhammad would win," Jerry fired him.

"Who you betting on right now?" Blood is demanding.

Bossman takes a deep breath, looks at the unfriendly faces around him and says quietly, "I bet on George."

"Goddamn!" Bundini shouts. "Give this nigger his plane ticket back home. We don't need this double agent."

They begin to shout and push Bossman toward the door.

I hold up my hand. "Wait a minute! Leave him alone! Angelo, get Bossman a ticket to Africa. I need him."

Heavyweights watch each other more than any class of fighter. I've heard some fighters say they want to know nothing about their opponent, won't read the papers or look at his movies. I've heard Rocky Marciano was like that, Jack Sharkey, Joey Maxim. But I like to judge and analyze an opponent. The more facts I know about him, the more comfortable I am. Not just simple facts, his punches or his ring life, but all about him. Even his political and domestic life, how he treats his wife. I put it together. I need to get the "feel" of him.

Never forget the man you're about to fight, he threatens your status, your job, your future, your past, your image. We'll have to fight, not in some dark hidden alley, but before the glare of TV, radio, the press, before the eyes of people all over the world, of everyone you've ever known or ever expect to meet, before those who haven't even been born who will judge how you fought a generation from now when they run the movies over. And those who don't see it or read about it will be told about it.

By the third day in Zaire, I've already set up a system to watch George, and I know he has one to watch me. My dressing room is directly across the street from the gym where we both train, a modern little one-story apartment in Nsele.

When I finish my workout, shadowboxing, rope-jumping and sparring, I wave to the swarms of Zairians and they follow me to my apartment until the guards block the way. Then I stretch out on the training table for Sarria to work over my muscles and to go through the calisthenics.

By then, George, whose own spies have been watching me train, will be notified that all's clear, and he'll march in to the sound of Aretha Franklin singing "Precious Lord."

I know the minute he enters because the loudspeakers, which have been filling the air with xylophones and drumbeats, suddenly change to George's favorite training records: gospel rock. Aretha Franklin may be the only thing George and I have in common.

He's in the gym, loosening up to the music. Bundini pulls back the drapes so he can see better across the street.

"What's he look like?" I say as Sarria rubs my muscles.

"He's still flabby, fat like he's pregnant. I wish the fight was tonight. You'd kill him."

"Who's his sparring partners?" I ask.

"He's got *six* sparring partners," Bingham, my photographer, announces. He, too, is looking through the drapes. "They're standing outside the ring, headgear and gloves on, waiting to go up, one by one . . . six of 'em."

"Give me those lenses." I reach for Bingham's telescopic lens and peer through it.

"Six sparring partners," says Bundini. "And we only got three."

I get the lens in focus and check out the sparring partners. All of them have, at one time or another, worked for me. "He's only got three," I say. "The other three are clowns. Elmo Henderson's forty-five years old, strictly a clown. Stan Ward keeps George laughing, and Bill McMurray can't punch. They use Terry Lee to imitate my style, but they never hit him. Frank Steele is fair. Henry Clark's the only one he really trains with.

I dismiss the six, but I watch George go through five sparring partners and I'm surprised. The Champion is faster on his feet than I thought.

"Good God!" Bundini cries after a while. "How long is them rounds?"

"His rounds're more than three minutes," Blood says. "Dick Sadler makes him go sometimes four-minute rounds with only half a minute rest. They train to build up his stamina. They ain't planning for him to get tired."

Angelo says, "But they ain't seen nobody like Muhammad."

I focus the lens on George's face. He's thundering into the big bag, sweat pouring from his head, but he keeps his back to me as though he suspects we may be watching.

In a few days I give up this post and depend more on reports my trainers and handlers bring back. We both have an open-door policy, which allows anyone to come in and watch. Some fighters train in secret, door guarded. Frazier does that a lot. No one enters without credentials. But here in Zaire the crews of both fighters are all together in hotels and gyms, and there will be no secrets when the bell rings for the clash.

ARCHIE, AM I TOO OLD?

The countdown of days until the fight is eight—eight more days—and now I put my sparring partners on notice to go all out. I tell Blood and Bundini to spur them on.

"I hear you talkin'!" Bundini shouts, and drives his sparring partners like a slave master:

"Lay it on him! Lay it on him, Holmes! Don't back off!"

"Come on, Bossman, mix it up! Mix it up! Earn your money!"

The crowds are delighted. The hall is packed every day as though we're putting on a real fight.

On this day I have three rounds of shadowboxing, five rounds on the speed bag, four skipping rope, three on the heavy bag. After that I go in the ring with my sparring partners, feeling the kind of fatigue I know will come in a real fight, but I drive myself through nine hot three-minute rounds of boxing. I'm ready.

Only eight days to go, and I'm nearing my peak. I remember lying down on the bed to rest and looking up at the picture of my four children on the wall. I wanted to bring them to Africa, but the baby is only one year old, and I didn't want them to have so many immunization shots. Besides, if they were here I would be huggin' and kissin' them; I'd have them in the bed with me right now. I need to get myself in the mood to face George. A vicious mood. It's hard to do that, huggin' and kissin' children all day.

"Ali! Ali!" I hear someone banging against my bedroom door.

"It's open!" I shout, and Howard Bingham breaks in.

"The fight's off!" Bingham, who ordinarily stutters, is speaking clear and straight. "The fight's off! It's over!"

I just look at him.

"Did you hear about George? He's got a big cut over his eye!" Lowell Riley, Herbert's photographer, comes in. His finger points to his right eye. "I saw the blood gushing out!"

I feel paralyzed.

"His sparring partner cut it," Bingham says. "The college boy, young Bill McMurray."

I roll out of bed and look them in the eye to see if they're acting. They're not. Now that I look back on it, I remember that for a split second I was pleased. George had been built up as an invincible monster; this shows he's human—like me. I'm thinking that nothing like that had ever happened to him in all his life. Then the full meaning of it hits me. "Oh, no!"

"Ali! The fight's off!" a Tunisian reporter rushes in.

Other reporters are coming down the hall. I tell Bingham to slam the door. I need time to think.

"Bill McMurray caught him with an elbow," Riley explains. "George was bobbing and weaving. McMurray was covering up and his elbow caught George's eye."

In a few seconds we hear that George has a cut over his right eye a quarter of an inch deep; that Dr. Peter Hacker, his private doctor, is saying it will take six weeks to three months for the cut to heal; that Dick Sadler has refused to allow the doctors to stitch George's eye, but has fixed it himself, sealing it with a "Sadler Special" butterfly bandage; that two planeloads of newsmen flying in for the fight have already been grounded in France and Germany, and are waiting for their publishers' decisions to go ahead or come home; that President Mobutu has called a special meeting of his Sports Committee to determine the next step; that the millions of dollars already put up for the fight hang in the balance.

That evening I talk to Bula and realize what the collapse of the fight would mean to Zaire as well as my chances of ever getting another shot at the title. I hear that the cut is not so deep or serious, that Sadler did an amazing job. I tell Bula, "I'll fight anyway and on schedule. I won't hit the eyes—if George loses because of the cut eye, I'll give him a rematch. His title will remain with him. I'll sign a paper to that effect now."

I watch the sun set over the wide Zaire River that flows just beyond my door, and I walk along the promenade with Hank Schwartz of Video Techniques, and Don King.

"This gives George his way out," King says. "There's been something pulling him away from taking this fight with you ever since it was made. Now fate comes in to help him."

"What does Sadler say?" I ask.

"If George is pressing to leave the country, Sadler will go with him," Schwartz says. "And we moved mountains to get this one."

"What can I do about it?"

"Nothing." King is depressed. "Nothing to do but wait and see what George is going to do."

Later that night we hear rumors that George and Dick Sadler are going off to Paris. In fact, there are rumors, circulated by some of the reporters who had opposed Africa as a site, that I was leaving, too, and quoting me as saying I wanted the fight moved to New York.

I know I can't let George make the first move. I have to act—fast. New York is my favorite fight city, but I don't want the work of honest promoters ruined for New York.

At the gym I go through my training routines just as though nothing had happened. Every member of the press in Kinshasa is jammed into the gym waiting to see what I will do. I refuse to say anything until I go through my schedule, shadowboxing, punching the heavy bag, skipping rope as though nothing has changed. Then I put on my robe and sit on the ringside steps. The reporters crowd around.

I say, "Listen, I have an open message to give to President Mobutu."

"Have you been talking to him?" a London newsman asks.

"No," I say. "I'm giving him this message today. I've heard a rumor that George and Dick Sadler are going to Paris now that George needs time to heal the scratch over his eye. I'm asking the President not to let George and Dick out of the city."

"Why?" another English reporter asks.

"They won't come back!"

The reporters see what I'm driving at and begin to laugh.

"George's eye ain't cut that bad," I go on. "It ain't the cut he's afraid of. It's me. I'm in shape and he ain't. You saw how fat he is. He's about to lose his title. Look at me!" I stand up and open the robe; I dance and throw jabs. "See how trim and pretty I am. Not an ounce of fat nowhere. Now, I appeal to the President not to let anyone connected with this fight out of the country. Be careful. George might sneak out at night. Watch the airports! Watch the train stations! Watch the elephant trails! Send boats to patrol the rivers. He'll never come back if you let him out, because George knows that I can't lose."

Everybody laughs. What has been a tense and confused atmosphere turns playful. Instead of writing obituaries and complaints about Zaire, they consider George.

"What do you think George will do if he leaves here?" an American reporter asks.

"He'll go home and think about the hell he's gonna catch fighting me," I say. "He's gonna say, 'Damn those five million dollars. I'll keep the title and let my eye rest for six months. I'll fight some unrated duck I can whip. One million is enough for me. The hell with the five million.' I'll stay in Zaire a year if necessary. *One whole year!* I'll stay here on the bank of the Zaire River just to keep George here, too. He wants to escape, Mr. President. Check all the luggage big enough for a big man to crawl in. Do whatever you have to do, Mr. President, but don't let George out of the country!"

Whether President Mobutu actually gave any orders preventing us from leaving, I'll never know, but after my press conference I am told that Sadler has changed his mind about flying to Paris.

In a few days George's eye is healed to the point that the bandages are taken off. Sadler's butterfly has done a miracle; you can't tell it was ever cut.

In two weeks George is back training in the gym. My spies are looking him over, and his are keeping their eyes glued on me.

George's reports on me should have been much better than mine on him. His chief spies are two of the greatest ex-champions in fight history: former Light Heavyweight Champion Archie Moore, and the most vicious Featherweight Champion of all times, Sandy Saddler. They have more than three hundred knockouts between them and a thousand victories.

On this day I start my shadowboxing and they ease in and sit down quietly in the crowd. Usually George pretends my spies are invisible, but Archie and Saddler won't dress like invisible men. Archie dresses like an Oklahoma farmer, overalls and suspenders, a red wool cap, and a picnic basket on his arm that he uses as his "file cabinet." Saddler stands behind Archie in big dark glasses and a white jockey cap on his head. He is as thin and tight as he was when he retired from the ring, still champion, seventeen years ago. They were both unmerciful finishers and some of it has rubbed off on George.

I call out to the crowd, "Folks, there's Archie Moore and Sandy

Saddler, two of the greatest of all time. Archie," I say, as I begin to shadowbox, "go back and tell George I'm goin' to throw on him some of the stuff you taught me in your camp. You remember? The cut eye gives George a chance to get in shape, but it won't change nothin'. He's never met a dancin' master before."

A smile crawls across Archie's face. He remembers me as an eighteen-year-old Olympic Champion, who my Louisville sponsoring group sent out to San Diego to be taught by Archie, the old master.

Now MY OLD boxing master has slipped in to study my weaknesses for his new student and I call out to him: "Archie, go back and tell George that when we fight, the greatest miracle of all time will take place, the greatest miracle since the Resurrection of Christ, the biggest upset of all time! Bring that sucker in here! I'll whip him now!"

The crowd roars. Even though most of them can't understand English, they understand the spirit. Archie sits through it all, a thin smile on his face.

I'm resting in my bedroom. C.B. brings in a letter. "One of George's men brought it to the door," he says.

I open it and read it:

Dear Ali:

Ali, George will half kill you. Why do you threaten him? I write this directly to you so that you can remember me as the kind, old man who helped you cut your wisdom tooth.

I see you added a few more tricks to the ones I taught you. You lifted the bolo punch from Kid Gavilan, who now serves as your handyman, you converted the Watson Shuffle to the widely advertised "Ali Shuffle." With those few tricks in your bag, you think you've got it all. Now, my student, here's my poem for you:

> Your poetry is nothing but rhyme,
> Fifteen rounds is a long time.
> Frazier couldn't even make two,
> Ken Norton was the victim of George's Coup.
> Foreman's left will make you dance
> Dance Turkey in the Straw.
> When his right connects with your lower mandible,
> Goodbye jaw.
>
> The truth must be told.
> You've gotten too old
> To win the Big Gold.

Ali, you remind me of the fable of the dog that had everything—the top dog. You had skill, the swiftest feet in your sport and a thinking man's brain. The dog in the fable had everything too. Then he looked down in the water and saw a bigger dog with a bigger bone. He dropped his own bone and leapt into the water.

For you, Ali, the bigger dog isn't just a reflection . . . it's George Foreman.

My former student, this leap isn't going to just cripple your future, it's going to cripple your ego. I think the big thing that is going to beat you is Foreman's total concentration.

George has concentrated totally to get in proper condition for this fight, and you have been distracted because you are a gullible young man.

I feel, Ali, you are being lured away from the subject, which is the Fight of the Century. It may enlighten you to know that Dick Sadler and his assistant trainer, Sandy Saddler, who retired as featherweight champion, have thought long and hard about this fight.

Sandy has the role of Minister of Strategy of Foreman's staff, working out techniques for cornering the most fleet-footed. The combined minds of Saddler, Moore and Dick Sadler are devising new approaches to force, to corner, fool, and browbeat you into a close confrontation with Foreman, who not only has the TNT in his mitts, but nuclearology as well.

Even if Foreman misses with a punch, the whoosh of the air will lower the ninety degree temperature of Zaire very considerably.

My logic, my dear ex-student, is that the quiet cunning and deadly patience of the Spider Family, in this case the Tarantula Family, whose game is really the big bananas, will settle this time for a mouthy, noisy bee.

Foreman is the most improved heavyweight since Joe Louis. In contrast, my loquacious ex-student, you have performed outlandishly, boring and bombarding the champion with threats.

Much of your prose is timeworn, an act now as thin as a Baltimore pimp's patent leather shoes. This time, you are in real trouble. I publicly and privately warn you.

After the fight, you can even hide out a few years in the jungle, then slide into Louisville about midnight and nobody will ever know.

The reason I'm writing this to you is that I don't want the blood of one of my talented ex-students on my otherwise clean and saintly hands.

Yours,
In prayer for your life,

Archie Moore

P.S. Remember, dear student: *You've gotten too old*
To win the Big Gold.

Of all the letters I've ever received before a fight, nothing gets to me more than these words from my old instructor. After I close the living room door and go back to my bedroom, I find myself looking up at the ceiling.

Is it time to retire? Am I too old? How does a fighter know when it's time to quit, time to leave the arena? When the end comes, will I know it before other people do? Will I be ready to leave the only "job" I've known since I was born? How will I know? Will it come to me down on the canvas, bleeding, unconscious, my face pulverized by some new Black or White Hope? Or will I go like Benny Paret—from a fractured skull?

What are the signs? Does Archie see real signs, as I know he can?

I've had defeats, but are defeats the end? A defeat can be a valuable experience, but I would like to go out a winner.

Certain fights are inevitable in my trade. If a fight produces enough profits for someone, then nothing can stop it. In public, I made it appear like I was chasing after George, and George's own strange drawback made him look not too anxious to clash with me. Five million dollars has too much pull for either of us to resist. How can you justify being a prizefighter and turn down the biggest prize of all? Neither one of us could have backed down.

I told everybody, "George don't hit hard." But I admit, I'm nervous wondering how hard he does hit. Can I really take a blow from George?

I see Archie and Saddler the next afternoon. They stand by the heavy bag, watching me pound it. Archie is avoiding my eye, but suddenly I look up and catch his smile and I stop punching the bag. I address the crowd: "Archie Moore, one of the greatest of all time." Then, to Archie directly, "You won the World Light Heavyweight Championship when you were forty-three. You had to wait so long because in those days they wouldn't let a black man fight for the title so fast. You knocked out the champions of four nations when you were forty-five, forty-six and forty-seven. You fought till you were fifty-four and you whipped the best till the end."

Archie is looking at me, his smile still on.

"Archie, am I too old at thirty-three?"

I see a soft, warm look in Archie's eyes.

"Am I too old?" I ask again.

He never answers. He and Saddler walk away.

BOMAYE

I wondered if it would feel strange to strip down for a fight at 4 A.M. in Zaire, Africa, but it feels the same as stripping down for a fight at 9 P.M. in Madison Square Garden, the corresponding time in New York, the usual fight time.

In the four months since the fight was announced, Zairian craftsmen have converted an old, dilapidated arena, built in 1917 by the Belgians, into a fresh, modern stadium. My dressing room is the cleanest and best I ever had for a fight.

Herbert and I step into the shower room, hold our last conference, give thanks to Allah, and briefly review what is at stake. We embrace warmly as only two old, close friends can, who have for eight years shared success and setbacks together, trials and triumphs, and are now at the crossroads.

In the dressing room I dance lightly, looking in the mirror. I feel the nervous tingle that comes when I know that whatever is about to happen will change my life.

"How much time, Blood?"

His hands are trembling as he seals my water bottles with adhesive so they look like little Egyptian mummies. Once they're sealed, only Blood and Bundini will be allowed to touch them.

Angelo's watch has stopped. Bundini says, "The clock on the wall is slow."

No one knows for sure until Blood sends out Lieutenant Bomba Nsakala, assigned to me since I flew here fifty-five days ago. Nsakala pushes through the crowd jammed around the dressing room door, goes directly to the timekeeper and synchronizes his watch, comes back out of breath and speaks low, as though there's some tactical advantage in only me knowing. "Fifteen minutes. The whole world's out there."

"Is President Mobutu out there?"

"Our President will view the fight from his home."

"Is George out there?"

"George wants you out first. He says he's The Champion."

"I'm The Champion before daybreak."

The lieutenant smiles.

An African reporter from Zambia, one of a handful of writers in the room, asks, "What goes through your mind before such a fight?"

I tell him, "I think over what's at stake. I go over every preparation I've made. My roadwork was right. My diet was right. The way I trained was right. My sleep was right. My timing was right. For thirty days I timed my roadwork to take place at 4 A.M., so when I step into the stadium at 4 A.M. it's like going for an exercise in the gym."

Then I speak to all my handlers. "This is just like an exercise in the gym, just another day."

But the mood in the dressing room doesn't change. Usually I'm the one who finds the dressing-room atmosphere before a fight too free, and usually I'm the one who brings the trainers and Angelo around to take these moments seriously. I feel uneasy and in danger when trainers and handlers take a fight lightly, but this morning they came into the dressing room as though they were walking behind a coffin. My coffin. Even Bundini is grim.

"It's just another exercise in the gym," I say. "From now on, time will fly."

I throw a flurry of punches at the mirror, and I see Dr. Pacheco. A close friend of Angelo's, he has been with me since the night I stopped Sonny Liston at Miami Beach, and with me for most of my fights. They call him "the boxing doctor," because he attends the fighters in Angelo's Fifth Street Gym. He's a sophisticated man, a painter, a musician and an artist. His eyes meet mine, and when the handful of writers are out of hearing range I take him to my inner dressing room.

It's about my hands.

Each fight I have to think of the shape my hands are in. Pain has tortured me through so many of my fights since I came back from exile. I hold up my hands to the light, flex them, wishing I could see what's inside them that might cripple me tonight. I'm fighting the youngest, most powerful opponent I've ever faced, and one with the highest knockout percentage in history. The odds are four to one against me in America, three to one in Europe—even three to one in Tokyo, where I'm popular. So pessimistic is the mood in Tokyo over my chances that actor-producer Shintaru Katsu, the "Marlon Brando" of Japan, has dropped his company's option to include the fight in Zaire in his documentary on my life. In England, where I was a favorite even when I was in exile, and even when I was fighting against their own champions, the odds this morning are two to one against me. And Angelo has handed me this week's Chicago *Tribune*, which says, ALI NEEDS A MIRACLE TO SURVIVE.

On the other hand, throughout all of Africa, cards, telegrams and greetings are pouring into my camp, hailing my victory even before I get in the ring and thanking my manager for his support of Black Africa's fight against South African racism. Herbert has refused to honor any contract which calls for me to fight inside South Africa until that country gives freedom to its black majority.

All this is flashing through my mind as I make a fist and bang my knuckles together harder and harder to arouse the pain. A trickle of sweat is coming from under my arms.

A fighter's only weapons are his hands. If they go, he goes. I've been using these hands in rings and gyms almost constantly for twenty-two years to strike against the hardest thing on a man's body, his head.

Sometimes something happens to the bones inside—microscopic chips, calcium deposits, so many things. It has changed my fighting style many times. Sometimes I've had to hold up on follow-through punches, because I can stand my opponent's blows easier than I can stand the pain when I deliver one to him.

I once heard Howard Cosell commenting on my fight with Dutch Heavyweight Champion Rudi Lubbers: "Ali hasn't used his right hand six times throughout the entire fight. Is something wrong with it? What is he saving it for? His fight with Joe Frazier?"

Yes. I was saving it for my second fight with Frazier, coming up next. But while training for Frazier the pain was almost unbearable. Even to be hit on the hands by sparring partners when blocking blows was torture. At first it was only the right hand, but then both hands.

Herbert had asked me to fly into Boston to see the famous hand specialist Dr. Richard Smith, at Massachusetts General Hospital. I knew my days as a fighter were numbered, but the treatment they prescribed seemed too costly, complex and long.

Besides, when I got back to camp, the pain had eased. I began tearing into sparring partners and the heavy bag to make up for lost time. Then suddenly it was back again and worse.

"Sparring partners now hit you with blows a baby could get away from," Bundini lamented. "Champ, if there's something wrong, let's leave boxing. We can make it somewhere else."

"Frazier is like a tank," Blood said. "You need anti-tank guns, Champ. You ain't got no anti-tank guns now. They broke."

It was less than three weeks before I was scheduled to go in the ring against Frazier. I wanted the return match with Joe Frazier not only to wipe out the first decision against me, but because Frazier was probably the most ruthless, aggressive and competitive heavyweight in modern times. I had to whip Frazier to establish any claim to a title fight. Then, too, a deep personal feud had grown up between us. Our fights were not just for money, but for our lives. Whatever would happen to me in the future, my body was now at its peak. I had everything it took to master Frazier or any other fighter.

Herbert was on the phone. "If the hands are no better in two weeks, we're calling the Garden to cancel the fight. It's better we bow out of boxing now than risk any injury. Nothing in boxing is worth that."

"I think they're getting better," I said. "They'll be all right."

"I hear what you say. I know why you say it," Herbert answered. "But just the same . . ."

Herbert had assigned C.B. to report on my hands early in training, not only during the Frazier training but during my training for Norton and Quarry. Now they had Blood and Bundini watching me for signs that might indicate danger.

I remember it was in mid-January of 1974 that I had a feeling close to desperation. I had just passed my thirty-second birthday, and I knew if I lost the chance to fight Frazier this time, I might never have another. I had wiped out a decision Norton held over me. I wanted to do the same with Frazier.

Joe stood like a stone wall against giving me a return match after our first "Fight of the Century," even when all those around him, including his manager and beloved "ring father" Yank Durham, were pleading with him to fight me again—if for no other reason than that it meant millions for both of us.

"I'll never fight that bastard for even money again," Frazier told

Yank, and he meant it. "I'd rather die and go to hell first."

But it was Yank who died and went somewhere first, only a month after he and Herbert had met secretly to maneuver a return match between Joe and me. Joe flew into a rage about that meeting and accused Yank of doublecrossing him.

Boxing officials had warned Joe that the year was almost up, that he must make a defense of his title against me or Foreman, the top-ranking contenders, or forfeit the title. He had a clear-cut choice between signing for four million dollars to fight me or eight hundred thousand to fight Foreman.

He overruled everybody, flew down to Jamaica, underprepared and overconfident, and George wiped him out, took the title.

But in January of 1974 I had not wiped out my defeat by Frazier and I was afraid that if Frazier fought a return match with Foreman and won, he would never get in the ring with me in this world or the next unless on terms too humiliating for me to accept. C.B. said Herbert wanted me to go back to Massachusetts General Hospital and have the treatment. But I refused; their verdict could end my career.

Rocky Aioka, a Japanese wrestling champion who was with me in the Rome Olympics, now owner of the Benihana restaurant empire, came up to the mountains around that time and saw me pawing away at sparring partners. He was so alarmed that he wired back to Tokyo for the leading Japanese orthopedic specialist. I refused to let him come.

But I knew I had to have help, so when Lou Beltrami, a friend since I moved up to the mountains, asked me to go to a nearby town to see his personal physician, Dr. Peter Greco, I agreed. "By the condition of your hands now," the doctor said, "I would say you should cancel the fight."

I felt hostile. "That's a judgment for me to make," I said. "All I want to know is if there's anything that can be done to help them before I fight Frazier."

He said he'd try. And almost every day he came to camp to give me cortisone and hot wax treatments. I bought a hot wax applicator, and all through the day and evening I doused my hands. Slowly, they seemed to improve.

But by the day of the weigh-in the New York Boxing Commission had heard reports of my trip to a doctor. Reporters who saw sparring partners push me around the ring wrote that something was wrong. For the first time in my career I was asked to have my hands x-rayed.

It was the quickest, most casual x-ray I'd ever taken. They found nothing.

Hal Conrad, Top Rank veteran boxing consultant, saw my puzzled look when I left the room. "They had to satisfy the reporters," he said. "The Garden's sold out. You can't beg, borrow or steal tickets. Nobody's gonna find anything wrong with the fighters at this late date. Two legs missing and one eye in the middle of your forehead might help. Otherwise, good luck."

In the quiet of my dressing room, twenty minutes before the fight, I held up my hands and flexed them. They felt better, but I decided to be careful.

This may have saved Frazier from a knockout in the second round of that last fight. I had him groggy and weaving, but did not follow up, not only because the timekeeper rang the bell too soon, but because I was saving my hands. I wasn't sure I had hit him that hard.

NSAKALA APPEARS in the doorway. "We go on in twelve minutes."

This may be the final fight of my life. I don't care how bad my hands hurt. I'll hit him until the pain tears them off at the wrists. I'll gamble on the weapons I got. Everything I want in life is on the line tonight.

"Countdown! Countdown is on!" Blood says in his intense, hushed way.

But my own countdown has already begun. I check over everything. One thing the countdown always brings is the urge to pee. I have the urge now, although I emptied myself before I left my villa. The urge is so overpowering that I get up from the training table and go to the toilet. I stand there over the bowl and try. I squeeze, but nothing comes out. Still the urge is there. I don't want to be in the ring during the seventh or eighth round in a hot exchange of blows with George and feel this urge. How could I say, "George, my black brother, hold that uppercut while I go over to my corner and pee in my bucket. I'd do the same for you." George would say, "Oh no you don't," hit me in the kidneys, and out it would come. I can see the late Jimmy Cannon rising from his grave and writing his most triumphant column: CHRISTIAN BEATS THE PEE OUT OF BLACK MUSLIM. Dick Young, New York *Daily News* sportswriter, banging out the beginning of his column: FOREMAN MAKES ALI WET HIS PANTS IN SEVENTH ROUND." Red Smith saying: ALI POURED OUT MORE PEE THAN PUNCHES TONIGHT.

It would be the same way when I finished fighting that morning, when they carried me through the screaming crowd back into the dressing room. There were two doctors I'd never seen before, one European and one Zairian, asking for urine specimens.

"Before you do anything else," the Zairian doctor said even before I undressed, "we need a urine specimen."

The European explained casually, "Since you took so many body blows, there is fear that your kidneys might be injured."

They gave me a flask. We went into the toilet and I tried. Not a drop came out. They looked disappointed.

"Maybe if you follow me home," I suggested, "maybe I can do better. Do you mind riding in my car?"

I took them in my caravan along the road to Nsele. The storm that had held off for four weeks broke out a half-hour after the fight. Of all the unexplained miracles in my life, the long-overdue torrential rain poured down in sheets so heavy that the very ring we fought in was wrecked and the stadium flooded. All of Hank Schwartz's Video Technique signal-bearing equipment went out of order. I sat back during the drive, wondering at the miracle; if it had come two hours earlier, I wouldn't be riding out of the stadium as World Heavyweight Champion. The fight would have been postponed for the final time. George would have gone back to his initial plan—to avoid me until I'm "a little older and slower." I'd be flying home as the old fighter who the oddsmakers said couldn't have beaten young George anyway.

But none of those tons of water got into me. When we reached the villa and I went to the bathroom to try again, nothing.

"You sweated it all out," one doctor said. "There is very little excess liquid left in your body."

I apologized and suggested that they come back in the morning when I woke up. "Tomorrow morning maybe I can do you justice."

But they gave up on it. They never came back.

I was told later they were doctors from the WBA. They were looking to examine my urine to see if I had taken any drugs that had enabled me to be so energetic while George seemed to wear down. And if they had found any, I was to be immediately disqualified and the title reverted back to George.

Dr. Williams, my own physician, said later, "They kept me in a room, quizzing me for two hours after the fight. Trying to get me to tell them if I had given you any medicine for any reason seventy-two hours before the fight. They were surprised that you seemed so strong and Foreman so weak. They wouldn't give up until they were certain they didn't have a leg to stand on to strip you of the title once more."

I SIT on the training table and Angelo tapes my hands with rows of thin gauze. Doc Nick Broadus comes over from George's camp to watch the wrapping, an ancient precaution designed to let each side see that no horseshoes or brass knuckles are taped on a fighter. We send Dr. Pacheco to George's room, but George has him kicked out. Broadus has to take him back to verify his credentials.

It's nice to know George is so suspicious and uneasy. Maybe it's because only last night a rumor circulated that George's aides tried to force an additional five hundred thousand from John Daly, the young London executive of Hemdale Leisure Corporation who advanced the original million and a half used by Don King and Hank Schwartz to start the mechanics of the title fight. According to the rumor, the aide told him that unless the five hundred thousand was delivered before the fight, George would not step into the ring. The Zaire venture, now up to a fifty-million-dollar outlay, would collapse.

George didn't know what I'd learned in my association with Daly, the son of a Welsh prizefighter. In spite of his rosy schoolboy look, Daly is as shrewd and tough in his business as George is in his—maybe more so.

"It was a delicate thing," Daly told me after the fight. "I felt the fight was in the balance. I had to give his man an empty suitcase and allow him to fly to London for the money."

Right now George's man is supposedly sitting in a London hotel, waiting to have the suitcase filled with five hundred thousand dollars in U.S. currency. Later we heard that Scotland Yard cooperated with Daly in having his outgoing phone calls cut off.

But another rumor in Kinshasa is that Daly was so certain I would be annihilated and George the dominant figure in boxing for years to come that he offered George the half-million if he would sign for Daly to handle his future title defenses. And crafty George insisted on having the money before the fight.

Somehow, I have no fear about George being foolish enough not to show up. Both The Champion and I have met President Mobutu Sese Seko, face to face, and if George is as feeble a judge of character as his aide, I would hate to be his wife, waiting for the day he gets out of Africa.

Nsakala whispers, "Seven minutes."

The countdown goes on.

I warm up before the mirror, throwing my punches, and two minutes later I go to the inside room with Herbert. We say a prayer of thanks to Allah. I come out and shadowbox again, lightly, keeping my body at a certain temperature.

"Five minutes."

Blood begins to stick his mummies in the water bucket. The only thing new in one of the bottles is a solution of honey, orange juice and water, a formula from Dr. Charles Williams of Chicago, who had analyzed the fatigue I felt while training in Philadelphia. I will do like Sugar Ray Robinson did when he fought, take a nip of sweets in between rounds.

Bundini throws the towels across his shoulders. The room is moving toward the door. A hand-picked squad of paratroopers is receiving last-second instructions from Lieutenant Nsakala. The line forms around me.

A young Zaire reporter with a scratch pad slips through to whisper to me, "What does a fighter think about these last minutes?" As though I'm a condemned man going for execution.

It's too late to answer. But I go over in my mind how I will pull every ounce of strength and endurance out of my body to defeat George.

I remember the signs President Mobutu has strung along the highway between the airport and the city, slogans to welcome visitors to Zaire. One describes this fight as a "Sport Between Two Brothers." But there's no one I feel more unbrotherly toward at this moment than George. I tighten my fist. I may not be able to stop the pain, but no pain will stop me from throwing blows at George.

We're at the door. Bundini has circled the editorial of a magazine, and reads it in my ear like a prayer: "So it boils down to this: 'Foreman-Ali, $5 million each in a battle in Zaire, Africa. Forget everything else, every fight that has been won or lost before and all of those that will be contested in years to come. Forget every battle of man against man, of mind against mind, of soul against soul. This is the one. This is the greatest.' "

I nod to him. The line is moving.

"This is it." Bundini's voice is husky. Then he cries out loud:

"THE LAMB'S COME BACK TO CLAIM HIS OWN!
GET THE PRETENDER OFF THE THRONE!"

"What does the fighter think these last minutes?" the reporter keeps trying to ask.

I think of who I am and who my opponent is. Who is he? He is White America, Christianity, the Flag, the White Man, Porkchops. But George is The Champion, and the world listens to The Champion. There are things I want to say, things I want the world to hear. I want to be in a position to fight for my people. Whatever I have to do tonight, George will not leave Africa The Champion.

"It's time!" Nsakala snaps, and the whole line moves faster.

I feel chilly, nervous. I want to pee. They push and pull us through the door, we're out into the hall now, and the people jammed in the corridor see me. The chants start:

"ALI! ALI! BOMAYE! ALI! ALI! BOMAYE!"

The sound booms through the corridor, stays with us until we make the turn up the ramp to the opening into the stadium. We move almost on the double, and burst into the grounds. Lights flood the stadium like poured-down sunshine. Zairians in bright clothes of all colors fill the arena and make it alive with chants, songs, cheers.

It's a quarter to four. The moon is still out, but the stadium is lit up like high noon. Spotlights crisscross, searching for my crew, and when the light finds them the stadium explodes from all sides:

"ALI! ALI! BOMAYE! ALI! ALI! BOMAYE!"

I'm behind Lieutenant Nsakala; Angelo is behind me, Bundini on my side, Blood and his bucket coming up. We swing down the aisle that leads to my corner.

I reach the four steps to the ring, climb up to my corner and see the full sweep of the stadium; people are on the walls, on the tracks, every space is filled. They cheer and I raise my hand and salute them back.

They respond as though we've been rehearsing together all our lives. I look up at the roof that stretches above us, forty feet across the field, so that if the overdue rains come, the fight will still go on. The people will be drenched, but the fighters will have no excuse. We fight for the Title to the World.

I raise my hand again and dance from one end of the ring to the other. I dance by George's empty corner. The crowd roars—they understand. I'm moving easy. Sweat comes down my chest and I feel good. I know George has already lost a heavy point by not coming into the ring at the same time.

"Maybe he's holding out for something," Blood says.

But I know he'll be here. There is no force on earth that can resist the power of these people and they want us both here.

"ALI! ALI! BOMAYE! ALI! ALI! BOMAYE!"

Bundini is frowning. "Champ," he whispers, "I forgot to do it."

"What?"

"I forgot the flags."

I smile. Bundini had planned that I would enter the ring with flags, in memory of George during the Olympics in Mexico when he waved an American flag to counteract the Black Power salutes of the black champions who were protesting race discrimination in America. I would enter the ring waving a Zairian flag, a flag representing the Organization of African Unity, and the UN flag. But Bundini had no time to get it together.

"George is playing prima donna," Angelo says. "He wants to make you wait."

I understand George's play. He thinks this will make me nervous, worn and edgy by the time the fight begins. But he has given me an edge I know how to take advantage of, a chance to study the crowd, to get to know their ego, their personality. Crowds exert pressure on you. Every crowd feels strange at first, no matter who they cheer for. But when I warm up, I feel their good vibrations, the pulsebeats.

George has given me time to test the ropes and to get the feel of the distance between the center and the corner. I circle the ring. I look at the crowd from different angles, from the corner, the center, all sides. I get used to the heat from the lights.

Newsmen who've described my circling the ring before the fight as all showmanship do not understand there's more to it than that. Instead of starting out cold, I will know more about the atmosphere than my opponent.

My feet get the feel of the canvas. I feel the soft spots, the firm spots. Ordinarily, there's no time to do this. Usually I try to enter a stadium the night before, as I did the ring in Madison Square Garden before I fought Frazier—move about and make myself known to the square I do my life's work in.

Angelo looks at his watch. "He's gonna be more than ten minutes late."

I look around at ringside, nod to people I know. I see Jim Brown, Miriam Makeba, Lloyd Price, Bill Withers. I nod to the press: Red Smith, Jack Griffin, Dave Anderson, Switzerland's Mario Widmar.

"The Champ's getting ready to cook!" Bundini is shouting. "Cook tonight, Champ! Cook!"

The longer The Champion lingers, the more I like it. By the time George comes out, he will be a total stranger in a house I know all about. I've looked into all the closets, the exits, the basement, the bedrooms. I'm at home. George will be my unwelcome guest, one I must not allow to stay too long.

"FOREMAN! FOREMAN! FOREMAN!"

I see Angelo's neck jerk. The audience on the west side starts a chant. It's for The Champion!

"THERE HE IS!"

The Champion is coming down the aisle, his entourage around him. His hands are up in the Olympic salute. I watch him climb up the steps behind his crew, Dick Sadler, Archie Moore, Sandy Saddler. He goes immediately to his stool. He doesn't move about the ring to get the feel of it. He doesn't test the ropes or get the feel of the crowd. He slumps on his stool and will stay there until the referee comes to the center of the ring.

I dance lightly and steadily. I glance across the ring and see Sadler whispering in George's ear. Now Zack Clayton, the referee, comes to the center. George is poised to get up.

The referee motions to us.

The greatest roar I've ever heard fills the air. We stand up face to face.

"ALI! ALI! BOMAYE! ALI! ALI! BOMAYE!"

"FOREMAN! FOREMAN! THE CHAMPION! THE CHAMPION!"

"ALI! ALI! BOMAYE! ALI! ALI! BOMAYE!"

Our eyes are locked like gunfighters' in a Wild West movie. Angelo and Bundini rub my shoulders. Sandy and Archie stand with George. In his eyes, I see Sonny Liston glaring at me ten years ago at Miami Beach, a fresh, young, powerful, taller, stronger Liston. Now I think this will answer the question critics have been asking since I first won the title from an "aging Liston": Could I have defeated a young Sonny Liston?

Clayton begins his instructions. "Now, both of you know the rules. When I step back, you break clean. No hitting on the breaks . . ."

But I draw my guns first. I lean close to George's ear, and since I obviously have his undivided attention, I think we should get a few things straight that the referee might overlook. "Chump," I say with all the contempt I can muster. "You're gonna get yourself beat tonight in front of all these Africans."

The referee's head jerks up. "Ali, no talking! Listen to the instructions." He goes on. "No hitting below the belt. No kidney punches . . ."

"Never mind that stuff, sucker." I speak low. "I'm gonna hit you everywhere but under the bottom of your big funky feet, Chump! You got to go, sucker!"

"Ali, I warned you," the referee snaps. "Be quiet!"

George bites his lips and his eyes glare.

"Ref," I say. "This sucker is in trouble. He ain't nobody's Champ!"

George's eyes go from me to the referee. He wants Clayton to chastise me, but I pull his eyes back to mine. The referee talks on mechanically while I say to George, "You heard about me for years, sucker! All your life you been hearing about Muhammad Ali. Now, Chump, you gotta face me!"

"Ali, I'm warning you for the last time!"

George's eyes are tight. His head is close to mine.

"You been hearing about how bad I am since you were a little kid with mess in your pants! Tonight"—I say it loud—"I'm gonna whip you till you cry like a baby."

"If you don't stop talking, I'll disqualify you." Clayton is furious, his hands shake. "I want a good, clean, sportsman fight, or I will absolutely call a halt to it."

"That's the only way you gonna save this sucker," I say. "He's doomed!"

Sweat is coming down George's forehead. Archie Moore is rubbing his shoulders.

"If you talk while fighting," the referee says, "I'm going to stop this fight, you hear? I'll stop it!"

I've been told this before, but where does it say in the rules that fighters can't have an orderly discussion while they work as long as they perform properly? Where does it say that they cannot discuss some personal problems or world problems?

The only other time objections were raised to my talking was when I fought Oscar Bonavena in Madison Square Garden, and the New York Boxing Commissioner, Dooley, put in a special rule aimed at me which declared that if either fighter talked during the fight a fine of five thousand dollars would be levied, which I thought was a compliment, since Bonavena understands no English and I speak no Spanish.

I keep talking. Too much is at stake to stop this fight. Too much has gone into making it; a billion people around the world are watching it. I'm not worried about the referee. After all, he knows I will not neglect my work while I lecture George. I will enlighten his mind while I whip him. The public will not be cheated. In fact, I will perform even better than if I go out slugging like a deadpan Frankenstein robot.

"Sucker," I explain, "I'm too fast for a big, slow mummy. Your title is gone. You never should have come to Africa."

"All right, all right!" Clayton gives up. "Go to your corners and come out fighting when you hear the bell, and may the best man . . ."

I flip around and dance to my corner. The thunderous roars come in waves, chants, yells, shouts.

"ALI! ALI! BOMAYE!

"FOREMAN! THE CHAMPION!"

I've never fought in a stadium like this. I feel at home. So much so, I look across at George and take his measurements as though I'm his undertaker's tailor, outfitting him for the suit he's to wear in his casket. How soon shall I go all out? How soon shall I gamble on getting him in the half-dream?

I've called it the half-dream room since I was a boy, boxing in Louisville, and was knocked down and almost out in the gym for the first time. I went home and thought about it all night. I had seen champions, contenders, professional boxers on TV get knocked down and out. Now I knew how it felt.

It's like in the Golden Gloves tournaments. I'm hit, knocked groggy. The feeling is like being half awake and half dreaming. And your awake half knows what you're dreaming about. In fact, it follows the whole scene. A heavy blow takes you to the door of this room. It opens, and you see neon, orange and green lights blinking. You see bats blowing trumpets, alligators play trombones, and snakes are screaming. Weird masks and actor's clothes hang on the wall.

The first time the blow sends you there, you panic and run, but when you wake up you say, "Well, since it was only a dream, why didn't I play it cool, put on the actor's clothes, the mask, and see what it's like? Only you have to fix it in your mind and plan to do it long before the half-dream comes. For when it comes, time stretches out slow. You have to put the plan in your mind long before you need it. The blow makes your mind vibrate like a tuning fork. You can't let your opponent follow up. You've got to stop the fork from vibrating.

I know how to do it now, like when Frazier knocked me down in the fifteenth round. I get up groggy. I go on the defensive. I act until my head clears, as I did when Norton broke my jaw in the second round and opened the door of the half-dream room. I acted it out until the fight was over.

I know George has never been hurt or dazed. He has never been behind in a single round. Shall I gamble in the first round? When should I go all out to take him to the dream room? Will he know what to do? Has The Champion thought it out as I have?

CLANG! ROUND ONE.

I move out and dance straight into George and throw a fast left. He's bearing down on me, and I dance away and flick out more jabs. I say nothing for the first full minute, but if he thinks this is going to be all work and no education, he's mistaken. Then:

"Come on, Chump! Now's your chance! Show me what you got!"

"You been hitting kindergarten kids!"

A quick jab in the face and his eyes blink.

"Here comes another one, Chump! Another one!"

"Didn't I tell you I was the fastest heavyweight that ever lived?"

"Didn't they tell you, sucker?"

"The round's half over, and you ain't landed a good shot yet."

But in the second half of the round George is executing what he's practiced for months. He's cutting the ring off and forcing me to move six steps to his two, and he's doing it better than anyone I've been up against. I've had fighters chase me—most fighters chase me—but I make them match me step for step. George is the first fighter to consistently cut me off.

He corners me for a few seconds, and I find myself lying against the ropes. The Champion moves in, throwing long rights and lefts, haymaker hooks. He's at the peak of his strength, and he hurls one left, his "anywhere" punch that strikes and makes me feel exactly as Boss-man Jones described it.

"DANCE, CHAMP! DANCE!" I hear Bundini crying out.

"MOVE, ALI! MOVE!" Angelo is calling.

All during training I had planned to stay off the ropes. Now I move off and circle the ring, but before the end of the round I know I've got to change my plans. Sadler and Archie have drilled George too well. He does his job like a robot, but he does it well.

I'm famous for being hard to hit in the first rounds, but no fighter can last fifteen if he has to take six steps to his opponent's three. When the first round is over, when I'm back in my corner, Angelo's voice is urgent: "Keep moving. You've got to stay off those ropes!"

The only thing my cornermen see out there is that I need to move, but I see something else. In the first three minutes I felt George's power, and I understand how Frazier and Norton were destroyed. I see what his Board of Strategy has planned.

I'm looking directly across into his corner when Blood alerts me that George's man, Doc Broadus, has come over and is standing at the foot of the stairs, directly under my corner, to hear what I'm saying. Blood wants to throw him out. I shake my head. "Leave him alone. I'm the only one George is listening to out there."

"Move and sting him!" Angelo is whispering. "Sting him!"

CLANG! ROUND TWO.

I move to the center, jab and dance and jab. But I know now that my danger is not in the corners or on the ropes, but in dancing six steps to George's three. His Board of Strategy knows at that pace he's forcing me to move. It won't be George who will be exhausted by round nine. It'll be me.

"ALI! DANCE! DANCE, CHAMP! DANCE!"

I dance, and in a clinch, glance down at those on ringside. My eyes fall for a split second on Eddie Futch, manager of Joe Frazier, once manager of Ken Norton, yelling up encouragement to George. New York newspapers are hailing Futch as the only trainer who has had fighters to defeat Ali, and Futch predicts: "George will corner Muhammad and destroy him. Nothing in the world can keep George from driving him into a corner, and when he does . . . George has the power of Joe Louis and Rocky Marciano combined. I pray for Ali's life."

I feel a shot of adrenalin. I have avenged my defeat by Futch's fighters. Now I will defeat Futch.

"DANCE, CHAMP! FLOAT LIKE A BUTTERFLY, STING LIKE A BEE!"

"ALI! ALI! BOMAYE!"

But I've moved into a corner, and my back is against the ropes. George eagerly comes in after me. For the first time in all my fights, I decide not to wait until I'm tired to play the ropes, but to take to the corners while I'm fresh and still strong, to gamble on the ropes all the way.

"Come on, sucker. Show me something, Chump!" . . . "They say you hit hard?" . . . "Is that the best you can do, sissy?"

My cornermen are screaming. I hear friends at ringside, pleading. Some get out of their chairs, come up to the lap of the ring.

"ALI! MOVE OUT OF THE ROPES!"

I taunt George. I goad him.

"You ain't got no punch, you phony!" . . . "Show me something, sucker!"

George roars in like a mob. He's throwing punches with tonnage I never thought a fist could carry. A crowbar in George's right hand crashes through my guard into my head, knocks me into the room of half-dream. My head vibrates like a tuning fork. Neon lights flash on and off.

I've been here before.

I say to myself: I've been hit. I've been hit.

I fight to open the door and go in the room.

"ALI, MOVE!" my cornermen are screaming. In all my life I've never heard the sound of fear from my corner before. "DANCE, CHAMP, DANCE!"

I hear them from far away, for I have crossed into another world and I will never come back to dance in this fight.

I tell myself: I must not get hit again. The tuning fork must stop vibrating. I must open the door of the room—the room I planned to take George into, the half-dream room. He has brought me here first. Only, I've been here before. I know about it. When I see the masks and the actor's clothes hanging on the walls, the lizards playing saxophones and the bats blowing trumpets, I don't panic and run out. I put on actor's clothes. I go on the defensive.

I know the best defense is an offense, that when you give up offense your opponent is free to take his best shots. George's blows explode into my kidneys, my ribs, my head. I lean back. I slip and slide. I catch some on my arms, off my elbows, but I stay on the ropes.

"GET OFF THE ROPES, CHAMP! MOVE!"

But they don't know what I know. I stay on the ropes. Then near the end of the round I rise up and shoot quick, straight jabs and right crosses directly into George's head. POW! POW! POW!

And I must carry on my educational program. I must not let him think his blows can stop me from talking. If I stop talking now, he knows I'm hurt.

"Sucker, is that all you got? Is that the hardest you can hit?"

When the bell rings, I go back to my corner. I see concern, confusion and fear in the eyes of my cornermen. They have strong advice about what I should do, but my head is on the line, not theirs. I've felt the hot breath of The Monster, and they do not know what

I know. Even Angelo doesn't remember that for years I've practiced blocking heavy punches at close range from heavyweights in the gym. For years my trainers and advisers have screamed and begged and pleaded in the gyms while I worked laying against the ropes to test the endurance of heavyweights.

I have a theory about speed and endurance in my own weight. I like to test a heavyweight when he's throwing his best shots wide open, to find out how long he can keep it up. I need to know, because I'll have to wear down an opponent stronger than me, and in the gym, practicing year after year, I've discovered something—that heavyweights usually burn down when the wide-open opportunity to punch and punch is in front of him. But this is a gamble now, because George is the strongest heavyweight in the world. Yet I know, too, that George is gambling on knocking me out, at least in the third round.

I've studied George too closely not to know that at times he's a fine, skillful boxer, who can execute the amazing moves and maneuvers he picked up from Saddler and Moore. I've seen him do it. But George has twenty-three knockout victims behind him. It's got to be hard for him to believe that the same methods he used on the others will not make me the twenty-fourth.

Can I make George the victim of his own fantastic success? It's not easy for him to change a habit that works so well.

In a few seconds the bell for round three will ring. George has not had to go beyond round three in five years. He will come at me now with all he's got. Everything in his ego and his psyche is at stake now.

"THE FLEA IN THREE!"

Suddenly the sound of a voice through a megaphone cuts across the arena. It takes my eyes off George and over to the left side of the ring. Elmo Henderson, The Champion's chief clown, is barking through a white megaphone. I expected it, but I still feel a chill. The secret inside Foreman's camp is that I will and must be destroyed by round three.

"OH, YEA! OH, YEA!

"THE FLEA IN THREE!"

Henderson, a tall, lanky retired heavyweight, a natural tout man, devotes his life to "giving the spirit to The Champion." All night he has walked through Kinshasa hotel lobbies and streets, screaming into his megaphone:

"OH, YEA! OH, YEA!

"TODAY IS THE DAY!

"THE FLEA IN THREE!

"GEORGE THE EAGLE WILL FLY!

"ALI THE BUTTERFLY WILL DIE!

"TODAY IS THE DAY!

"OH, YEA! OH, YEA!"

Bundini clashed with Henderson in the hotel lobbies and tried to outshout him: "You can't beat God's son! Put your money where your mouth is!" But Henderson's voice is even louder than Bundini's. He would stand before a crowd and shout until Bundini would fade away saying, "I can't deal with a nut."

Angelo is pleading in my ear, "Keep off the ropes. Keep in the center of the ring. Make him box!"

And Elmo rings out his prophecy:

"THE FLEA IN THREE!"

CLANG! ROUND THREE.

I move quick and shoot jabs with sting. POW! POW! POW! George blinks, but moves forward like a big tank. He controls the center of the ring, as though he expects me to challenge him, but I go back to the ropes and to the corner. And I call to him: "All right, sucker! This is where you want me. Come on, man!"

I'm talking louder and louder, and the referee is hissing at me, "Be quiet, Ali. Be quiet. I warned you the last time! Stop talking!"

His voice makes me look at his face. It's tight, tense. Zack has refereed a thousand fights. He was the third man in the ring when I knocked out Sonny Liston in Maine. He anticipates the action in a fight better than any referee in the ring, and he knows this is George's "murder" round. But if he expects me to be quiet on the day I'm supposed to die, he's mistaken.

I'm snapping jabs in George's face and talking through my mouthpiece: "Where's your punch, sucker? Show me! You ain't got nothin'! Show me somethin'!" . . . "Here I am! Come and get me!"

My corner is screaming, "ALI, GET OFF THE ROPES! STICK HIM! JAB! MOVE OFF THE ROPES!"

George is throwing bombs at my head. I lean back, but he stays on top of me. I'm amazed at how he can pack power into every punch. Every punch is a haymaker. I block them from my head, and suddenly he switches, comes up from the floor with an uppercut that seems to blow my jaw off. I'm hurt. I try to hold on.

"GET OFF THE ROPES! DANCE, CHAMP, DANCE!"

I try to move off, but he pushes me back like a rag doll. The tuning fork in my head is humming. I've got to hold on. I've got to keep him from following up. George senses that I'm hurt, and he's coming in for the kill. I block, move back and weave. It's the longest round I've ever fought in my life, but near the end my head begins to clear.

George keeps roaring in with his head straight up, confident all I will do is take cover. Suddenly I come out from under with straight lefts and rights directly into his face. WHAM! WHAM! WHAM!

The crowd roars. They come to life as if they're seeing me rise from the dead.

WHAM! WHAM! WHAM! They're not powerful punches, but they shake him up.

"MOVE, CHAMP! DANCE! MOVE, CHAMP!"

George looks startled. He throws his heaviest bomb, it curls around my head and we clinch so tight I feel his heart pounding. I bite his ear. "Is that the best you can do, sucker? Is that all you got, Chump? You ain't got no punch! You in big trouble, boy!"

I feel his breath coming in gasps, and I know I'm taking something out of him. I know this round will go down on the judges' scorecards as belonging to George, but there's something in it that belongs to me.

When the round ends, my head is humming. But the round of my execution is over, and all I will do now is plot the time when my turn comes. I take a deep swig from my water bottle and wash the blood out of my mouth.

Bundini is crying, "Champ, you got to move! You got to stick and move!"

"He wants you on the ropes. Don't let him!" Angelo is desperate.

I rarely ask for advice from my corner, and seldom accept what they say. And now, more than any time, I know they do not understand what's happening out there.

The stadium crowd is all I'm listening to:

"ALI! ALI! BOMAYE! ALI! ALI! BOMAYE!"

They chant in Lingala, but I know that "Bomaye" means:

"KNOCK HIM DOWN! KILL HIM DEAD!"

They've seen me take the worst shelling I've had in my life, and they still believe I can take the fight. It's like a charge of electricity.

"ALI! ALI! BOMAYE! ALI! ALI! BOMAYE!"

I remember looking down at ringside. My eyes meet Jim Brown's. Brown has publicly predicted George would knock me out. I lean out of the ring. "Jim Brown! You bet on the wrong horse! This sucker don't have a chance! You lost your money! He can't fight no better than you can act!"

"George is going to lynch you!" a disbeliever next to Brown jumps up and screams.

I can see all of George's corner looking over at me, shocked that instead of resting I'm taking the entire time educating the disbelievers around the ring. Before the bell rings, I stand up and wave my gloves to direct my choir.

"ALI! ALI! BOMAYE!"

CLANG! ROUND FOUR.
CLANG! ROUND FIVE.

CLANG! ROUND SIX.
CLANG! ROUND SEVEN.

I lay on the ropes through them all, and I come to life near the end of each round just when George thinks my life is over.

WHAM! WHAM! WHAM! WHAM! into The Champion's face and head. In the clinches, I measure his heavy breathing. The slowdown in his punches, the weakening of his recoil. And I talk to him like an old friend, louder and louder: "You gone six rounds, sucker, and you ain't hit me yet! Who said you could hit? Come on! I'll give you a chance. Swing, sucker! Swing!"

Then, WHAM! WHAM! WHAM! I pop him straight in the eye. "Look at your eye, sucker! I ain't even touched the cut eye yet. I'm hittin' the good eye!"

But George keeps driving on like a one-way tank, every ounce of his 220 pounds behind his blows. I'm draining him, but it's coming near time when I've got to go all out before he gets his second wind. Tired as he is, it will take the heaviest blows I've ever thrown to bring him down.

When the seventh round nears the end, I clinch him tightly and give my best advice: "You got eight more rounds to go, sucker! Eight more rounds, and look how tired you are. I ain't even got started, and you out of breath! Look at you! Out of gas, and I'm whippin' you."

He throws a long, almost slow-motion swing, and I block it and come in with two quick jabs to his face. POP! POP! "Look at your eye, chump! Ain't you 'shamed? Those pretty African girls sittin' out there lookin' at your eye all messed up?"

Sadler is yelling at him from the corner. Archie Moore is trying to say something to him. But I know he's listening to me. "Don't listen to those fools in your corner. Don't listen to Archie and Sadler. They're foolin' you. They didn't tell you how bad I was, did they? They didn't tell you I was the baddest in the world. They lied to you. You got eight —EIGHT—long rounds to go, sucker! And you can hardly make it past this one."

The bell rings, and I feel pain all over me. Even my cornermen now sense something is being turned around.

I sit down, but I feel uneasy. The pace is killing George, but it's also taking a heavy toll on me. I've got to go for the kill before he gets his second wind. I know The Champion is more exhausted than I am, but how long can I stand up under this barrage? I look at George's corner. He's had to go into the eighth round only three times in his life. Every minute now will be strange, unsure.

I remember catching the eye of a tall African girl walking by, flashing the number of the upcoming round. She winks at me. I wink back and feel better.

• • •

CLANG! ROUND EIGHT.

George storms out, still only one thing on his mind: knockout. But now his blows come slower, take longer to reach me. I know fire and pain are inside his stomach and lungs, and every breath is torture, just as it is for me. I see him draw back for a mighty swing with all his power, and I slip aside and he tangles himself in the ropes. "Sucker!" I say. "You missed by a mile! You look bad, chump!"

I keep my eyes pinned on his eyes. I never even blink. I don't want to miss anything his face might say, and his eyes tell me everything. As I watch him pull himself back into the ring, I suddenly think of Joe Frazier. Have I been treating George as though he's another Frazier? If you knock Frazier down, he'll get up almost before he hits the canvas and come back at you. His heart is a lion. When Frazier comes at you, his blood and marrow and muscles all scream at you: "If you can't kill me, get out of my way, or I'll kill you!" He'll fight way beyond exhaustion and still come on. Even when his lungs are tired and burning, when every ounce of blood is drained out of him, he still keeps coming. Whatever the price, he'll pay it. You can knock him down a dozen times, and he'll still bounce back up and come again.

George *looks* like King Kong when he comes at you, but does he have the heart—of a Joe Louis, Rocky Marciano, Henry Armstrong? A Joe Frazier?

Only a man who knows what it is to be defeated can reach down to the bottom of his soul and come up with the extra ounce of power it takes to win when the match is even. I know George wants to keep The Champion's crown. He wants the crown, but is he willing to pay the price? Would he lay out his life?

It's time to go all out. Toe to toe. George pours out a long left, and I cross my right over it. Now I've got to lay it all down on the line. If the price of winning is to be a broken jaw, a smashed nose, a cracked skull, a disfigured face, you pay it if you want to be King of the Heavyweights. If you want to wear the crown, you can play it careful only until you meet a man who will die before he lets you win. Then you have to lay it all on the line or back down and be damned forever.

The crowd eggs me on: "ALI! ALI! BOMAYE!"

I hear Kid Gavilan, the old Cuban Champion of a thousand fights, telling me, "Ali, the crowd'll push you on like they own a piece of you, like there's something in their life that depends on whether you live or die. And you'll get into something too deep to back down. You've been calling out, 'I'm the prettiest. I'm the greatest. See how pretty I am. Not a scratch!' They laugh, but one day the people will test you out. They will send you into a den to take meat out of the lion's mouth and see who comes out the prettiest. If you die trying, they'll be sorry for you, but if you back down, they'll remember you as a phony forever. When you fight for the title, you lay it all on the line."

I know it's time for the test. I see George trying to lumber back, to regain his poise. I shoot a straight right to his jaw with all the snap and power that's in me. I strike him almost flush on the chin, and he stands still.

Archie Moore will say the blow would have knocked out anybody, but I know, had I thrown it in the earlier rounds, George would have been strong enough to shake it off.

I'm ready to follow through with combinations, but I see he's slowly falling, a dazed look in his eyes. I know he's entering the room of the half-dream for the first time in his life. George is down, his eyes glazed. He's listening to the tuning forks humming in his head, bats blowing saxophones, alligators whistling, neon signs blinking.

The referee begins the count. George will later protest that he was the victim of a short count, and I can understand why. In the half-dream room time seems to stretch out slow, like rubber, and unless you've been there before, you'll never know how fast it goes by.

I watch every lift of the referee's arm. I remember thinking again of Frazier. He would never lose the crown lying on the floor. No referee could count over his body as long as he had blood in it.

"Six . . . seven . . . eight . . ."

George is turning over slowly.

"Nine . . . ten!"

George is on his feet, but it's over. The referee raises my hand in victory.

And the stadium explodes. People break past the paratroopers and climb over the press tables, climb into the ring.

Archie has wrapped his arms around George, and I holler, "Archie, am I too old?"

Archie jerks his head my way. There's a gleam in his eye. He raises his fists and shouts, "Your time is coming! Your day will come!"

And this I know. But the referee is raising *my* hand, and the whole world is screaming, "ALI! ALI! ALI! ALI!"

A reporter claws his way through the crowd and yells at me, "How did you do it, World Heavyweight Champion? What you think of George now?"

I shake my head. I want to go to my dressing room. I don't want to tell him what George has taught me. That too many victories weaken you. That the defeated can rise up stronger than the victor.

But I take nothing away from George. He can still beat any man in the world.

Except me.

MANILA:
September 30, 1975

If I talk about it now, they say, we can phone it to New York and get it in the book. They can add it on to the end if they get it before noon New York time. They want me to talk about the fight, right now, so the book will be up to date. This will be the last tape, they tell me.

That's good, because me and Joe Frazier have rumbled together this night for the last time. And it's over. The dinosaurs met for the last time, and I'm still The Champion.

So I'm going to talk about it, about the hardest fight I've ever had in my life—the deadliest and the most vicious. About how for the third time Joe Frazier surprises me with his stamina, his relentlessness and the gunpowder in his blows. How I open his lip and close his eye but he still keeps coming, forcing me into the ropes, making me deliver power when I don't even know if it's still there. How this time the butterfly has to stop floating so the bee can sting. Because it's the same old Joe. The same Joe who dropped me in Madison Square Garden four years ago; who shook me in January, 1974, round after round, before I could take him out.

Should I say that the fight we had tonight is the next thing to death? That I felt like fainting and throwing up? Frazier is a helluva fighter and when Carlos Padilla, the referee, looks at Joe's face, and his manager, Eddie Futch, won't let him out of his corner for the fifteenth round, I'm so relieved, so tired, and in so much pain that my knees buckle and I stretch out right where I am—right there in the middle of the ring. Laying there, drained, I hear the blood pounding in my ears, and in the middle of the pounding, Joe's words come back to me: "You one bad nigger. We both bad niggers. We don't do no crawlin'. "

Bundini lifts me up while Angelo cradles my legs to haul me back to my stool. The screams are so loud they sound far away. Then the crowd, pushing, shoving, reporters shouting. They want something from me. Something more. Some word or comment. But I'm too tired. Besides, I already told them. And I already told you. Didn't you hear me? I said I was The Greatest.

ABOUT RICHARD DURHAM

Mr. Durham is a prizewinning journalist and TV playwright, among whose awards are the Peabody, the first National Five Arts Award for radio and television dramas, and an Emmy for his dramatic series "Bird of the Iron Feather." A former editor of *Muhammad Speaks* newspaper, he has been intimately acquainted with Muhammad Ali and his manager Herbert Muhammad since 1962 and has traveled extensively with them for the past five years. His articles have appeared in *Life, The Saturday Evening Post, Ebony* and *The London Observer.*